Baedeker's Rail Guide to Europe

Baedeker's
RAIL GUIDE
TO EUROPE

Sources of illustrations:
Austrian National Tourist Office
Belgian National Railways
Belgian National Tourist Office
Britain On View
British Railways Board
Danish Tourist Board
Finnish Tourist Board
French Government Tourist Board
German Federal Railways
German National Tourist Office
Goethe Institute
Italian State Tourist Board
Luxembourg National Tourist & Trade Office
Netherlands Board of Tourism
Netherlands Railways
Norwegian Tourist Board
Orient-Express
Tom Stephenson
Swedish National Tourist Office
Swiss National Tourist Office and Swiss Federal
   Railways
Claire Wheeler
Professor White
Yugoslav National Tourist Office

Cover photo © The Stock Shop.

Source of maps and artwork:
British Rail (pp. 27, 40, lower; 55, 69, 101, lower; 124,
   160, 202, lower; 217, 232, 243, lower; 259, top;
   279, pull-out map).
Netherlands Railways (p.191).
Thomas Cook Ltd (pp. 10–11, 15, 16, 40, top; 56, 68,
   81, 101, top; 123, 141, 161, 174, 190, 202, top;
   216, 231, 243, top; 258–9, 278, 293).

How to Use this Guide

In the lists of hotels b.=beds and r.=rooms.

The symbol (i) at the beginning of an entry or on a
town plan indicates the local tourist office or other
organisation from which further information can be
obtained. The post-horn symbol on a town plan
indicates a post office.

Only a selection of hotels and restaurants can be
given. No reflection is implied on establishments not
included.

Contents

Introduction

In a world where, for most people, international travel means being squashed into jumbos, endless waiting and lunches one would rather forget, it is refreshing to rediscover the joys of travelling by rail. In many parts of Europe, recent advances in speed and comfort for rail travellers have been significant. It would be foolish to allow these developments to be eclipsed by the popularity of air travel. Even in countries where services are slow and facilities are basic, many people still maintain that travelling by train is the only way to see the countryside properly. The 'progress' of the twentieth century must surely be questioned by those intrepid travellers who venture through the Alps by rail rather than 30,000 feet over them.

Speed is not the only advantage. For people who wish to work in transit, there really is no better choice than the train. The space, the seating arrangements and the smooth, quiet ride can present the traveller with a mobile office or conference room.

Being able to eat and sleep en route is a valuable time saver, too. The paradox here is that greater speed has tended to lessen the need for proper dining and sleeping facilities, for often there simply isn't the time. The trend on many expresses therefore is to grills, buffet-style service or snack trolleys. A number of services, however, still uphold traditional standards of gracious dining, particularly over long distances.

Admittedly, the modern traveller can cross much of Europe by car,

Private Mountain Railway

using the efficient system of autoroutes, autobahns, autostrades and so forth. But driving a car on roads does not allow much opportunity for sightseeing. Rail travel is still a relaxing way to enjoy all the diversity of town and countryside.

It is no wonder that people are finding rail travel more attractive! Europe offers an amazing range of contrasting scenery and cultural heritage, and this guide will help you to plan a memorable visit. Illustrated in full colour throughout, with valuable city maps, the guide whets the appetite to explore Europe, country by country.

What the Guide Covers
To afford maximum coverage within the space such a volume allows, the guide concentrates on the 17 countries most likely to be visited by the reader; all of these are in Western Europe except Yugoslavia. The guide is divided into 18 chapters, 17 of which provide tourist and rail information country by country; the countries are covered in alphabetical order. The first chapter is an international section providing information of particular value to the train traveller who plans to tour.

Each country chapter starts with background information to establish the essential character of the country. Then, the rail information provides facts and practical advice to enable the traveller to explore using the country's rail network. Great centres of interest that can be readily and enjoyably reached by rail have been selected for more detailed coverage. Maps, plans and illustrations complement handy sightseeing lists, with descriptions of what to see and how to get there.

An accurate picture of the country's rail system may be gained both from the general opening comments and from specific details given of scenic routes, frequency of trains and station and train facilities.

Fares and other prices are given in local currency or the Sterling or US dollar equivalent, where appropriate. Unless indicated to the contrary, the prices were based on 1990 rates, which were operational at the time of going to press. Passengers are advised to check prices with the appropriate rail company before budgeting a journey.

For those on a limited budget, there is a whole range of special offers and passes which, with a little planning, will make rail the only way to travel. In their efforts to increase their share of the market, the various rail companies are constantly thinking up new ways to make travel by rail more attractive – especially to the non-business traveller at off-peak hours. There is no denying that the restrictions on special tickets are often quite complicated. Do not let this put you off. Use this book to educate yourself to the possibilities. Always check the latest information before you book, as you cannot always rely on busy ticket clerks to have the time, inclination or knowledge to give you the cheapest ticket without being specifically asked for it.

The 'Major International Services' tables are intended to provide a skeletal impression of the services available. The figures indicate direct express trains only. Many minor services exist as well, of course, and information relating to these may be found in the time-table published by the appropriate rail company. The 'Major Internal Services' tables also exclude local and indirect services, and passengers should refer to a local time-table for further details.

Information on the purchase of tickets – whether inside the country concerned, in Great Britain, or in the USA or Canada – is given where relevant.

Before you plan your trip, get to know the possibilities of where to go and how, at the same time, to save money. This guide will provide an excellent framework for the first stage of planning. Good travel agents, national tourist and rail offices will confirm fare details at the second stage, when you have a good idea of where you want to go and what you want to do. Finally, to plan in day-to-day detail, use the latest edition of the international timetable published by Thomas Cook and known as the *Thomas Cook Continental Timetable*. This is very detailed and is published monthly at £4.95 (obtainable from any branch of Cook's either directly or by post). If your journey is straightforward, using major expresses between major centres, you could manage with British Rail's *International Passenger Timetable,* published 3 times a year and costing only £1.50. It is available from British Rail Travel Centres or major stations.

While this guide does not claim to be totally comprehensive, it does provide the ideal framework of reference for every rail traveller, whether planning for business or for pleasure. The wealth of information on reduced fares alone should repay the cover price many times over. Use the guide to make the most of all that Europe has to offer. *Bon voyage!*

International Section

The *TGV* runs from Paris to Geneva or Lausanne

Most European countries have their own autonomous rail network and each rail company, therefore, decides on its own fare policies, reduction schemes, train facilities and so on. Someone intending to travel by train through Europe will consequently encounter not only varying standards of service but also a number of different fare options. The choice of tickets avail-able is dependent on the passenger's age, the distance of the journey, the number of people travelling and a host of additional criteria.

Travelling by train from Britain to Europe is considerably eased by British Rail's InterCity Europe services. These offer a wide range of integrated rail/sea routes to bring more than 100

INTERNATIONAL SERVICES

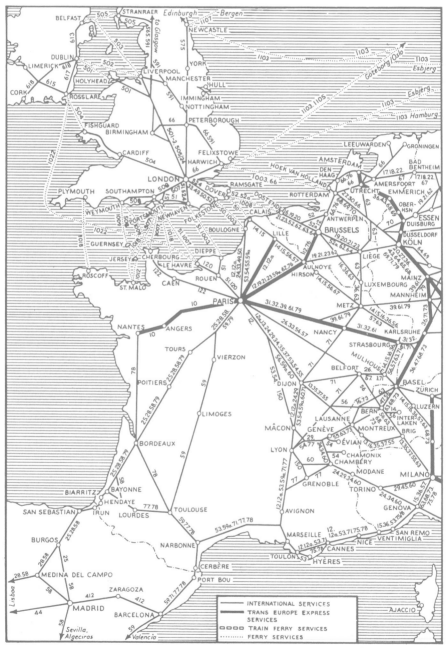

Map supplied by kind permission of Thomas Cook Ltd. The numbers along the lines refer to tables in the *Thomas Cook Continental Timetable*.

key centres within daytime reach of London. Jetfoil services between Dover and Ostend have cut the Channel crossing time to just 100 minutes. Improved shipping and boat-train carriages make the journey to Europe quicker and more comfortable. Using Hoverspeed hovercraft and French Railways 'turbo-trains' from Boulogne, Paris is now just over 5 hours 30 minutes from London. (From May 31 1987, InterCity Europe combined with the Trans-Europe Express [TEE] network to form the new Euro-City network.)

Many tourists who intend to travel some distance by rail find that they are best served by some form of rail pass; after the initial investment, these

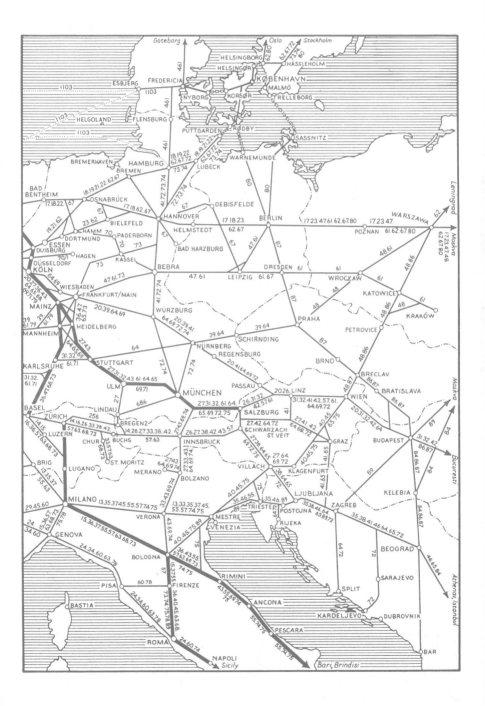

generally offer unlimited travel in a chosen area for a specified time period. They have the added advantage, in many cases, of being available for purchase outside the country in which they will be used. These unlimited travel passes (often called rover passes) are good value even for passengers who intend to limit their travel to one country as many European countries offer some form of internal pass. The passes provide great flexibility by permitting travel on additional coach, ferry and tram services within the country. Some 'groups' of countries (like the Scandinavian and Benelux countries) have combined to produce a pass which allows 'free' travel throughout the particular region (for information on these refer to the fare structure of the country you are visiting). European passes are listed at the end of this section.

If the passenger's journey really only merits an ordinary single or return ticket within a certain country these, too, are available. This can be an expensive exercise, although some organisations charge as little as £1 per ticket for point-to-point travel on the continent. The vast majority of point-to-point tickets can be issued in England. Those that can't usually mean that it would be cheaper and easier to buy the ticket in that particular country.

Practical Travel Information

1st and 2nd class

Most European trains offer both 1st and 2nd class accommodation, although the precise facilities will vary from train to train. 1st class carriages are usually identified by a yellow band, but on some trains there is simply a figure 1 near the door at the end of the coach. British Rail identify their 1st class coaches by means of a yellow band above the doors and windows of the carriage and the figure '1' on the doors.

Identification of trains

Most trains in Europe carry a destination plate which is usually located on the side of each coach. This will show the major calling points. Many trains divide 'en route', so it is always worth checking that you settle in the right part of the train.

Supplementary fees

Faster trains in Europe (like the TEE trains, the Euro-City trains, most IC trains in Germany and some TGV

A Netherlands Railway locomotive

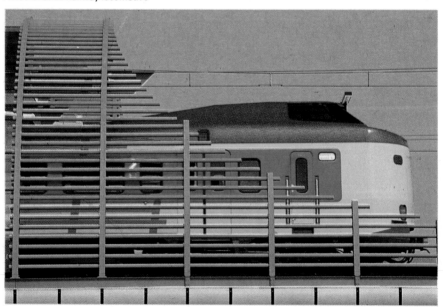

trains in France) are subject to a supplementary payment on the fare.

Reservations

Accommodation on international services is limited and if a passenger wishes to travel at a definite time and on a specific service, advance reservation is strongly recommended. In some cases, if this is not done, passengers may not be able to travel. On some train services, reservation is compulsory. Look out for an indication of this on the timetable. Passengers must have reservations on Townsend Thoresen Jetfoil and Hoverspeed hovercraft cross-Channel services.

Luggage

Most major stations in Europe have left luggage facilities, although this service has been temporarily suspended in Spain. The larger ones have left luggage lockers of various sizes as well as the ordinary deposit system.

An average load of hand luggage is carried free when it is in the possession of international ticket-holding passengers. However, on some journeys where space is limited it may be necessary for the baggage to be placed in a designated area. Larger items, like bicycles, non-folding prams etc. are generally only conveyed as registered luggage for which an appropriate fee must be paid. British Rail operates a Registered Luggage system which is designed to save passengers the chore of hauling hand luggage around when changing trains or transferring to a ferry. The charges are based on the distance the luggage has to be transported. No single item should weigh more than 60kg. For luggage routed to or via France, you are limited to 3 items, none of which should weigh more than 30kg. In most cases your luggage will travel on the same train as you, although this cannot be guaranteed, especially during peak periods.

Elderly and disabled

While every effort is made to ease travelling problems for the elderly and disabled, facilities vary considerably from country to country. It is generally advisable to give written notice to the rail company concerned well before the date of travel. When travelling from Britain to the Continent, applications should be made to:
Correspondence Section
European Rail Travel Centre
PO Box 303
Victoria Station
London SW1V 1JY

Travelling by night

TEN (Trans Europe Night) is a network of sleeping car services which runs between major cities in Western Europe. In general, there are 3 types of accommodation available in the sleeping cars: the 'single' (one-berth), the 'double' (two-berth) and the 'tourist' (two-, three- or four-berth). Normally, 1st class tickets are required for the 'single' or 'double' and 2nd class tickets for the 'tourist'. In addition, a supplement which varies according to the distance travelled, will be charged. The compartments have basins, razor sockets and space for clothes and luggage. The conductor can provide light refreshments. During the day, the berths fold back to form a long settee.

Couchettes are another form of night-time accommodation for which a small supplement must be paid. 1st class couchettes come in a compartment which accommodates 4 berths while 2nd class couchettes come in a compartment which accommodates 6. In some countries, it is possible to use the 6-berth compartments for 4 on payment of an additional supplement. Blankets and pillows are supplied and washing facilities are available at the end of each couchette coach.

SNCF have recently introduced the 'Cabine 8' to their overnight services. Refer to Facilities on Trains in the French section for further information.

Car hire

Europcar has an extensive network of offices throughout Europe and self-drive cars can be made available to InterCity Europe passengers at all principal destinations.

Cars should be reserved in advance and bookings can be made through most Europcar offices (many British Rail stations have these) or by phoning Central Reservations on (081) 950 5050.

Crossing the English Channel

There are now through services to the English ports (and beyond) not only from the main London stations but also from towns in other parts of England. These new high-speed inter-city services will save time and the inconvenience of cross-London interchange between British Rail stations.

Travel between Dover and Ostend on the Jetfoil

Although it is possible to travel to the English ports by other than the direct train-connected services, using domestic rail links and car ferries/hovercraft/Jetfoil, connections are not guaranteed. In practice, most people purchase an all-in-one ticket which pays for all rail and sea travel and guarantees connections.

In addition to the numerous ferry services which operate between England and the continent, hovercraft and Jetfoil services now provide a fast and competitive alternative. The Dover to Boulogne crossing takes 35 minutes by hovercraft. Or, if you are heading further north, the 100-minute Jetfoil crossing from Dover to Ostend is convenient. Passengers must have reservations on Townsend Thoresen Jetfoil and Hoverspeed hovercraft services.

Motorail

Motorail is a European network of special overnight trains which carry passengers and their cars or motorbikes over distances of up to 900 miles. It is a fast, efficient and relaxing way of travelling to, and across, the European continent. There is a wide range of sleeping accommodation available to suit all budgets.

International motorail routes are now established all over Europe. Boulogne to Milan, Paris to Madrid, Brussels to Ljubljana, 's-Hertogenbosch to Avignon, Cologne to Salzburg, are some of these. In addition, many domestic routes are possible throughout Great Britain, Austria, Yugoslavia, West Germany, Italy, Switzerland, and France.

For further details and booking information, contact your travel agent, motoring organisation, or British Rail Travel Centre. If you are travelling to or through the Continent, French Railways ([071] 409 3518) or DER Travel Service ([071] 408 0111) will be able to advise you.

Fares

Standard European fares to destinations in Europe are valid for 2 months and allow for stop-over en-route. Standard return fares are approximately double the single fare. Children under 4 travel free. Children aged 4 travel free on British Rail services only. Children aged 5–15 inclusive travel at reduced rates. Before deciding to buy a standard European fare it is worth investigating the numerous ways of obtaining reductions on fares. Here are some of the more popular schemes.

Special fare schemes

Rail Europ Senior Card

Men over 65 and women over 60, who are resident in one of the European countries which participates in the scheme, are eligible to apply for the RES card which costs £5 (in Great Britain you must already hold a BR Senior Citizens Railcard). Reductions are on single, return, or circular journeys, 1st or 2nd class, and are based on full standard fares. (Where a special rate fare to a destination exists, the RES reduction will be based on the higher original fare.)

The amount you save varies:
* Up to 50% on railways in Belgium, Finland, France, Greece, Luxembourg, the Netherlands, Norway, Portugal, Republic of Ireland, Spain, Sweden; and most Swiss railways.
* Up to 30% on railways in Austria, Denmark, West Germany, Hungary, Italy and Yugoslavia.
* Up to 50% on British Rail when you buy a through international rail/sea ticket.

CROSS-CHANNEL SERVICES

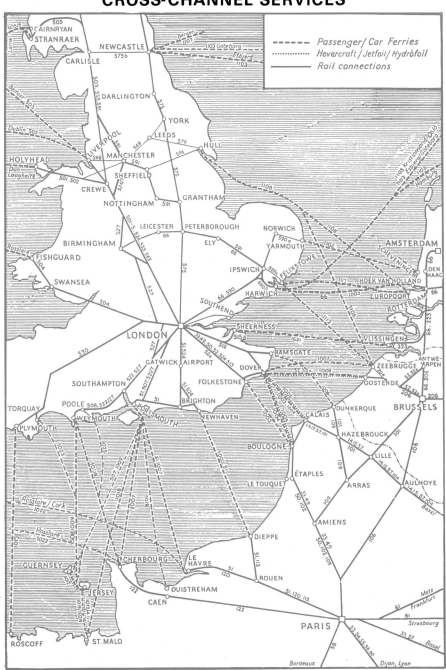

Map supplied by kind permission of Thomas Cook Ltd. The numbers along the lines refer to tables in the *Thomas Cook Continental Timetable.*

* Up to 30% on sea crossings to the Continent by Sealink, Hoverspeed hovercraft, and Townsend Thoresen services between Dover and Ostend or between Portsmouth and Le Havre when these are part of a through rail/sea journey.

Once you have your card it is valid for one year. To benefit from the reductions, your card must be valid not only

CAR-SLEEPER TRAINS
and local car-carrier routes through Alpine tunnels

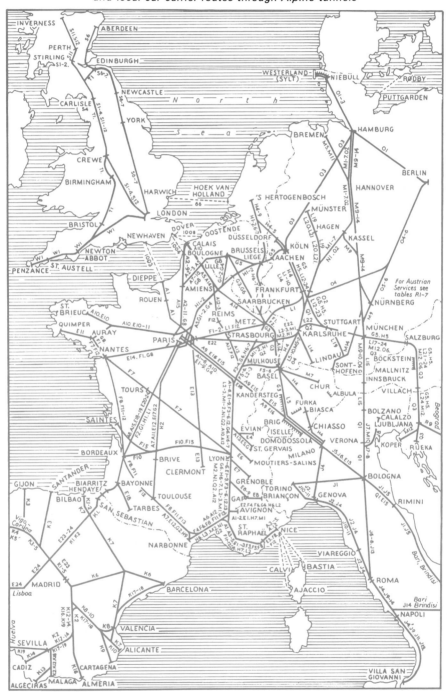

Map supplied by kind permission of Thomas Cook Ltd. The numbers along the lines refer to tables in the *Thomas Cook Continental Timetable*.

when you buy your ticket but also for the return journey. Reduced rate tickets issued in Britain are not subject to travel restrictions. However, reduced rate tickets issued in France cannot be used for journeys starting between 3pm Friday and 12 noon Saturday or between 3pm Sunday and 12 noon Monday. There may also be local restrictions on tickets issued in Spain and West Germany.

A number of private rail companies do not participate in the scheme and will not be able to offer reduced rate fare on production of a RES card.

Rail Europ Family Card

Another discount card for £5, the REF card is available to groups of up to 8 people who are resident at the same address, which must be in one of the participating countries. A minimum of 3 named people including an adult must travel together to qualify for the discounts. The holder of the card (who must be an adult) pays the full fare while the others can get the following reductions:

* Up to 50% on railways in Austria, Belgium, Denmark, France, Greece, Italy, Luxembourg, the Netherlands, Portugal, Republic of Ireland, Spain, Turkey (European lines), West Germany and Yugoslavia – and most Swiss railways.
* Up to 50% on British Rail when you buy a through international rail/sea ticket.
* Up to 30% on sea crossings to the continent by Sealink, Hoverspeed hovercraft and Townsend Thoresen (via Dover/Ostend or Portsmouth/Le Havre) when these are part of through rail/sea journeys.

Children aged between 5 and 11 (inclusive) pay half the reduced adult fare.

Your card is valid for a year and entitles you to buy reduced rate tickets from issuing offices in Britain or in any of the participating countries. To benefit from the reductions your REF card must be valid not only when you buy your tickets but also when you make the return journey.

Private Swiss Railway

Tickets bought in France, Spain and West Germany may be subject to restrictions with regard to travelling time. Some private rail companies in Europe do not belong to the scheme and are therefore unable to offer reduced rate fares on production of a REF card.

Inter-Rail

The Inter-Rail card gives unlimited 2nd class travel through 21 countries to under-26-year-olds. It costs £145 and is valid for one month which makes it ideal for touring the major cultural centres of Europe or for using local trains to explore one region in depth.

In addition to free travel in most European countries and Morocco, Inter-Rail card holders are also entitled to buy rail tickets at up to 50% discount in Great Britain and Northern Ireland as well as reduced price tickets on Hoverspeed hovercraft, Sealink and other shipping services. The countries in which free travel is possible are Austria, Belgium, France, Denmark, Finland, Greece, Hungary, Italy, Luxembourg, Morocco, the Netherlands, Norway, Portugal, Republic of Ireland, Roumania, Spain, Sweden, Switzerland, Turkey (European lines only), West Germany and Yugoslavia.

Although the card is available to under-26-year-olds in each of the participat-

ing countries, you must purchase it in the country in which you are permanently resident (minimum residence period is 6 months).

The Inter-Rail card permits 2nd class travel in the participating countries but 1st class travel is possible if the cardholder is prepared to pay the difference between the full 2nd class fare and the full 1st class fare for the journey. Some Continental trains can only be used if you pay a supplement. Card-holders must pay this and the fee for any additional services, such as couchettes and sleeping berths.

The Inter-Rail and Boat card costs £180 It offers all the facilities of the basic Inter-Rail card plus free travel on some Mediterranean, Scandinavian and Irish shipping routes.

Eurotrain

A Eurotrain ticket is available to anyone under the age of 26 and costs almost half the price of the normal rail fare. You can stop off at any one of 2000 stations en-route provided that you do not exceed the 2 month validity of the ticket. Your seat will be reserved at no extra charge.

The Eurotrain circle fares are return tickets designed for people who want to make a small tour within Europe without having to double back. There are 5 circle tours to choose from.

Eurotrain has numerous offices in Western Europe. In London, tickets and information are available from: 52 Grosvenor Gardens, London SW1W 0AG. Tel: (reservations) (071) 730 3402.

The newly-opened Schipol station

In the United States, information can be obtained from the Council for International Educational Exchange (CEE) and in Canada from the Canadian Travel Service (CTS).

Group rates

Passengers travelling in a group of 6 or more to a European destination are eligible for a 20–30% discount on rail fares. Group leaders travel free when the group consists of 16 or more people. Seat reservations are made free of charge and meals can be arranged if required. For further information, contact the Group Sales Section, European Rail Travel Centre, PO Box 303, Victoria Station, London SW1V 1JY (Tel: (071) 630 8133).

Narbonne Station, France

Other special deals

In addition to the passes and cards described above, there are many other 'special deals' available for travel to Europe. Most of these are for people of all ages, but there may be restrictions with regard to the time of travel, duration of stay, validity etc.

European Savers (5-day returns)

European Savers provide an economical way of making a short trip from Britain to selected countries on the continent. These low-price fares are available to any station in the Netherlands, Belgium, Denmark, or West Germany, to most stations in France and to selected destinations in Switzerland

and Luxembourg. You can spend up to 4 nights at your chosen destination. Some examples of European Saver fares are: £46 London to Paris; £59 London to Cologne; and £50 London to Amsterdam (via The Hook of Holland).

European Super Savers (Mini-excursions)

These provide the opportunity to travel overnight and spend a day in Paris (winter only), Amsterdam, Cologne or Brussels. You leave London in the evening, arrive in time for a full day at your chosen destination and return to London early the following morning.

Economy Night Fares

These allow cheap travel to any *SNCF* station in France via the Newhaven–Dieppe service. The minimum journey requirement is London–Paris. Economy Night Fares are also available to destinations in Belgium, Luxembourg and West Germany during the summer season when the rail-connected night service between Dover and Ostend is in operation. Example of EN 2nd class return is Paris £46.50. Tickets are valid for 2 months.

Economy Day Fares

These are available to passengers travelling to the Netherlands and West Germany using day sailings between Harwich and the Hook of Holland. ED fares are available to any station in the Netherlands for £26.10 (2nd class single) and to selected stations in West Germany. Tickets are valid for 2 months.

Holiday Return (Séjour)

These tickets offer reductions for travellers making return or circular journeys of more than 1000 km in France, or through France to Austria, Italy, Morocco, Portugal, or Switzerland, provided that a Sunday is included in the stay or in the journey.

Starlight Fares

Starlight fares are available for return journeys only, on certain overnight trains to selected destinations in Austria, West Germany, and Switzerland. Reduced rates are available to children aged 4–11 years inclusive. The tickets can only be used in conjunction with seat, sleeping car or couchette reservations, which are available at normal prices.

Travel Passes for Passengers Resident Outside Europe

Eurail Youth Pass

This pass is on sale outside Europe and may be bought by passengers under 26 who are permanently resident outside Europe. The holder is entitled to unlimited 2nd class travel – free of charge – on the rail systems of the 16 participating countries. These are Austria, Belgium, Denmark, Finland, France, Greece, Italy, Luxembourg, the Netherlands, Norway, Portugal, Republic of Ireland, Spain, Sweden, Switzerland and West Germany. The pass is available for periods of 1 or 2 months. A number of bonuses are open to pass-holders including travel on certain buses and ferries run by the rail companies. The pass costs $320 for 1 month and $500 for 2 months.

Trains near Châteaux d'oeux, France

Eurail Pass

This pass is for passengers over 26 years old. The holder must travel 1st class and is entitled to the same benefits as the Youth Pass holder (above). The pass costs $340 for 15 days, $440 for 21 days and $550 for 1 month.

BritRail Pass

BritRail Passes are available to overseas visitors to Britain only. They allow unlimited travel on British Rail services and are valid for periods of 4, 8, 15, 22 days or one month. The passes can only be bought abroad – either from travel agencies or major train stations. Two passes are available: the Gold (1st class) or Silver (2nd/Economy class). Young people (aged 16–25) can buy a BritRail Youth Pass at a price lower than that of the Adult Silver Pass. For senior citizens, there are lower prices for 1st class Gold Passes. Children aged 5–15 pay half the adult rate and children under 5 travel free. The passes are priced in local currency (or US dollars) and as exchange rates are always fluctuating, we offer a rough price guide only – an Adult Pass is around the same price as a Standard Return from London to Edinburgh. The Pass is validated from a starting date chosen by you after your arrival in Britain.

Extra benefits for the BritRail Pass holder (other than visitors from North America and Japan) include vouchers for free hotel or Youth Hostel accommodation, generous discounts on Europcar hire, cross-Channel ferry, hovercraft and Jetfoil services and free wine with lunch when taken in a restaurant car.

For further information, contact BritRail Travel International offices:

New York

630 Third Avenue,
New York, NY 10017
Tel: (212) 599 1467

Chicago

333 North Michigan Avenue,
Chicago, Ill. 60601
Tel: (312) 263 1910

Dallas

Cedar Maple Plaza,
2305 Cedar Springs,
Dallas TX 75201
Tel: (214) 748 0860

Los Angeles

Suite 603,
800 South Hope Street,
Los Angeles, Cal. 90017
Tel: (213) 624 8787

Toronto

94 Cumberland Street,
Suite 601, Toronto M5R 1A3
Tel: (416) 929 3333

Vancouver

409 Granville Street,
Vancouver, BC V6C 1T2
Tel: (604) 683 6896

Denmark

Danish Tourist Board
Sceptre House
169–173 Regent Street
London W1R 8PY
Tel: (071) 734 2637

Danish State Railways
c/o DFDS Seaways
Scandinavia House
Parkeston Quay
Harwich
Essex CO12 4QG
Tel: (0255) 554681

Finland

Finnish Tourist Board
66–68 Haymarket
London SW1Y 4RF
Tel: (01) 839 4048

Finnish State Railways
c/o Finlandia Travel Agency
130 Jermyn Street
London SW1Y 4UJ
Tel: (01) 839 4741

Tourist and Railway Representatives in Great Britain

Austria

Austrian National Tourist Office
30 St George Street
London W1R 0AL
Tel: (01) 629 0461

DER Travel Service
18 Conduit Street
London W1R 9TD
Tel: (071) 499 0577/78

Container Train at Perpignan, France

Belgium

Belgian National Tourist Office
38 Dover Street
London W1X 3RB
Tel: (01) 499 5379

Belgian National Railways
Premier House, 10 Greycoat Place
London SW1P 1SB
Tel: (071) 233 0360

France

French Government Tourist Office
178 Piccadilly
London W1V 0AL
Tel: (071) 491 7622

French Railways Ltd
179 Piccadilly
London W1V 0BA
Tel: (071) 409 1224

Greece

National Tourist Organisation of
Greece
4 Conduit Street
London W1R 9TD
Tel: (071) 734 5997

Portugal

National Tourist Office
New Bond Street House
1–5 New Bond Street
London W1Y 0NP
Tel: (071) 493 3873

Italy

Italian State Tourist Office
1 Princes Street
London W1R 8AY
Tel: (071) 408 1254

Italian State Railways
CIT England Ltd
50–51 Conduit Street
London W1R 9FB
Tel: (071) 434 3844

Spain

Spanish National Tourist Office
57–58 St James' Street
London SW1A 1LD
Tel: (071) 499 0901

Sweden

Swedish National Tourist Office
3 Cork Street
London W1X 1HA
Tel: (071) 437 5816

Swedish State Railways
c/o Norwegian State Railways Travel
Bureau.
21–24 Cockspur Street
London SW1Y 5DA
Tel: (071) 930 6666

Luxembourg

Luxembourg National Trade & Tourist
Office
36–37 Piccadilly
London W1V 9PA
Tel: (071) 434 2800

The Netherlands

Netherlands Board of Tourism
25–28 Buckingham Gate
London SW1E 6LD
Tel: (071) 630 0451

Netherlands Railways
25–28 Buckingham Gate
London SW1E 6LD
Tel: (071) 630 1735

Switzerland

Swiss National Tourist Office and
Swiss Federal Railways
Swiss Centre
1 New Coventry Street
London W1V 8EE
Tel: (071) 734 1921

A spectacular journey through the Alps

Norway

Norwegian Tourist Board
20 Pall Mall
London SW1Y 5NE
Tel: (071) 839 6255

Norwegian State Railways Travel
Bureau
Norway House
21–24 Cockspur Street
London SW1Y 5DA
Tel: (071) 930 6666

West Germany

German National Tourist Office
61 Conduit Street
London W1R 0EN
Tel: (01) 734 2600

German Federal Railways
10 Old Bond Street
London W1X 4EN
Tel: (01) 499 5078

Yugoslavia

Yugoslav National Tourist Office
143 Regent Street
London W1R 8AE
Tel: (01) 734 5243

Tourist and Railway Representatives in the United States and Canada

Austria

500 Fifth Avenue
Suite 2009
New York
NY 10110
Tel: (212) 944 6880

3440 Wilshire Boulevard
Suite 906
Los Angeles
CA 90010
Tel: (213) 380 3309

Belgium

745 Fifth Avenue
New York
NY 10151
Tel: (212) 758 8130

Denmark

655 Third Avenue
New York
NY 10017
Tel: (212) 949 2333

Scandinavia Tourist Board
150 North Michigan Avenue
Suite 2110
Chicago
Illinois 60601
Tel: (312) 726 1120

Scandinavia Tourist Board
8929 Wilshire Boulevard
Los Angeles
CA 90211
Tel: (213) 854 1549

Danish Tourist Board
151 Bloor St. West
8th Floor
Toronto
Ontario M5S 1S4
Tel: (416) 960 3305

Finland

655 Third Avenue
New York
NY 10017
Tel: (212) 949 2333

Narrow gauge railway, Cerdagne, France

France

610 Fifth Avenue
New York
NY 10020
Tel: (212) 582 2110

645 North Michigan Avenue
Suite 630
Chicago
Illinois 60611
Tel: (312) 337 6301

360 Post Street
San Francisco
CA 94108
Tel: (415) 982 1993

9465 Wilshire Boulevard
Beverley Hills
Los Angeles
CA 90212
Tel: (213) 272 7967

World Trade Centre No. 103
2050 Stammons Freeway
PO Box 58610
Dallas
Texas 75258
Tel: (214) 742 7011

1982 McGill College Avenue
Suite 490
Montreal
Quebec H3A 2W9
Tel: (514) 931 3855

1 Dundas Street W.
Suite 2405
Box 8
Toronto
Ontario M5G 1Z3
Tel: (416) 593 4717

Great Britain

40 West 57th Street
New York
NY 10019
Tel: (212) 581 4700

World Trade Centre
350 South Figueroa Street
Suite 450
Los Angeles
CA 90071
Tel: (213) 628 3525

John Hancock Centre
Suite 3320
875 North Michigan Avenue
Chicago
Illinois 60611
Tel: (312) 787 0490

Cedar Maple Plaza
2305 Cedar Springs Road
Dallas
TX 75201
Tel: (214) 720 4040

94 Cumberland Street,
Suite 600
Toronto
Ontario M5R 3N3
Tel: (416) 925 6326

Greece

645 Fifth Avenue
Olympic Tower
New York
NY 10022
Tel: (212) 421 5777

611 West Sixth Street
Los Angeles
CA 90017
Tel: (213) 626 6696

Italy

630 Fifth Avenue
Suite 1565
New York
NY 10111
Tel: (212) 245 4961

500 North Michigan
Suite 1046
Chicago 1
Illinois 60611
Tel: (312) 644 0990

360 Post Street,
Suite 801
San Francisco
CA 94108
Tel: (415) 392 6206

Luxembourg

801 Second Avenue
New York
NY 10017
Tel: (212) 370 9850

The Netherlands

355 Lexington Avenue
New York
NY 10017
Tel: (212) 370 7363

605 Market Street
San Francisco
CA 94105
Tel: (415) 543 6772

225N Michigan Avenue
Suite 326
Chicago
Illinois 60601
Tel: (312) 819 0300

25 Adelaide Street East
Suite 710
Toronto
Ontario M5C 1Y2
Tel: (416) 363 1577

Norway

655 Third Avenue
New York
NY 10017
Tel: (212) 949 2333

Portugal

548 Fifth Avenue
New York
NY 10036
Tel: (212) 354 4403

1801 McGill College Avenue
Suite 1150
Montreal
PQ H3A 2N4
Tel: (514) 282 1264

Spain

665 Fifth Avenue
New York
NY 10022
Tel: (212) 759 8822

180 North Michigan Avenue
Chicago
Illinois 60601
Tel: (312) 641 1842

4800 The Galleria
5085 West Heimer
Houston
Texas 77056
Tel: (713) 840 7411

8383 Wilshire Boulevard
Suite 960
Beverley Hills
Los Angeles
CA 90211
Tel: (213) 658 7188

Casa del Hidalgo
Hipolita and St George Street
San Agustin
Florida 32084
Tel: (904) 829 6460

60 Bloor Street West
201 Toronto
Ontario M4W 3B8
Tel: (416) 961 3131

Sweden

655 Third Avenue
New York
NY 10017
Tel: (212) 949 2333

Scandinavia Tourist Board
150 North Michigan Avenue
Suite 2110
Chicago
Illinois 60601
Tel: (312) 726 1120

Scandinavia Tourist Board
8929 Wilshire Boulevard
Los Angeles
CA 90211
Tel: (213) 854 1549

Switzerland

Swiss Centre
608 Fifth Avenue
New York
NY 10020
Tel: (212) 757 5944

250 Stockton Street
San Francisco
CA 94108
Tel: (415) 362 2260

PO Box 215
Commerce Court
Toronto
Ontario M5L 1E8
Tel: (416) 868 0584

West Germany

747 Third Avenue
New York
NY 10017
Tel: (212) 308 3300

444 South Flower Street
Suite 2230
Los Angeles
CA 90071
Tel: (213) 688 7332

No. 2 Fundy
PO Box 417
Place Bonaventure
Montreal
PQ H5A 1B8
Tel: (514) 878 9885

Yugoslavia

630 Fifth Avenue
Rockefeller Center,
Suite 210
New York
NY 10020
Tel: (212) 757 2801

Landwasser Viaduct, Switzerland

International Rail Symbols

These are the more commonly used pictograms to be found on most European railway stations and trains.

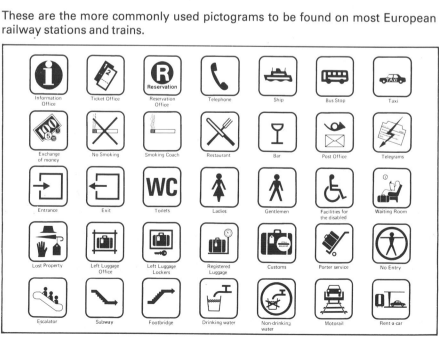

Time Zones

This table indicates the difference between local time and Greenwich Mean Time in European countries.

COUNTRY	SUMMER	WINTER	COUNTRY	SUMMER	WINTER
Austria	+2	+1	Monaco	+2	+1
Belgium	+2	+1	Netherlands	+2	+1
Denmark	+2	+1	Norway	+2	+1
Finland	+3	+2	Portugal	+1	GMT
France	+2	+1	Spain	+2	+1
Great Britain	+1	GMT	Sweden	+2	+1
Greece	+3	+2	Switzerland	+2	+1
Italy	+2	+1	West Germany	+2	+1
Luxembourg	+2	+1	Yugoslavia	+2	+1

The Orient-Express

The Orient-Express is one of the most famous trains ever to run in Europe. Its story began in 1883, when an enterprising Belgian by the name of Georges Nagelmacker, the founder of the *Compagnie Internationale des Wagons-Lits et des Grands Express Européans*, arranged for the first luxurious express from Paris to the Danube, with connections to the Bulgarian coast and Constantinople (now Istanbul). In its heyday, the service ran to Athens, Istanbul and beyond, continuing as the 'Taurus Express' to Aleppo, Haifa, Baghdad and Mosul. Numerous stories have grown up about this exceptional train and it has been the setting for a number of books and films.

The service enjoyed its finest period between 1900 and 1914, when it was much used by the rich and the powerful and extended its routes. The company sustained some loss during World War I but there was a revival of interest between the wars. World War II, however, brought massive damage to rails, routes and even the rolling stock itself, and although some service was maintained until 1962, the Orient-Express was a shadow of its former self. Happily, the service has now been resurrected, with many of the original coaches expensively refurbished, and is available for scheduled services, day trips and charters.

The Orient-Express

In Britain

The service in Britain is made up of eight Pullman coaches, many of which were originally part of Britain's famous trains, like the *Brighton Belle* or the *Golden Arrow*. As well as providing the first leg of the main route to Venice, the Pullman coaches are available for charter and for the following day trips:

ORIENT EXPRESS

Return Prices

Alternate Wednesdays			**Lunch in the Garden of England**	
Bath			**Every Wednesday**	
4 April to 14 November	£145		10 January to 28 March	£95
Bristol			**Every Friday**	
4 April to 14 November	£145		6 April to 16 November	£110
Arundel Castle			**Special Events**	
11 April to 7 November	£145		St. Valentine's Day	£120
Every Thursday and Sunday			**Lunch or Dinner**	
Folkestone			Christmas Luncheon Trips	£135
1 March to 15 November	£125			
			A Day at the Races	
Hever Castle			Royal Ascot	£295
1 April to 15 November	£95		Ascot – Diamond Day	£295
			Newmarket 2000 Guineas	£295
Alternate Fridays			Newmarket July Meeting	£295
Salisbury				
13 April to 9 November	£145			

Venice Simplon Orient-Express

Probably the most luxurious way – and one of the most expensive – of getting from London to Venice, this service must be a rare experience for lovers of old trains and fine food. The service runs twice weekly to Venice, via Boulogne, Paris, Zurich, St Anton, Innsbruck and Verona. The train originally ran through the Simplon tunnel, via Milan, but the new oeprators have altered the route to take in the spectacular mountain views over the Alps; the train now travels through the Alberg Tunnel and the Brenner Pass,

so the name is something of a misnomer. One advantage of the new route is that it takes longer – so you get an extra meal!

The train journey takes two days and a night from London to Venice, or *vice versa*. Southbound trains leave London Victoria at 11.00 on Sundays and Thursdays, arriving in Venice at 18.50 the following day. Northbound trains leave Venice Santa Lucia at 10.55 on Wednesdays and Saturdays and arrive in London at 16.50 the next day.

Day trips are also available on the Continent, in Pullman coaches or restaurant cars: London to Paris (£250);

Zurich to Innsbruck (£155); Zurich to Venice (£225); Innsbruck to Venice (£155). All prices are inclusive of meals on the train.

The company that owns the train also controls hotels in Venice, Florence, York, Stratford-upon-Avon and Scotland, which means that all-in prices are available for British Pullman overnight trips, with dinner and a night's stay in one of the company's hotels. Special prices are also quoted for holidays taking the train to or from Venice, with air travel one-way and a hotel stay of up to 7 nights. Prices for 2 nights in Venice, including train travel one-way and a flight, range from £960 to £1570 – depending on the quality of hotel and whether you choose to take the train southbound or northbound; it is cheaper to fly south and take the train north.

Now it is possible to plan extravagant winter holidays with V-S-O-E. Connections at Chur or Landquart with the picturesque Swiss Mountain Railway make the ski resorts of Arosa, Klosters, Davos and St Moritz accessible in a very elegant and spectacular way. Connections, transfers, and hotel reservations are all taken care of and the quality of the hotels and service is in keeping with the standards upheld in the train itself.

Further information

For further information on booking, charters and hotel reservations, contact one of the following:

In Great Britain
Venice Simplon – Orient-Express
Suite 200
Hudsons Place
Victoria Station
London SW1V 1JL
Tel: (071) 928 6000

In the United States
Orient-Express
Suite 1235
1 World Trade Centre
New York
NY 10048
Tel: (800) 524 2420/(212) 938 6830

Reservation Systems Inc
6 East 46th Street
New York
NY 10017
Tel: (800) 1588/(212) 661 4540

British Transport Hotels
185 Madison Avenue
New York
NY 10016
Tel: (800) 221 1074/(212) 684 1820

In other European countries
Orient-Express
Dr W Lueftner Reiseburo
Sterzinger Strasse 8
A6020 Innsbruck
Austria
Tel: (5222) 33566

Orient-Express
De Keyser Thornton
Rue de la Madeleine 63
1000 Brussels
Belgium
Tel: (02) 513 96 46

Orient-Express
DSB-Rejsebureau Terminus
Vesterbrogade 5
DK 1620 Copenhagen V
Denmark
Tel: (1) 141126

Orient-Express
15 rue Boissey d'Anglais
75008 Paris
France
Tel: (1) 742 3628

Orient-Express
Deutsches Reiseburo GmbH
Im Hauptbahnhof
6000 Frankfurt-am-Main
West Germany
Tel: (069) 230911

Orient-Express
Travelclub
Via Cernaia 2
20121 Milan
Italy
Tel: (02) 6291

Orient-Express
Travelclub
San Marco 2568
30124 Venice
Italy
Tel: (041) 30603/85811

Orient-Express
Reiseburo Mittelthurgau
CH8570 Weinfelden
Switzerland
Tel: (72) 224677

Austria

The Murtal Railway (Murtalbahn)

Introduction

Austria is now one of the most popular holiday centres in Europe, not least because it attracts visitors all year round. A major European destination for winter sports enthusiasts, its mountains are equally popular during the spring and summer, as are the many spas which have been used for medicinal purposes since the Roman occupation. Besides the beauty of its mountains and countryside, Austria's visitors are also attracted by the two major cities of Vienna and Salzburg. Both centres of the great Habsburg Empire, they offer many glimpses of Austria's glorious past.

Austria contains a great variety of landscapes within a relatively small area, from low plains in the east, to high Alpine peaks in the west. Almost two-thirds of the country's total area of 83,853sq km is taken up by the Austrian section of the Eastern Alps, whilst a little more than a quarter of the country consists of terrain suitable for human settlement. The population of 7.5 million is concentrated in the lower areas in the east of Austria. The diverse terrain has meant that there is a marked social difference between the Viennese and the people who live in the west of Austria. It is only because the Austrian Alps are relatively easy to cross that Austria has managed to survive as a coherent state.

The Austrian climate is determined by the fact that much of the country is mountainous. In the east, warm summers and moderately cold winters are the norm, while in the west the summers are cold and the winters severe. Atlantic influences become weaker the further east one travels, where warmer influences predominate.

Austria is made up of nine different provinces. Each has its own distinct regional characteristics, people and traditions. The provinces are well defined geographical units of considerable internal stability, and thus form a firm foundation for the Austrian Federal system. Each Federal province elects its own assembly and head of government. The Austrian Federal Assembly of Parliament consists of two houses: the Federal Council in which members are appointed by provincial assemblies; and the National Council, which is elected by the population as a whole.

The Head of State is the directly elected Federal President who appoints a Federal Chancellor and a Federal Government over which the Chancellor presides.

The Austrian economy is still changing from an agricultural economy to an industrial one. After the industrial expansion brought about by Hitler's introduction of industry to west Austria (which was continued by the allied forces of occupation) the proportion of the population employed in agriculture declined. As a result of the post-war exodus of agricultural workers into industry, Austrian agriculture underwent a period of mechanisation and nationalisation. Despite the continued decline, agriculture and forestry are still important elements in the economy. More than three-quarters of domestic requirements are met by home-produced food, and in the case of wine, beef, butter and cheese, Austria produces more than it can consume. Tourism is perhaps the most important contributor to the economy, since its large foreign currency earnings serve to

View from Rathaus tower, Vienna

alleviate the massive deficit on its balance of trade. Around 15 million visitors come to Austria each year making it more dependent than most European countries on its tourists. Also, the nature of the trade in Austria ensures that revenue is widely spread, and that those living in remote areas in the Alps have employment.

Austria has frontiers with six different countries, and its culture has been influenced to a great extent by developments outside these borders. In fact it was not until the 17th century that any national style can be said to have evolved. This is particularly true with regard to Austrian music. The emergence of the Viennese classical school in the 18th century made Vienna the capital of the European musical world. Haydn (1732–1809), Mozart (1756–91), Beethoven (1770–1827) and Schubert (1797–1828) were the major composers and the tradition of Viennese music was continued by Johann Strauss (1804–49) and his son of the same name, who developed the famous Viennese Waltz. In the 20th century, the twelve tone music, arguably at its best in the works of Arnold Schönberg (1874–1951) has been internationally recognised as a major contribution to contemporary classical music.

In recent years the great tradition of Austrian music has been carried on by the musicians of Vienna. The Vienna Philharmonic is one of the leading orchestras in the world and the Salzburg Festival (founded by Hugo von Hofmannsthal, Richard Strauss and Max Reinhardt) is of international renown.

There were three great eras of Austrian literature: the 13th and 14th centuries, the early 19th century, and the late 19th and early 20th centuries. Notable figures of these eras were:

Walther **von der Vogelweide** (c1170–1230), poet
Franz **Grillpartzer** (1791–1872), classical writer
Adalbert **Stifter** (1805–68), novelist
Arthur **Schnitzler** (1862–1931), dramatist
Hermann **Bahr** (1863–1934), novelist and playwright
Hugo **von Hofmannsthal** (1874–1929), dramatist

The great flowerings of Austrian art and architecture coincided with the two great Austrian dynasties – Babenberg and Habsburg. During the Babenberg era, through the crusades and Byzantine marriage alliances, Eastern influences predominated. The Gothic art and architecture of the late 13th and early 14th centuries produced some notable landmarks, for example the Leechkirche in Graz, and the Augustinian Church in Vienna. The 15th century was a prolific period of late Gothic architecture, the most notable example being St Stephens Cathedral in Vienna. This was also a rich period for painting and sculpture. Because the struggle against the Turks was often waged on Austrian soil, the Renaissance took several years to establish itself in Austria. It was the Baroque period that followed it, however, that was the most brilliant period of Austrian art and architecture. The consolidation of the absolutist state and the resurgence of the Roman Catholic faith resulted in a great burst of building activity. Vienna was the centre of this activity and the oustanding figures were Lukas von Hildebrandt and Johann Fischer von Erlach.

Vienna Philharmonic Orchestra

This building activity was accompanied by an increase in the output of Baroque painting and sculpture that continued in full strength well into the period normally regarded as Rococo. These traditions of fine art and architecture have continued into the modern era culminating in the Expressionist movement and the often harrowing representations of people depicted, for example, in the work of Egon Schiele.

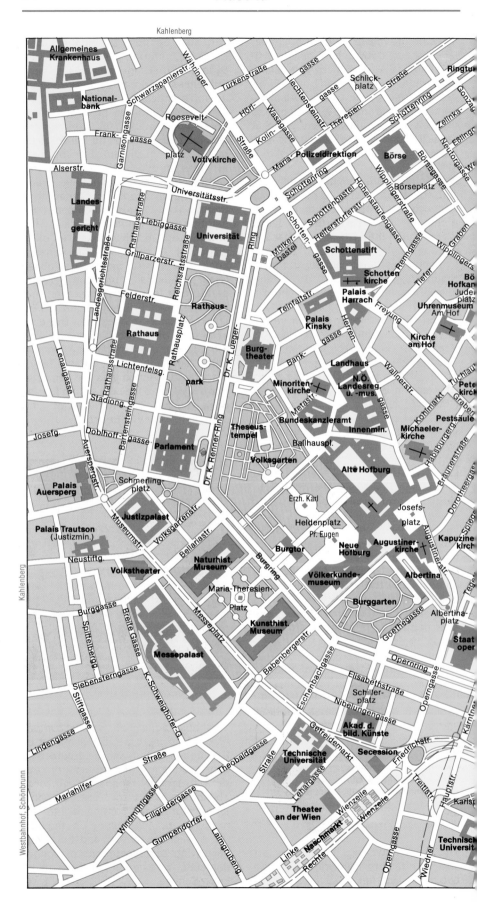

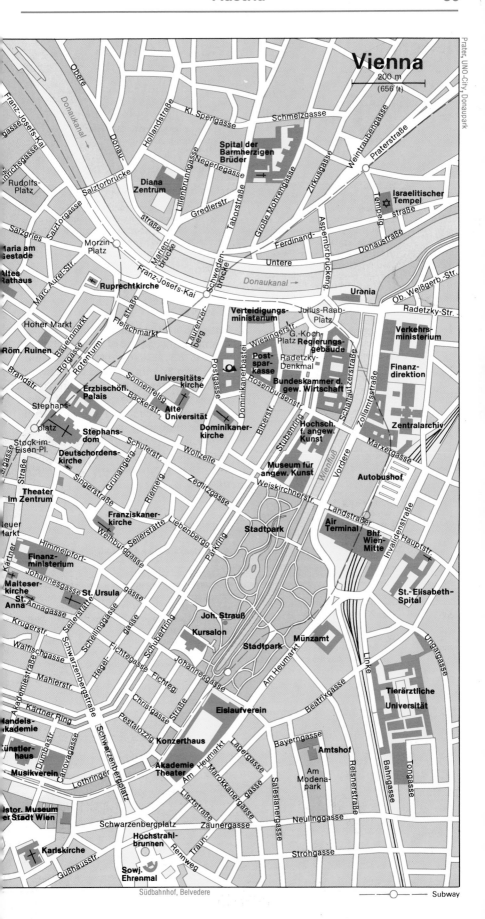

History

15 BC–AD 500	Roman occupation
788	Austrian territories incorporated into Carolingian Empire
976	Babenbergs become Margraves of Ostmark
1156	Ostmark becomes an independent hereditary duchy, with Vienna as its capital
1278	Rudolf of Habsburg establishes Habsburg dynasty
1453	The Emperor Frederick III makes Austria an archduchy
1521	Diet of Worms. Martin Luther is outlawed. Spread of Reformation
1699	Establishment of the dual monarchy of Austria and Hungary
1742–80	Vienna becomes focal point of classical music in Europe
1814–15	Congress of Vienna
1849	Austria granted a constitution
1914	Assassination of the heir to Austrian throne sparks off First World War
1918	Revolution in Vienna, proclamation of Republic of German Austria
1920	New constitution. Austria becomes a federal state
1938	The *Anschluss*. Austria is incorporated into the German Reich
1939–45	Second World War in which Austrians fight in the German army
1945	Vienna occupied by Soviet army. Renner elected as Federal President
1955	Full sovereignty restored to Austria
1972	Free trade treaty with EEC
1975	Socialist Party wins absolute majority in National Council
1978	A national referendum prohibits the further building of nuclear power stations
1983	General election returns a two-party coalition government
1985	Major wine scandal dents Austria's prestige as a producer and damages export market
1986	Dr. Kurt Waldheim elected President of Austria on a second ballot

Major Centres

Vienna

Fremdenverkehrsverband für Wien
IX Kinderspitalgasse 5,
Tel: (222) 43 16 08/(222) 42 65 65

Stadtinformation
Rathaus, Schmidthalle
Tel: (222) 43 89 89 (branch in Karlsplatz Passage)

Tourist Information in Opernpassage (Tel:(222) 43 16 08) at Westbahnhof (upper concourse) and Süd-bahnhof (lower concourse) and (summer only) on west and south motorways.

Embassies:
UK: Reisnerstrasse 40
Tel: (222) 73 15 75 79
USA: Boltzmanngasse 16
Tel: (222) 31 55 11

Situated on the banks of the Danube, Vienna is the capital of the Republic of Austria. It was also centre of the great Habsburg Empire, located as it was at the intersection of the important trade routes. The city has buildings providing ample evidence of the past, and many interesting museums exhibit artistic treasures. Vienna also offers a wide range of cultural activities including the internationally renowned opera.

Sightseeing

Archbishop's Palace – rebuilt in Baroque style 1631–41
Belvedere and Belvedere Gardens – the master-piece of Baroque by architect J. L. von Hildebrandt
Burgtheater – massive late Renaissance theatre, reopened in 1955 after heavy war damage
Giant Wheel, Prater – perhaps Vienna's best-known landmark
Hofburg and Neue Hofburg – previously the seat of the rulers of Austria and for two centuries the residence of the German Emperors. See perform-ances of the famous **Spanish Riding School** here

Schönbrunn Palace, Vienna

Kunsthistorisches Museum (Museum of Art), Vienna

Josefplatz – Austrian National Library, Spanish Riding School
Karlskirche – one of the finest high Baroque churches, built by J B Fischer von Erlach
Kärntner Strasse – perhaps the best-known street in Vienna, lined with offices, shops, hotels and cafés
Museum of Art – a fine collection of sculpture and applied art

Museum of the 20th Century – exhibiting painters and sculptors from the beginnings of Art Nouveau to the present day
Natural History Museum – one of the largest of its kind, noted for its collection of meteorites
Neuer Markt – Imperial Vault, Donner Fountain
Opera House – built 1861–9 in an early French Renaissance style
Ringstrasse – magnificent circular boulevard
St Peters Church – believed to have been founded by Charlemagne in 792
St Stephens Cathedral – the finest Gothic building in Austria
Schönbrunn Palace and Park – well-preserved French-style gardens of the Baroque period containing the Emperor's summer residence
Secession Building – a fine example of Art Nouveau architecture

Salzburg

Stadtverkehrbüra
Auerspergstrasse 7
Tel: (662) 8072 0

Branches:
Mozartplatz 5
Tel: (662) 84 75 68

Hauptbahnhof (Central Station)
Tel: (662) 7 17 12/7 36 38

Müncher Bundesstrasse 1
Tel: (662) 3 22 28 and 3 31 10

Salzburg, birthplace of Wolfgang Amadeus Mozart and graced by the magnificent Baroque architecture of Fischer von Erlach and Lukas von Hildebrandt, is one of the most beautiful

Panoramic view of Salzburg

cities in Europe. Situated on the banks of the Salzach and dominated by the Salzburg Alps, it has, for many years, been the cultural hub of central Austria.

Sightseeing

Cathedral – begun in 1614, it was the first deliberately Italian-style church built north of the Alps. Damaged by bombs in 1944, restored by 1959
Getreidegasse – busy shopping street lined with burghers' houses of 15th–18th centuries. At No. 9 is Mozart's birthplace, now a museum
Hohensalzburg – picturesque fortress situated 120m above the Salzach. First built in 1077, in its present form it dates from 1500
Museum Carolino Augusteum – contains a wide range of material of artistic and cultural interest
Residenz – Palace of the Prince Bishops, built 1596–1619
Residenzbrunnen – finest Baroque fountain outside Italy; it stands 15m high and is made of Unterberg marble
St Peters Church – built 1130–43, altered 1605–25 and decorated in Rococo style 1757–83
Schloss Mirabell and Mirabellgarten built 1606, remodelled in Baroque by J L von Hildebrandt. Fine marble staircase in west wing. An excellent example of Baroque landscape gardening

Innsbruck

Städtisches Verkehrsbüro (Tourist Office)
Burggraben 3
6020 Innsbruck
Tel: (52 22) 25 7 15

The town of two Olympic Winter Games, a university town, the see of a bishop, centre of sports, and capital of the province Tyrol, Innsbruck lies in the wide Inn valley and is surrounded by magnificent mountains. The town still preserves its medieval core, with its narrow and irregular streets and tall houses in late Gothic style, many of them with handsome oriel windows and fine doorways.

Sightseeing

Goldenes Dachl (Golden Roof) – magnificent late Gothic oriel window with 2657 gold-plated tiles. Built under Emperor Maximilian I in 1500 as a royal box for spectacles held in the square below
Stadtturm (City Tower) – built in the early 14th century as a Gothic tower, in 1560 the spire was replaced by a dome. Excellent views
Dom zu St Jakob (St Jakob's Cathedral) – Baroque architecture, built in place of the decaying gold parish church in 1720. Altarpiece with famous paintings by Lucas Cranach. Magnificent pulpit and ceiling paintings

Hofburg (Imperial Palace) – Viennese late Rococo style, with four wings, originally built in the 15th and 16th century and remodelled in Baroque and Rococo style in the 18th century. Magnificent hall with splendid ornamentation and ceiling frescoes. Valuable pictures and tapestry
Hofkirche (Court Church) – built 1553–1563 in the local late Gothic style. In the middle of the nave is the tomb of Emperor Maximilian I, the finest work of German Renaissance sculpture, conceived as a glorification of the Holy Roman Empire: Massive black marble sarcophagus with a bronze figure of the Emperor (1584), the sides are covered with 24 scenes (1562–66) depicting his deeds, and around the sarcophagus are 28 over-life-size bronze statues (1508–50) of the Emperor's ancestors and contemporaries
Tyrolean State Museum Ferdinandeum – ancient and early history. Largest Gothic collection in Austria. Baroque gallery. Old German and Dutch Gallery (Rembrandt), Modern Art
Tyrolean Regional Museum – cultural and natural history covering a very wide field (mineralogy, mining, coining, cartography, hunting, technology, field sports)
Tiroler Volkskunstmuseum (Museum of Tyrolean Folk Art) – most important folk museum in Austria. National costumes, peasant farmhouse rooms and furniture, collection of Christmas cribs
Basilika Wilten (Wilten Basilica) – most beautiful Rococo church in Tyrol; containing famous statue of the Virgin dating from the 14th century

Accommodation

Hotels, Inns, Pensions

The hotels in the larger Austrian towns and tourist resorts are well up to the normal international standards of comfort and amenity; but the inns (*Gasthöfe*) in the smaller places also offer excellent accommodation and food. There are many *Schlosshotels* in old castles and country houses. And all over the country there are large numbers of pensions. It is advisable to book accommodation in advance, particularly during the main tourist season and on public holidays.

Holidays on the Farm

Farm holidays have become increasingly popular in Austria in recent years. The movement has been actively promoted by the Hauptverband der Österreichischen Sparkassen (Federation of Austrian Savings Banks), which publishes an annual list of farms (at present almost 4000 in number) offering holiday accommodation.

Holiday Villages
(Erholungsdörfer)

These are villages, still predominantly agricultural, which provide holiday accommodation in quiet and relaxing surroundings, enabling visitors to see something of the local way of life. Frequently they offer shooting and fishing.

Camping

Camping is now a very popular form of holiday in Austria, and there are large numbers of officially recognised camping sites, often in very beautiful settings and equipped with modern facilities, in the mountain regions (particularly in the high valleys with their Alpine meadows and on the passes), on the shores of the warm Carinthian lakes and the lakes of the Salzkammergut, on the banks of the Danube and in many other parts of the country. Members of camping clubs are usually entitled to reductions on the normal charges. Campers who prefer to find their own sites should ask the owner's permission before pitching their tent on private land. In some places (eg on the Grossglockner Road) this freelance camping is not permitted.

Information may be obtained from Österreichischer Camping-Club, Mariahilfer Str. 180, A-1015 Wien.

Hotels, inns and pensions are officially classified in five categories, from A1 to D, as follows:

Introduction to Rail Information

The Austrian rail system is very extensive and most of it is run by the Austrian Federal Railways (*Österreichische Bundesbahnen, ÖBB*). The system comprises:

Expresszüge – international expresses.

Schnellzüge – long distance expresses.

Eilzüge – fast local trains which stop only at major stations.

Personenzüge – slow local trains which stop at all stations.

The Semmering Line (Semmeringstrecke)

Hotel Price Range	
Price per person for 1 night in Austrian Schillings	
A1 Luxury hotels	755–2400
A First class hotels	500–1400
B Excellent middle class hotels, etc	250– 700
C Good middle class hotels, etc	200– 450
D Modest hotels, inns and pensions	150– 250
Rates in Vienna are considerably higher. These prices are intended to act as a rough guide only.	

Extra charges are applicable for special services such as transport of guests or luggage to and from the hotel or pension, local or long distance calls, use of garage facilities, etc.

In areas geared to winter sports, the hotels are frequently closed in summer, while in the summer resort areas they may be open only from spring to autumn.

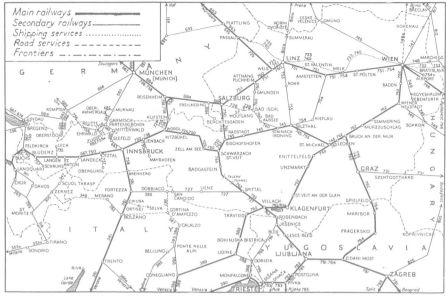

Map supplied by kind permission of Thomas Cook Ltd. The numbers along the lines refer to tables in the *Thomas Cook Continental Timetable*.

Passengers who use express trains for short journeys have to pay about 30AS more than on local trains. The standard of service, in general, is high and the trains are clean and comfortable. However, the booking procedure is time consuming.

Major International Services

Connection	Duration	Frequency
London–Vienna	23–30hrs	twice daily
Paris–Vienna	14–16hrs	4 times daily
Vienna–Cologne	10–12hrs	4 times daily

Major Internal Services

Connection	Duration	Frequency
Salzburg–Vienna	3–4hrs	24 times daily
Innsbruck–Salzburg	3–4hrs	17 times daily
Vienna–Graz	2–4hrs	12 times daily
Vienna–Klagenfurt	4–5hrs	10 times daily
Graz–Linz	3–4hrs	6 times daily
Salzburg–Klagenfurt	3–4hrs	9 times daily

Scenic Routes

The Austrian rail network offers many opportunities for viewing the country's spectacular landscape. The Schneeburg rack railway runs between Puch-

The Murtal Railway (Murtalbahn), Murau

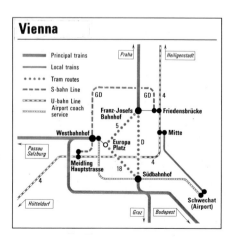

berg and Hochschneeburg through dramatic mountainous landscape and the Innsbruck–Brennero run offers equally impressive mountain views. Try also the Linz–Kerens route, the Salzburg–Villaen route or the Selzthal–Heiflau–Steyr route which travels through the Enns Valley.

Veteran railways

150 Years of Rail

1987 marked the 150th anniversary of the year in which Austria's first railway train pulled away from a platform in Floridsdorf on the outskirts of Vienna.

The event was celebrated in a variety of ways throughout the year, one of which was the Birthday Train. This travelling exhibition presented rail information from the past and into the future in an amusing and innovative way. The train stopped at over 40 stations, and at each stop a big birthday party was held. Trains, locomotives, and rolling stock through the ages were on show in countless excursions, parades and displays.

Other steam railways

1. **Murtalbahn**
   Route: Unzmark – Tamsweg (Styria and Salzburg provinces)
   Length: 65km/40 miles
   Gauge: 760mm/30in
   Diesel and steam traction
   Operates throughout the year; special trips for steam enthusiasts and amateur engine-drivers by arrangement with management (Murau). On the narrow gauge Murtal line, you can get a feel for steam train driving at close hand. As well as learning about how a train is constructed, visitors also travel in the cab of a heavy diesel train – and even have a go at driving. The trip includes a visit to the railway museum at Frojach and a ride on a slow steam train from Murau to Tamsweg and back (in July and August). This train has a buffet-car which used to be the saloon carriage of Kaiser Franz Josef.

2. **Feistritztalbahn**
   Route: Weiz – Birkfeld
   Length: 24.12km/15 miles
   Gauge: 760mm/30in
   Diesel and steam traction
   Operates Saturday, July–September; special steam trips by arrangement with management (Weiz). The Feistritztal line is one of the few on which you can still experience 'old time' journeys just as they used to be. The old passenger carriages, which are pulled by a steam train, still have the original wooden seats. The narrow gauge track winds over viaducts and through tunnels carrying passengers through a particularly beautiful region of the country. The 'Felistritsztal Public House' ensures that the travellers are well catered for and the atmosphere is enlivened by folk music.

3. **Bregenzerwaldbahn**
Route: Bregenz – Bezau (Vorarlberg)
Length: 35km/22 miles
Gauge: 730mm/29in
Steam traction
During summer, mostly at weekends; also 30 December to 6 January.

4. **Montafonerbahn**
Route: Bludenz – Schruns (Vorarlberg)
Length: 12.7km/8 miles
Gauge: 1435mm/56½in
Steam traction
At weekends in summer

5. **Achenseebahn**
Route: Jenbach – Seespitz (Tirol)
Length: 6.7km/4 miles
Gauge: 1000mm/39½in
Cog railway, steam traction
May–September

6. **Zillertalbahn**
Route: Jenbach – Mayrhofen (Tirol)
Length: 32km/20 miles
Gauge: 760mm/30in
Steam and diesel traction
Throughout the year

7. **Schafbergbahn**
Route: St Wolfgang – Schafberg (Salzburg province)
Length: 5.9km/3½ miles
Gauge: 1000mm/39½in
Steam and diesel traction
May–October

8. **Linz – Urfahr – Pöstlingberg Railway** (Upper Austria)
Length: 2.9km/1¾ miles
Gauge: 1000mm/39½in
Electric traction
Throughout the year

9. **Gurktalbahn**
Route: Traibach – Zwischenwässern (Carinthia)
Length: 3.3km/2 miles
Gauge: 760mm/30in
Steam and diesel traction
Saturdays in summer

10. **Preding – Stainz Railway** (Styria)
Length: 11.3km/7 miles
Gauge: 760mm/30in
Steam and diesel traction
According to demand, special trips for steam enthusiasts and amateur engine-drivers by arrangement (apply to Stainz station)

Internal Fare Structure

Standard Rate Fares

Austrian standard rate tickets come in a variety of forms: cardboard tickets, EDV tickets, tickets for automatic machines, printed or hand-written tickets and books of tickets. Ordinary 1st and 2nd class tickets may be purchased for local and semi-fast trains; some high speed trains (marked on the time-table with EX, D or MIT) require high-speed train tickets. Tickets for distances between 1 and 70km are valid for 1 day. Tickets for distances over 70km are valid for 2 months. If you buy a ticket with a maximum validity of 4 days you can get up to a 20% reduction.

Child Reductions

Children below the age of 6 travel free as long as they do not take up a seat and children under 15 travel for half fare.

Student Reductions

Austrian students up to the age of 27 are entitled to 50% reductions on the production of their student railcard. Visiting students who intend to do a lot of rail travel are best served by one of the European student passes (see the International Section). See also the information on the Austria Ticket under Railrover Passes in this section.

Family Cards

Visiting families travelling by rail in Austria may well benefit from the Rail Europ Family Card (see International Section).

Senior Citizen Reductions

Senior citizens visiting Austria are advised to purchase the Rail Europ Senior Card (see International Section).

Party/Group Savers

Groups of 6 or more people travelling in the same class to the same destination can obtain a reduction of 30%. Special reductions are available for groups of students or young people. Reservations are generally recommended and they are compulsory for groups of more than 24 travellers.

Railrover Passes

Country and Federal State Season Tickets

These passes are valid for 9 days, 16 days or 1 month. The Country Season Ticket is valid for the whole *ÖBB* network while the Federal State Season Ticket only permits travel within one of the states, plus further half price travel for up to 70km in the connecting regions.

Austria Tickets

These are bargain tickets for those under 26 and are valid for 9 or 16 days. They give 'free' 2nd class travel on all *ÖBB* lines, domestic railway and post bus lines. They also cover travel on *ÖBB* ships which sail the Wolfgang Lake and the Donau Steamship Company whose ships sail between Vienna and Passau and cheap travel on Lake Constance and on a number of cable railways.

Austrian General Season Tickets
(Bundesnetz Karten)

These tickets give unlimited travel in 1st or 2nd class on the whole network and certain shipping services. Children must be accompanied by an adult. Prices for 1990 are as follows: 9 days 2nd class £74 (adult), £37 (child); 9 days 1st class £148 (adult); £74 (child); 16 days 2nd class £100 (adult), £50 (child); 16 days 1st class £200 (adult), £50 (child); 1 month 2nd class £158 (adult), £79 (child); 1 month 1st class £316 (adult), £158 (child).

The Austria ticket and Austrian General Season Ticket are both issued in the form of coupons which must be exchanged upon arrival in Austria at principal stations.

Rover Tickets

This ticket gives the traveller 1000km of travel but must be used on journeys over 71km. The ticket may be used on all trains and when exhausted will have given a reduction of 35% of the regular cost for the distance travelled.

Where to buy tickets

In Austria

Tickets may be purchased from any station booking office, some tourist agencies and from ticket machines. Alternatively, if tickets are unavailable for purchase at a station, they may be bought from the train conductor.

In Great Britain

European Rail Travel Centre
PO Box 303
Victoria Station
London SW1V 1JY
Tel: (071) 834 2345

Most tickets are available from:
DER Travel Service
18 Conduit Street
London W1R 9TD
Tel: (071) 499 0577/78

In the USA

From ÖBB representatives (see International Section).

Facilities on Trains

Sleepers and Couchettes

Austrian trains have 1, 2 or 3 berth sleepers. A 1st class ticket is required for all single compartments and some 2 berths. A 2nd class ticket is sufficient for tourist class compartments. There are reductions for children. Couchettes are included on most high speed and semi-fast night trains (they will be marked on the timetable).

Food

There are restaurant cars on the inter-city trains and expresses but facilities on local services are rare.

Luggage

Hand luggage is carried free. In Vienna and Innsbruck you can arrange for luggage to be taken from your residence to the station (or vice versa) for a reasonable fee. This service must be booked one working day in advance.

Disabled

Wheelchairs designed specially to fit into the train carriages may be booked up to 3 days before departure. Station staff will help with boarding and disembarking from the train.

Bicycle Carriage

Bikes can be taken as accompanied luggage on trains for a modest fee. Sent as unaccompanied luggage the charge is double and if the bike travels on a separate train it may arrive up to 3 days later.

Motorail

Motorail services operate from Vienna, Salzburg and Villach to various destinations in Europe. In the summer, motorail trains leave Salzburg and Villach for Germany, Belgium and the Netherlands and they leave Vienna for Venice, Rimini, Rijeka and Split. Bookings are available up to 2 months before departure date at the larger rail stations and at selected travel agents. Reductions are obtainable depending on the number of passengers travelling.

Animals

Animals carried in baskets and small dogs travel free. However, other dogs will be charged at half the normal 2nd class fare on local and semi-fast trains.

Telephone

On some trains, as a special service, a 'phone is linked to the public telephone system. The 'phones will connect to all numbers available within the country or abroad. The service is indicated in Section B of the timetable.

Facilities at Stations

Food

Most stations have restaurants which are open during normal working hours.

Reservations

The booking system enables passengers to book tickets and other facilities by 'phone, teleprinter or post. For passengers intent on a problem-free journey the 'train service pass' may also be booked. This service takes care of seat reservation, luggage organisation, porter service, luggage insurance and complimentary drinks.

Tourist Information

Tourist offices can be found in stations at major centres like Vienna, Salzburg and Innsbruck. The offices are normally open between 8am and 5pm.

Luggage

At most major stations there are luggage offices, left luggage lockers and trolleys.

Bureau de Change

Most major stations have facilities for changing foreign currency, travellers cheques or Eurocheques into Austrian schillings.

Car Hire

Stations which are marked with a car on the timetable offer car hire facilities from Monday to Friday (8am to 6pm). Cars can be ordered from all *ÖBB* stations, selected travel agencies and from conductors on fast or semi-fast trains. The booking must be made at least 2 hours before the arrival of the train. The maximum period of hire is 3 days and the car must be returned to the station from which it was hired.

Bicycle Hire

Stations which are marked with a bicycle in the timetable offer bicycle hire facilities between April and November. To hire a bike you will be asked to produce an identity card or passport. Bicycles can be returned to any station within opening hours. It is advisable to make advance reservations by 'phone, especially in the height of summer.

Belgium

Illuminated Grand' Place, Brussels

Introduction

Belgium, the major battle-ground of Europe for centuries, is a country with rich cultural and historical associations. Of particular interest are the Gothic University cities that were at the centre of the great era of Flemish naval and commercial supremacy. These cities, whose wealth was abruptly cut short by the silting up of the rivers on which they depended, have changed little in appearance since those times.

Belgium can be geographically divided into three parallel east-west bands: lower Belgium, with its lowlands reclaimed from the sea and its many dunes; middle Belgium, with its more fertile hilly landscapes; and upper Belgium, which is characterised by the steep hills and deep valleys of the Ardennes. Being a small country, and with no regions over 700 m in height, the Belgian climate is a temperate oceanic one and is determined by the prevalent westerly and south-westerly winds.

Belgium occupies an area of some 30,500 sq km and has a population of 10 million. Half of this population live in the country's many towns, and a further 38% live in urbanised communities. These figures underline the highly developed nature of the Belgian economy, and the fact that the population is very diverse. This has led to much internal strife. The country is divided linguistically into Flemish and French. There is also a small German-speaking community in the east border regions. Brussels, the capital, is officially bi-lingual. The conflicts arise over linguistic discrimination and economic injustice. These conflicts, however, do not extend to religion, as over 8 million Belgians join in belonging to the Roman Catholic church.

Under the provisions of the 1831 constitution, which was revised in 1921, Belgium is a constitutional monarchy in which the monarch's role is limited to representative and official functions. The governing of the country is directed by the Council of Ministers, headed by the Prime Minister, and is carried out in Parliament. The Belgian parliament consists of two chambers, the Senate and the Lower House. The members of both chambers are elected for four years. Brussels, the capital and centre of government, is also a major centre for international organisations, among them the Secretariat of NATO and the Commission of the EEC.

The Belgian economy is industrially based and is now one of the most modern industrial economies in the world. Initially, the basis of the economy was the mining of coal and iron ore. Now the export-orientated metal processing industry is the most important section of the economy. The more traditional textile and glass industries also flourish. The glass works supply 25% of total world production. Only 6% of the population are employed in agriculture. But modern techniques and the increasing use of technology enables the sector to supply the majority of the basic foodstuffs that the population requires. Tourism makes a relatively small contribution to the economy, and the visitors that do come tend to head for the sandy beaches of the north-west or to the old historic cities such as Antwerp or Bruges.

Belgium did not attain full independence until 1830 so it is impossible to disassociate its artistic achievements of the Middle Ages from those of the Dutch. A host of outstanding artists worked in Flanders during the 15th and 16th centuries, among them the van Eyck brothers, Hubert (c 1370–1426) and Jan (c 1390–1441), Rogier van der

'Head of Christ' in the Cathedral of Antwerp

Weyden (c 1400–64), Hans Memling (1430–95) a German who worked in Bruges, Quentin Metsys (1466–1530), a member of the St Lukes Guild in Antwerp and Joos van Cleve (d. about 1540) who became the court painter of Francis I of France. Pieter Breughel (c 1525–69) painted peasant scenes and seasonal landscapes.

The Gothic period also saw the zenith of Flemish architecture, both religious and secular. The cathedrals of Tournai (begun in 1140) and Antwerp (begun in 1352) are two fine examples as are the many town houses, guildhalls and belfries, often built for wealthy Flemish cloth-makers. Such ostentatious design was repeated during the Baroque era, particularly in Brussels, in huge architectural projects such as the National Bank (built 1859–64) and the Law Courts (1866–83). In modern architecture the influence of Henry van der Velde (1863–1957) was extensive. One of the founders of the Art Nouveau style, he achieved his main success in Germany where he designed the College of Applied Art in Weimar.

The dividing line between the Flemish and French linguistic areas runs right across Belgium and ever since the Middle Ages, a bilingual literature has developed on the territory of the present kingdom. Flemish literature, and French writing in the Walloon linguistic area represent independent literary branches. The French-language literature of Belgium was for centuries closely connected with France, and Paris in particular. Attempts to foster a specifically 'Belgian-French' style led to the appearance of the journal 'La Jeune Belgique' founded by Max Waller in the late 19th century. Among the best known names associated with the journal were the poet Albert Giraud (1860–1929) and Emile Verhaeren (1855–1916). In the 20th century, the novelist Georges Simenon (b 1903) is perhaps the best known.

Within the field of music, several Walloon composers made a name for themselves in Paris in the 18th century, among them André Gréty (1742–1813), one of the founders of the French 'Opéra Comique'. In the 19th century, César Franck from Liège was perhaps the only Belgian-born composer to acquire international recognition but he took French citizenship and worked for most of his life in Paris. Generally, Belgian music is better known for its interpreters than for its composers.

Royal Palace, Brussels

History

58 BC–AD 500	Roman occupation
10th–14th centuries	Emergence of counties, duchies and towns in Low Countries
1384–1473	Low Countries united under the Dukes of Burgundy
1550	Calvinism becomes dominant creed, endangering cohesion of the state
1568	Northern Netherlands begin to fight Spanish rule
1604	Split of northern and southern parts – later still under Spanish rule
1714	Spanish Netherlands becomes Austrian
1789	Popular uprising. Republic of the United Belgian States formed
1815–30	Kingdom of United Netherlands. Popular uprising in Belgium against the Dutch
1830	Belgium declares its independence
1908	Congo becomes a Belgian colony
1914–18	German occupation
1939–45	German occupation
1951	Baudouin becomes King after abdication of Leopold III
1958	Customs and Economic Union of the Benelux countries
1960	Belgian Congo becomes an independent republic
1963	Linguistic barriers between Flemings and Walloons fixed

1981	New four-party coalition government formed under premiership of Dr Wilfried Martens
1984	Three-year austerity programme launched by the government
1985	Prime Minister, Dr Wilfried Martens, forms new government
1985	41 killed in soccer riot in Brussels

Major Centres

Brussels

Commissariat-Général au Tourisme
Rue du Marché aux Herbes
Tel: (2) 513 9090

Tourisme Information Bruxelles
Rue du Marché aux Herbes
Tel: (2) 513 8940

Embassies:
UK: Britannia House
28 Rue Joseph II
Tel: (2) 217900

USA: 27 Boulevard du Régent
Tel: (2) 513 4450

Brussels is the capital of Belgium and is also the headquarters of NATO, the EEC, and numerous other international organisations. Once the centre of the Emperor Charles V's court, it developed rapidly after it was made the Belgian capital in 1830. It is now the financial and economic hub of the country. Officially Brussels is a bilingual city, but in the central section French is the language predominantly used.

Mannekin Pis, Brussels

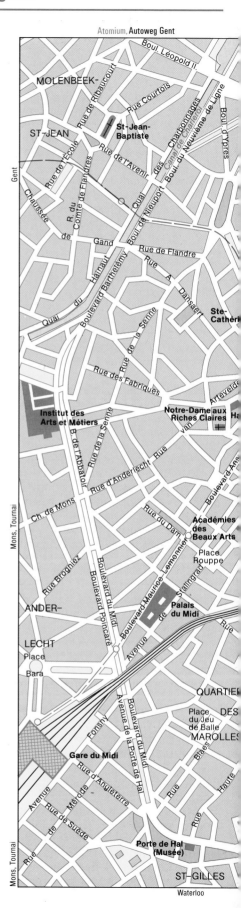

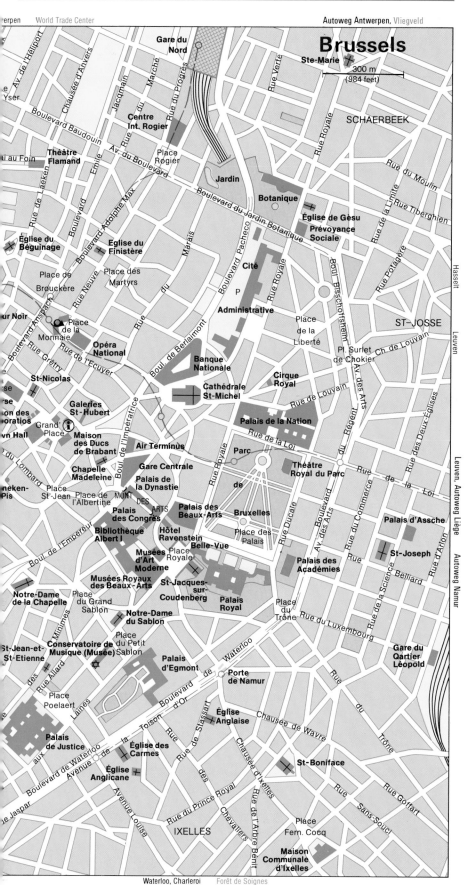

Antwerp

300 m (984 feet)

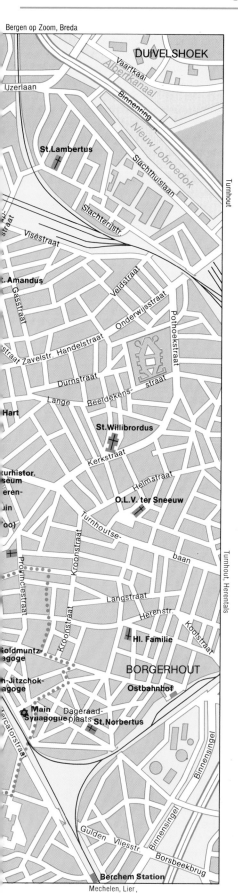

Sightseeing

Atomium – built as a model of an atom of iron for the World Exhibition of 1958; it measures 110m high and weighs 2500 tons

Basilique Nationale du Sacré Coeur – enormous church, begun in 1926 and consecrated in 1951

Bois de la Cambre – a superb wooded park, 2km long and 500m wide

Cathedral – a majestic structure, dating from the 13th–15th centuries

Grand' Place – the main square in the middle of the Old Town surrounded by Baroque and Gothic buildings

Hotel Ravenstein – dating from the 15th–16th centuries, it is the last surviving mansion from the Burgundy period in Brussels

Law Courts – the largest building of the 19th century with an area of 26,000sq m, bigger than St Peter's in Rome

Manneken Pis – the famous fountain with a bronze statue of a little boy relieving himself, created in 1619

Place Royale – Museum of Modern Art, Royal Museum of Fine Arts

Royal Museum of Arts and History – housed within the Palais du Cinquantenaire and containing an excellent summary of Belgian history from early times

Royal Palace – built 1827–9 on the site of the old Ducal Palace, which was destroyed by fire in 1731

Town Hall – 60m long and 50m wide, it is one of the largest and most beautiful of its kind in Belgium

Antwerp

Dienst voor Toerisme
Gildekamerstraat, 9
Tel: (3) 232 0103/232 2284

Information Office
Koningin Astridplein
Tel: (3) 233 0570

The Brabo Fountain with Cathedral in background, Antwerp

One of the largest sea ports in the world, Antwerp has been an important commercial city for centuries. Positioned like Ghent on the river Schelde, it lies 88km from the Schelde estuary and the North Sea. Antwerp boasts a splendid Gothic Cathedral, and is also an important centre of the diamond industry.

Sightseeing

Cathedral – largest Gothic Church in Belgium, containing three works by Rubens

Church of St Jacob – dates from the 15th–16th centuries, decorated in a rich Baroque style; a side chapel contains a fine altarpiece by Rubens and the artist's tomb

Exchange – built 1868–72 by J Schadde in the style of the old Stock Exchange which was destroyed by fire in 1858

National Maritime Museum – has numerous models of ships, and a large collection of nautical instruments and old sea charts

Plantin Moretus Museum – fine example of Flemish Renaissance architecture, with well-preserved interior

Royal Museum of Fine Arts – some 1800 paintings and sculptures from the 19th–20th centuries, and a collection of old masters from the Dutch and Flemish schools

Town Hall – richly decorated interior, including tapestries by H Leys depicting the history of Antwerp

Zoo – with an Aquarium, Dolphinarium, Reptile House, Nocturnal House and Planetarium

Brugge

Tourist Information Office
Markt 7
Tel: (50) 33 07 11

Lace-maker in Brugge

Brugge is a city of medieval splendour characterised by soaring belfries and an intricate network of canals. There is a pleasant air of tranquillity throughout the city and plenty to discover. Numerous galleries provide the opportunity to see some of the world's greatest art. The Beguinage, a magnificent town hall and the 353ft belfry are just some of the remarkable sights which make Brugge such a fascinating place to visit.

Sightseeing

Belfry and Halles – a remarkable monument dated 13th–16th century. A 260-ft-high tower can be climbed by means of 366 steps. On the second storey is a wrought iron railing, all that is left of the former medieval treasure room. Also on display is the triumph-bell which weighs 11,400lbs

Town Hall – one of the oldest Gothic town halls in the Low Countries. Particularly prized is the Gothic Hall with its graceful hanging-vault ceiling and wall-paintings

Groeninge Museum – masterpieces housed here include works by J Van Eyck, P Christus, H Van der Goes, H Memling, R Van der Weyden, G David, H Bosch, P Bruegel the Younger and many others

Church of Our Lady – the church is famous for its paintings, carvings and the white marble statue of the Madonna and Child by Michelangelo

St John's Hospital and Memling Museum – originally a charitable institution of the 12th century. Masterpieces by Hans Memling can be viewed in an adjoining chapel

Beguinage – the 'Princely Beguinage of the Vineyard' was founded in 1245. Today it is lived in by the Benedictine Sisters

Jerusalem Church – built in the 15th century following the plans of the Holy Sepulchre in Jerusalem

Lace Centre – training centre where lace-makers of all ages are instructed in the ancient craft of making bobbin lace. There is an impressive lace collection

Ghent

Dienst voor Toerisme
Borluutstraat 9
Tel: (91) 25 3641 and 23 36 41

This beautiful old university city is the capital of the province of East Flanders. Once one of the largest commercial cities in Europe, Ghent lies at the confluence of the rivers Schelde and Leie. After a period of decline, it is now the site of many major industries, and is once again an important commercial city. The city boasts a fine cathedral and an imposing medieval fortress.

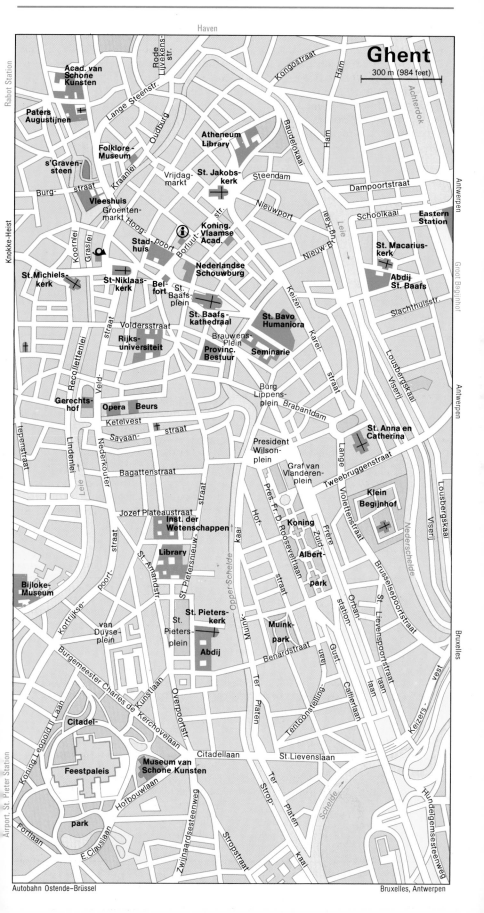

Haven

Ghent

300 m (984 feet)

Rabot Station

Acad. van Schone Kunsten

Paters Augustijnen

s'Graven-steen

Folklore-Museum

Lange Steenstr.

Oudburg

Rode Lievekens-str.

Kongostraat

Ham

Achterdok

Antwerpen

Atheneum Library

Baudelokaai

Vrijdag-markt

St. Jakobs-kerk

Steendam

Dampoortstraat

Burg-straat

Kraanlei

Groenten-markt

Nieuwport

Schoolkaai

Eastern Station

Vleeshuis

Koornlei

Graslei

Hoog-poort

Koning. Vlaamse Acad.

Borluut

Nieuw-B.

Stad-huis

St. Macarius-kerk

St. Michiels-kerk

St-Niklaas-kerk

Bel-fort

St. Baafs-plein

Nederlandse Schouwburg

Keizer

Abdij St. Baafs

Slachthuisstr.

St. Baafs-kathedraal

St. Bavo Humaniora

Karel-straat

Lousbergskaai

Viserij

Voldersstraat

Rijks-universiteit

Brauwens Plein

Provinc. Bestuur

Seminarie

Veld-straat

Recollettenlei

Gerechts-hof

Opera

Beurs

Ketelvest

Savaan-straat

Burg Lippens-plein

Brabantdam

St. Anna en Catherina

Iepenstraat

Lindenlei

Lele

Nederkouter

Bagattenstraat

President Wilson-plein

Graf van Vlanderen-plein

Lange

Violettenstraat

Tweebruggenstraat

Klein Begijnhof

Lousbergskaai

Viserij

Jozef Plateaustraat

Inst. der Wetenschappen

Koning

Frère

Nederschelde

St.-Amandstr.

poort-straat

Library

Opper-Schelde

Hof-straat

Pres. Fr. D. Rooseveltlaan

Albert-park

Zuid-station

Brusselsepoortstraat

St. Lievenspoortstraat

Bruxelles

Bijloke-Museum

Kortrijkse-poort-straat

van Duyse-plein

St. Pieters-kerk

St. Pieters-plein

Muink-park

Benardstraat

Orban-laan

Gust. Callierlaan

Citadel-

Feestpaleis

Burgemeester Charles de Kerchovelaan

Overpoortstr.

Abdij

Munk-

Ter Platen

Tentoonstelling-laan

Koning Leopold II Laan

Fortlaan

E. Clausiaan

park

Museum van Schone Kunsten

Hofbouwlaan

Zwijnaardsesteenweg

Citadellaan

St.Lievenslaan

Strop-straat

Ter Platen

Scheide

Strop-kaai

Stropstraat

Keizers-vest

Hundelgemsesteenweg

Airport, St. Pieter Station

Knokke-Heist

Groot Begijnhof

Antwerpen

Begonia show in Lochristi, near Ghent

Sightseeing

Abbey of St Bavon – by legend founded in 642 by Saint Amandus, it now houses a lapidary collection

Cathedral of St Bavon – begun in the 10th century, it contains the Altar of Ghent, the greatest masterpiece of old Flemish painting by Jan van Eyck and his brother Hubert

Church of St Michael – begun in 1440 and completed in the 17th century, except for the massive tower which remains unfinished; the impressive interior houses a number of altarpieces including one by Van Dyck

House of Free Boatman – perhaps the most beautiful Gothic guildhall in Belgium

Museum of Fine Arts – holds a number of interesting old and modern paintings, tapestries and sculptures

Museum voor Volkskunde – provides a vivid picture of Flemish life; previously it was a children's hospital founded in 1363 and restored in 1962

's Gravensteen – one of the strongest moated fortresses in Western Europe, built 1180–1200 on the foundation of a 9th-century structure

Town Hall – one of the best examples of Gothic secular architecture in Belgium

Accommodation

Hotels and Inns

Hotels in the larger towns and resorts in Belgium provide the usual international comfort. Advanced booking is recommended, especially in high season. In Belgium, the houses bearing the appellation 'Hotel', 'Pension', 'Hostellerie', 'Auberge', 'Gasthof', 'Motel', must satisfy the standards for amenities and comfort laid down by law.

Prices and particulars of the rooms should be posted up both at the reception desk and in the rooms. The price of meals must be exhibited in the entrance of the restaurant.

The tourist season is considered to begin on July 1st and to end on August 31st including, in addition, Easter, Whitsun, Christmas and New Year Holidays.

Children are particularly welcomed in Belgium. The majority of hotels provide special prices for young children.

If you make your reservation by telephone, confirmation must be made in writing detailing:
– the number of rooms required, single or double beds, with or without private bath or shower
– the number of people to be accommodated
– any personal preferences (overlooking street or garden, etc)
– day and time of arrival and day of departure.

Country House Hotels

In Belgium, there are a number of country-house hotels well known for their high standards and for their attractive locations. Frequently, they provide opportunities for fishing, hunting or riding. Generally, they have only a limited number of rooms and advance booking is therefore recommended.

Hotel Price Range

Benelux classification	Price for 1 night in francs	
	1 Person	2 Persons
****	2800	3959
***	1200	2000
**	800	1500
*	600	1000

These prices are intended to act as a rough guide only.

Youth Hostels

Youth hostels in Belgium provide low-priced accommodation for young people. There is no age limit and no restriction on the length of time you can stay. A youth hostel card from the country of origin is required.

Information:
Vlaamse Jeugdherbergcentrale
Van Stralenstraat 40
B-2000 Antwerpen
Tel: (03) 232 7218

Centrale Wallonne des Auberges de la Jeunesse
Rue Van Oost 52
B-1030 Bruxelles
Tel: (02) 215 3100

Holiday Flats and Villas
(Vacation Rentals)

Numerous vacation apartments and villas are available on the coast as well as inland. Here also, advance booking is recommended in high season. Information can be obtained from the Tourist Bureaux.

Farm Vacations

Opportunities for farm vacations (*Agrivacances*) are widely available in Belgium. Camping at farms is also possible.

Camping and Caravanning

Belgium is particularly well-suited to camping and caravanning. There are well-appointed camp sites in most tourist resorts and off the beaten track in quiet river valleys or in the dune areas on the coast. Holders of an international camping card qualify for a range of price reductions. In high season, many sites are filled to capacity. Camping in the open is limited to a few areas because of the population density. It requires permission from the owner of the land.

Introduction to Rail Information

Belgium has one of the densest rail systems in the world with a large network of just under 4000km in a country of 30,000sq km. The rail company goes by two names: *Nationale Maatschappij der Belgische Spoorwegen (NMBS)* in Dutch and *Société Nationale des Chemins de Fer Belges (SNCB)* in French. As the country is so small it only takes 3 hours 50 minutes to cross it and trains leave for most destinations at regular intervals. The rail company is treated very much like a government department with the Minister of Transport also taking the position of Chairman of the Board. Perhaps because of the close relationship between the two, most Belgians do not pay the full fare as so many groups are eligible for reductions.

Major International Services

Trains

Connection	Duration	Frequency
Paris–Brussels	2–3hrs	12 times daily
Cologne–Brussels	2–3hrs	15 times daily
Amsterdam–Brussels	2–3hrs	20 times daily
Maastricht–Brussels	2hrs	14 times daily
Luxembourg–Brussels	2½–3hrs	15 times daily
Lille–Brussels	1½–2hrs	8 times daily
Lille–Antwerpen	1hr 50m	7 times daily

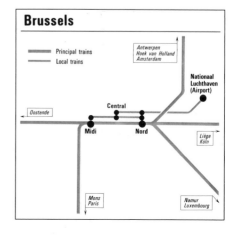

Brussels

Principal trains
Local trains

Antwerpen
Hoek van Holland
Amsterdam

Nationaal Luchthaven (Airport)

Oostende

Central

Midi   Nord

Liège Köln

Mons Paris

Namur Luxembourg

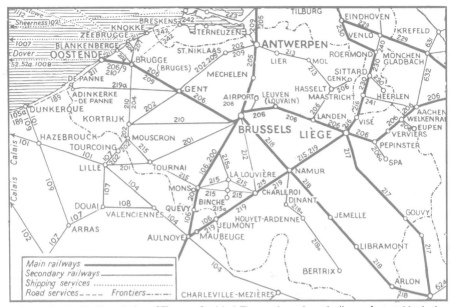

Map supplied by kind permission of Thomas Cook Ltd. The numbers along the lines refer to tables in the *Thomas Cook Continental Timetable.*

Castle's Gravensteen in Ghent

Zurich/Basle–Brussels

Two very fast trains, the IC 'Iris' and 'Edelweis' along with three other trains link Belgium with Switzerland. One of these is a night train.

Train/Ferry Connections

London–Brussels
By train and boat via Dover/Folkestone –Ostend and by rail from Ostend to Brussels. (About 8–10 hours.)

Dover–Ostend (by Jetfoil)
Up to 5 times a day a Jetfoil (hydrofoil) crosses from Dover to Ostend, to co-incide with immediate train connec-tions to the most important cities of the country. It takes 5 hours to get from London to Brussels. For the return jour-ney there are also immediate train con-

nections from the principal railway sta-tions and even from Roosendaal and Cologne. It is recommended to book your seat in advance (compulsory for groups of 10 passengers and more). The same rates apply as on other boats. A 'speed supplement' is usually payable per passenger per crossing; children aged between 1 and 4 pay this supplement alone.

Ostend Harbour

Major Internal Services

Connection	Duration	Frequency
Zeebrugge–Bruges– Roeselare–Kortrijk	1–2hrs	16 times daily

SNCB rolling stock

Brussels–Kortrijk	1–2hrs	15 times daily
Kortrijk–Ieper–Poperinge	½–1hr	16 times daily
Antwerpen–Mechelen–Brussels–Charleroi	1–2hrs	29 times daily
Brussels–Mons	½–1hr	15 times daily
Knokke–Blankenberge–Bruges–Ghent St P–Brussels–Leuven–Hasselt–Genk–Liège	2–3hrs	14 times daily
Ostend–Brussels–Liège–Verviers	2–3hrs	15 times daily
Verviers–Spa	½hr	15 times daily
Ostend–Ghent–Antwerpen	1–2hrs	17 times daily
Brussels–Namur–Marloie–Jemelle–Libramont–Arlon	2–3hrs	15 times daily
Namur–Dinant	½hr	14 times daily

The Meuse near Profondeville

Scenic Routes

There are certain routes which are recommended by *SNCB* as being particularly picturesque. These are Namur to Givet which runs along the valley of the River Meuse; then Namur to Luxembourg and Liège to Luxembourg which both run through the Ardennes.

Internal Fare Structure

Standard Rate Fares

The ordinary single fares per kilometre are: 4.10BF in 1st class and 2.75BF in 2nd class. The return fare for a journey between 2 *SNCB* stations is double the single fare. These return tickets, obtainable at rail stations, are valid for 2 consecutive days, including the day of issue. The outward journey must be made on the date mentioned on the ticket. The return journey must be commenced at the latest at midnight on the second day. The validity of the return ticket is, however, extended by one day for each Sunday or Public Holiday following immediately thereafter.

Child Reductions

Children under 6 travel free. Children between 6 and 11 are entitled to half fares.

Student Reductions

There are special reductions for Belgian students but visiting students are eligible only for the international student rate fares (see details in the International Section).

Family Reductions

Families travelling in Belgium in groups of between 3 and 8 are advised to invest in the Rail Europ Family Card (see International Section).

Senior Citizen Reductions

Senior Citizens travelling in Belgium are advised to invest in the Rail Europ Senior Card (see details in the International Section).

Party/Group Savers

Reductions are available for school-children travelling in parties of 10 or over. The reduction is usually 50%, but the group may be entitled to free tickets depending on the nature of the group and the numbers involved.

Adults travelling in groups of 10 or more may also be eligible for reductions of 25% or more depending on the size of the group and the mileage covered.

Special Excursion/Holiday Rates

Day Excursions

'A Lovely Day in . . .' tickets give considerable reductions (50% adults, 75% children) not only on train and bus tickets, but also on tickets for visiting museums, castles, grottos, sightseeing trips, boat trips, ski-lifts, cablecars, etc. Tickets are on sale until departure time in main stations; they must be requested 48 hours in advance in other stations. Tours are available to Antwerp Zoo, the seaside, the Ardennes and many other tourist spots.

The reductions are subject to certain restrictions, depending primarily on the time and distance you travel. Please note also that you may not break your journey with these tickets. A Belgian Rail Station should be contacted for full details of these restrictions.

A rural scene in the Ardennes

Minitrips

SNCB run a number of inclusive minitrips during the summer and winter. These consist of 2, 3, 4, 5 or 7 day visits to towns in Austria, Belgium, Denmark, France, West Germany, Holland, Italy, Luxembourg, Spain, Sweden and Switzerland. The Minitrips brochure which is available at all main line stations gives full details.

Railrover Passes

Runabout Tickets

The following runabout tickets enable you to travel freely on the whole SNCB network without any distance limit but within their period of validity. They can be used for travel to and from the national border. A supplement must be paid when travelling on TEE and IC trains.

a) 16 consecutive day runabout ticket; issued all year round, available only at a fixed adult rate. Fares are 2920BF (2nd class) and 4380BF (1st class).

b) 5-day B-Tourrail ticket; valid within a period of 16 days issued as from the 15th day before Easter until September 30th and from December 15th–31st.

2nd class fares are 780BF (6–11 year olds); 1170BF (12–25 year olds) and 1550BF (adults). 1st class fares are 1170BF (6–11 year olds); 1760BF (12–25 year olds); 2350BF (adults).

c) 8-day B-Tourrail ticket valid within a period of 16 days issued as from the 15th day before Easter until September 30th and from December 15th–31st. 2nd class fares are 1030BF (6–11 year olds); 1540BF (12–25 year olds) and 2050BF (adults). 1st class fares are 1550BF (6–11 year olds); 2310BF (12–25 year olds) and 3080BF (adults).

Passengers should ensure that they understand the 'shading square' validation procedure. If the holder omits to shade a square the ticket is considered invalid and the holder must pay the fare and an additional surtax of 600BF. Also, you must sign the ticket on receipt.

The 50% Reduction Card

The 50% reduction card is valid for one month on the whole of the *SNCB*. It is obtainable all the year round and enables you to buy – during the valid period – an unlimited number of single tickets at half fare. It can also be used for travel to and from adjoining countries, as long as it is valid as far as, or from the border. To be valid, the 50% reduction card must be signed by the holder as soon as he/she receives it.

With a total distance potential of 454km in 1st class and 435km in 2nd class travel, it is often cheaper to use a 50% reduction card than to buy ordinary single tickets.

Tourist Reductions

Especially attractive for tourists is the Benelux Tourrail Card which is available between 1 April and 31 October. It entitles the holder to unlimited travel on any self-selected 5 days out of a specified validity of 17 days over all Netherlands Railways (*NS*), Belgian Railways (*SNCB*), Luxembourg Railways (*CFL*) and by *CFL* country buses in Luxembourg. It cannot be used in the Netherlands in conjunction with the Public Transport Link Rover. It can be used for travel by D and IC trains without supplement. Holders of this card are required to carry a valid passport for identification purposes. The price of the card for 2nd class travel is £31 for 4–25 year olds, and £43·50 adults; for 1st class travel the price is approximately 50% extra. Tickets are available from railway stations in the countries concerned and from Netherlands Railways offices in Great Britain and the United States (see International Section). In Great Britain, the card may also be bought at Youth Hostels Association Travel, 14 Southampton Street, London WC2.

Where to buy tickets

In Belgium

At any *SNCB* station.

In Great Britain

European Rail Travel Centre
PO Box 303
Victoria Station
London SW1V 1JY
Tel: (071) 834 2345

or

Youth Hostel Association
14 Southampton Street
London WC2E YHY

In USA

From *SNCB* rail representatives (see International Section).

Facilities on Trains

Luggage

Each passenger may keep with him, free of charge and at his own risk, as much luggage as he can reasonably carry by hand. All other luggage must be registered. The rates vary according to distance and are applied per fraction

Two *SNCB* trains

of 10kg with a minimum of 186BF up to 10kg and 280BF over 10kg.

Bicycle Carriage

Bicycles can be registered between any two points in Belgium to be transported for a moderate fee. Bike tickets must be purchased from the luggage office, or on local trains, from the guard. The bicycles must be wheeled into the station and the passenger is responsible for loading and transferring the bicycle.

Motorail

SNCB run motorail services from Brussels to Milan, Salzburg, Brig, Villach, Ljubljana, Avignon, St Raphael, Toulouse, Narbonne, Brive, Biarritz, Bordeaux, Nantes and Auray. All services have sleeping cars and couchettes. In Britain, detailed information

SNCB train set against urban landscape

about the services is available from the Belgian National Railways office (please refer to the International Section).

Animals

Accompanied dogs and other small animals carried without cages are conveyed on trains upon payment of 50% of the 2nd class passenger fare with a maximum fare of 50BF per animal and per single journey. They cannot occupy a seat. If they are kept in cages, dogs and other small animals are conveyed free of charge (there are certain cage dimension restrictions).

Facilities at Stations

Left Luggage

Luggage can be left at any station in Belgium for a moderate fee.

Bicycle Hire

Bicycles can be hired all the year round from most major *SNCB* stations. When making a booking, passengers must state the number of bicycles required and also their arrival time at the station. Bicycles can either be returned to the station from which they were hired or to any of the 101 selected stations in Belgium. A list of the selected stations will be provided, upon request, by the bicycle-hire service station.

Denmark

The Little Mermaid, Copenhagen

Introduction

Denmark provides the stepping stone from continental Europe to the Scandinavian peninsula. Jutland, its largest province, is the only area of Scandinavia attached to mainland Europe and is, in turn, closely linked to the island of Denmark by a system of road bridges and ferries. Copenhagen, on the island of Zealand, is the capital of Denmark and also Scandinavia's largest city.

As the southernmost country of Scandinavia, Denmark also has the most temperate climate. Temperatures vary very little within a small area, although it is much cooler in the north than in the south. In Copenhagen, the temperature averages from −1.2°C in February to 17.2°C in July. August is invariably the wettest month and the winter is usually stormy and changeable. The coast of Denmark usually remains ice-free.

The Exchange, Copenhagen

The total area of Denmark is just over 43,000sq km. Today, the population of some 5 million is largely urbanised, though there are few large towns apart from Copenhagen. The religion is predominantly Lutheran.

Agriculture is still a major sector of the Danish economy and the processing of agricultural products is the most important part of Danish industry. Since Denmark's entry into the EEC in 1972, however, a massive investment programme has almost doubled Denmark's industrial production and drawn more young people to the towns. The fishing industry has declined owing to over-fishing of the North Sea and West Baltic and Denmark's lack of raw material resources has resulted in a concentration on the processing industries such as machinery, shipping, furniture, glass, textiles, chemicals and pharmaceuticals. The main industrial areas are around Copenhagen and rely on the excellent shipping and ferry services which connect the islands with the mainland of Europe and Scandinavia.

The flowering of Scandinavian art followed the spread of Christianity in the 11th century. Churches are the lasting monuments to the Romanesque period notably Ribe and Viborg Cathedrals and Lund Cathedral (now in Sweden but architecturally belonging to Denmark). Gothic architecture is sparse in Denmark, but later Dutch, German and French influences were important, as the Prince's Palace (now a National Museum and modelled on the Hôtel de Ville in Paris) manifests.

The Dutch also left their mark on Danish sculpture and painting. Today, Danish painters are trying to break through the artistic isolation of Denmark, with financial support from the government Art Foundation.

History

7th and 8th centuries	Emergence of the Danish state during the Viking Age
9th to 11th centuries	Formation of the state, Christianisation and Viking expeditions
1000–1042	Danish Empire under Swein (985–1014) and Canute (1018–1035) conquer Norway and England, but the Empire falls to pieces after Canute's death
1157–1375	The Age of the Valdemars brings internal consolidation and external power
1375–1523	The unification of Denmark, Norway and Sweden under Danish rule
1660	Denmark becomes an unlimited hereditary monarchy

1720–1807	A long period of peace during which time Copenhagen becomes an important international and commercial centre
1807	British bombardment of Copenhagen in an attempt to involve Denmark in the Napoleonic Wars
1814	Treaty of Kiel. Denmark loses Norway and Heligoland
1849	Introduction of a constitution
1914–1945	Denmark remains neutral during both world wars, but is occupied during the Second World War
1944	Iceland breaks free of Denmark and becomes a republic
1949	Denmark abandons its neutral position after Second World War and joins NATO
1951	Denmark becomes a founding member of the Nordic Council
1972	Denmark joins the EEC
1979	Greenland is given its own administration but remains under Danish sovereignty
1982	Greenland votes to leave the EEC in a referendum
1984	Elections produce a minority four-party government under Prime Minister Poul Schlüter
1985	The Danish Parliament votes to end all trade with South Africa

Major Centres

Copenhagen

Danmarks Turistråd
(Danish Tourist Board)
H C Andersens Boulevard 22
DK-1553 København V
Tel: (1) 11 13 25

Embassies:
UK: 36/38/40 Kastelsvej
Tel: (1) 26 46 00
USA: Dag Hammarskjölds Alie 24
Tel: (1) 42 31 44

Copenhagen has been Denmark's capital city since 1445 and is today an important commercial and industrial city as well as the seat of government. It is also an exciting city, elegant and entertaining and with many distinctive features such as the famous Tivoli Gardens. The city centre comprises the medieval Rådhuspladsen (Town Hall Square) with Strøget – the main

shopping street open to pedestrians only – running off it. Visitors to Copenhagen can vary tours of the city with trips into the beautiful surrounding countryside. There is a national and international airport at nearby Kastrup.

The Chinese Tower, Tivoli

Sightseeing

Amalienborg Palace – Rococo-style residence of the Queen, built around an octagonal Palace Square

Christiansborg Palace – seat of the Danish government and Parliament (rebuilt 1907–16)

Exchange (Børsen, 1619–20) – a picturesque building in Dutch Renaissance style facing the harbour

National Museum – finely situated on the Frederiksholms Canal, houses a remarkable Danish collection of prehistoric material, antiquities and old coins and medals

Ny Carlsberg Glyptotek – perhaps Copenhagen's finest art collection

Rådhus – Town Hall, dominating the central square. At the main entrance the World Clock shows the time and date and astronomical constellations

Tivoli Amusement Park – best visited in the evening, a unique meeting-place with a carefree atmosphere

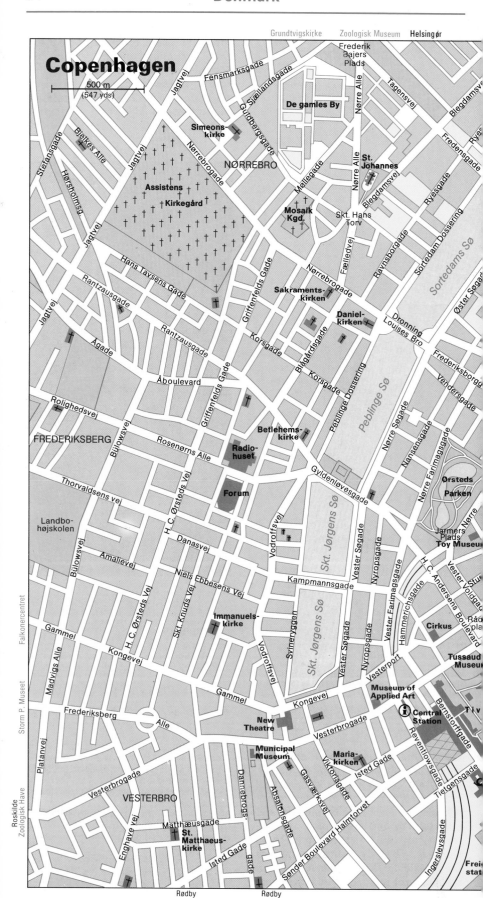

Copenhagen

500 m
(547 yds)

Grundtvigskirke   Zoologisk Museum   **Helsingør**

Frederik
Bajers
Plads

Fensmarksgade

Jagtvej

Guldbergsgade

Sjællandsgade

De gamles By

Nørre Alle

Tagensvej

Blegdamsv

**Simeons-
kirke**

Nørrebrogade

NØRREBRO

Møllegade

Nørre Alle

St.
Johannes

Fredensgade

Assistens
Kirkegård

Mosaik
Kgd.

Skt. Hans
Torv

Blegdamsvej

Ryesgade

Sortedam Dossering

Sortedams Sø

Stefansgade

Bjelkes Alle

Hørsholmsg.

Jagtvej

Hans Tavsens Gade

Sakraments-
kirken

Nørrebrogade

Fælledvej

Ravnsborggade

Øster Søgade

Rantzausgade

Jagtvej

Griffenfelds Gade

Daniel-
kirken

Dronning
Louises Bro

Frederiksborgg

Ågade

Rantzausgade

Korsgade

Blågårdsgade

Korsgade

Peblinge Dossering

Peblinge Sø

Vendersgade

Åboulevard

Griffenfelds Gade

Nørre Søgade

Nansensgade

Nørre Farimagsgade

Rolighedsvej

Betlehems-
kirke

FREDERIKSBERG

Bülowsvej

Rosenørns Alle

Radio-
huset

Gyldenløvesgade

Ørsteds
Parken

Thorvaldsens vej

H. C. Ørsteds Vej

Forum

Skt. Jørgens Sø

Jarmers
Plads
Toy Museum

Landbo-
højskolen

Danasvej

Vodroffsvej

Vester Søgade

Nørre

Bülowsvej

Amalievej

Niels Ebbesens Vej

Kampmannsgade

Vester Søgade

Nyropsgade

Vester Farimagsgade

Hammerichsgade

H. C. Andersens

Cirkus

Vester Voldga

Rå
pla

Falkonercentret

Gammel

H. C. Ørsteds Vej

Skt. Knuds Vej

Immanuels-
kirke

Vodroffsvej

Svineryggen

Skt. Jørgens Sø

Nyropsgade

Boulevard

Storm P. Museet

Kongevej

Gammel

Kongevej

Vesterport

Tussaud
Museu

Madvigs Alle

Frederiksberg

Alle

New
Theatre

Vesterbrogade

Museum of
Applied Art

Bernstorffsgade

Ti v

Platanvej

Municipal
Museum

Maria-
kirken

Central
Station

Reventlowsgade

Roskilde
Zoologisk Have

Vesterbrogade

VESTERBRO

Dannebrogs-
gade

Absalonsgade

Viktoriagade

Gasværksvej

Isted Gade

Tietgensgade

Ingerslevsgade

Enghave vej

Matthæusgade

St.
Matthaeus-
kirke

Isted Gade

Sønder Boulevard Halmtorvet

Freir
stat

Rødby   Rødby

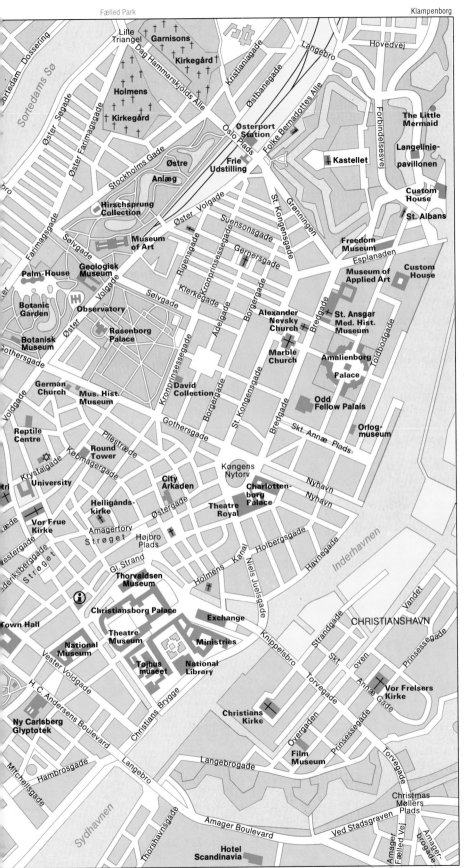

Fælled Park

Klampenborg

Sortedams Sø

Lille Triangel
Garnisons
Kirkegård
Holmens
Kirkegård
Østre Anlæg
Hirschsprung Collection
Museum of Art
Geologisk Museum
Palm-House
Botanic Garden
Observatory
Botanisk Museum
Rosenborg Palace
German Church
Mus. Hist. Museum
David Collection
Reptile Centre
Round Tower
University
Vor Frue Kirke
Helligånds-kirke
Amagertorv
Strøget
Højbro Plads
Gl. Strand
Thorvaldsen Museum
Christiansborg Palace
Town Hall
Theatre Museum
National Museum
Tøjhus museet
Ny Carlsberg Glyptotek

Østerport Station
Oslo Plads
Frie Udstilling

Øster Søgade
Øster Farimagsgade
Stockholms Gade
Dag Hammarskjölds Alle
Østbanegade
Kristianiagade
Solvgade
Øster Voldgade
Suensonsgade
Gernersgade
Klerkegade
Rigensgade
Kronprinsessegade
Borgergade
Adelgade
St. Kongensgade
Grønningen
Folke Bernadottes Alle
Langebro
Hovedvej
Forbindelsesvej

The Little Mermaid
Langelinie-pavillonen
Custom House
St. Albans
Kastellet
Freedom Museum
Esplanaden
Museum of Applied Art
Custom House
Alexander Nevsky Church
St. Ansgar Med. Hist. Museum
Marble Church
Amalienborg Palace
Odd Fellow Palais
Orlog-museum
Bredgade
Toldbodgade

Gothersgade
Pilestræde
Købmagergade
Krystalgade
Østergade
Strøget
Kongens Nytorv
Charlotten-borg Palace
Theatre Royal
Nyhavn
City Arkaden
Exchange
Ministries
Holbergsgade
Niels Juelsgade
Havnegade
Inderhavnen

CHRISTIANSHAVN
Strandgade
Prinsessegade
Vandet
Knippelsbro
Skt. Annæ Plads
Skt. oven
Torvegade
Annæ Gade
Vor Frelsers Kirke
Overgaden
Torvegade

National Library
H. C. Andersens Boulevard
Ny Carlsberg Glyptotek
Vester Voldgade
Christians Brygge
Christians Kirke
Film Museum
Langebro
Hambrosgade
Mitchellsgade
Sydhavnen
Thorshavnsgade
Langebrogade
Amager Boulevard
Ved Stadsgraven
Christmas Møllers Plads
Amager Fælled Vej
Amager brogade

Hotel Scandinavia

University, Bella Center, Airport

Museums and places of interest

Applied Art, Museum of
(Kunstindustrimuseet),
Bredgate 68.

Arsenal Museum
(Tøjhusmuseet),
Tøjhusgade 3.

Bakkehus Literary Museum
(Bakkehusmuseet),
Bahbeks Allé 23.

Botanic Garden, Palm House
(Botanisk Haves Palmehus),
Gothersgade 130.

Brøste Collection
(Brøstes Samling),
Christianshavn.

Carlsberg Brewery Museum,
Valby Langgade 1.

David Collection
(C L Davids Samling, European and Oriental handicrafts),
Kronprinsessegade 30.

Film Museum
(Det Danske Filmmuseum),
Store Søndervolstræde.

Freedom Museum
(Frihedsmuseet, Denmark's memorial to the Resistance, 1940–45),
Churchillparken.

Fyrskib XVII
(Lightship XVII),
Nyhavn 2.

Geological Museum
(Geologisk Museum),
Øster Voldgade 7.

Grundtvig Church
(Grundtvigs Kirke, modern cathedral in the style of a Danish village church),
På Bjerget.

Hirschsprung Collection
(Hirschsprungske Samling, 19th c. Danish art),
Stockholmsgade 20.

Holmen Church
(Holmens Kirke, the Church Royal),
Holmens Kanal.

Kastellet,
Langelinie.

Marble Church/Frederick Church
(Marmorkirken/Frederikskirken),
Frederiksgade 1.

Medical History, Museum of
(Medicinsk-historisk Museum),
Bredgate 62.

Motor Ship Museum
(B & W Museum),
Strandgade 4.

Municipal Museum and Kierkegaard Collection
(Bymuseum og Søren-Kierkegård-Samlingen),
Vesterbrogade 59.

Musical History Museum and Carl Claudius Collection
(Musikhistorisk Museum og Carl Claudius' Samling),
Åbenrå 34.

Naval Museum
(Orlogsmuseet),
Qvinti Lynette, Refshaleveg.

Postal and Telegraph Museum
(Post- og Telegrafmuseet),
Vesterbrogade 59.

Puppet Theatre Museum
(Dukketeatermuseet),
Købmagergade 52.

Railway Museum
(Jernbanemuseet),
Sølvgade 40.

Rosenborg Castle *(Crown Jewels)*
(Rosenborg Slot),
Østervoldgade 4A.

Round Tower
(Rundetårn),
Købmagergade.
Observatory: at present closed.

Royal Library
(Kongelige Bibliotek),
Christians Brygge 8.

Royal Stables
(Kongelige Stalde og Kareter),
Christiansborg Ridebane.

St Ansgar's Church Museum
(Museet ved Skt. Ansgars Kike),
Bredgade 64.

St Peter's Church
(Skt. Petri Kirke),
Nørregade/Sankt Peders Stæde.

State Museum of Art
(Statens Museum for Kunst),
Sølvgade.

Theatre Museum
(Teatermuseet),
Christiansborg Ridebane 18.

Thorvaldsen Museum
(Thorvaldsens Museum),
Slotsholmen, beside Christiansborg Palace.

Tobacco Museum
(Tobaksmuseet),
Amagertorv 9.

Toy Museum
(Legetøjsmuseet),
Teglgårdstræde 13.

Tussaud's Wax Museum
(Louis Tussauds Voksmuseum),
H C Andersens Boulevard 22.

Vor Frelsers Kirk
(Church of Our Saviour),
Prinsessegade.

Vor Frue Kirke
(Church of Our Lady),
Nørregade 6.

Zoological Garden
(Zoologisk Have),
Roskildevej 32.

Zoological Museum
(Zoologisk Museum)
Universitetsparken 15.

Town Hall Square, Copenhagen

Accommodation

Hotels

The hotels in Denmark, noted for their cleanliness, are right up to international standards of comfort and service for the different price categories. The large towns (advance reservations recommended) have luxury establishments, but many smaller places have excellent hotels combining international standards of comfort with distinctive national features. Even in the far north, there are good hotels and well-equipped inns which provide a very adequate standard of comfort. Many establishments have 'family rooms' with 3–5 beds which provide reasonably priced accommodation for a family group. Some mountain hotels in Denmark are open for only part of the year, during the summer and winter seasons. There are also special summer hotels.

For a stay of some length, it is more economical to take a room in a pension (guest-house). There are also a large number of motels in Denmark.

Youth Hostels

Youth hostels admit adults as well as young people, and have family rooms. An international youth hostel card is required. Information about vacation houses, vacation villages and farmhouse vacations can be obtained from the national tourist organisations.

The *kroer* (singular *kro*) of Denmark offer pleasant and comfortable accommodation. Some of the rooms are old and some new; all are full of character. The mission hotels (members of the Danish Mission Hotels Federation) are good and reasonably priced. They can be found in most Danish towns.

Hotel Price Range	
Type of hotel	Price in kroner for a double room for 1 night
Luxury	950–1400
Middle-grade	280– 700
Modest	220– 440

These prices are intended to act as a rough guide only.

Camping and Caravanning

Denmark is an ideal camping country, and there are numerous official campsites (*campingplads*). Campers should have an international camping carnet or the membership card of a national camping organisation. Lists of camp sites are issued annually by the national tourist organisations, motoring organisations and camping clubs, giving the location, size, facilities and category (1–3 stars) of the sites. In addition to the usual sanitary and cooking facilities, the larger sites normally have showers and shops selling provisions. On many sites there are also camping huts or chalets (simple wooden huts with sleeping accommodation). In areas of particular natural beauty, there are also vacation villages with chalets and log cabins.

Campers who want to camp on their own should always ask the owner's permission before camping on or near private property. In the sparsely populated northern areas, care should be taken to maintain an adequate supply of water. On the coast and on the shore of a fjord, it is advisable to pitch the tent so that the entrance is sheltered from the wind.

Introduction to Rail Information

The *Danske Statsbaner (DSB)* comprises over 2000km of track which is serviced mostly by diesel engines. The system is important not only as a means of transport on the mainland but also because, with the ferries, it

Lyntog at Copenhagen

provides an important link with surrounding islands and with Sweden. The services are divided into four types:

Lyntog – express trains used on long haul journeys

IC or Inter-city trains – these serve the shorter distances between the main centres

Regionaltoget – slower, regional trains

S-tog – Copenhagen's underground

Map supplied by kind permission of Thomas Cook Ltd. The numbers along the lines refer to tables in the *Thomas Cook Continental Timetable*.

Major International Services

Connection	Duration	Frequency
Copenhagen–Oslo	9–10hrs	4 times daily
Copenhagen–Stockholm	8–9hrs	8 times daily
Copenhagen–Paris	16–18hrs	3 times daily
Copenhagen–Hamburg	5–7hrs	12 times daily
Copenhagen–Gothenburg	4–5hrs	5 times daily

Major Internal Services

Connection	Duration	Frequency
Fredrikshavn–Fredericia	4–5hrs	14 times daily

Fredericia–Copenhagen	3–4hrs	30 times daily
Esbjerg–Fredericia	1–2hrs	27 times daily
Thyborøn–Vemb	1–2hrs	8 times daily

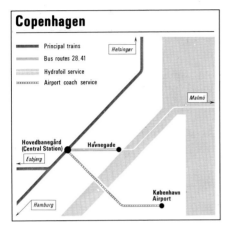

Copenhagen

▬▬▬	Principal trains
═══	Bus routes 28, 41
▬▬▬	Hydrofoil service
┅┅┅	Airport coach service

Helsingør

Malmö

Hovedbanegård (Central Station)   Havnegade

Esbjerg

København Airport

Hamburg

Scenic Routes

The nature of the landscape with its many islands, bridges and ferry crossings means that most lines are of scenic interest. The Fredericia–Odense route and the Nykøbing–Naestved route are particularly renowned for their beauty.

Hans Christian Anderson Monument, Odense

A series of special trains runs from Copenhagen Central Station to Odense where tourists can visit the Hans Christian Andersen Museum, the Railway Museum, and the Falck Museum. They run hourly during the peak period and the journey takes about 3 hours.

There is also a special service to Legoland. The Legoland model park was constructed from 25 million lego pieces and has examples of buildings

and monuments from all over the world. Other attractions include 'Legogredo', a miniature wild west town and 'Tiberius Palace'. Fares including seat reservation and admission are 225.00DK for adults and 112.50DK for children.

'Around the sound' tickets are available for tourists who wish to make their own way around the sound that divides Sweden and Denmark. The ticket enables visitors to use the train, hydrofoil and ferry to visit the tourist attractions in this area.

Veteran Railways

1. Mariager – Handest Veteran Railway
Length: 17km
This tourist railway is part of the former Mariager–Faarup–Viborg railway which was opened as late as 1927. In 1970 a veteran railway was established on the route. Stock consists of private and state first-class carriages dating from 1900–1935. Every second trip is generally run using a steam engine or motor car as the driving force. In addition, the railway owns a complete rail bus from 1947–48. The journey lasts about 50 minutes and travels through very scenic countryside, particularly near Mariager, where the tracks are laid in high plateaux alongside the banks of the fjord.
Operated by: Danish Railway Club (Jutland Section).

2. Byrup–Vrads Veteran Railway
Length: 5km
The line runs along part of what used to be the Horsens–Byrup–Silkeborg track which closed in 1968. The tracks are laid through very beautiful national trust countryside and the journey takes about 15 minutes. During dry periods, the train is pulled by a motor car but periodically steam engines are used as well. The oldest carriages are a freight van dating from about 1912 and a locomotive from 1918. The railway also owns a couple of rail buses.
The railway is manned by members of the Railway Club.

3. Helsingør–Gilleleje Veteran Railway
Length: 24km
This railway, known as the 'milk-train' runs along a scenic coastal route. The train stops *en route* at Hornbaek and on request at the other stations with whistle stops along the way. The carriages are pulled by a steam engine and the cars and locomotives date from 1885–1920. They are operated by members of the Helsingør Railway Club who all appear in traditional uniforms.
Operated by: Helsingør Railway Club in co-operation with Hornbaek Railway.

4. Maribo–Bandholm Veteran Railway
Length: 7km
The station at Bandholm is the oldest, for private railways, in Denmark. The route is run today as a combination of a freight route and a museum route with passenger transport. It

opened in 1962 and is the oldest veteran railway of all. The railway owns four steam locomotives, two of which were built between 1878 and 1879. In addition, they boast a splendid passenger carriage from 1869. The journey takes you through unspoilt countryside passing by several streams and small stations on the way.

5. **Aalholm Castle Veteran Railway**
This veteran railway runs from the hall (which houses a model railway) through the park and down to the beach. The train is a reconstruction of a steam engine from 1850, built partly with rejected materials from the old sugar beet freight railway.

Railway Museums

1. **Danish State Railway Museum, Copenhagen**
The Danish railway museum is housed in the headquarters of the Danish State Railways, Sølvgade 40. It displays illustrations and objects which show the development of the Danish railways. There are models of the two oldest stations and of the present mail railway station in Copenhagen, as well as models of older and newer locomotives, carriages, ferries and railway bridges. There is also a collection of telegraphs, signals and tools, plaques, medals, tickets, etc. The interior of King Frederik VII's royal carriage is also on show to the public.

2. **Danish Railway Museum, Odense**
The museum is housed in an old round-house. In contrast to the museum for Railway History in Copenhagen, it displays real locomotives and carriages. The museum started in 1975 by displaying a collection of steam engines, the oldest of which dated from 1869. Now, in addition, there are two diesel locomotives from 1932 and 1936, a number of passenger carriages (of which one is two storey), two royal carriages from 1871 and 1902 (containing original furniture, silk wallpaper and sundry equipment), a freight car from 1865 and a mail van from 1856.

Internal Fare Structure

Standard Rate Fares

Single tickets are valid only for the day of sale but returns are valid for 2 months. With a single ticket you are allowed to break the journey once and with a return ticket the journey may be broken once in each direction.

Child Reductions

Children under 4 travel free and under 12s are entitled to a 50% reduction.

Student Reductions

There are no special reductions for students but the usual international reductions are available (see the International Section for full details).

Senior Citizen Reductions

The '65-billet' is for people aged 65 and over and enables them to buy a return ticket for the price of a single. The return journey must be made within a period of 3 months and the card is subject to certain restrictions during rush hours.

Party/Group Savers

Passengers travelling in groups of 3 or more can claim a discount of between 20% and 50% with special group tickets.

Train entering ferry at Helsingør

Railrover Passes

The Copenhagen Card

This is a combined bus/rail pass which gives unlimited travel in the Copenhagen area. The card costs: 80DK for one day; 140DK for 2 days and 180DK for 3 days. The pass also allows free admission to a number of museums and other places of interest in the area and offers a 50% reduction on the *DSB* ferries to Sweden.

Tourist Reductions

Nordic Tourist Ticket

The Nordic Tourist Ticket is valid for 21 days and entitles the holder to unlimited rail travel throughout Denmark, Finland, Norway and Sweden. It also permits unlimited travel on certain ferry services including Helsingor–Helsingborg; Rodby Faerge–Puttgarden Mitte See; Goteborg–Frederikshaven; Stockholm–Turku; Kristiansand–Hirtshals; Gedser–Warnemunde; and the *NSB* bus section Trondheim–Storlein. Prices are: 2nd class £135 (adult), £101 (12–25) and £67 (4–11); 1st class £181 (adult), £136 (12–25) and £90.50 (4–11). Normal prices apply for seat, sleeper and couchette reservation.

Where to buy tickets

In Denmark

Tickets can be bought at any railway station in Denmark.

In Great Britain

European Rail Travel Centre
PO Box 303
Victoria Station
London SW1V 1JY
Tel: (071) 934 2345

Booking for *DSB* tickets can also be made at most British Rail stations, DFDS Seaways Offices and at many travel agencies.

In USA

From *DSB* representatives (see International Section).

Facilities on Trains

Sleepers and Couchettes

The only sleeper service available is on the Copenhagen–Frederikshavn route. The cost is 200DK for a 2nd class double sleeper and 300DK for a 1st class

Inner city train

single sleeper. The price for a couchette is 100DK.

Food

A wide range of food and drink is available on the *Lyntog* and IC trains.

Luggage

All luggage travels free.

Disabled

There are special lifts and special compartments for disabled travellers on the new *DSB* trains which serve the Copenhagen–Ålborg and Copenhagen–Esbjerg routes.

Bicycle Carriage

Most Danish trains do not have a luggage compartment so bicycles cannot be accompanied on trains but they can be sent in advance as registered luggage. This means that the bicycle will not necessarily arrive at the destination at the same time as the passenger. In addition, the bicycles may be registered for travel between the major stations only.

Facilities at Stations

Food

Most major stations have shops, kiosks, restaurants and mini-bars which are open from early morning to late in the evening.

Train leaves Copenhagen station

Reservations

These are not usually compulsory but it is obviously advisable to book in advance if you are planning to travel on the major routes or during the tourist season. On some journeys which involve a ferry crossing it is compulsory to reserve a seat and the cost of reservation is 10DK.

Luggage

Left luggage facilities are open in the major stations from early in the morning to late at night.

Coach Links

DSB operate a coach service to the larger towns that do not have their own railway station. Passengers buy a through ticket to their destination, take the train to the nearest station and from there continue their journey by coach.

Car Hire

'Intercitycar' is the name of the car rental service run in conjunction with Avis. The car can be booked at any *DSB* or private station and the car will then be kept at one of the following stations: Copenhagen, Helsingør, Odense, Fredericia, Esbjerg, Artus or Ålborg.

Bicycle Hire

Bicycles can be hired from bicycle shops or tourist offices at the stations. The charge is 30DK per day with a 100DK deposit. The bicycle must be returned to the station from which it was hired during opening hours.

Finland

Finlandia Hall, Helsinki

Introduction

Finland is a low-lying country of un-spoilt natural beauty. It is called the 'land of a thousand lakes', but in reality it has about 180,000 of them inter-woven with dense and austere wood-land. The Finns are not of Germanic origin like the majority of the Scan-dinavian population, but instead moved into Finland from the Baltic area in the early Christian era, driving back the Lapps. Yet today the country has close links with its Scandinavian neighbours through trade and mem-bership of the Nordic Council.

In common with other Scandinavian countries, Finland has an Arctic Zone which experiences the midnight sun. In this northern region, winter lasts for up to 7 months of the year and tempera-tures can reach −30°C. In the south, winter lasts for 3 months during which ports, waterways and lakes freeze over. Summer is warm, however, be-cause of continental and Gulf Stream influences and temperatures can reach up to 30°C. Rainfall is heaviest in the south and in the month of July.

The Finns had a long struggle for inde-pendence from their neighbours and their determined character reflects this. There have been many notable Finnish scientists and artists. A num-ber of architects have achieved particu-lar renown and the composer Sibelius has achieved world-wide fame for his musical achievement. Finland has a population of 4.8 million, who, through the Nordic Council, can travel and work in the rest of Scandinavia without res-triction. Visitors to Finland are un-failingly treated to a particularly gener-ous brand of hospitality.

Finland is a republic governed by a single chamber (*Eduskunta*) which is composed of 200 elected members. Legislative power is vested in the chamber and in the President, who is elected for a six-year term.

The economy of Finland relies to a large extent on the enormous wealth of it's forests. Some 70% of the country is coniferous forest providing the raw materials for the manufacture of a vari-ety of timber products, such as paper, furniture and cellulose. Out of a total area of 337,000sq km, only 9% can be used for cultivation. Finland has also developed some heavy industry cen-tred around the capital, Helsinki, and imports large quantities of raw mate-rials and energy to fill its needs. As most economic activity is centred in the south, the communications net-work is more extensive here than in the north. Finland is, on the whole, less prosperous than its partners in the Nordic Council and suffers from high unemployment and above-average inflation.

Although the Finns are not of Germa-nic origin, the development of their art in the early and medieval periods was closely connected with that of other northern European countries. Folk art predominated in Finland until the 18th century, when German influences on painting and architecture encouraged the development of a distinctive Fin-nish national style. Axeli Gallén-Kallela's (1865–1931) illustrations for the Finnish national epic *'Kalevala'* are particularly distinctive. Today Finnish architecture has established an inter-national reputation for its clear, calm forms, which are easily visible in the capital, Helsinki.

Punkaharju nature reserve, Finland

History

9th–13th centuries	Sweden gains control of Finland and promotes the spread of Christianity
14th century	Finland becomes a Swedish province with same rights as other parts of the country
1495–1595	Russian invasions cause devastation and loss of trading links
1700–1809	Swedish wars with Russia, culminating in the occupation of Finland by Russian troops
1809	Finland becomes the Russian Grand Duchy of Finland; Tsar Alexander I promises to maintain Finnish rights and privileges

1880–1912	Gradual suppression of Finnish self-government: postal services, customs and currency are taken over, the army is abolished and Russian becomes the official language of government
1917	Finland is declared an independent Republic
1918	War of Liberation. Finnish volunteer forces defeat a combined army of Russian Bolsheviks and Finnish Communists
1919	Formation of a republican constitution
1939–1944	Renewed conflict with the Soviet Union and resulting loss of territories
1948	Treaty of friendship and mutual assistance with the Soviet Union
1955	Finland becomes a member of the Nordic Council and the United Nations
1961	Finland becomes an associate member of the European Free Trade Association
1982	Mauno Koivisto (Social Democratic Party) becomes the new President of Finland
1983	Coalition government formed by Prime Minister Kalen Sorsa
1985	150th anniversary of the publication of *Kalevala*
1986	Acceptance of women priests by main authoritative body of Finnish church

Major Centres

Helsinki

Suomen Matkailun Edistämiskeskus
(Finnish Tourist Board)
Asemapäällikönkatu 12B
PB 53
00521 Helsinki
Tel: (0) 01 44 511

Helsingin Kaupungin Matkailutoimisto
(Helsinki Tourist Information Office)
Pohjoisesplanadi 19
SF-00100 Helsinki
Tel: (0) 17 40 88/(0) 69 37 57

Embassies:
UK: Uudenmaankatu 16-20,
Tel: (0) 64 79 22
USA: Itainen Puistotie 14A,
Tel: (0) 17 19 31

Helsinki is the world's most northerly capital city, after Reykjavik. It lies on a rugged peninsula on the northern shores of the Gulf of Finland and has a population of just under half a million.

Sibelius Memorial, Helsinki

Centred around the Market Square and Cathedral, Helsinki was built in neo-classical style in the first half of the 19th century and is called the 'white city of the north' because of its white building façades. It is Finland's largest industrial town and port as well as being its cultural centre.

Sightseeing

Ateneum (built by Theodor Höijer in 1884–7) – houses the finest collection of art in Finland
Market Square – the heart of Helsinki, particularly on market mornings (Monday to Saturday, 7am to 2pm)
National Museum – contains an interesting record of the history of ethnography in Finland
Rock Church (1968–9) – an unusual underground church hewn from rock, with a 13m high dome
Senate Square – an imposing square containing a bronze statue of Tsar Alexander II. On one side of the square stands the Lutheran Cathedral and on another, the University built from 1828–32. Opposite the University is the Government Palace, which housed the Senate of the Grand Duchy of Finland from 1809 to 1918
Sibelius Memorial – in the Sibelius Park; constructed in 1967 by Eila Hiltunen
Uspensky Cathedral – icons and paintings inside

Uspensky Orthodox Cathedral, Helsinki

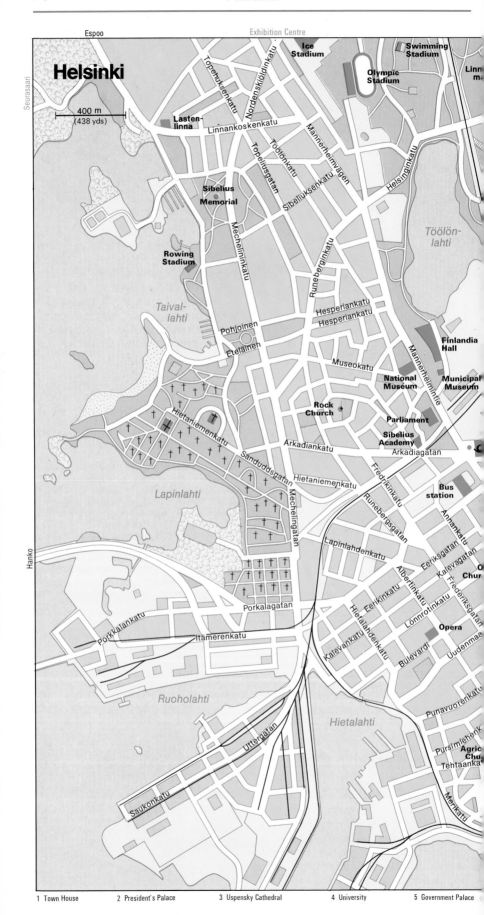

Helsinki

Espoo

Exhibition Centre

Seurasaari

400 m
(438 yds)

Ice Stadium

Swimming Stadium

Olympic Stadium

Linn m.

Topeliuksenkatu

Nordenskiöldinkatu

Lasten-linna

Linnankoskenkatu

Mannerheimvägen

Töölönkatu

Topeliusgatan

Sibeliuksenkatu

Helsinginkatu

Sibelius Memorial

Mechelininkatu

Rowing Stadium

Runeberginkatu

Töölön-lahti

Taival-lahti

Pohjoinen

Eteläinen

Hesperiankatu

Hesperiankatu

Museokatu

Finlandia Hall

Mannerheimintie

National Museum

Municipal Museum

Hietaniemenkatu

Rock Church

Sibelius Academy

Parliament

Sanduddsgatan

Arkadiankatu

Arkadiagatan

Lapinlahti

Hietaniemenkatu

Mechelingatan

Fredrikinkatu

Runebergsgatan

Bus station

Annankatu

Eeriksgatan

Kalevagatan

Lapinlahdenkatu

Chur

Hanko

Albertinkatu

Eerikinkatu

Fredriksgatan

Porkalagatan

Hietalahdenkatu

Lönnrotinkatu

Opera

Porkkalankatu

Itämerenkatu

Kalevankatu

Bulevardi

Uudenmaa

Ruoholahti

Hietalahti

Punavuorenkatu

Uttergatan

Pursimiehenk

Agric Chu

Tehtaanka

Saukonkatu

Merikatu

1　Town House　　　2　President's Palace　　　3　Uspensky Cathedral　　　4　University　　　5　Government Palace

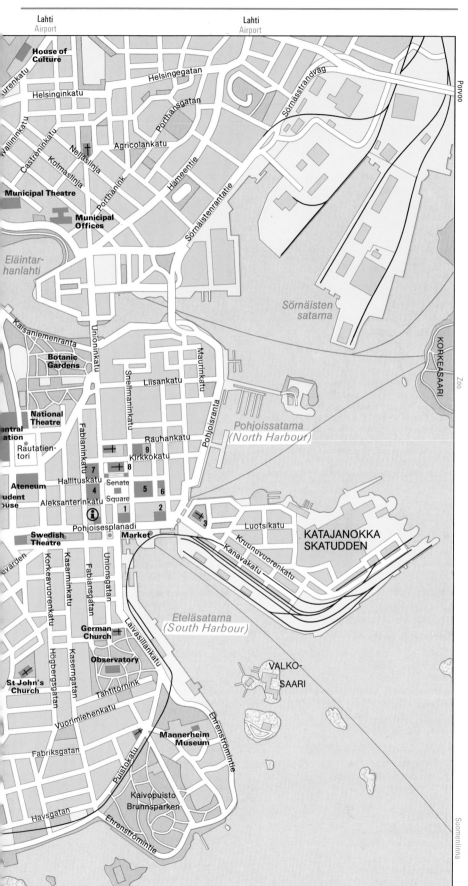

Lahti
Airport

Lahti
Airport

House of
Culture

Helsingegatan

Sörnässtrandväg

Porvoo

Helsinginkatu

Porthansgatan

Agricolankatu

Neljäslinja

Kolmaslinja

Castréninkatu

Hämeentie

Sörnäistenrantatie

Porthanink.

Municipal Theatre

Municipal
Offices

Eläintar-
hanlahti

Sörnäisten
satama

KORKEASAARI

Zoo

Kaisaniemenranta

Unioninkatu

Botanic
Gardens

Maurinkatu

Snellmaninkatu

Liisankatu

Pohjoisranta

National
Theatre

Pohjoissatama
(North Harbour)

entral
ation

Rautatien-
tori

Fabianinkatu

Rauhankatu

9

Kirkkokatu

7

8

Hallituskatu

Senate

4

Ateneum
udent
ouse

5

6

Aleksanterinkatu

Square

1

2

Pohjoisesplanadi

3

Luotsikatu

KATAJANOKKA
SKATUDDEN

Swedish
Theatre

Market

Kruununvuorenkatu

evärden

Kasarminkatu

Korkeavuorenkatu

Unionsgatan

Fabiansgatan

Kanavakatu

Eteläsatama
(South Harbour)

German
Church

Laivasillankatu

Högbergsgatan

Kaserngatan

Observatory

VALKO-
SAARI

St John's
Church

Tähtitornink.

Vuorimiehenkatu

Ehrenströmintie

Fabriksgatan

Puistokatu

Mannerheim
Museum

Kaivopuisto
Brunnsparken

Havsgatan

Ehrenströmintie

Suomenlinna

Knights' House   7 University Library   8 Cathedral   9 House of Estates

South Harbour, Helsinki

Opening Times

In general, the opening times for Sundays apply also to public holidays. Almost all institutions are closed on 1 January, 6 January (Epiphany), Good Friday, Easter Day, 1 May, Ascension Day (usually mid-May), the Saturday closest to 24 June (midsummer Day and Finnish Flag Day), All Saints Day (Saturday nearest end of October or beginning of November), Independence Day (6 December) and almost continuously from Christmas Eve to New Year.

Other Places of Interest

Activity Centre of the Helsinki Artists' Society,
Katariinankatu 2.

Amos Anderson Museum of Art,
Yrjönkatu 27.

Arabia-Nuutajärvii (glass and porcelain),
Hämeentie 135; by appointment.

Museum of Architecture,
Kasarmikatu 24.

Art Gallery *(Taidenhalli)*,
Nervanderinkatu 3.

Athenaeum (Ateneum) Museum of Art,
Kaivokatu 2–4.

Museum of Aviation,
Helsinki-Vantaa Airport.

Bank Museum *(Union Bank of Finland)*,
Aleksanterinkatu 30.

Botanic Garden of University,
Unioninkatu 44.

Cathedral
Senaattitori (Senate Square).

Coastal Defence Museum,
Kustanmiekka works, island of Suomenlinna.

**Coins and Banknotes
Exhibition of** *(KOP Bank)*,
Pohjoisesplanadi 29.

Didrichsen Museum of Art,
Kuusilahdenkuja 3 (buses from Bus Station, platform 50).

Finnish Design Center,
Kasarmikatu 19B.

Friends of Finnish Handicrafts (textiles),
Seurasrentie, Meilahti 7.

Gallén-Kallela Museum
Gallén-Kallelantie 27.

Herttoniemi Museum (manor-house and farm),
Linnanrakentajantie 14.

Kluuvi Gallery,
Unioninkatu 28B, 3rd floor.

Linnanmäki Amusement Park,
Tivolintie.

Mannerheim Museum,
Kalliolinnantie 14.

Market Square *(Kauppatori)*.

Military Museum *(Sotamuseo)*,
Maurinkatu 1.

Mineralogical Museum,
Kivimiehentie 1, Otaniemi (buses from Bus Station).

Municipal Art Collection,
Meilahti, Tamminiementie 6.

Municipal Horticultural Centre
(with gardens)
Hammareskjöldintie 1.

Municipal Museum
Karamzininkatu 2.

National Museum *(Kansallismuseo)*,
Mannerheimintie 34.

Observatory,
Kaivopuisto Park, Ullanlinnanmäki.

Parliament Building,
Mannerheimintie 30.

Photographic Museum,
Korkeavuorenkatu 2B, F 72.

Pijlajasaari
(island with swimming and recreation area);
motorboats from Laivurinkatu (tel: 63 00 65).

Postal and Telegraph Museum,
Tehtaankatu 21B.

President's Palace,
Pohjoisesplanadi 1. By appointment only.

Seurasaari *Open-Air Museum and Nature Park,*
island of Seurasaari (terminus of No. 24 bus).

Sport Museum of Finland,
Olympic Stadium.

Strindberg Art Gallery,
Pohjoissesplanadi 33.

Submarine 'Vesikkö',
island of Suomenlinna, Tykistölahti Bay.

Suomenlinna Castle,
island of Suomenlinna.

Museum of Technology,
Viikintie 1.

Temppeliaukio Church,
Lutherinkatu 3.

Theatre Museum,
Aleksanterinkatu 12A.

Tuomarinkylä Manor-House *Municipal Museum,*
Tuomarinkylä.

Uspensky Cathedral (Orthodox),
Kanavakatu 1.
By appointment only.

Zoo,
island of Korkeasaari (ferry from North Harbour
from beginning of May to around end of September; rest of year, footbridge from Mustasaari).

Zoological Museum,
Pohjoinen Rautatiekatu 13.

Parliament Building, Helsinki

Accommodation

Hotels

The hotels in Finland, noted for their cleanliness, are right up to international standards of comfort and service for the different price categories. The large towns (advance reservation very desirable) have luxury establishments, but many smaller places have excellent hotels combining international standards of comfort with distinctive national features. Even in the far north, there are good hotels and well-equipped inns which provide a very adequate standard of comfort. Many establishments have 'family rooms' with 3–5 beds which provide reasonably priced accommodation for a family group. Some mountain hotels in Finland are open for only part of the year, during the summer and winter seasons. There are also special summer hotels.

In Finland, there are luxury hotels in Helsinki and other large towns. The Finnish Tourist Board also runs tourist hotels offering a high standard of comfort, in the main tourist areas (reservations advisable). In the remoter parts of the country, there are inns (*matkustajakoti*), which are of a more modest standard but are usually clean. A *majatalo* is a country inn.

Finland also has a useful hotel cheque system. The Finncheque costs 115FM per person per night and can be used in 160 hotels and 80 localities. Only the first night can be reserved in advance. Reservation to the next hotel is free of charge. Finncheques are valid from June 1 to August 31 and there are no restrictions on the number that can be bought.

Finland is the home of the sauna. In the traditional Finnish sauna, a simple

Hotel Price Range		
	Price for 1 night in FM	
Type of hotel	Single	Double
Luxury	350–400	450–700
Middle-grade	200–450	230–600
Modest	100–200	180–300

These prices are intended to act as a rough guide only.

wooden hut, stones are heated in a wood fire and water is thrown over them to produce steam and fierce heat. This regular alternation of dry and moist heat distinguishes the Finnish sauna from other types of steam bath. In order to enhance the sweat-producing effect and promote the circulation of blood, the bathers whip themselves with birch twigs. Many hotels and other forms of accommodation offer the use of a sauna.

Youth Hostels

Youth hostels admit adults as well as young people, and have family rooms. An international youth hostel card is required. Information about vacation houses and vacation villages can be obtained from the national tourist organisations.

Farmhouse holidays

There are about 150 farmhouses in Finland which take guests on a full board basis. They are in rural settings and, almost without exception, close to water. The guest rooms are always clean even if without modern conveniences, but there is usually a bathroom in the house. Accommodation is in the main

Lake Inari, Finnish Lapland

building, separate barns or outhouses. Some farms also have individual cottages for full board guests, or apartments with kitchen including fridge and electric stove for those who wish to cater for themselves. The guest is almost a member of the family and joins them for their meals. He can have a sauna bath twice a week, wander in the forest, row, fish or take part in the work of the farm, haymaking or looking after the cattle.

Prices: Full board rates including two hot meals, coffee twice a day, sauna twice a week, adults: 900–1000FM per week, 600–670FM incl. bed and breakfast, children 50–75% reduction. The majority of the farms are in Central and East Finland, some on the coast and in the Aland Islands.

Reservations:
Suomen 4H-liitto,
Bulevardi 28,
00120 Helsinki,
Tel: (9)0 645 133.

Camping and Caravanning

There are about 350 camping sites and about 5500 camp cabins and holiday cottages in Finland, spread out over the whole country. The majority have cooking facilities, kiosks and canteens where food, cigarettes and sweets can be bought. Camping sites are generally along the waterways, within easy reach of main roads and towns. Camping other than on official camping sites, and making a campfire are forbidden without the permission of the landowner. The present tendency is for camping to be more and more confined to camping sites only.

The camping season starts in late May or early June, and ends in late August or early September. In southern Finland you can sleep under canvas for about 3 months in summer and in the north for about 2 months. A few sites are open all the year.

It costs 20–48FM depending on the site classification, for an overnight stay at a camping site for a family ie. two adults, children, car, tent or trailer. The charge includes the basic facilities: eg. cooking, washing, washing up etc.

Introduction to Rail Information

The Finnish rail system is run by *Valtionrautatiet (VR)*, or Finnish State Railways. It is as extensive as many in Europe with 6000km of passenger carrying track. In recent years there have been extensive improvements to the system increasing the speed of trains and the general efficiency of the service. The passenger rolling stock is new, modern and comparable with other European services. There are 3 types of train:

Erikoispikajuna – special express
Pikajuna – regular express
Henkilöjuna – local train

Major International Routes

Connection	Duration	Frequency
Helsinki–Leningrad	7hrs	once daily
Helsinki–Moscow	15hrs	once daily
Helsinki–Stockholm	12–15hrs	3 times daily

Major Internal Routes

Connection	Duration	Frequency
Helsinki–Turku	2–3hrs	twice daily
Helsinki-Rovaniemi	10–12hrs	4 times daily
Helsinki–Tampere	2–3hrs	4 times daily

Scenic Routes

Most of the rail trips in Finland are scenically interesting but the Kuovola–Joensuu line is particularly renowned for its beauty.

Veteran railways

1. **Jokioinen Museum Railway**
   This is the most northern museum line in the world. The steam engines are regularly in operation. The museum line is a part of a 750mm gauge light railway built in 1898. The remaining section was rescued by Finnish railway enthusiasts, who now operate the trains.

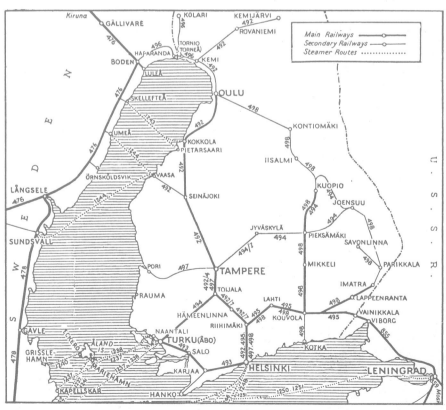

Map supplied by kind permission of Thomas Cook Ltd. The numbers along the lines refer to tables in the *Thomas Cook Continental Timetable*.

2. Minkiön Station

This station houses the only narrow gauge museum in Finland. All mail deposited in the letter box at Minkiön Station can be stamped with a special marker featuring a steam locomotive with the inscription 'Jokioinen Museorautatie'.

The Railway Museum

The Railway Museum, founded in 1898, was transferred from Helsinki to Hyvinkää in the spring of 1974. At present, the museum occupies all the buildings situated in the museum grounds.

The permanent exhibitions of the Railway Museum are on display in four different buildings. The oldest and historically most interesting locomotives and rolling stock are exhibited in the engine shed and outside in. Other buildings contain scale models, various small exhibits, photographs, etc. the engine shed houses the oldest steam locomotive preserved in Finland (1868); the imperial train; a first and second class passenger coach (1873); a steam locomotive (1903); the oldest track motor car in Finland (1914); and some of the oldest gangers' trolleys. The three-coach imperial train dates from the 1870s. It was built for the journeys of the tsar of Russia and his suite to Finland. The imperial train originally consisted of five coaches: the tsar's and the tsarina's coaches; a saloon; a dining saloon; and a kitchen coach.

Locomotives and rolling stock preserved in the Railway Museum in Hyvinkää: a shunting locomotive Bl No 9 (1868); mixed train locomotive G 11/Sk 3 No 400 (1903); rail tractor (1914); track motor car Fiat (1914); internal combustion locomotive Vk 11 No 101 (1931); Diesel railcar Dm 2 No 13 (1936); the tsar's coach (1870); the tsarina's coach (1875); imperial saloon (1876); service coach No 80 (1877); first and second class passenger coach (1873); guard's van (1905); luggage van (1901); mail van (1871); first class passenger coach (1896); car-carrier of Marsha Mannerheim's train; fire-engine car and water tank (1930–1); steam-driven excavator (1918); snow-plough (1920–1).

Exhibition II consists of nine rooms, introducing the visitor to the history of the railway in Finland, the history and architecture of stations and other railway buildings; the history of locomotives and rolling stock; and the history of the Railway Museum itself. A special section is devoted to the Helsinki–Hämeenlinna (1862) and Riihimäki–St Petersburg (1870) lines. Upstairs there are photographs of railway bridges, a display of the

Flower market, Turku

museum railways in Finland, and a model railway. The model railway, one of the largest in Finland, displays scale models of the Riihimäki and Hämeenlinna Railway Stations. The fully automated railway was built for the centenary celebrations of the Finnish State Railways in 1962. Exhibition III contains furniture from stations, waiting rooms, the Railway Board and railway offices as well as group photographs of railway staff.

Exhibition IV consists of nine rooms, containing mainly scale models.

Internal Fare Structure

Standard Rate Fares

Finnish rail fares are based on the number of kilometres travelled. For example, 100km is charged at the rate of 30FM. Single tickets for distances under 75km are valid on the day of issue only but tickets for longer journeys are valid for one month. Return tickets for distances under 75km are valid for 3 days and those over 75km are valid for one month. Passengers are allowed to break their journey once in addition to breaks for changes of train but in these cases they must have their ticket stamped at the station where the journey is broken.

Child Reductions

As with most other rail systems children under 4 travel free but are not entitled to a seat and children over 4 but under 12 pay half fare and are entitled to a seat.

Student Reductions

There are no special student reduction cards. Students travelling by rail in Finland are advised to read the International Section for information on the international reductions available.

Senior Citizen Reductions

There are no special Senior Citizen reduction cards. However, Senior Citizens are advised to read the International Section for information on the Rail Europ Senior Card.

Party/Group Savers

The group reduction is 20% for a group of at least 3 people, 25% for a group of at least 10 people and 30% for a group of at least 25 people. The reduction for groups of students and children is 30%. The group tickets are valid for one month and they can be bought for both a single and return journey. The minimum cost is the fare for a journey of 76km one way. All members of a group must travel on the same train and in the same class.

Tourist Reductions

Tourist Tickets

These are sold throughout the year and are valid for 2 months. In the summer, in addition to travel by train, they cover travel by coach, plane or boat. The ticket should be ordered well in advance from a railway station or travel agency in Finland and be picked up within 14 days. The precise section of the route required, the date of departure and the class of ticket must be indicated.

Finnrail Pass

These are most useful for visitors intending to travel a great deal by train while in the country. The prices for a 2nd class pass are 400FM for an 8-day pass 600FM for a 15-day pass, and 750FM for a 22-day pass. The pass will be issued only on production of a foreign passport. It can be bought in railway stations and at ports of arrival in Finland either for cash or against vouchers issued by certain authorised agencies.

Nordic Tourist Ticket

The Nordic Tourist Ticket is valid for 21 days and entitles the holder to unlimited rail travel throughout Denmark, Finland, Norway and Sweden. It also permits unlimited travel on certain ferry services including Helsingor–Helsingborg; Rodby Faerge–Puttgarden Mitte See; Goteborg–Frederikshavn; Stockholm–Turku; Kristiansand–Hirtshals; Gedser–Warnemunde; and the *NSB* bus section Trondheim–Storlein. Prices are: 2nd class £135 (adult), £101 (12–25) and £67 (4–11); 1st class £181 (adult), £136 (12–25) and £90.50 (4–11). Normal prices apply for seat, sleeper and couchette reservation.

Where to buy tickets

In Finland

At any railway station and at selected travel agencies.

In Great Britain

Finlandia Travel Agency
130 Jermyn Street
London SW1Y 4UJ
and
European Rail Travel Centre
PO Box 303
Victoria Station
London SW1V 1JY
Tel: (071) 834 2345

In USA

From Finnish State Railways representatives (see International Section).

Kuopio – general view from Puijomaki

Facilities on Trains

Sleepers and Couchettes

There are no couchettes on Finnish trains but sleepers are available. The cost of a bed in a double berth is 63FM and in a triple berth 42FM.

Luggage

This may be sent in advance to a specified destination provided the baggage is labelled and checked in.

Motorail

The Finnish State Railways have a motorail service on the Helsinki–Rovaniemi route and the Turku–Rovaniemi route. Reservations have to be made in advance. In addition to the car charges, at least one full fare ticket has to be purchased per car. Charges per car range from 46FM to 69FM.

Bicycle Carriage

Most trains will carry bikes and the loading and unloading is done by the railway staff. You pay for the bike according to distance and there is a minimum and maximum fare. If you want to send it unaccompanied you must register it at the baggage office.

Facilities in Stations

Helsinki and other major stations are well equipped with train information, tourist information, restaurants, left-luggage lockers, shops and post offices.

France

The outskirts of Marseilles

Introduction

France is a country rich in cultural heritage and scenic beauty. The scenery ranges from the snow-capped peaks of the Alps and the Pyrénées to the picturesque river valleys of the Loire and the Dordogne; from the wild and rocky Brittany coast to the golden sands of the Côte d'Azur. France has a varied though mild climate. In the south, the Mediterranean coast with its hot summers and mild winters enjoys sub-tropical conditions. The temperature in the inland regions of France is kept moderate owing to the prevalent westerly winds which blow from the extensive coastline. In the north the weather is less predictable and alternates between areas of low pressure and high pressure.

The population of France is a little over 54 million, of which 4.2 million are foreigners, mostly from other European countries. The notable exceptions are some 50,000 Vietnamese and considerable numbers of North Africans from Morocco and Tunisia. Despite the limitations on immigration, the native population of France is far from uniform. 1.2 million people in Alsace and Lorraine speak a German dialect, a similar number in Brittany speak Breton, and the people of Corsica have their own language which has an affinity to Italian. Of the 54 million population, 45 million are nominally Catholics. From the once strong Protestant Church, 900,000 believers remain, still practising their faith in the centres that survived the religious persecutions of the 16th and 17th centuries.

France has had five republics since the first one in 1792. The Head of State is the President, elected by popular vote for a seven-year term. He appoints the Prime Minister and presides over the Council of Ministers. He is also Commander-in-Chief of the Armed Forces. Ever since the fifth republic of 1958, the President has had substantial powers, but the election of 1981 brought Mitterand to power and a comprehensive programme of decentralisation was introduced, presaging a reversal of the traditionally highly centralised form of government. The French parliament consists of two chambers, the National Assembly which serves a five-year term, and the Senate, which serves a nine-year term. The National Assembly discusses and, together with the Senate, passes laws.

The French economy is largely industrial and this makes up 40% of the gross national product. Agriculture contributes only 5% in spite of the fact that it employs almost a quarter of the population, and agriculture land makes up 60% of the country's total area. The principal industrial exports are machinery and cars. Peugeot-Citroen and Renault are among the world's largest industrial enterprises. Much of French industry is located in the Paris basin, and Paris itself accounts for a quarter of all industrial production. Recently, deposits of oil and natural gas have been discovered in the Garonne basin, and this region is now playing a more important role in the French economy. Tourism is also a major source of income for the French, with Paris, Provence and the Côte d'Azur constituting the major centres. However, in recent years the winter resorts of the French Alps have been very popular. Many tourists also come to France to sample the delights of its cuisine and above all its wines. Visiting vineyards and tasting their wines is a tourist attraction in itself.

The Eiffel Tower, Paris

Throughout France's long and illustrious history the arts have always been well patronised. Architecturally there is ample evidence of this wherever you travel in France. From the early Romanesque architecture of Burgundy, the splendid Gothic cathedrals that are to be found all over France, the majestic Renaissance châteaux of the Loire Valley, the unique Rococo style of the Palace of Versailles, to the modern Pompidou Centre in Paris.

Porte du Croux, Nevers, Burgundy

French painting did not really come to the fore until the 17th century. At the same time as Louis XIV was transforming Versailles into a Rococo Palace, three French artists – Jean-Antoine Watteau, François Boucher and Nicolas Poussin – were reflecting the life of their time with a new sense of movement and grace. The events of the latter part of the 18th century led to a more severe classical style particularly in the work of Jacques-Louis David, who used themes from antiquity to express the ideas of the French Revolution. There was also a Romantic School of French painting represented in the first half of the 19th century by Eugène Delacroix.

The Romantic School was followed by a new realism in the work of Camille Corot, Jean-François Millet and Gustave Courbet. Using themes from everyday French life, their characters were a far cry from the mythological and religious figures portrayed by the Classicists. However, the next generation of French painting broke totally new ground, stimulated by the invention of the camera by Louis-Jacques Daguerre in 1837.

Edouard Manet marked out new directions in his employment of colour and started a school of Impressionism, literally the recording of the fleeting impression by the use of colour. He was followed by the 'father' of the movement, Claude Monet and a whole series of great artists – Auguste Renoir, Edgar Degas, Camille Pissarro, Alfred Sisley and later the Pointillists Georges Seurat and Paul Signac. The work of the Impressionists can be seen to its best effect in the Musée d'Orsay, Paris.

An even more radical break with the past was heralded by the work of Paul Cézanne and his followers Paul Gauguin and the Dutchman Vincent van Gogh, who lived and worked in Provence. Cézanne's work moves much further away from nature than any of his contemporaries and is a forerunner to the greatest 20th century painter Pablo Picasso, who spent most of his working life in France.

Twentieth-century French painting contains a wide collection of different movements from the Fauvism of Rouault, Dufy and Derain, to the naive painting of Henri Rousseau, the Cubism of Georges Braque and the Surrealism of Russian-born Marc Chagall. The field of sculpture is equally rich with the work of Auguste Rodin in the late 19th century and also the work of Aristide Maillol.

French literature has also been extremely productive throughout the ages. Again, the 17th century was a great time for the theatre and three playwrights in particular, Pierre Corneille, Jean Racine and Molière excelled in this period. In the field of philosophy, René Descartes helped to free science from its theological fetters. The 18th century witnessed a group of political thinkers called the Physiocrats led by Montesquieu, author of 'L'Esprit des Lois' and championed by Voltaire, Diderot and Rousseau; they were entertained by royalty and their thoughts were applied to current political problems.

Nineteenth-century literature in France was dominated by the novelist Honoré de Balzac and the poet Victor Hugo. They were followed by Gustave Flaubert and Emile Zola and in the 20th century principally by Marcel Proust, André Gide and Albert Camus. In the theatre, Jean Girardoux, Jean Anouilh and above all Jean-Paul Sartre continually provided fresh ideas and new impulses.

In the field of music, France has for the most part been overshadowed by Germany and Austria, although it has a great tradition of its own. In the 17th century, there was a great flowering of French music with Jean-Baptiste Lully who wrote ballets and operas and the composer François Couperin. Then there was a gap until the 19th century and the romantic symphonies of Hector Berlioz, the lyrical operas of Georges Bizet and the operettas of Jacques Offenbach. In the 20th century, Claude Debussy, Maurice Ravel and later Pierre Boulez were the main figures.

Wine grapes, Alsace

History

51 BC	Caesar conquers Gaul and puts the country under Roman civil administration
AD 200	The conversion to Christianity begins
400–800	Establishment of the Frankish kingdom of the Merovingians and Carolingians. Charlemagne is crowned Emperor in 800
843	Soon after Charlemagne's death, the Frankish Empire is partitioned; the boundary between eastern and western parts remains in all essentials the frontier between France and Germany
987	Start of the Capetian line who rule France until 1328
1066	William, Duke of Normandy, conquers England
1096–1250	France plays a leading part in the Crusades
1309–77	The 'Babylonian captivity' of the Popes in Avignon
1339–1453	Hundred Years War between France and England
1430	Joan of Arc is captured by the English after the Siege of Orléans and is burned at the stake as a heretic
By 1453	England loses all its possessions on the continent apart from Calais
After 1603	Establishment of the first French colony in Canada
From 1635	France becomes involved in the Thirty Years War
From 1661	French absolutist monarchy reaches its height under Louis XIV, the 'Sun King'
After 1715	The death of Louis XIV leaves the country in economic ruin after years of war and court extravagance
1789	Outbreak of the French Revolution and the Storming of the Bastille (July 14th)
1803–15	Napoleonic Wars with the European powers. Napoleon Bonaparte is crowned Emperor of the French in 1804 and at the height of his Empire is sovereign to over 87 million people
1815	Napoleon is defeated at Waterloo and sent into exile
1830–47	French conquest of Algeria
After 1879	Extension of France's colonial possessions in Central Africa (1879–94), Tunis (1881), Incohina (1887 onwards) and Madagascar (1896)
1914–18	First World War, largely fought on French soil. At the end of the war, France becomes a founder member of the League of Nations
1939–45	Second World War. France is divided into occupied and un-occupied zones
1944	The liberation of France begins with the Allied Landings
1954–6	Loss of Indochina, Vietnam, Tunisia, Morocco, French West Africa and French Equitorial Africa
1958	Fifth Republic. De Gaulle is appointed prime minister and given special powers
1962	Algeria becomes independent after seven years of war
1968	Student unrest in Paris and a general strike in May, provoked by economic and social injustices
1969	De Gaulle steps down from the Presidency and is replaced by Georges Pompidou
1981	François Mitterand, a socialist, becomes President
1984	Mitterand pledges support for deployment of US nuclear missiles in Europe
1985	M Laurent Fabius, the French Prime Minister, admits that the sinking of the 'Rainbow Warrior' has been carried out by French agents
1986	President Mitterand appoints M Jacques Chirac, the neo-Gaullist leader, to become the new Prime Minister

Food and Wine

French cuisine is world-famed both for its quality and variety. The average Frenchman attaches great importance to a well-chosen meal, whether he is eating *haute cuisine* or a cheap meal at a *brasserie*. Herbs and spices are used on a large scale and French sauces, often using butter and cream, are deservedly famous. Recently, there has been a trend towards *la nouvelle cuisine* which relies on the best ingredients without over-elaboration. The French café is an excellent place to enjoy coffee accompanied by one of the range of cakes or pastries that make shopping at a *pâtisserie* such an exciting experience.

No French meal is complete without a good bottle of wine and France can boast probably the best selection of wines anywhere in the world. Other spirits well worth sampling are the famous brandies – *cognac, armagnac* and *calvados* – and liqueurs such as Bénédictine, Grand Marnier and Cointreau; and, of course, champagne. France is also famed for its cheeses, including creamy *camembert*, crumbly *chèvre* and blue-veined *roquefort*.

Types of Grape

(Source: Comité National des Vins de France, Paris)

Aligoté – a Regional grape grown in Burgundy.

Aramon – A regional grape grown in Languedoc.

Auxerrois – A regional grape grown round Cahors.

Breton: see Cabernet Franc.

Cabernet Franc – The grape which produces the great red wines of Bordeaux. Also grown in the Loire valley under the name of *Breton* and used in making the red wines of Bourgueil, Chinon and Saumur-Champigny.

Cabernet-Sauvignon – A grape grown in the Bordeaux region, particularly in Médoc and Graves, which produces 50–70% of the great wines of the area. It makes full-bodied, full-coloured red wines rich in tannic acid which improve with age.

In Anjou it is used along with Cabernet Franc to produce semi-dry rosé wines.

Carignan – A grape used in the great white wines of Burgundy (Montrachet, Meursault, Chablis, Pouilly-Fuissé) and Champagne (Blanc de Blancs). It produces light, fruity, transparent wines.

Chasselas – Used in Alsace, under the name of *Gutedel*, to produce light white wines. Also a good table grape.

Chenin – Also known as *Pineau de la Loire*. Grown in Anjou and Touraine, it produces in some years full-bodied but mild white wines which keep well.

Cinsaut – A grape grown in the Mediterranean region which produces delicate, soft, aromatic wines.

Clairette – A white grape grown in the S of France. It produces wines of high alcohol content which tend to take on a taste of 'age'. Also a table grape.

Folle Blanche – Also known as *Gros Plant du Pays Nantais*. An even older grape than Melon, from the Charentes and Gers; it was formerly used to produce cognac and armagnac in the Nantes area.

Gamay – This black grape with white juice does best on the granitic soils of Beaujolais. The wines it yields are light, fruity, palatable and full of charm. It is also found in the Mâconnais and in some wines of Auvergne, St-Pourçain, Châteaumeillant, etc.

Gewürztraminer – A grape grown in Alsace which produces a strong, full-bodied white wine with a delicate bouquet and full aroma.

Grauklevner: see Tokay.

Grenache – Grown in the S of France (Châteauneuf du Pape; dessert wines of Banyuls and Rivesaltes). In combination with Cinsaut, Mourvèdre and Syrah it produces the delicate wines of Languedoc.

Frolleau – A regional grape grown in the Loire valley.

Gros Plant du Pays Nantais: see Folle Blanche.

Gutadel: see Chasselas.

Jacquère – A regional grape grown in Savoy.

Knipperlé – A regional grape grown in Alsace. Little aroma.

A flourishing vineyard

Maccabéo – A regional grape grown in Roussillon.

Malbec – A regional grape grown in the Bordeaux area.

Malvoisie – A regional grape grown in Roussillon.

Manseng – A regional grape grown in the Pyrenean foreland.

Mauzac – A regional grape grown round Gaillac and Limoux.

Melon – Formerly grown in Burgundy, it is now used to produce the fresh, dry, fruity white wines of Muscadet in the area round Nantes.

Merlot – A black grape which is used to supplement the Cabernet grapes of the Bordeaux area. It is the dominant element in Pomerol and St-Emilion, giving fire and fullness to the wine.

Meunier – A regional grape grown in Champagne.

Mondeuse – A regional grape grown in Savoy.

Mourvèdra – A grape grown in the southern Côtes du Rhône (Châteauneuf du Pape), E of the Rhine (Côteaux de Tricastin, Côtes du Ventoux) and in Côtes de Provence. It is found at its best round Bandol, giving the wine soul, distinction and keeping quality.

Muscadelle – A regional grape grown in the Bordeaux area.

Muscat – There are many kinds of muscatel grapes, used both as table grapes and for the production of wine, which all have a strong and unmistakable aroma of muscatel but produce very different kinds of wine: *Muscat d'Alsace* is a dry fruity wine. *Muscat de Hambourg* is both a table grape and (in S and SW France) a wine grape. *Muscat doré à petits grains* (small-berried golden muscatel) produces the famous dessert wines Muscat de Frontignan, Muscat de Rivesaltes, Muscat de Lunel and Muscat de Beaumes de Venise. In the Die area, E of the Rhône, Muscat is used along with clairette to produce a popular sparkling wine, Clairette de Die. *Muscat d'Alexandrie* is used in Roussillon to produce excellent dessert wines.

Neilluclo – A regional grape grown in Corsica.

Pécoul-Touar – A regional grape grown in Provence.

Picpoul – A regional grape grown in Languedoc.

Pineau de la Loire: see Chenin.

Pinot Blanc – Grown in Alsace, under the name of *Weissklevner* or *Weissburgunder*, to produce a dry, flowery white wine.

Pinot Gris: see Tokay.

Pinot Noir – Produces the great red wines of Burgundy; also grown in Champagne. It is also found in Alsace, under the name of *Spätburgunder*, in the Mâconnais and in the rosé wines of Sancerre and Alsace.

Poulsard – Grown in the Jura, and used in combination with Trousseau, Pinot or Chardonnay to produce red and rosé wines.

Riesling – The best known of the grapes grown in Alsace. It produces a distinguished dry white wine, fruity and with a delicate bouquet.

Roussanne – A regional grape grown in the Rhône valley.

Roussette – A regional grape grown in Savoy.

Sauvignon – An excellent white grape which produces wines of some distinction. It is grown in the Bordeaux area (Graves) and in the Loire Valley (Pouilly-Fumé, Sancerre, Quincy, Reuilly, etc.).

Savagnin – A late-ripening grape which is sometimes not harvested until November. It gives the 'ice wines' or *vins jaunes* (yellow wines) of the Jura, Château-Chalon, L'Etoile and Côtes du Jura their distinctive character.

Sciaccarello – A regional grape grown in Corsica.

Semillon – The commonest white grape of the Bordeaux area, the basis for the great white wines of Bordeaux, either dry like Graves or sweet like Sauternes, Barsac, etc.

Spätburgunder: see Pinot Noir.

St-Emilion des Charentes: see Ugni Blanc.

Sylvaner – Grown in Alsace. It produces fresh, fruity white wines.

Tannat – A regional grape grown in the Pyrenean foreland.

Terret – A regional grape grown in Languedoc.

Tilbouren – A regional grape grown in Provence.

Tokay – Grown in Alsace, where it is also known as *Grauklevner* or *Pinot Gris*. It produces a full-bodied dry white wine.

Tressot – A regional grape grown in Burgundy.

Ugni Blanc – This grape is widely grown in Provence, and gives the wines of southern Languedoc the tannic acid which they often lack. It is also used in western France, under the name of *St-Emilion des Charentes*, to produce cognac.

Vermentino – A regional grape grown in Corsica.

Viognier – A regional grape grown in the Rhône valley.

Weissburgunder, Weissklevner: see Pinot Blanc.

Major Centres

Paris

Office de Tourisme
Syndicat d'Initiative et Accueil de France
127 Avenue des Champs Elysées
Tel: 46 23 61 72

Embassies:
UK: 35 Rue du Faubourg St Honoré
USA: 2 Avenue Gabriel
Tel: 42 96 12 02/42 61 80 75

One of the most beautiful cities in the world, a centre of western culture since the 12th century, an economic metropolis of international importance, and the centre of European fashion for many years, Paris offers the foreign visitor a bewildering array of sights and experiences.

Bird's-eye view of the Arc de Triomphe

Sightseeing

Paris boasts some of the world's most famous museums, and architecture of unparalleled majesty. It is also a city of many beautiful squares and tree-lined avenues. Much of the modern city was planned by Georges-Eugéne Haussmann in the second half of the 19th century.

Bibliothèque Nationale – Houses one of the world's richest collections of books
Champs Elysées – famous avenue, on which lies the Elysée Palace, the residence of the President of the Republic. It leads to the Place Charles de Gaulle and the Arc de Triomphe, the largest triumphal arch in the world
Eiffel Tower – built for the Exhibition of 1889 by Gustave Eiffel
Hôtel des Invalides – built in 1671 at Louis XIV's request to house old soldiers, now a fascinating Military Museum
La Bastille – built in 1370, served as a royal prison until it was destroyed at the beginning of the French Revolution
Montmartre – centre of Paris nightlife, famous for its street painters
Notre Dame – founded in 1183, finished in the 14th century, severely damaged during the French Revolution. Famous for its Rose Window. Contains a bell weighing 15,000kg cast in 1686
Musée d'Orsay – this magnificent former railway station houses French art from the late 19th and early 20th centuries and in particular the collection of Impressionist paintings which used to hang in the Jeu de Paume
Palais de Justice – the law courts, the majority of the building dates from the 18th century
Place de la Concorde – one of the world's largest and most beautiful squares. Also in its time one of the most terrifying. Between 1793 and 1795 the guillotine claimed 2800 victims here
Sacré Coeur – huge Romanesque-Byzantine style church. Building started in 1875 and was completed in 1914. Fine views of Paris from the front of the Church
The Louvre – covering 198,000sq m, opened 1793, in many ways Europe's finest museum
Picasso Museum – a relatively new museum, this houses a collection of Picasso's works – drawings, prints, pottery, *collages*, paintings in relief, sculptures and oil paintings

Hall of Mirrors, Versailles

The Seine and Notre Dame

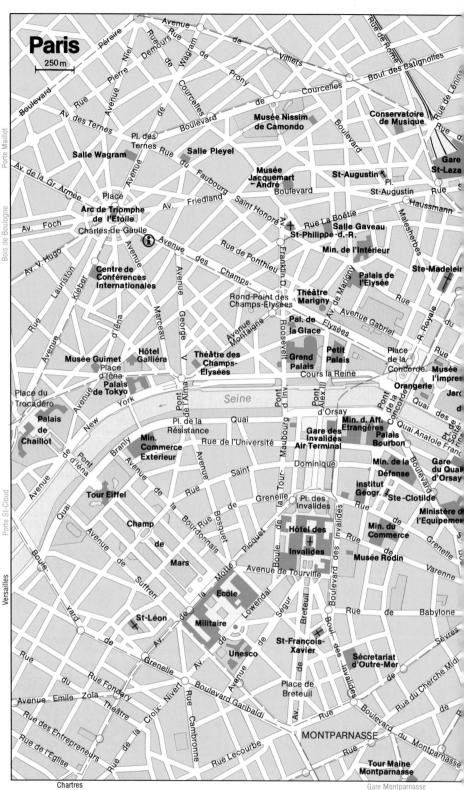

Moulin Rouge   MONTMARTRE
Boul. de Clichy
Place Pigalle   Boul.   Boulevard   de   la   Chapelle
Rue Blanche
R. Pigalle
Casino   Rue   Av. Trudaine
de Paris   Rue N.-D. de Lorette
Rue   Condorcet
Gare du Nord
St-Vincent-de-Paul
Fayette   St-Joseph
ste-Trinité
Musée Gustave Moreau
Notre-Dame-de-Lorette
Fayette
Rue de la Grange
Gare de l'Est
St. Laurent
Folies Bergère
Rue de Paradis
R. d. Petites Ecuries
Boul.
Opéra national
Haussmann
Boul. des Italiens
Musée Grevin
Olympia
Boulevard des Capucines
Salle Favart
Bourse des Valeurs
Min. de la Justice
R. du 4 Septembre   Rue   Boul. Bonne Nouvelle
Bibl. Nationale   N. D. des Victoires
Place Vendôme   R. des Champs
Noveau Carré   Boul. St-Martin   Place de la République
Conservatoire des Arts et Métiers
St-Roch
R. Etienne   Turbigo
Cirque d'Hiver
Comédie Française   Palais Royal   Banque de France
St-Eustache   Marcel
Musée de la Chasse
Musée Tuileries   Min. des Finances   Bourse du Commerce
Forum des Halles
Pl. du Carrousel   Palais du Louvre
Centre Pompidou
Archives Nationales
St. Honoré   Rivoli
Egl. St-Denis
St-Germain   Théâtre du Châtelet   St-Merry
Musée Carnavalet
Inst. de France   Théâtre de la Ville
Tour St-Jacques
Pl. des Vosges
cole Nationale des Beaux-Arts
Monnaie   Palais de Justice   Rathaus
St-Gervais
niversité aris V
ÎLE DE LA CITÉ   St-Paul
St-Germain-des-Prés   Préf. de Police   Hôtel-Dieu
Notre-Dame
ÎLE ST-LOUIS
Boul. Henri IV.
Université Paris V-VI   St-Séverin   St-Julien-le-Pauvre   St-Louis
St-Sulpice
Hôtel de Cluny
Odéon
Palais du Luxembourg   Sorbonne   QUARTIER LATIN
Universités Paris VI
Jardin du   St-Etienne-du-Mont
Ecole Polytechnique
Luxembourg   Panthéon   Arènes de Lutèce   Paris VII
Ecole des Mines
Jardin des Plantes
Mosquée
Gare d'Austerlitz

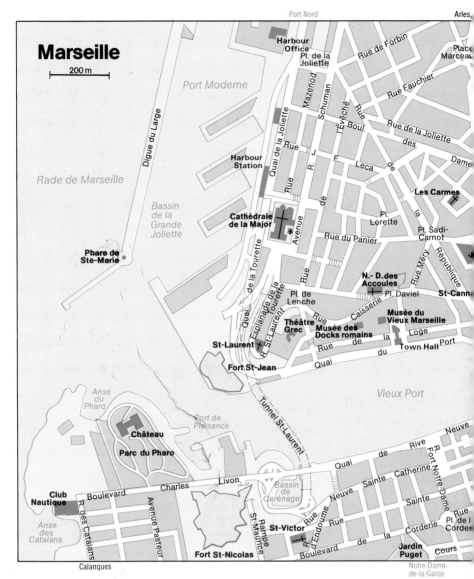

Marseille

200 m

Port Nord

Arles

Harbour Office
Pl. de la Joliette
Rue de Forbin
Place Marceau
Rue Fauchier

Port Moderne

Mazenod
Schuman
Rue de la Joliette
des
Dame

Quai de la Joliette
Rue   J.   F.   Leca

Rade de Marseille

Harbour Station

Les Carmes

Bassin de la Grande Joliette

Cathédrale de la Major

Avenue

Pl. Lorette
Pl. Sadi-Carnot

Rue du Panier

Phare de Stè-Marie

Rade de Marseille
Digue du Large

N.- D.des Accoules

Rue Méry
République

Quai de la Tourette
Esplanade de la Tourette

Rue de

Pl. de Lenche
Théâtre Grec

Pl. Daviel   St-Cann

Caisserie

Musée du Vieux Marseille

St-Laurent
Quai St-Laurent
Rue St-Laurent

Musée des Docks romains

Loge
Town Hall Port

Fort St-Jean

la de
du
Quai

Vieux Port

Anse du Pharo

Port de Plaisance

Tunnel St-Laurent

Neuve

Château

Quai   de   Rive
Fort Notre-Dame

Parc du Pharo

Livon

Charles

Bassin de Carénage

Sainte   Catherine

Neuve   Sainte

Club Nautique
Boulevard
R. des Catalans
Avenue Pasteur

Rampe St-Maurice

St-Victor

Rue d'Endoume
Rue

Corderie
Pl. de l Corder

Anse des Catalans

Fort St-Nicolas

Jardin Puget

Rue
Cours

Boulevard   de   la

Calanques

Notre-Dame-de-la-Garde

Versailles

Office de Tourisme
7 Rue de Réservoirs
Tel: 39 50 36 22

20km south west of Paris, Versailles is famed for its magnificent Palace, the last home of the French monarchy and its court. As well as the Palace there is an 18th century cathedral, the Lambinet Museum, and the Municipal Library, which are all of interest.

Sightseeing

Palace of Versailles – the largest and perhaps most magnificent palace ever built. Its interior is particularly lavish and includes the world-famous Hall of Mirrors. There are also some beautiful gardens and several outbuildings worthy of mention in its grounds

Lambinet Museum – built in the 18th century it contains furniture, pictures and prints

Municipal Library – famed for its highly decorated interior

Notre Dame – a Church built by Mansart in 1844–46

Salle du Jeu de Paume – tennis-court built for the King in 1686 where the National Assembly met in 1789

Marseilles

Office de Tourisme
4 La Canebière
Tel: 91 54 91 11

Founded in the 6th century by the Greeks, Marseilles, France's oldest and second largest town, is also its most important port. It has two har-

en Provence,

Lazare

Boul. G. Desplaces

Av. Gal. Leclerc

Place V. Hugo

Honnorat

St-Charles Station

Rue

Boul. M. Bourdet

Av. P. Sémard

Place des Marseillaises

Liberté

Boul. Ch. Nedelec

Boul. Voltaire

Boul. National

Camille

Rue d'Isoard

de Bernardy

Longchamp

Consolat

Libération

Flammarion

Jardin Zoologique

Musée des Beaux-Arts

Palais Longchamp

Musée Grobet-Labadié

Rue J.

de

la

St-Théodore

Rue des Dominicaines

Rue

Nationale

Boulevard d'Athènes

Boul. de la

Place A. Labadié

Rue St- Bazile

Rue

Boulevard

de

Boulevard

St-Théodore

Longue

Rue d'Aix- Cours

Rue

des

Vert

Allées L. Gambetta

Cours Roosevelt

Rue Monte-Cristo

LSUNCE

Tapis

Capucins

Bus Station

Canebière

St-Vincent-de-Paul

Rue St-Savournin

Rue

Boul.

Eugène

Rue du Camas

vations

Belsunce

La

Rue Adolphe Thiers

Rue

Terrusse

St-Michel

Ferréol

Musée de la Marine

urse

Canebière

Rue

de

Rue Cartol

Rue

de

Pierre

Chave

a

Rue

St

de

Rue d'Aubagne

Cours Lieutaud

Rue des Trois Mages

Place J. Jaurès

Boulevard

Bruys

Rue

Paradis

Rome

Cours

Julien

Rue des 3 Frères Barthélemy

Rue

St-Pierre

Rue

Ferrari

éra

ue F. Davso

Grignan

Ste-Trinité

Calvaire

R. Estelle

R. Dieudé

Pl. Cézanne

Château Payan

Rue des Vertus

St-Charles

Ferréol

Rue

Cours

Rue de

Rue

de la

ignan

Musée Cantini

Pl. F. Baret

Rue

Rue des Lodi

Loubière

Palais de Justice

onthyon

Paradis

B. Salvator

Notre-Dame du Mont

Tilsit

erre

Puget

Rome

Préfecture

Lieutaud

St-Sacrement

Cité Radieuse,Toulon

———○——— Métro

Train from Briançon at Marseilles station

bours. The Vieux Port is for the fishing fleet and is surrounded by restaurants serving the famous 'bouillabaisse' (fish soup). The Porte Moderne copes with the commercial traffic. Marseilles has several museums; of particular interest are the Museum of Fine Arts and the Shipping Museum

Sightseeing

Cathédrale de la Major – the largest church built in the 19th century
Cathédrale St Lazare – built in the 11th–12th centuries, originally founded in the 4th century
Château d'If – reached by boat from the Vieux Port, this island fortress, built in 1529, is famous for its association with Alexander Dumas' 'Count of Monte Cristo'
Museum of Fine Arts – situated in the Palais Longchamp, it contains a good collection of paintings and sculpture
Notre-Dame-de-la-Garde – built 1853–4, it affords a fine view of the city
Shipping Museum – situated in the State Exchange building

Summer on the Riviera

Côte d'Azur

The Côte d'Azur or 'French Riviera' is now a long succession of beach resorts from Marseilles to the Italian border. Every summer, thousands of tourists flock to the beaches of Nice, St Raphael and St Tropez. In the winter, attracted by the mild climate, visitors come to see the historical coastal towns of Fréjus and Hyères.

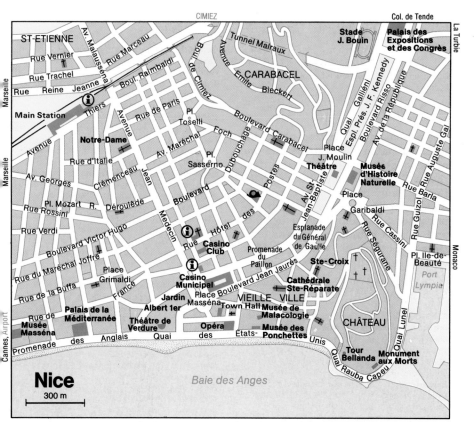

Nice

300 m

Baie des Anges

Sightseeing

Cannes – an excellent beach makes this a busy tourist centre. It contains the Musée de la Castre and a 16th–17th century church

Fréjus – its Roman remains include the oldest amphitheatre in France. There is also a cathedral and a 4th–5th century baptistery which adjoins the cathedral

Hyères – the oldest winter resort on the Côte d'Azur. A very picturesque old town, containing a Municipal Museum with exhibits of Greek and Roman origin

Monaco – home of the famous Grand Prix (May), an independent principality with a hereditary constitutional monarchy

Nice – a popular resort in both summer and winter with a particularly attractive townscape. Chagall Museum contains a comprehensive collection of his works

St Raphael – another popular winter resort. There is a museum here which has archaeological finds some dating back to the 5th century BC

St Tropez – a very popular beach resort. Has an excellent modern art collection in the Musée de l'Annonciade, and a Maritime Museum. It also boasts a busy and interesting harbour

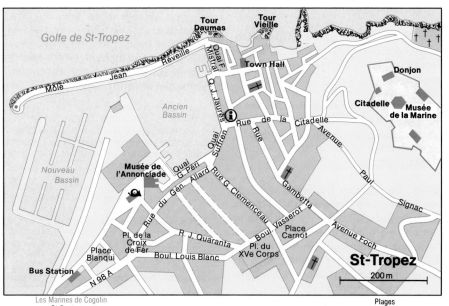

St-Tropez

200 m

Monaco and Monte Carlo

Direction du Tourisme et des Congrès
Monte Carlo
2, bis Boulevard des Moulins
Tel: 30 87 01

The principality of Monaco, one of the smallest states in Europe, is also one of the most luxurious tourist resorts in the world. Attractively situated on the Côte d'Azur, between Nice and the Italian border, it offers a number of attractions including sandy beaches and a busy marina, an international Grand Prix through its streets in May, and the world famous Place du Casino.

Sightseeing

Palais du Prince – a 13th century building containing sumptuous state apartments; there is a daily changing of the guard at 11.55am
Oceanographic Museum – rises to a height of 87m above the sea, and contains important scientific collections of marine life
Exotic Garden – contains a great variety of delicate tropical plants with stalactitic caves and a Museum of Prehistoric Anthropology
Monte-Carlo Congress Centre – opened in 1978, a massive hexagonal complex incorporating hotels and flats
Casino – built in 1878 by the architect of the Opéra in Paris, Charles Garnier

Strasbourg

Office de Tourisme
10 Place Gutenberg
Strasbourg F-67000
Tel: (88) 32 57 07

The Rhine frontier gateway to France, and the crossroads of Europe, Strasbourg is an economic, cultural and sightseeing centre. It is the capital of Alsace, a university town, the see of a bishop, headquarters of the Council of Europe, the European Court of Justice and the European Science Foundation, and meeting place of the European Parliament.

With its soaring Cathedral and its many burghers' houses of the 16th and 17th century, Strasbourg still retains something of the character of an old free city of the Holy Roman Empire, but is also typically French with its handsome buildings in Louis XV style, and its numerous mansard roofs.

Sightseeing

Cathedral – begun in 1015 it reflects the organic development of the whole range of styles from Romanesque to late Gothic (12th–15th century). The interior contains beautiful stained glass and the famous Astronomical Clock. Magnificent views of the city from the tower
Château des Rohan (1728–42) – prior to the Revolution the Château was the residence of the Cardinal-Bishops of the great house of Rohan. On the ground and first floors are the bishop's apartments in Rococo style. The Château also houses the **Archaeological Museum**, the **Museum of Fine Arts** (works by Italian, Spanish, Flemish, Dutch and French masters), and the **Museum of Decorative Arts** (principally ceramics and porcelain)
Maison de l'Oeuvre Notre-Dame – has housed the Oeuvre Notre Dame (the authority responsible for the maintenance of the Cathedral) since 1349. It contains the **Musèe de l'Oeuvre Notre Dame**, with the originals of sculpture from the cathedral and many paintings
Museum of Modern Art – 19th and 20th century pictures and sculpture, including work by Hans Arp, Braque, Klee, Max Ernst, Rodin, Renoir and Degas. Housed in the **Ancienne Douane** (Old Custom House)
Ponts Couverts – four bridges, formerly roofed, crossing the River Ill, which is here divided into four arms. Four of the medieval defence towers are also preserved here
Palais de L'Europe – built in 1972–77 this is a fortress-like structure of 9 storeys with an interior courtyard containing the tent-like chamber in which the Council of Europe and the Europeän Parliament meet

Bordeaux

Office de Tourisme
12 Cours du 30-Juillet
Bordeaux F-33000
Tel: (56) 44 28 41

This lively commercial and industrial town lies in the heart of the world's biggest vintage-wine growing area. Chief town of Aquitaine and a busy port, Bordeaux has preserved much handsome and attractive 18th-century architecture in the city centre and along the Garonne.

Sightseeing

Grand Théâtre (1773–80) – situated in the Place de la Comédie (the former Roman forum), the theatre has a spectacular colonnaded façade and elaborate internal appointments
Esplanade des Quinconces (1818–28) – the largest square in Europe (29 acres). Monument to the Girondists (1895) as well as statues to Montaigne and Montesquieu
Cathédrale St André – begun in the 12th century. On the north side is the Porte Royale (first-class sculpture of the 13th century), and near the choir of the Cathedral is the richly decorated Tour Pey Berland
Musée des Beaux Arts – includes work by Perugino, Botticelli, Tiepolo, Cranach

Strasbourg: view over 'Little France' to the Cathedral

Accommodation

Hotels

French hotels are categorised into five grades by the Ministry of Tourism. These hotels show a sign recording their classification on the outside of the premises. Hotels charge by the room, not by the person, so prices for two sharing are much better than for one. Refer to the table below for information about prices.

Hotels which belong to the Logis de France association are good value for those on a moderate budget. They are family-run and generally clean but with few frills.

Relais du Silence hotels are particularly recommended for travellers who are looking for peace and quiet in comfortable surroundings with good food and a friendly welcome. The standard of these hotels corresponds generally to an equal split between two- and three-star grading in France.

The Relais Routiers are mainly used by long-distance drivers. They are generally simple restaurants, but some offer rooms.

Information and leaflets available from:

French Government
Tourist Office,
178 Piccadilly
London W1V 0AL

(Send 50p in stamps to cover postage and packing.)

Hotel Price Range	
Type of hotel	Price for 1 night in francs for two persons
*****	800–2000
****	500–1000
***	200– 400
**	120– 240
*	60– 160

These prices are intended to act as a rough guide only.

Hotels with facilities for the handicapped *handicapés physiques* are indicated by the wheel-chair symbol in the official Hotel Guides.

Gîtes de France

Gîtes de France provide reasonably-priced self-catering accommodation in or near small country villages (but very rarely near the sea). A gîte may be anything from a village cottage to a wing of a farmhouse. Average rent is £60–£100 a week for a house for 4–6. For details, send s.a.e. to:
Gîtes de France Ltd
178 Piccadilly
London W1V 0PQ

Youth Hostels

France has over 300 youth hostels (*auberges de jeunesse*), which can be used by foreign visitors with an international youth hostel card (obtainable from the youth hostels association in the visitor's own country). Advance booking is advisable in July and August: the maximum stay permitted is usually 3 nights.

Information

UK: Youth Hostels Association
           14 Southampton Street
           London WC2
           Tel: (071) 836 8541

France: Federation Unie des
           Auberges de Jeunesse
           6 Rue Mesnil
           75116 Paris
           Tel: (45) 53 51 14/(45) 05 13 14

Camping and Caravanning

France enjoys a high reputation for the quality of its camping with some 10,000 officially graded sites. Sites graded ** and above must have communal buildings lit (and roads for *** and ****), games areas (with equipment for *** and ****), a central meeting-place, points for electric razors, surrounding fence with guard (night watchman for *** and ****). Sites graded *** and **** also have washing facilities in cubicles, hot showers, safety deposits, telephones and good shops on or close by the site. For a family of 4 with a tent and car, allow 60F for a * site and 105F for a **** site per day.

Introduction to Rail Information

The *Société Nationale des Chemins de Fer Français (SNCF)* is one of the most progressive and well organised services in the world. Some 10,500km of line is equipped to carry trains at speeds of 160km/h or more. Passenger traffic is handled by several different classes of train:

Train à grande vitesse (TGV) – this type of train is regarded as the *SNCF*'s flagship. It is the fastest train in the world and reaches speeds of up to 270km/h in commercial service between Paris and SE France. Passengers using this service are charged a fare supplement during peak hours.

Rapides – fast, inter-city trains which make few intermediate stops.

Express – fast, inter-city trains which make a number of intermediate stops. NB Both the *Rapides* and *Express* services generally use 'Corail' rolling stock. The trains are air-conditioned and offer a high standard of comfort.

Omnibus – local stopping trains.

Major International Services

Connection	Duration	Frequency
Paris–London	7–10hrs	up to 11 times daily
Paris–Copenhagen	16hrs	once daily
Paris–Amsterdam	5–6hrs	10 times daily
Paris–Moscow	46hrs	once daily
Paris–Brussels	2½–3hrs	11 times daily
Paris–Cologne	5–6hrs	8 times daily
Paris–Vienna	15–18hrs	4 times daily
Paris–Geneva	3½–4hrs	5 times daily

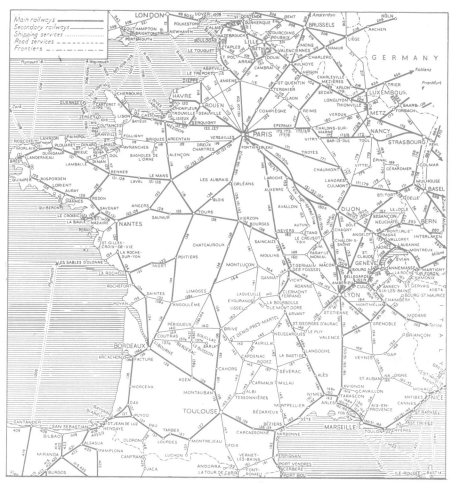

Map supplied by kind permission of Thomas Cook Ltd. The numbers along the lines refer to tables in the *Thomas Cook Continental Timetable.*

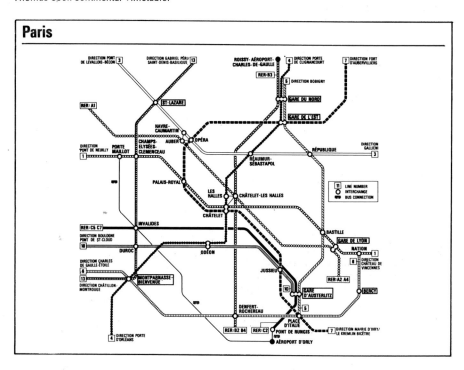

Major Internal Services

Connection	Duration	Frequency
Le Havre–Paris	2–3hrs	up to 10 times daily
Paris–Quimper	6–7hrs	7 times daily
St Malo–Quimper	4–5hrs	4 times daily
St Malo–Bordeaux	8–10hrs	2/3 times daily
Paris–Marseilles	5hrs	up to 12 times daily
Paris–Grenoble	3–4hrs	8 times daily
Paris–Lyon	2–3hrs	12 times daily

Montpellier Cathedral

Scenic Routes

Southern France is the area most re-nowned for scenic trips, with the Alps providing a spectacular backdrop on virtually any run. The train from Paris to Chamonix (change at Culoz or Aix-les-Bains and at St Gervais) is one of the finest of these. Alternatively, the Grenoble to Genoa run (via Marseilles) follows the Côte d'Azur and covers some beautiful coastal scenery. For up-land scenery, try the lines between Clermont-Ferrand and Bêziers. In addi-tion, there are a number of privately operated steam train routes which are interesting both scenically and histor-ically. The shortest is the Chemin de Fer de Marcilly, which covers 1.5km in the Loire Valley. The longest antique rail service is the Chemin de Fer de Provence, which runs from Nice to

Digne for 151km over the Alpes Maritimes.

Other lines renowned for their scenic attractions include:
Aurillac–Neussargues
Chambéry–Bourg St Maurice
Culoz–Modane
Gap–Briançon
Nice/Ventimiglia–Cuneo
Perpignan–La Tour de Carol
Port Bou–Perpignan
Vichy–Nîmes

Veteran Railways

1. **Chemin de Fer Touristique Froissy–Dompierre** (Somme)
   Route: Froissy–Dompierre
   Length: 7km
   Gauge: V60
   Steam train and diesel
   Operates Sundays, May and June and selected days during July and August
   Operated by: *Association Picarde pour la Pre-servation et l'Entretien des Véhicules Anciens (APPEVA), BP 106, 800001 Amiens Cedex. Tel:* (22) 44 55 40

2. **Chemin de Fer Touristique du Vermandois** (Aisne)
   Route: Origny–Sainte-Benoîte
   Length: 22km
   Gauge: VN
   Steam train and diesel
   Operates on selected dates during June, July and September
   Operated by: *Cercle Ferrovaire et Touristique du Vermandois (CFTV), BP 262, 02104 Saint-Quentin Cedex. Tel: (23) 67 05 00*

3. **Chemin de Fer Touristique de la Vallée de la Doller** (Haut-Rhin)
   Route: Cernay–Sentheim
   Length: 14km
   Gauge: VN
   Steam engines and diesel trains
   Operates Sundays from May to September and every day (except Monday and Tuesday) in July and August
   Operated by: *Chemin de Fer Touristique de la Vallée de la Doller (CFTVD), 10 rue de la Gare, BP 5, 68780 Sentheim. Tel: (89) 82 88 48*

4. **Chemin de Fer Touristique de la Vallée de la Canner** (Moselle)
   Route: Vigy–Hombourg-Budange
   Length: 12km
   Gauge: VN
   Steam train: Operates weekends May to October
   Operated by: *Association Lorraine d'Exploita-tion et de Modélisme Ferroviaire (ALEMF), rue Mal-de-Lattre-de-Tassigny, 54340 Pompey. Tel: (8) 349 07 64*

5. **Regie Ferroviaire de Richelieu** (Indre-et-Loire)
   Route: Richelieu–Ligne–Rivière–Chinon
   Length: 21km
   Gauge: VN
   Steam train: Operates weekends June to mid-September

Operated by: *Trains à Vapeur de Touraine (TVT)*, Gare de Richelieu, 37120 Richelieu. Tel: (47) 58 36 29

6. **Train à Vapeur du Puy-du-Fou** (Vendée)
Route: Mortagne-sur-Sèvre–Epesses–Herbiers
Length: 21km
Gauge: VN
Steam: Operates weekends June–mid-October.
Operated by: *Association du Chemin de Fer du Puy-du-Fou*, c/o M. Ribemont, 21 rue Delille, 85022 La Roche-sur-Yon. Tel: (51) 05 06 92

7. **Chemin de Fer de Marcilly** (Indre-et-Loire)
Route: Marcilly-sur-Maulne
Length: 1.5km
Gauge: V60
Steam and diesel trains. Operates Sundays May to mid-September
Operated by: *Association d'Exploitation du CF de Marcilly (CFM)*, Marcilly s/Maulne, 37330 Château-la-Vallière. Tel: (47) 24 07 95/ (47) 24 04 46

8. **Chemin de Fer de Saint-Eutrope** (Essonne)
Route: Parc de Saint-Eutrope à Evry
Length: 2.5km
Gauge: V60
Steam and diesel trains. Operated Wednesday and weekends until mid-November.
Operated by: *Société Etudes et Equipements (Département Chemin de Fer)*, 5 square Montsouris, 75014 Paris. Tel: (1) 569 76 49

9. **Chemin de Fer Touristique de la Sendre**
Route: Saujon–La Tremblade
Length: 20km
Gauge: VN
Steam and diesel trains. Operates Sundays May to October and, in addition, Saturdays during August
Operated by: *Association des Amis de Chemin de Fer de la Vallée de l'Isle Nord Libournais*, c/o M P Meriet, Résidence Chartrons tour B, rue Leybardie, 33300 Bordeaux. Tel: (56) 39 10 78/(57) 69 01 47

10. **Chemin de Fer de la Vallée de L'Ouche** (Côte-d'Or)
Route: Bilgny-sur-Ouche–Pré–Magnien
Length: 4km
Gauge: V60
Steam and diesel trains. Operates Sundays, May to September and Tuesday, Thursday, Saturday through August
Operated by: *Chemin de Fer de la Vallée de L'Ouche (CFVO)*, 4 rue Pasumot, 21200 Beaune. Tel: (80) 22 86 35 (afternoons)

11. **Chemin de Fer Touristique du Breda** (Isère Savoie)
Route: Pontcharra–La Rochette
Length: 14km
Gauge: VN
Steam train. Operates Sundays, July to beginning of September
Operated by: *Chemin de Fer Touristique de Bréda (CFTB)*, BP 21, 38530 Pontcharra. Tel: (76) 97 69 54 or Mairie de Pontcharra (76) 97 61 39

12. **Train à Vapeur des Cévennes** (Gard)
Route: Anduze–Saint-Jean-du-Gard
Length: 13km
Gauge: VN
Steam train. Operates Thursday, Friday, Sunday from May to September and, in addition,

Saturdays in July and August
Operated by: *Régie Municipale du Train à Vapeur des Cévennes*, La Gare, 30270 St-Jean-du-Gard. Tel: (66) 85 13 17

Internal Fare Structure

Standard Rate Fares

The price of a standard fare is determined by two factors: the distance of the journey, and the class in which you choose to travel. The approximate kilometric rate is 60c for 1st class travel and 40c for 2nd class.

Some restrictions concerning the day and time of travel may operate for passengers using special-rate passes and reduced fares. *SNCF* have divided the year into a tariff calendar which is colour-coded as follows:

Blue (off-peak) period: generally from 12 noon Monday to 3pm Friday and from 12 noon Saturday to 3pm Sunday. All reduced fares are valid.

White (standard) period: generally from 3pm Friday to 12 noon Saturday and from 3pm Sunday to 12 noon Monday plus some French public holidays. Some reduced fares are not valid.

Red (peak) period: approximately 24 days in the year when no reduction is available.

Child Reductions

Children under the age of 4 travel free. Children between the ages of 4 and 12 travel at 50% of the price of an adult ticket. If the child is travelling with a family who are using a Couple/Family Card, he or she travels at 75% reduction on the basic fare.

Train for Briançon at Veynes

Youth Card Reductions

Young people who are not resident in France are advised to consult the International Section. The Carré Jeune allows reduced price travel anywhere on the *SNCF* network for 12–25 year olds. The holder is entitled to a 50% discount in an off-peak period or a 20% discount in a standard period on 4 single (or 2 return) journeys. The cost of the pass is equivalent to £15 and it is valid for a year. The Carte Jeune, at the same price, is available from the 1st June to 30th September and gives 50% discount off-peak.

Family Cards

The Rail Europ Family Card is the most suitable pass for a family visiting France by train. Refer to the International Section for details.

Senior Citizen Reductions

Senior Citizens from countries outside France are best served by the Rail Europ Senior Card (please refer to the International Section).

Party/Group Savers

These are designed for return, circular or transit journeys on the *SNCF* network. They give 20% reductions for parties of at least 6 adults and 30% reductions for parties of at least 25 adults. Validity is for 2 months. Free tickets are issued for leaders of parties travelling on party tickets, subject to certain conditions.

Special Excursion/Holiday Rates

The holiday return (Séjour) tickets represent a 25% reduction on ordinary return fares. The distance covered must be at least 1000km and the return journey may not be started until the Sunday following the outward journey. Séjour fares are valid only from Monday midday–Friday midday and from Saturday midday–Sunday midday.

Tourist Reductions

The 'France Vacances Pass' special railrover card is available to all passengers who are not resident in France or French overseas territories. It covers the entire *SNCF* network and can be used on any train. The card can be purchased and used at any time of the year and offers unlimited 1st or 2nd class travel for 4 days during a period of 15 days or for 9 or 16 days during a period of 1 month.

Validation of Ticket

Tickets must be validated by the passenger before boarding the train by using one of the orange-coloured automatic date-stamping machines at the platform entrance. Failure to do so may result in a supplementary fee. Following a break of journey of 24 hours or more, passengers must revalidate their ticket. (This procedure does not apply to tickets purchased outside France.)

Where to Buy Tickets

In France

Tickets can be obtained in person at principal rail stations, or by letter.

In Great Britain

Tickets can be obtained from:
European Rail Travel Centre
PO Box 303
Victoria Station
London SW1V 1JY
Tel: (071) 834 2345 for enquiries and credit card bookings.

Motorail forms and some of the passes are available from the French Railways office at:
French Railways Ltd
179 Piccadilly
London W1V 0BA
Tel: (Motorail) (071) 409 3518

In the USA

SNCF offices in New York, Los Angeles, San Francisco, Chicago and Dallas (see International Section).

Facilities on Trains

Sleepers and Couchettes

Sleepers and couchettes are fitted on many of the *SNCF* routes but accommodation is generally limited and reservations should be made in advance. Sleepers comprise 1, 2 or 3 bed compartments equipped with sheets, blankets and pillows. Both 1st and 2nd class compartments have a corner basin with hot and cold running water and a razor outlet. All couchettes are equipped with blankets, pillows and sheets.

SNCF have recently introduced a popular alternative to the sleeper and couchette in the form of specially-built air-conditioned compartments with semi-reclining bunks called 'Cabine 8'. A 'Cabine 8' bunk is available with a 2nd class ticket without paying a supplement of any kind. A bunk may be reserved at the cost of a normal seat reservation fee.

Food

On *TGV*s a bar/buffet is open offering packed meals and hot and cold drinks. Both *TGV*s and 'Corail' trains also operate an at-your-seat meal service. Reservations are required for the restaurant cars. As well as full restaurant cars, many self-service vehicles and buffet cars providing hot meals are now in operation.

Luggage

On *TGV*, 'Corail' and fast trains, luggage compartments are provided at the entrance to each carriage.

Disabled Passengers

On *TGV*s and certain inter-city trains a disabled passenger in a wheelchair may travel 1st class with a 2nd class ticket.

Bicycle Carriage

Bicycles should normally be registered for each journey undertaken (current charge 30F). A delay of up to 5 days is possible before the bicycle arrives at the destination. There are, however, a limited number of local trains on which cyclists may take their bike free of charge. Details are available locally.

Motorail

Motorail is particularly convenient for passengers travelling with their cars from England to the continent. From embarkation at the English port to your holiday destination, everything is taken care of and you arrive well-fed, rested and relaxed. Created for the British market in 1957, French Motorail nowadays boasts over 1,000,000 passengers a year on 130 routes. For further information, see the International Section.

Animals

Pets require a special ticket which is half the price of the accompanying passenger's ticket. However, if the animal is small (under 6 kilos or able to fit into a bag or basket 45cm × 30cm × 25cm) it goes free. In a sleeping compartment, passengers may only carry a pet if they are the sole occupant.

Train for Villefranche at Perpignan station

Facilities at Stations

Food

The larger *SNCF* stations have excellent restaurant facilities. The provincial capitals usually have a bar/restaurant or self-service bar. The smaller stations will have only kiosks.

Reservations

Reservations are recommended for couchettes and sleepers and can be made at the station or through travel agents. Reservations are compulsory for motorail travellers, and on TGV services.

Disabled Passengers

In larger stations there are information panels designed particularly for disabled people. They show the best routes to use within the station. There are also special welcome points designated by their orange colour, where uniformed staff are happy to help. There are special toilets, paths and lifts in the major stations designed to accommodate those in wheelchairs.

Coach Links

There is a wide network of coach services which ties into the rail timetables. *SNCF* operates tours lasting several days as well as day or half-day excursions. For further information contact French rail stations.

Car Hire

There are over 200 stations which provide car-hire facilities.

Bike Hire

French Railways operate a nationwide *train+vélo* service in 250 stations. Step off the train, collect your bike, cycle to your destination and hand your bike in at the nearest station that participates in the system. You can book in advance by writing to a station stating your date and time of arrival.

Great Britain

Ffestiniog Railway, Wales

Introduction

Steeped in history and tradition, Great Britain has plenty to attract visitors to its shores. London, a vast city with many famous landmarks, is the most popular destination. However, Britain is visited very often on account of its delightful countryside, a patchwork of many different landscapes, which is dotted with castles, cathedrals, and country houses from past ages.

Great Britain is made up of England, Wales and Scotland. There are many smaller islands, from the Channel islands and Scilly Isles in the south to the Shetlands and Orkney Islands off Scotland which give Britain yet another title – the British Isles. A kingdom of 95,000sq miles, the mainland extends for more than 600 miles and is 300 miles across at its broadest point. This surface area includes some 1200sq miles of inland waters, an important scenic feature of the British countryside.

A country with an extraordinarily varied and beautiful coastline, England, Scotland and Wales can roughly be divided into two regions; the highland region in the north and west, and the lowland region in the south and east, with the Pennines forming a spine between the two. The highest mountain ranges are in Scotland (Ben Nevis 4406ft) and in Wales (Snowdon 3560ft). Popular areas like the Lake District and Cumbrian Hills in the north west, and the North and South Downs in the south east, provide centres for the famous British pastime of walking.

Ben Nevis, Britain's highest mountain

Both areas are also renowned for their public houses. The British climate is best described as temperate with winters that are generally mild and summers that only occasionally scorch.

The population of Great Britain is nearly 54½ million, 46½ million in England, 5½ million in Scotland and 2½ million in Wales. Of the 54½ million, half live in the country's sixty largest towns. So despite a high density of population, there are many areas in Great Britain which are sparsely populated.

Land's End, the most westerly point of Britain

Britain's political system has changed minimally over the last 500 years. Those changes that have occurred did so gradually and there were few major upheavals. Even today there is still no written constitution. There are, however, a series of legal judgements that have been made at various times that provide a core around which the country is governed. Britain is one of the few European countries that has retained its monarchy. The British monarch plays a primarily ceremonial role in government and despite being able to veto laws and dismiss ministers in theory, in practice she must act on the advice of her ministers.

The country is governed by Parliament. Established in its modern form in 1295, Parliament consists of two houses, the House of Commons and the House of Lords, and legislation must be passed by both Houses to become an Act of Law.

The Government, which is responsible to Parliament, consists of the Prime Minister, usually the leader of the majority party, and the ministers selected by him or her. The 600 Members of the House of Commons are elected by popular vote, and the 900 Members of the House of Lords are predominantly hereditary peers, who have the power to delay legislation but not to veto it.

Britain has an industrial economy. Once the leading industrial nation in the world, it now produces only 7% of the world's industrial goods. It is, however, still the leading processor of imported raw materials, which underlines the decline in its mineral wealth. The major industries are involved with textiles, chemicals and electrical and mechanical engineering. They are mainly located in the Midlands and the North of England. The discovery of oil in the North Sea has been of mixed benefit to the economy and in a declining world market, the value of the £ has suffered as the price of oil has fallen. Other industries have been allowed to decline. The North, once the centre of the industrial world, is now suffering severely in the recession, and new industries are being introduced there in an attempt to try to stem the flow of the young labour force from these areas. Tourism also plays an important part in the British economy, and is a useful earner of foreign currency. About 12 million visitors come to the UK each year, bringing in an estimated £4500 million.

The history of British culture is predominantly the history of its architecture and literature. The most productive period of British painting was the late 18th and early 19th centuries, a time when the two landscapists John Constable (1776–1837) and J M W Turner (1775–1851) made their mark. The 18th century was also a time when the decorative arts flourished; of special interest were the furniture of Thomas Chippendale (1707–79) and the ceramics of Josiah Wedgwood (1730–95) and both are still popular today. Sculpture, never a field favoured by British artists, nor seen in any frequency in religious buildings, produced Britain's best known modern artist, Henry Moore (1898–1986).

British architecture has always been well represented and there are examples all over the country, dating from as early as 1800 BC (Stonehenge). Of particular interest are the remains from the period of Roman occupation, the Norman cathedrals, churches and castles, and the Medieval castles and Gothic cathedrals of the Middle Ages. The Tudor and Elizabethan country houses represent the British form of the Renaissance. The Baroque period produced Britain's greatest architect Sir Christopher Wren (1632–1723) who had a unique opportunity to rebuild the city of London after much of it was destroyed in the Great Fire in 1666.

However, perhaps Britain's greatest contribution to the cultural world has been in the field of literature. From Chaucer right through to the modern day, British literary output has been prodigious. William Shakespeare (1564–1616), is probably still Britain's best known poet and dramatist. Judging by the frequency with which they are still performed the plays are as relevant today as they were in the 16th century. He was followed by many leading literary figures including John Milton (1608–74) who wrote the epic poem 'Paradise Lost', Jonathan Swift (1667–1745), world-famous for his satirical 'Gullivers Travels' and Daniel Defoe (1660–1731), author of 'Robinson Crusoe'.

In the 18th and early 19th centuries the sonnets of William Wordsworth (1771–1850), the ballads of Samuel Taylor Coleridge (1772–1834) and the romantic poetry of Lord Byron (1788–1824), Percy Bysshe Shelley (1792–1822) and John Keats (1795–1821) were written. The 19th century also saw the socially critical novels of Charles Dickens (1812–70).

The late 19th and early 20th centuries were dominated in literary terms by the Irish. The poet William Butler Yeats (1865–1939), novelist James Joyce (1882–1941) and playwright George Bernard Shaw (1856–1950) all in their different fields typified the great wealth of British literary talent.

Musically Britain has had few major figures. The composers to achieve most international recognition are Henry Purcell (1658–95), Sir Edward Elgar (1857–1934) and Benjamin Britten (1913–76).

History

55 BC–AD 412	Roman occupation of Britain
596	St Augustine is sent from Rome to convert Britain to Christianity
1016–42	England a Danish kingdom under Canute and his sons
1066	Duke of Normandy conquers England and establishes Norman line of kings
1215	King John is forced to sign Magna Carta, foundation stone of English Constitution
1295	Parliament is established in its modern form
1540	Henry VIII breaks with the Church of Rome. Monarch becomes Head of the Church in England
1588	Destruction of the Spanish Armada
1640–49	English Civil War – Charles I beheaded
1707	Act of Union between Scotland and England
1777	Britain loses its American colonies in the war of American Independence
1815	Napoleon is defeated by Wellington at the Battle of Waterloo
1837–1901	Reign of Queen Victoria, the golden age of the British Empire
1914–18	First World War. Britain declares war on Germany
1922	Establishment of the Irish Free State
1936	Edward VII abdicates in favour of his brother George VI
1939–45	Second World War. Churchill heads an all-party government Germany defeated by the Allies
1952	Accession of Queen Elizabeth II
1969	Disturbances in Northern Ireland
1973	Britain joins the EEC
1979	Margaret Thatcher is elected as first woman Prime Minister
1982	War with Argentina over possession of the Falklands
1984	Margaret Thatcher, is re-elected for a further five-year term
1986	Agreement signed with France to build a rail tunnel beneath the English Channel.
1987	Conservatives under Margaret Thatcher win the General Election for the third time.
1988	Oil rig Piper Alpha catches fire in North Sea with the loss of over 130 lives.

Kings and Queens of England (before 1603) and the United Kingdom (since 1603)

Anglo-Saxon and Danish kings

Alfred the Great	871– 899
Edward the Elder	899– 924
Athelstan	924– 939
Edmund	939– 946
Edred	946– 955
Edwy	955– 956
Edgar	959– 975
Edward the Martyr	975– 978
Ethelred	978–1016
Edmund Ironside	1016
Knut (Canute)	1016–1035
Harold Harefoot	1035–1040
Harthaknut	1040–1042
Edward the Confessor	1042–1066
Harold Godwinson	1066

Norman kings

William I, the Conqueror	1066–1087
William II	1087–1100
Henry I	1100–1135
Stephen	1135–1154

House of Anjou-Plantagenet

Henry II	1154–1189
Richard I, Cœur-de-Lion	1189–1199
John	1199–1216
Henry III	1216–1272
Edward I	1272–1307
Edward II	1307–1327
Edward III	1327–1377
Richard II	1377–1399

House of Lancaster

Henry IV	1399–1413
Henry V	1413–1422
Henry VI	1422–1461

House of York

Edward IV	1461–1483
Edward V	1483
Richard III	1483–1485

House of Tudor

Henry VII	1485–1509
Henry VIII	1509–1547
Edward VI	1547–1553
Mary I	1553–1558
Elizabeth I	1558–1603

House of Stuart

James I	1603–1625
Charles I	1625–1649
Republic	1649–1659
Oliver Cromwell, Lord Protector	1653–1658
Richard Cromwell, Lord Protector	1658–1659
Charles II	1660–1685
James II	1685–1688
William III, and Mary II	1689–1702
Anne	1702–1714

House of Hanover/Windsor

George I	1714–1727
George II	1727–1760
George III	1760–1820
George IV	1820–1830
William IV	1830–1837
Victoria	1837–1901
Edward VII	1901–1910
George V	1910–1936
Edward VIII	1936
George VI	1936–1952
Elizabeth II	since 1952

Major Centres

London

Tourist Information Centres
HM Tower of London
West Gate, EC3

Victoria Station
Forecourt, SW1

Selfridges
Oxford Street, W1

Harrods
Knightsbridge, SW1

Teletourist Service
Tel: (071) 246 8041

US Embassy
24/31 Grosvenor Square, W1A 1AE
Tel: (071) 499 9000

A cosmopolitan city with a population of 6.7 million, London is one of the largest cities in the world. It is situated on the banks of the River Thames, which is the site of many of London's most famous landmarks. Although parts were damaged by German air raids during the 1840s, particularly in the area of the docks, London still remains a city full of historic buildings and museums. It is also a city famed for its many beautiful parks.

Tower of London

Sightseeing

British Museum – one of the world's largest museums founded by the Act of Parliament of 1753

Imperial War Museum – contains a large collection of material used in the two world wars

Kensington Palace – still a royal residence; State Apartments and Court Dress Collection can be visited

Madam Tussauds – the famous waxworks exhibition

Natural History Museum – contains a vast range of exhibits in the fields of zoology, mineralogy, botany, entomology and palaeontology

Parliament Square – Houses of Parliament, Big Ben and Westminster Abbey

Kensington Palace

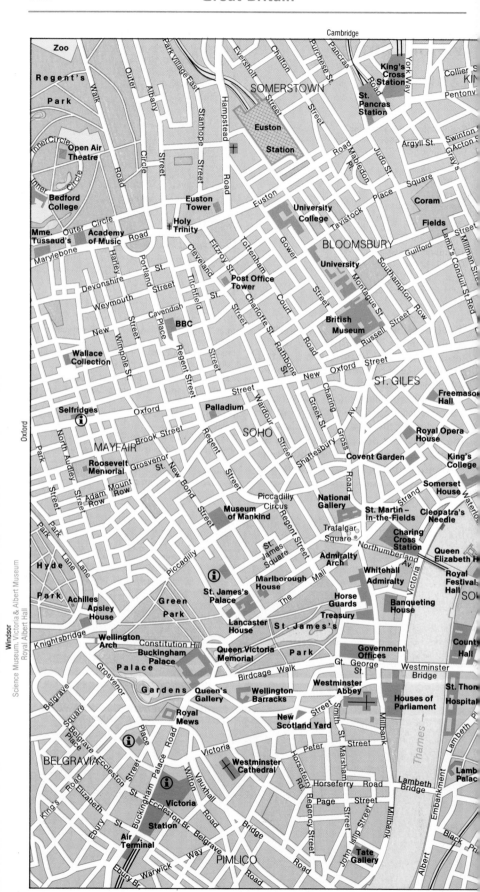

Cambridge

Zoo

Regent's Park

SOMERSTOWN

King's Cross Station

St. Pancras Station

Open Air Theatre

Euston Station

Euston Tower

Holy Trinity

University College

BLOOMSBURY

Coram Fields

Bedford College

Mme. Tussaud's

Academy of Music

University

Post Office Tower

British Museum

ST. GILES

BBC

Wallace Collection

Freemason Hall

Selfridges

Palladium

SOHO

Royal Opera House

MAYFAIR

Roosevelt Memorial

Covent Garden

King's College

Somerset House

Museum of Mankind

Piccadilly Circus

National Gallery

St. Martin-in-the-Fields

Cleopatra's Needle

Trafalgar Square

Charing Cross Station

Queen Elizabeth H

Hyde Park

St. James's Square

Admiralty Arch

Royal Festival Hall

SO

Marlborough House

Whitehall

Admiralty

Achilles

Apsley House

Green Park

Horse Guards

Banqueting House

St. James's Palace

Lancaster House

St. James's

Treasury

Wellington Arch

Constitution Hill

Buckingham Palace

Queen Victoria Memorial

Park

Government Offices

County Hall

Palace

Gt. George St.

Westminster Bridge

Gardens

Queen's Gallery

Wellington Barracks

Birdcage Walk

Westminster Abbey

St. Thom Hospital

Royal Mews

New Scotland Yard

Houses of Parliament

BELGRAVIA

Westminster Cathedral

Lamb Palac

Victoria Station

Air Terminal

PIMLICO

Tate Gallery

Windsor
Science Museum, Victoria & Albert Museum
Royal Albert Hall

Oxford

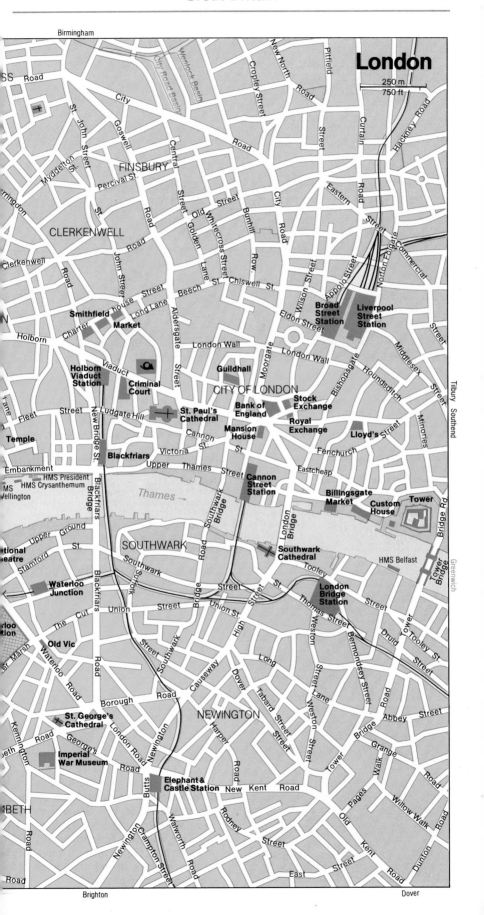

Birmingham

London

250 m
750 ft

City Road Basin

Wenlock Basin

City Road

Cropley Street

New North Road

Pitfield Street

SS Road

St. John Street

Goswell Road

Central Street

FINSBURY

Myddelton St.

Percival St.

Curtain Road

Hackney Road

rrington Road

Clerkenwell

CLERKENWELL

John Street

Clerkenwell Road

Old Street

Golden Lane

Whitecross Street

Bunhill Row

City Road

Chiswell St.

Eastern Street

Nonton Gate

Commercial Street

Holborn

Charterhouse Street

Long Lane

Beech St.

Aldersgate Street

London Wall

Wilson Street

Eldon Street

Appold Street

Moorgate

London Wall

Bishopsgate

Houndsditch

Middlesex Street

Tilbury Southend

Smithfield Market

Broad Street Station

Liverpool Street Station

Holborn Viaduct Station

Viaduct

Criminal Court

New Bridge St.

Ludgate Hill

Guildhall

CITY OF LONDON

Stock Exchange

Fleet Street

Street

St. Paul's Cathedral

Bank of England

Royal Exchange

Lloyd's Street

Minories

Temple

Cannon St.

Mansion House

Fenchurch Street

Blackfriars

Victoria

Upper Thames Street

St.

Eastcheap

Embankment

HMS President

HMS Crysanthemum

MS Wellington

Blackfriars Bridge

Thames →

Cannon Street Station

London Bridge

Billingsgate Market

Custom House

Tower

Bridge Rd

Upper Ground

SOUTHWARK

Southwark Bridge

Southwark Cathedral

HMS Belfast

Greenwich

tional eatre

Stamford St.

Waterloo Junction

Blackfriars Road

Southwark Street

Tooley St.

London Bridge Station

Tower Bridge

loo tion

Union Street

Southwark Street

Union St.

High Street

Thomas Street

Street

Tower

Tooley St.

The Cut

Old Vic

Waterloo Road

Borough Road

Southwark Bridge Road

Causeway

Dover

Long Lane

Tabard Street

Weston Street

Bermondsey Street

Druid Street

Road

Tooley St.

er Marsh

St. George's Cathedral

George's Road

London Road

Newington

NEWINGTON

Harper Road

Bridge

Grange

Abbey Street

Imperial War Museum

Butts

Elephant & Castle Station

New Kent Road

Road

Old Kent Road

Willow Walk

BETH

Road

Newington

Crampton Street

Walworth Road

Rodney Road

Street

Pages Walk

Dunton Road

Road

East Street

Kent Street

Road

Brighton

Dover

St Paul's Cathedral, London

Regents Park and Zoological Gardens – London's most famous park which also contains London Zoo, opened in 1826

Royal Albert Hall – famous for its annual promenade concerts and huge 10,000 pipe organ

Science Museum – covers every aspect of science and technology

St Pauls Cathedral – the City of London's largest and most famous Church, totally destroyed by fire in 1666 and rebuilt by Sir Christopher Wren

Tate Gallery – opened in 1897, concentrates mainly on British painting, modern foreign art and modern sculpture

'Big Ben', Houses of Parliament

The Mall – Admiralty Arch, St James' Palace, Marlborough House, Buckingham Palace

Piccadilly Circus – the centre of the West End with its bright neon lights and new Trocadero Centre

Tower of London – the fortress of the capital, first conceived by William the Conqueror in 1068

Trafalgar Square – National Gallery, National Portrait Gallery, Nelson's Column

Victoria and Albert Museum – contains one of the greatest collections of fine and applied art in the world

Wallace Collection – a rich and varied collection of art, porcelain, furniture, jewellery and armour

Wellington Museum – residence of the great Duke of Wellington and opened as a museum in 1952

Westminster Cathedral – one of the major Roman Catholic churches in Britain

Whitehall – Changing of the Guard, Downing Street, Banqueting House

Cardiff

Wales Tourist Board
3 Castle Street
Tel: (0222) 27281

Train Information
Cardiff Station
Tel: (0222) 499811

Cardiff, capital of Wales, lies on the wide estuary of the Severn and is traversed by two much smaller rivers, the Taff and the Rhymmey. An important port, it is also a university town and the cultural as well as the economic centre of Wales.

Sightseeing

Civic Centre – an imposing building, the first of its kind in Britain. The complex includes:
City Hall – built in 1904, this elaborate building features a bell-tower and a dome crowned with a dragon, the emblem of Wales. The *Marble Hall* is embellished with figures from Wales's turbulent history
War Memorial – in the centre of the complex
Law Courts – the centre of Welsh justice
National Museum of Wales – founded in 1907 to be a repository of Welsh history and culture. It contains archaeological exhibits, from the earliest periods of the country, plus early Christian artefacts, tools and implements of pre-industrial crafts and domestic items, as well as musical instruments. Included in the National Museum is an *Art Gallery*, which gives an excellent survey of Welsh painting as well as housing a fine collection of English and foreign art

City Hall, Cardiff

Llandaff Cathedral – founded under the aegis of Bishop Urban (1107–34), the see is one of the oldest in Britain. The main part of the cathedral is 13th century, although the tower was rebuilt in the 15th. After several centuries of decay, the cathedral again became a focal point when John Wood of Bath built an 'Italian temple' within its walls in 1734. Badly bomb-damaged in World War II, the cathedral has now been extensively renovated and contains a notable 'Christ' by Epstein
Cardiff Castle – in the centre of the city, this castle stands on the site of a Roman fort, and part of the Roman walls and bastion (4th century) have been preserved. A fortress was built here in 1090 by Robert Fitzhammon, and then greatly extended by his successor. Owen Glendower razed it in 1404. The whole complex – Roman and Medieval – was skilfully restored at the end of the last century
The State Apartments – including the Library, are decorated in Pre-Raphaelite style
Greyfriars Church – built in 1280, only the foundations can still be seen, with the ruins of a mansion built on the site after the Reformation
Queen Street – main shopping street, bustling with life; this is the busiest street in Wales
Welsh Folk Museum – 4 miles out of Cardiff to the west, in a beautiful park in St Fagans. Exhibitions include furniture and crafts of former times and modern craftsmen can sometimes be seen at work.
Caerphilly Castle – 7½ miles north of Cardiff in a large industrial town, this well restored castle dates from 1268 and has the most elaborate system of defences of any British castle. It has been enlarged several times, and includes two drawbridges, massive walls, round towers and a moat

Edinburgh

Tourist Information Centres
Waverley Market, Princes Street
Tel: (031) 577 2727

Edinburgh Airport
Tel: (031) 333 2167

British Rail Travel Centre
Waverley Station
Tel: (031) 556 2451

Edinburgh Castle from Princes Street Gardens

Edinburgh, dominated by the splendid 11th century castle is the capital and cultural centre of Scotland. Ever since the building of the New Town to the north in the 18th century, it has been two towns not one, with the Old Town to the south huddling round the Royal Mile and the Palace of Holyrood at the bottom. Set in particularly beautiful countryside, Edinburgh has many historic buildings, museums and galleries.

Sightseeing

Edinburgh Castle – offers a marvellous view of the city. Site of St Margaret's Chapel, built in 1090, the oldest building in Edinburgh. Around Crown Square to the south of the chapel are the main

Royal Botanic Garden

Edinburgh

300 m
600 ft

Water of Leith

Forth

Bridge

Royal Circus

Great King Street

Northumberland Street

Dundas Street

Gloucester La.

Moray Place

Heriot Row

Street

Garde

Queen Str

Queen Street

Queen Street

Hill Street

Thistle

St. And

St

Dean Br.

Castle Street

Frederick St.

Hanover Street

St

Randolph C.

George

Music Hall

Queensferry Street

Charlotte

Street

Rose

Royal Scottish Academy

Glentin Hope Street

Square

Rose

Princes Street

Scott Monument

Garden

Drumsheugh

Melville Street

Princes Street Garden

Natio Galle

Shandwick Pl.

St. John

St. Cuthbert

St. Mary's Cathedral

Kings Stables

Castle

Esplanade

Lothian Road

Road

Grassma

West Port

Forth

Park

Zoological

Morrison Street

Morrison Street

Bread Street

Lauriston

Pl

Fountainbridge

Earl Grey St

Home St.

North

Fountainbridge

Gilmore

Canal

Place

Leven St

Melville

Union

Gilmore

Park

Leamington Ter.

Bruntsfield Links

historic apartments and the Scottish National War Memorial, built by Sir Robert Lorimer in 1927

St Giles Cathedral – begun in 1387, contains numerous monuments commemorating eminent Scots. Lead equestrian statue of Charles II (1685) in Parliament Square behind the church is probably the oldest of its kind in Britain

Parliament Hall – built 1632–40 but considerably altered in 1808. Building in which Scottish Parliament met from 1639 until the Union in 1707

Royal Scottish Museum – contains a fine exhibition of primitive art

Holyrood Palace – building begun by James IV, the palace was devastated by fire in 1544 and 1630. The present building dates from the 1670s. State apartments contain valuable furniture, tapestries and pictures. Beyond the Palace in Holyrood Park is Arthur's Seat, an extinct volcano with magnificent views of the city

National Gallery – a fine collection including works by Rubens, Rembrandt and the French Impressionists

Events – Edinburgh Festival of Music and Drama (August–September)

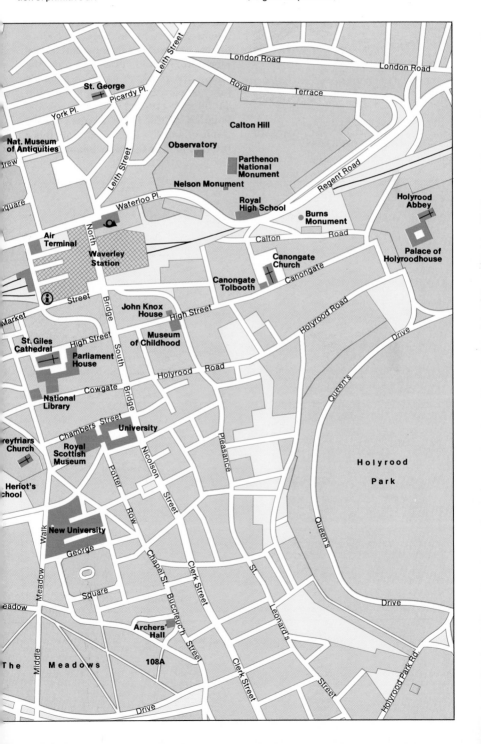

Hertford Bridge, Oxford

Oxford

Tourist Information Centre
St Aldate's Chambers
St Aldates
Tel: (0865) 726871

British Rail Travel Centre
Oxford Station
Tel: (0865) 722333

One of the oldest and most famous university towns in Europe, Oxford boasts some of the finest architectural works in England. It has also been the university at which some of Britain's most celebrated intellectuals and public figures studied. Situated at the junction of the River Thames (called the Isis) and the River Charwell, it is a town of immense scenic beauty.

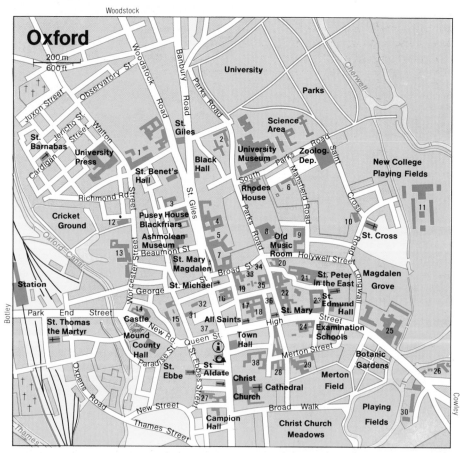

Oxford

COLLEGES				OTHER BUILDINGS
1 Somerville	11 St. Catherine's	21 New College	31 Frewin Hall
2 Keble	12 Ruskin	22 All Souls	32 Union Soc Rooms
3 Regents Park	13 Worcester	23 Queen's	33 Sheldonian Theatre
4 St. John's	14 Nuffield	24 University	34 Clarendon Building
5 Trinity	15 St. Peter's	25 Magdalen	35 Bodleian Library
6 Mansfield	16 Jesus	26 Wayneflete	36 Radcliffe Camera
7 Balliol	17 Lincoln	27 Pembroke	37 St. Martin's Tower
8 Wadham	18 Brasenose	28 Corpus Christi	38 Peckwater Quad
9 Manchester	19 Exeter	29 Merton	
10 St. Cross	20 Hertford	30 St. Hilda's	

Radcliffe Camera, Oxford

Sightseeing

Ashmolean Museum – oldest museum in the country. Magnificent collection of art and antiquities
Bodleian Library – contains over two million volumes, and some 40,000 manuscripts
Cathedral – also the Chapel of Christ Church. Dates from the second half of the 12th century. Spire is one of the oldest in England
Christ Church College – founded in 1525 by Cardinal Wolsey. Wren's Tower contains the huge bell called Great Tom which peals 101 times every evening at five minutes past nine. The hall is the largest in Oxford
High Street – American writer Nathaniel Hawthorne (1804–64) called it 'the finest street in England'
Magdalen College – one of the most beautiful colleges. Founded in 1458. Contains a fine late 15th century tower. Famous choir
Merton College – founded about 1266 in Surrey, and moved to Oxford in 1284. Chapel contains some fine stained glass
Radcliffe Camera – rotunda designed by James Gibbs (1762–1854), the most prominent representative of the Anglo-Italian style of architecture

Shakespeare's birthplace, Stratford

Stratford-upon-Avon

Tourist Information Centre
Judith Shakespeare's House
1 High Street
Tel: (0789) 293127

Birthplace of William Shakespeare, Stratford is a delightful town situated on the River Avon. It owes its popularity to its greatest son, and it is for this reason alone that the thousands of visitors come every year. It has virtually become a place of literary pilgrimage.

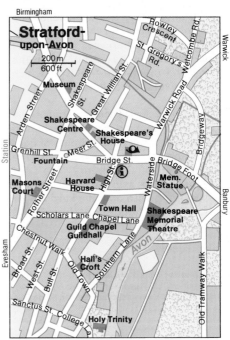

Statue of Hamlet, Stratford

Sightseeing

Shakespeare's Birthplace – contains the 1623 First Folio and is also a museum
Halls Croft – one of the finest Tudor houses in Stratford. Probably the home of Shakespeare's son-in-law Dr John Hall
Church of Holy Trinity – where Shakespeare is buried. Early English tower (c 1210), with a spire added in 1763

Royal Shakespeare Theatre – contains a Picture Gallery and Museum which exhibits a unique collection of portraits of Shakespeare and famous actors who have appeared in his plays

York

York Tourist Information Centre
De Grey Rooms
Exhibition Square
York YO1 2HB
Tel: (0904) 21756/7

The county town of Yorkshire before it was divided in 1974 into four separate counties. Few cities look as completely medieval; York has been called the 'City of Churches' for there are 17 pre-Reformation churches within its boundaries. But the pride of York is the huge and magnificent Minster which towers over the whole city.

It is the ecclesiastical capital of the Church of England, the archbishop of York, with the style of Primate of England, being second only to the archbishop of Canterbury. The Lord Mayor of York also has a special status, sharing with only the Lord Mayor of London the honorific prefix of 'Right Honourable'.

Sightseeing

York Minster – one of the largest and most beautiful medieval churches North of the Alps, it contains England's greatest concentration of medieval stained glass. Famous also for the twin-towered west facade, the octagonal chapter house and

York Minster

15th-century choir screen. The present Minster, the fifth on the site, took 250 years to build and was completed and consecrated in 1472

York Minster Undercroft – exposes the 20th-century engineering that has saved the Minster, and shows the unearthed sections of several of the earlier cathedrals

Town Walls – encircling the city the walls date from the time of Henry III (1216–72). They run for a total of 3 miles, with 6 gates or 'bars', 4 of which have been preserved

City Art Gallery – houses an important collection of English and European paintings from the 14th to the 20th centuries. Particularly rich in Italian works

Guildhall – built between 1447–53 as the civic hall of York, partially destroyed in an air raid in 1942 and since restored. Fine timbered roof and modern stained glass

Clifford Tower – of unusual quatrefoil shape, the Tower was built in the 13th century by Henry III. The original Norman keep was destroyed by fire during the Jewish massacre in 1190

Castle Folk Museum – contains the 'Kirk Collection': a series of period rooms and reconstructed streets from Tudor to Edwardian times. Also contains an 18th-century watermill, Yorkshire crafts, costume and military history

Jorvik Viking Centre – an underground reconstruction taking the visitor back through 10 centuries to the very heart of the Viking kingdom in York

National Railway Museum – fascinating collection of old locomotives, rolling stock, equipment and other paraphernalia covering the history of steam trains, their ancestors and their successors

York Story – the former 15th-century church of St Mary's, Castlegate, was restored as part of the city's contribution to European Architectural Heritage Year. It now houses a fascinating exhibition including colourful models of historic buildings and a lively slide presentation bringing together York's centuries of change under one roof

The Shambles – one of the finest preserved medieval streets in Europe, where the upper storeys of the houses lean precariously towards each other across the roadway. Antique shops and art shops

Accommodation

Hotels

The British Automobile Association's full-time and highly qualified team of inspectors regularly visit all AA-recommended hotels in Britain.

The hotels are classified by stars; each classification reflects the provision of facilities and services rather than comparative merit. The range of menus, service and hours of service are appropriate to the classification, although hotels often satisfy several of the requirements of a classification higher than that awarded.

* Good hotels and inns, generally of small scale and with modest facilities and furnishings, frequently run by the proprietor himself. All bedrooms with hot and cold water; adequate bath and lavatory arrangements; main meals with a choice of dishes served to residents; menus for residents and meal facilities for non-residents may be limited, especially at weekends.

** Hotels offering a higher standard of accommodation, more baths and perhaps a few private bathrooms/ showers; lavatories on all floors; wider choice of meals (but these may be restricted, especially to non-residents).

*** Well-appointed hotels with more spacious accommodation and at least 40% of the bedrooms with private bathrooms/showers; full meal facilities for residents every day of the week, but at weekends service to non-residents may be restricted.

**** Exceptionally well-appointed hotels offering a high standard of comfort and cooking with 80% of the bedrooms providing private bathrooms/ showers. At weekends meal service to non-residents may be restricted.

***** Luxury hotels, offering a very high standard of accommodation, service and comfort. All bedrooms have private bathrooms/showers.

Approved hotels which do not conform to the minimum classification requirements in respect of porterage, reception facilities, and choice of dishes; facilities for non-residents are often limited

---

Hotel Price Range

The enormous range and variety of accommodation makes an average hotel price difficult to establish. As a general guideline, prices in large or popular tourist towns are much higher than in rural areas and, almost invariably, the split cost of a double room is much lower than that of two single rooms.

It is advisable to telephone the tourist office in advance, especially in the high season (June–August) to avoid overbooking or inconvenience.

Bath: Tourist Office (0225) 62831 — 2/3* rooms are around £50 a double.

Cambridge: Tourist Office (0223) 322640 — 2/3* rooms are around £45 a double.

Chester: Tourist Office (0244) 40144 — 2/3* rooms are around £40 a double.

Edinburgh: Tourist Office (031) 577 2727 — 2/3* rooms are around £55 a double.

London: Tourist Office (01) 730 0791 — 2/3* rooms are around £55–65 a double.

Oxford: Tourist Office (0865) 726871 — 2/3* rooms are around £50 a double.

Stratford: Tourist Office (0789) 293127 — 2/3* rooms are around £45 a double.

Windsor: Tourist Office (0753) 852010 — 2/3* rooms are around £55 a double.

York: Tourist Office (0904) 21756 — 2/3* rooms are around £50 a double.

For those on a limited budget, double rooms can be found in guest houses for around £20/25 plus breakfast. In each case, the tourist office can assist you. Those prepared to stay less centrally will find lower prices.

Red stars

★ The award of red stars is based on a subjective assessment to highlight hotels considered to be of outstanding merit within their normal star ratings, offering something special in the way of welcome and hospitality. The award is normally withdrawn when the hotel undergoes a change of ownership.

Pubs and Inns

Pubs and inns are suitable places to stay for tourists on a limited budget. They are generally cheaper than hotels and the standards of comfort and cleanliness are more than adequate. Many inns and public houses are old and have an individual charm which makes them unique stops for an over-night stay.

Bed and Breakfast/Guest Houses

This form of accommodation is also ideal for the traveller on a limited budget. Visitors to Bed and Breakfast and Guest House accommodation sometimes eat with the family. The meals available are breakfast and, sometimes, an evening meal. In rural areas there are a number of farmhouse bed and breakfasts who provide their visitors with the produce of the land.

Youth Hostels

Members of the Youth Hostel Association are able to find very reasonably priced accommodation in Youth Hostels which are spread all over the country. Most tourist resorts and major towns have at least one Youth Hostel. Reduced price accommodation is granted in exchange for a few house-hold chores.

Camping and Caravanning

Camping and caravanning remains a popular pastime in Great Britain despite the inclement weather conditions. There are a number of organised sites in most of the popular resorts. Some of these are very well-equipped with shop, shower block, amusement centre, washing facilities and so on. Others are very basic, some offering just a river, perhaps, and a field of level ground. Rates vary according to the standard of the facilities supplied.

Introduction to Rail Information

British Rail (BR) meets the needs of the traveller very well with 14,000 trains a day to service over 2350 stations. Long-distance services are provided by InterCity trains. Almost half of these services use InterCity 125 high-speed trains which have a maximum speed of 125mph (200km/h). Most other Inter-City trains have a top speed of 100mph (160km/h). Nearly all InterCity trains provide refreshments, the most luxu-rious being the Pullman trains where 1st class ticket holders can have meals served at their seats. Cross-country and local trains connect into the In-terCity network while around major conurbations commuter and suburban services are in operation. In the heavily populated area around London, the in-tensive rail system is known as Net-work SouthEast.

British Rail, like most other European railways have been investing heavily in rolling stock, thus improving their ser-vice in terms of both comfort and speed.

Major International Services

Connection	Duration	Frequency
London–Paris	5½–9hrs	10 times daily
London–Brussels	5–9hrs	9 times daily
London–Amsterdam	8–12hrs	8 times daily
London–Geneva	12–14hrs	3 times daily
London–Rome	22hrs	twice daily
London–Munich	14–21hrs	9 times daily

Major Internal Services

Connection	Duration	Frequency
London–Aberdeen	7½hrs	4 times daily twice nightly
London–Birmingham	1½hrs	29 times daily
London–Cardiff	1¾–2hrs	23 times daily
London–Dover	1½hrs	hourly
London–Edinburgh	4¾hrs	16 times daily 3 nightly
London–Manchester	2½hrs	14 times daily
London–Oxford	1hr	16 times daily
London–York	2hrs	26 times daily

Map supplied by kind permission of Thomas Cook Ltd. The numbers along the lines refer to tables in the *Thomas Cook Continental Timetable*.

London

Inter-terminal links by London Underground ⊖

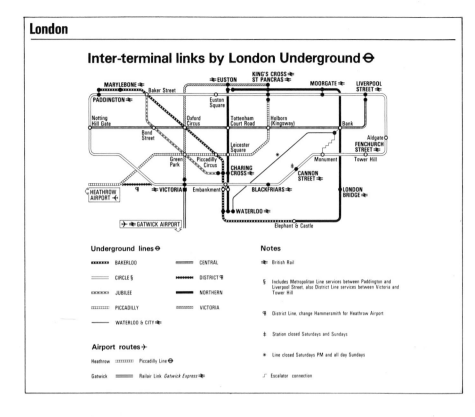

Veteran Railways

The construction of the railways had a greater impact and caused deeper changes in the shape of society than any engineering project before or since. Never before had everyday life been so dramatically changed.

Britain was the first country in the world to have a railway system, with the result that the designs for stations and bridges, engines and carriages were copied all over the world.

Today, it is easy to forget how much is owed to the past, which established the rail age with no more than iron and steam. Much of this historical legacy still remains to be appreciated by those who know where to look. Traces of early beginnings carefully recorded are preserved to be enjoyed today. Here are some of the preserved railway lines and museums which are open to the public.

1. **Vale of Rheidol** (South Wales)
   Route: Aberystwyth–Devils Bridge
   Length: 12 miles
   Gauge: 2ft
   The Vale of Rheidol Railway opened in 1902 to carry minerals from the Rheidol Valley to the harbour at Aberystwyth. As this business declined after World War I tourism grew. Today the line exists solely for the enjoyment of the holiday visitor. 'Prince of Wales', one of the original locomotives, dating from 1902, is still in regular service in its original yellow-ochre livery. The other locomotives and coaches have also been restored to historic colours. Operates weekdays April to October and selected weekends.
   Operated by: Vale of Rheidol Narrow Gauge Steam Railway, British Rail, Aberystwyth Station, Aberystwyth, Dyfed. Tel: (0970) 612378

2. **Ffestiniog Railway** (North Wales)
   Route: Porthmadog–Blaenau Ffestiniog
   Length: 13 miles
   Gauge: narrow
   This narrow gauge railway was originally built in 1836 to link the slate quarries around Blaenau Ffestiniog with Porthmadog Harbour. Constructing reliable locomotives for its small gauge had originally been considered too difficult a task, but in 1863 two very small locomotives were successfully put to work. Operates to its own timetable, connecting at both ends of the route with British Rail services.
   Operated by: Ffestiniog Railway, Porthmadog, Gwynedd, North Wales. Tel: (0766) 2384

3. **The Dart Valley Railway Co Ltd** (South Devon)
   Route: Totnes–Buckfastleigh
   Length: 7 miles
   Gauge: Originally 7ft; now standard gauge
   Steam trains and a collection of GWR engines run alongside the River Dart. Operates on selected days April–October.
   Operated by: Dart Valley Railway Co Ltd, Buckfastleigh, South Devon. Tel: (03644) 2338

4. Torbay Steam Railway (South Devon)
Route: Paignton–Kingswear
Length: 7 miles
Gauge: originally 7ft; now standard gauge
Four steam locos and three diesel locos run along the line. Passengers can enjoy fine views of the red cliffs of East Devon and the varied rock formations around the bay as the descent begins towards the Dart Estuary and the train heads along the rocky foreshore to Dartmouth. Operates daily May to September.
Operated by: Torbay and Dartmouth Railway, Queens Park Station, Torbay Road, Paignton. Tel: (0803) 555872

5. Keighley and Worth Valley Railway (West Yorkshire)
Route: Keighley–Haworth–Oxenhope
Length: 5 miles
Gauge: standard gauge
Steam trains run regular services. The Worth Valley line follows a particularly gruelling route with a continuous up-gradient and long stretches of very steep climbs. Operates weekends, holidays and daily during July and August.
Operated by: Keighley and Worth Valley Railways, Haworth, West Yorkshire. Tel: (0535) 43629/45214

6. Bluebell Railway
This 5-mile line runs from Sheffield Park to Horsted Keynes through the beautiful Sussex Weald. It is steam operated and uses a variety of locomotives ranging from the 1870s to the 1950s. The collection of coaches and wagons adds to the excitement of this historic spectacle. It operates every day from June to September; weekends in March, April, May, October and November; Wednesdays in May and October; and Sundays in December, January and February. Operated by The Bluebell Railway, Sheffield Park Station, East Sussex, TN22 3QL. Tel: (082 572) 2370.

7. Watercress Line
An historic steam railway line which runs from Alton to Alresford in the middle of Hampshire. The route passes through interesting countryside dotted with woods, historic houses, a wildfowl collection and an engine shed. Alresford has a picturesque riverside walk, a costume museum and famous watercress beds. The service operates: Saturdays, Sundays, Bank Holidays, 8 March–26 May; daily except Monday, 27 May–20 July; daily, 21 July–31 August; Saturdays and Sundays only, 1 September–26 October.

8. The Shakespeare Limited
This special Sunday Luncheon Express departs London (Marylebone) at 10.55am and calls at High Wycombe about 40 minutes later *en route* for Warwick or Stratford-upon-Avon. Trains are steam hauled as far as Banbury on the outward journey and throughout on the return journey. The trains are generally hauled by one of the following steam locomotives – *Sir Nigel Gresley, Clan Line, Flying Scotsman, Sir Lamiel* and *Green Arrow*. The return train arrives in London by 8pm.
The fares include 1st class return travel, a reserved seat, morning coffee, a roast beef 3-course lunch and afternoon tea.
The train runs on selected Sundays only and information and booking is available on Tel: (0524) 734220.

Railway Museums

1. The National Railway Museum, York
A short walk from York Station and you have free entry to one of the most comprehensive displays of historic locomotive and passenger coaches to be found anywhere in Britain. Many of these are maintained in working order and

Vale of Rheidol, South Wales

taken out for special runs. Every aspect of railways is represented here from cap badges and whistles to one of the world's few surviving examples of wooden railway track.

2. Didcot Railway Centre

Within 45 minutes by train from London Paddington, Didcot Railway Centre, adjacent to the main British Rail station is home to a large collection of GWR locomotives and rolling stock and it includes the original locomotive depot, a country branch-line station, signalbox and a goods shed which was originally used for the transfer of freight from broad to standard gauge wagons.

Didcot Railway Centre is usually open every weekend from the beginning of March to the end of October. On the first and last Sunday of each month visitors can ride in vintage carriages behind a steam locomotive.

3. Railways and Royalty – The Queen Victoria Exhibition, Windsor and Eton Central Station

Visitors to Windsor will believe they have stepped back into history. The date is 1897 and England is celebrating Queen Victoria's Diamond Jubilee.

In this year the GWR Company re-built Windsor Central Station and provided a royal waiting room for the Queen and her entourage. This has been restored to its former glory to become part of an enthralling exhibition of Victorian times.

Using careful reconstruction and many original exhibits, Madame Tussaud's have provided visitors with a fascinating glimpse of 19th century travel centred on the Royal Train of 1897. Full size replicas have been made of the locomotive and Queen Victoria's Day Saloon with meticulous attention to detail. There is also an original carriage from the Royal Train.

By train, Windsor can easily be reached from London Waterloo or Paddington Stations in under 1 hour.

4. National Science Museum, London

Early locomotives are rarer, as they were usually broken up for scrap at the end of their working lives. Miraculously though, the original Puffing Billy built about 1812 has survived. Alongside stands a modern replica of Robert Stephenson's Rocket, winner of the 1829 trials to select an engine for the Liverpool to Manchester Railway. Both engines show the development of coupling all the wheels together to overcome the tendency for one pair to spin on its own.

Internal Fare Structure

BR follows a policy on fares that leads to an almost bewildering choice of options. If possible, it is wise to check at a BR Travel Centre or appointed agent since conditions and prices may also change at short notice. For travellers from overseas who are doing a reasonable amount of travelling the best deal is probably a BritRail Pass (see International Section) which has to be bought before travelling to Britain. For those who don't have a BritRail Pass, pre-planning can afford considerable savings; some of the current ticket schemes are detailed below.

National Railway Museum, York

Standard Rate Fares

Standard fares allow the passenger maximum flexibility. They are available for any train, on any day, whether 1st or 2nd class. A Standard Single has a 3 day validity except for short distances and in restricted validity areas, where the ticket may be used only on the day of sale. A Standard Return is priced at double the single fare and has a 3 month validity. The Standard Day Return is also double the single fare but has only a one day validity.

100 mph electric train

Below are details of various reduced fares. Those wishing to travel 1st class should note that, except where specifically stated, reductions are not available in 1st class.

Savers

Saver fares offer a reduced rate for medium- and long-distance return trips in 2nd class only. They are valid for outward travel on the date shown on the ticket and return travel on any day within a month. There are restrictions on the use of Savers dependent primarily upon route and time of travel. The cost of Savers varies according to whether you travel on a 'white day' (every Friday and some busy holiday days) or a 'blue day' (all other days). For example, a 2nd Class Return Saver from London to Leeds costs £37 on a 'white day' and £30 on a 'blue day'.

Cheap Day Returns

Reduced prices available for a journey travelling off-peak, and returning the same day.

Young Person's Railcard

These cost £16 and are valid for one year from the date of purchase. Passengers under 24 and 'mature students' qualify for the card which allows them to buy 2nd class Cheap Day Returns, Standard Day Returns, Savers, Standard Returns and Standard Singles at one third discount. Holders of the Young Person's Railcard can also purchase Railrovers at one third discount, get a £10 discount on an Inter-Rail Card (see International Section) for European travel, and also get certain extra discounts in the Network South East area.

Foreign students should see the information on reductions in the International Section.

Family Railcard

A Family Railcard costs £20 and is valid for 12 months from the date of purchase. Either 1 or 2 adults can be nominated on the card allowing them and up to 2 other adults to travel at half fare (on 2nd class Cheap Day Returns and Standard Day Returns) with at least 1 and up to 4 children at a flat fare of £1 each. The reduction on Savers, Standard Returns and Standard Singles is one third. Minimum party size is one adult railcard holder at half fare and one child travelling for £1.

Senior Citizen Reductions

The Senior Citizen Railcard. This provides a year's reduced price travel for British Senior Citizens. With a £16 Card you can buy 1st or 2nd class Standard Day Returns and 2nd class Cheap Day Returns for half price. The reduction on Standard Singles, Standard Returns (2nd class) and Savers is one third. You may be accompanied by up to 4 children at a flat rate of £1 each for rail journeys only. Cards are valid for 12 months from date of purchase. Senior Citizens who are not resident in Britain should see the information on reduced price travel in the International Section.

A new 'Sprinter' train leaving Harlech, Wales

Disabled Person's Railcard

The blind and severely disabled are eligible to apply for a £12 Railcard which allows the disabled person and an adult escort to travel on 1st and 2nd class Standard Day Returns and on 2nd class Cheap Day Returns at a 50% discount. The reduction on Standard Singles, Standard Returns (1st or 2nd class) and Savers (2nd class) is one third. Cards are valid for 12 months from the date of purchase. Certain reductions are also available to wheelchair-users who do not have a Railcard. Even when travelling with a companion, disabled people are advised to tell British Rail about their journey in advance so that a member of staff can help them safely on board.

Special excursion/holiday rates

Britainshrinkers

These Road and Rail Tours are operated during the summer in co-operation with British Rail. Fully escorted, they offer a combination of fast train and motorcoach services to several specified destinations. Most of the trips are one day only and include a pub lunch. In addition, there are selected 'Overnighters' to Scotland and York which include accommodation, dinner, breakfast and lunch.

Golden Rail Holidays and Short Breaks

The enormous range of Golden Rail Holidays is designed to suit all tastes with accommodation in hotels, guest houses and self-catering flats. There are participating resorts in all parts of Britain and the Channel Islands. The long breaks range from 7 to 14 nights. Short Breaks of 2 to 5 nights are also available in cities, picturesque towns and small village inns.

Copies of the Golden Rail and Short Break brochures are available at principal British Rail stations, at Golden Rail appointed travel agents or by writing to Golden Rail Holidays, PO Box 12, York, YO1 1YX.

Railrover Passes

All-Line Railrover

The All-Line Railrover gives unlimited rail travel anywhere in Britain, including the Isle of Wight. It is available for 7 or 14 days. Sealink Shipping services for the Isle of Wight, Windermere (20% reduction), and between Tilbury and Gravesend, are also included. After the initial investment, travel is 'free'. Children under 5 travel free; those aged between 5–16 get a one third discount on the adult fare. Holders of Young Person's, Senior Citizen's and Disabled Railcards also get one third off. 1990 fares: 7 days 1st class £250, 2nd class £150. 14 days 1st class £380, 2nd class £240.

Freedom of Scotland Railrover

This gives unlimited 2nd class rail travel anywhere in Scotland after the initial investment. It is available for 7 days (£46) or 14 days (£77). Over-the-border crossings to Carlisle and Berwick-on-Tweed are included. The same reduction rates for children and some Railcard holders apply as for the 'All-Line Railrover'.

Local Rovers

These are suitable for those who want to explore selected parts of Britain rather than the whole country. There are 18 different local Rover tickets covering holiday and tourist areas. They are available for 2nd class travel on any 7 consecutive days between Easter and October. There are restrictions in some cases on weekday morning rush hour travel. Some examples of prices include: North East £33; North West Rover £26; Anglia Rover £24. Again children and many Railcard holders get a one third discount.

One Day Travelcard

The One Day Travelcard allows you unlimited off-peak travel for the day throughout the whole of Greater London by train, underground, and bus.

The cards are available from British Rail and Underground Stations within Greater London at a cost of £2.60 (90p for under 16s). They can be bought up to 24 hours in advance, or on the day of use. You can travel any time after the weekday morning rush. One day Travelcards can also be 'added on' (at bargain rates) to Cheap Day Returns from BR stations outside Greater London.

Network Card

For just £12 anyone can buy a Network Card which gives a one third reduction on Standard Singles, Standard Returns, Cheap Day Returns and Network Savers throughout the Network SouthEast area. It also gives a reduction on One Day Travelcards. Up to 4 accompanying children can travel for £1 each. One person's Network Card entitles up to 8 people (4 must be children) to travel together; all of the adults will enjoy the special discounts. Network SouthEast extends as far as Northampton and Kings Lynn in the North; Harwich and Dover on the East coast; Eastbourne and Weymouth on the South coast; and beyond Newbury and Salisbury to the West. The Network Card is valid for 12 months and tickets bought with it can be used for travel anytime after 10am Monday to Friday and as early as required on weekends and bank holidays.

The Scottish Highlands

Intercity 125

Night Time Reductions

InterCity Nightrider

This is a special InterCity service for travellers, offering reduced fares for night travel between London and Aberdeen and London and Glasgow, and intermediate stops. The Aberdeen train runs nightly all week from King's Cross, Stevenage, or Peterborough to Edinburgh, Kirkcaldy, Dundee, Arbroath, Montrose and Aberdeen. Glasgow trains also run each night from Euston and Watford Junction to Carlisle, Dumfries, Kilmarnock and Glasgow. The tickets are one way only (though a return fare may be booked at the same time) and it is 1st class. Seats must be reserved. A buffet service (without alcohol) is available.

Tourist Reductions

BritRail Pass

BritRail Passes are available to overseas visitors to Britain only. They allow unlimited travel on British Rail for varying periods up to 1 month. Refer to the International Section for full details.

Where to buy tickets

In Great Britain

British Rail Travel Centres

Expert staff are available to help with all aspects of travel planning: itineraries, rail tickets for travel in Great Britain, Ireland and Europe (including Sealink car ferries), seat reservations, InterCity sleeper reservations, motorail services, etc. The principal London centre is:
The British Travel Centre,
4–12 Lower Regent Street
London SW1Y 4PQ
Tel: (071) 730 3400
Open 9am–6.30pm (Mon–Sat); 10am–4pm Sun

Other centres in London:
14 Kingsgate Parade, Victoria Street
London SW1
407 Oxford Street
London W1
170B, Strand
London WC2
87 King William Street
London EC4

Station Travel Centres:

Cannon Street, Charing Cross, Euston, King's Cross, London Bridge, Paddington, St Pancras, Victoria, Waterloo, and cities and major towns within Britain. Many travel agencies also sell BR tickets.

In USA

From British Rail representatives (see International Section).

Facilities on Trains

Sleepers

Air-conditioned sleepers operate from London and central England to many Scottish destinations. They also run between London and Newcastle, North West England, North Wales and the West of England. Reservations can be made at British Rail Travel Centres.

Food

Most InterCity trains have a buffet car on them and many have full restaurant service serving meals at appropriate times. On major routes there are Pullman services where passengers travelling 1st class can have meals at their seats. On some cross-country services there are mini-buffet or trolley services.

100 mph diesel train

Luggage

A passenger travelling 1st class can carry up to 70kg in luggage and passengers in 2nd class are entitled to

carry up to 50kg. Anyone wishing to carry more than the limit can do so by paying an excess luggage charge.

Disabled

The new designs of British Rail trains have taken into account the needs of the disabled passenger. Modern coaches incorporate grab handles, wide access, automatic interior doors, lower steps and removable seats. Passengers in wheelchairs and their escort may travel at a reduced fare (see Disabled Person's Railcard). Guide dogs accompanying blind people always travel free and can generally be taken into stations, train restaurants and buffet cars.

Bicycle Carriage

Bikes (whether carried free of charge or not) are conveyed providing a) space is available and b) machines are properly labelled. The same conditions apply to tandems, tricycles and the Rann' trailer attachment to bikes.

Accompanied cycles are carried *free of charge* on many InterCity trains and on the majority of suburban services outside peak travelling times on Mondays to Fridays. (Peak hours: to London, arriving between 7.45–9.45am; from London, departing 4.30–6.30pm).

On InterCity 125 routes, because of limited luggage space, there are certain restrictions and charges (powered bicycles are always charged). Passengers are advised to contact the station before planning a journey with a bike.

Motorail

The motorail services carry privately owned cars and motor caravans subject to a height limit, between London and Scotland and on other selected routes. Cars are loaded well in advance of departure time, and reporting times will be quoted when booking is made.

For day-time services, accommodation will consist either of compartments or of individual seats reserved for each fee-paying member. For overnight passengers, there is usually a choice of single berth (1st class) or double berth (2nd class) sleeper accommodation with, on some routes, alternative seating. Exclusive use of a compartment can usually be arranged.

Tray meals are available on the service and must be booked at least 8 days before the journey. They range from a salad dinner with wine to a picnic or breakfast tray.

Booking must be made well in advance and should be made to the motorail terminal from which you intend to start your journey. Booking forms can also be returned to principal BR stations or appointed travel agents, AA or RAC offices. Telephone bookings may be made to the relevant office, but must be confirmed within 3 days with a deposit or full payment.

On receipt of the completed booking form, reservation confirmation will be posted. When full payment is made, you will receive your motorail ticket and information sheet showing reporting time, arrangements for loading the car and details of facilities at the terminal and on the train.

Facilities at Stations

Food

All major stations have self-service restaurants and bars. In addition, several of the larger stations are adjacent to hotels with restaurants. There are also kiosks offering hot and cold snacks.

Reservations

Seats on all InterCity trains can be reserved in advance. Apply in person at the station where the train starts its journey or write to the station or any British Rail Travel Centre or appointed travel agent. At departure stations, bookings may be made until 2 hours

Bath Spa Station

before the train leaves and the fee is £1 (£2 for most 1st class journeys) even if your journey requires a change of trains. If you are travelling in a group of 2–4 people, the £1 will cover the group for a single journey. A computerised seat reservation system, which gives a more comprehensive service is in operation on trains to and from Euston, King's Cross and Paddington.

For sleeper reservations:
These may be made by visiting a British Rail Travel Centre or by telephoning the departure station. London numbers are:

Euston (071) 388 6061
King's Cross (071) 278 2411
Paddington (071) 723 7681

Car Hire

Europcar has Rail Drive offices at 81 InterCity rail stations in Britain. The leading makes of car used include Fiesta, Renault 5, Granada, BMW, and Mercedes. This service can be particularly useful for an out-of-the-way business meeting or for a touring holiday. You travel the longest part of the journey by train and then pick up a rented car at the station with which to continue to your destination. You can leave the car at any of the 280 offices which allows for even greater flexibility. Central reservations: (081) 950 5050.

Greece

Temple of Athena Lindia, Rhodes

Introduction

Greece, the cradle of western culture, has always attracted scholars and others interested in its classical past. In recent years, however, the multitude of largely unspoilt Greek Islands, with their beautiful beaches and scenery, have also become an increasingly popular holiday destination.

The Greek mainland reaches out from the Balkan landmass into the Eastern Mediterranean in a series of mountain ranges running from north to south, contained by an intricately carved coastline of inlets and peninsulas. The islands, spread across the Aegean Sea in the east and the Ionian Sea in the west, account for about one fifth of the total land area of Greece. The largest island, Crete, is also the most southerly outpost of Europe.

Except in the northern mainland, where continental influences predominate, Greece has a Mediterranean climate with high winter and summer temperatures, and rain mainly in the winter. The summer is dry everywhere on account of the dry *etesian* winds which blow from the north and northeast, and the *meltemi* which blows from the north-west between May and September. In effect, this means Greece has only three seasons – spring from March to June, a very dry summer from June to October, and a rainy season from October to March.

Just under half of the Greek population still live in rural areas. Yet in recent years, the large towns have begun to grow quite rapidly, and of the 9.7 million people in Greece, 3 million now live in the urban area of the capital, Athens, and in Piraeus, its port. Despite modern developments, the family is still the central unit governing Greek life. The majority of the population are country folk and life in many of the towns still preserves a rural atmosphere. This is one reason why visitors to Greece are accorded such a warm and friendly welcome.

In spite of the regional differences within Greece, religion remains a unifying force. The Greek Orthodox Church has been the established state church since 1864 and its supreme head is the Archbishop of Athens. Apart from small groups of Muslims, Jews, Roman Catholics and Protestants, some 94% of the population profess the Greek Orthodox faith.

Since the fall of the military dictatorship in 1974 and the referendum on the monarchy in which the great majority of the population voted for the abdication of the exiled King Constantine, Greece has been a Democratic Republic. The new constitution of 1975 gives considerable power to the President, who is elected for a 5 year term; he appoints the head of government and he can dissolve Parliament. The Parliament of 300 members, elected for a 4 year term is dominated by the New Democracy Party and the Pan Hellenic Socialist movement. An associate member of the EEC since 1962, Greece became a full member in January 1981.

View of Kythira

The Greek economy is still heavily dependent on agriculture which employs a quarter of the working population. The main products are olives, olive oil, corn, fruit, wine, tobacco and honey. Yet farming is still hampered by the poor quality of the land, the small size of holdings and the old fashioned methods. Minerals are fairly abundant in Greece, and include the world famous marble, but further development of the extractive industries is restricted by the shortage of power supplies. Considerable reserves of oil and natural gas were discovered in 1974 off Thasos, but these have been claimed by Turkey, adding further strain to the relations between the two countries. Industry is concentrated on processing the agricultural produce for export and sale, the most important being the production of foodstuffs and textiles, leather goods and tobacco. Shipping is a vitally important area and Greece has the fifth largest tonnage in the world. Greek merchant ships play an important role in international shipping and there are large shipyards in the port of Piraeus and in the Bay of Elensis. Finally, tourism which brings in over 7 million visitors a year is naturally a major sector of the economy.

The ancient civilizations of Greece, the remains of which attract so many visitors to Greece today, were a powerful formative influence on all future developments in European culture and intellectual life. In art, architecture, philosophy, literature and science, the Greek cultures, from the early Minoan period, through the Golden Age of Athens in the 5th century BC, to the Roman and Byzantine period, produced such renowned and influential figures as:

Homer (c 800 BC)
Pythagoras (c 570–497 BC)
Socrates (c 470–399 BC)
Euripides (c 406 BC)
Hippokrates (c 460–375 BC)
Aristophanes (c 420 BC)
Plato (c 427–347 BC)
Aristotle (c 384–322 BC)

Ceiling fresco in Perivieptos Monastery, Mistra

History

From the earliest times to the Persian Wars 3rd Millennium–c 500 BC

c 1800	Heyday of the Minoan culture
c 1400	Collapse of Minoan empire, perhaps as a result of an earthquake
1194–1184	Trojan War
c 950	Foundation of Sparta
776	Traditional date of foundation of the Olympic Games

From the Persian Wars to the destruction of Corinth (c 500–146 BC).

480	Battles of Thermopylai and Salamis; Greek victory arouses consciousness of their national identity
442–429	Golden Age of Athens
336	Alexander the Great founds the Macedonian world empire
146	Destruction of Corinth; beginning of Roman and Byzantine rule

Greece under Roman and Byzantine rule (2nd–1st century BC–AD 1453).

31 BC–AD 14	Augustus sole ruler of Rome. Greece becomes province of Achaea
AD 49–54	Apostle Paul preaches Christianity in Thessalonica, Athens and Corinth
323–337	Under Constantine the Great Byzantium becomes capital of the Roman Empire
1204	Crusaders take Constantinople and found the Latin Empire

Greece under the Turks (c 1450–1828) and the Kingdom of Greece (1830–1974).

1456	The Turks besiege Athens; beginning of almost 400 years of Turkish rule in Greece
1830	Greece becomes a sovereign kingdom
1920–22	Graeco-Turkish war ends in the defeat of Greece
1924	Declaration of Republic
1935	Restoration of the monarchy; return of King George II
1936	Coup d'état by Colonel Metaxas; establishment of dictatorship
1941–4	German and Italian occupation
1945–9	Civil war between government forces and Communists
1967	Coup d'état by Colonel Papadopoulos, followed by military dictatorship
1973	Abolition of the monarchy and proclamation of a Republic
1974	Referendum in favour of a democratic Republic
1981	Greece joins the EEC
1984	Greece withdraws from NATO exercises
1986	Earthquake in Kalamata, killing 20 people

Major Centres

Athens

Greek National Tourist Organisation
Amerikis 2
Tel: (1) 3 22 31 11

Information Bureau Sýntagma
Karageórgi Sérvias 2
Tel: (1) 3 22 25 45

Tourist Police
Leofóros Sýngrou 7
Tel: 171

Embassies:
UK: Ploutárkhou 1
Tel: (1) 723 62 11
USA: 91 Vasilissis Sophias Blvd.
Tel: (1) 7212951

The official capital of Greece since 1834, Athens has long been the largest and most important city in Greece. Dominated by the Acropolis, and boasting many museums full of art treasures of incalculable worth, Athens is one of the most important tourist centres in Europe. The numerous visitors to the city are well catered for by ever increasing numbers of hotels, and by the recent development of the coastal strip along the Bay of Fáliron known as the Apollo Coast.

Sightseeing

Acropolis – originally a royal fortress, later the exclusive stronghold of the gods, it is the religious centre of Ancient Athens

The Acropolis

Acropolis Museum – built 1949–53, contains one of the world's finest collections of Greek sculpture
Agora – excavated 1931–41 and 1946–60, the remains are incorporated in an attractive park, and there is also an interesting museum
Erechtheion – built between 421 and 406 BC, on the north side of the Acropolis
Hephaisteion – one of the best preserved of all surviving Greek temples, dedicated to Hephaistos and Athena
Hill of the Muses – affords a magnificent view of the Acropolis
Little Mitrópolis – a 12th century church of great interest in the city
National Archaeological Museum – houses the finest collection of Greek art in the world
Odeon of Herodes Atticus – a fine Roman theatre still used today for concerts and dramatic performances
Olympieion – a temple to the supreme god of the Greek pantheon, it took 700 years for it to be completed
Parthenon – temple of Athena, built between 447 and 438 BC
Stadion – the first *modern* Olympic Games were staged here in 1896
Temple of Athena Nike – built between 432 and 421 BC on the west side of the Acropolis

Other places of interest

Argo Gallery
Merlin 8;
pictures.

Monument of Philopappos, Hill of the Muses

Art Centre
Glykonos 4;
art exhibitions.

Astor Gallery
Karageórgis Sérvias 16;
pictures.

Benaki Museum
Koumbari 1;

Byzantine Museum
Vasilissis Sofias 22;

Desmos Art Gallery
Akadimias 28;
art exhibitions.

Tomb of Dionysios of Kollytos, Kerameikos

Academy, Athens

Desmos Gallery
Syngrou 4;
art exhibitions.

Diogenes Gallery
Diogenou 12;
pictures and sculpture.

Diogenes Gallery
Tsakalof 10;
pictures.

Fine Art Centre
Zaimis 18;
special exhibitions.

Folk Art Museum
Kydathinaion 17;

Greek Women's Lyceum
Dimokritou 17;
special exhibitions.

Iolas Zoumboulakis Gallery
Kolonaki 20;
pictures.

Jewish Museum
Melidoni 5;

Kerameikos Museum
Ermoú 148;

National Archaeological Museum
Corner of Patission and Tositsa;

National Gallery
Mikhalakopoulou 1;

National Historical Museum
Stadiou 13;

Ora Cultural Centre
Xenophontos 7;
pictures.

Rotonda Gallery
Skoufa 20;
pictures.

Stoa Tekhnis
Solonos 13;
pictures by Greek artists.

Tholos Gallery
Filellinon 20;
pictures.

Zappion
Special exhibitions.

Zygos Art Gallery
Iofontos 33;
special exhibitions.

Archaeological sites and national museums are closed on January 1, 25 March, Good Friday, Easter Day and Christmas Day.

The Peloponnese

Tourist Police
Sidéras Merarkhias
Náfplion
Tel: 2 77 76

Tourist Police
Koliátsou 33
Corinth
Tel: 2 32 83

Tourist Police
Khilonos 8
Sparta
Tel: 2 87 01

The Peloponnese is the most southerly part of the Greek mainland. It is a peninsula and linked to the mainland by the Isthmus of Corinth, but has been known since ancient times as an island. Its famous cities, Sparta, Corinth and Olympia, steeped in the history of the Greek civilizations attract many visitors as do the sandy beaches of the resorts of the Gulf of Corinth.

Mountain landscape in the Peloponnese

Sightseeing

Corinth – the new city moved to its present site in 1858, the ancient city, which lies 7km away, contains extensive remains mostly from the Roman period. The site is dominated by the Temple of Apollo. There is also a Museum which gives a comprehensive view of the art of Corinth

Mistra – positioned 7km from Sparta, the new town lies beneath the ruins of the medieval town. The remains provide the most complete picture we have of a town of the late Byzantine period

Mycenae – excavated from 1864 onwards, this fortified city dates from the 2nd millenium BC. Of particular note are the Treasury of Atreus and the Lion Gate

Náfplion – has a magnificent situation in the Gulf of Argolis. A flourishing tourist centre, the town is within easy reach of several historical sites. It also has an interesting museum and a Byzantine gatehouse with a fine frescoed interior

Neméa – linked with one of the labours of Hercules, the killing of the Nemean lion, the main feature of the site is the Doric Temple

Olympia – the venue of the Olympic Games, it is one of the great achievements of archaeological

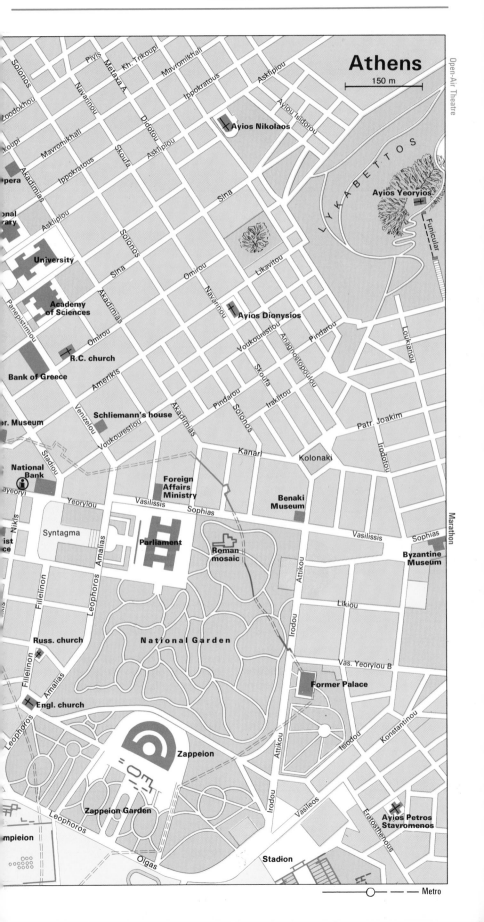

Open-Air Theatre

Athens

150 m

Solonos

Zoodokhou

Navarinou

Piyis Metaxa A.

Kh. Trikoupi

Mavromikhali

Ayios Nikolaos

Ayiou Isidorou

Asklipiou

L Y K A B E T T O S

koupi

Mavromikhali

Didotou

Skoufa

Asklipiou

Sina

Ayios Yeoryios.

Ippokratous

pera

Akadimias

nal
rary

Asklipiou

Sina

Omirou

Likavitou

Funicular

University

Akadimias

Sina

Navarinou

**Academy
of Sciences**

Omirou

Ayios Dionysios

Pindarou

Panepistimiou

R.C. church

Amerikis

Voukourestiou

Anagnostopoulou

Skoufa

Traklitou

Loukianou

Bank of Greece

Venzelou

Voukourestiou

Pindarou

Solonos

Patr. Joakim

or. Museum

Schliemann's house

Akadimias

Kanari

Kolonaki

Irodotou

Stadiou

**National
Bank**

ayeoryi

Yeoryiou

Vasilissis

**Foreign
Affairs
Ministry**

Sophias

**Benaki
Museum**

Vasilissis

Sophias

Marathon

Nikis

Syntagma

Amalias

Parliament

**Roman
mosaic**

Attikou

**Byzantine
Museum**

ist
ce

Fillelinon

Leophoros

Amalias

Irodou

Likiou

N a t i o n a l   G a r d e n

Russ. church

Fillelinon

Vas. Yeoryiou B

Konstantinou

Engl. church

Amalias

Former Palace

Attikou

Istodou

Leophoros

Zappeion

Irodou

Vasileos

Eratosthenous

**Ayios Petros
Stavromenos**

mpieion

Zappeion Garden

Leophoros

Olgas

Stadion

Metro

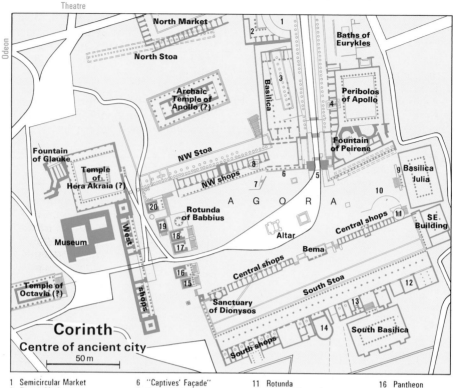

Corinth
Centre of ancient city
50 m

1 Semicircular Market	6 "Captives' Façade"	11 Rotunda	16 Pantheon
2 Roman Market	7 Sacred Spring	12 Office of Agonothetes	17 Temple of Herakles
3 Greek Market	8 Oracle	(mosaic pavement)	18 Temple of Poseidon
4 Greek temple of	9 Starting-line in	13 Fountain-house	19 Temple of Apollo
4th c. B.C.	Stadion	14 Bouleuterion	20 Temple of Hermes
5 Propylaia	10 Retaining wall	15 Temple of Venus Fortuna	

excavation, and as a direct consequence the Games were revived in 1896 in Athens. The museum at the site contains a large collection of bronzes, pottery and sculpture

Sparta – the town was refounded on the ancient site in 1834, and lies in the fertile Eviotas plain. The site has a very interesting Archaeological Museum

Accommodation

Hotels

Greece possesses some 3500 hotels all affiliated to the Hellenic Chamber of Hotels. In addition to the hotels there are numerous bungalow villages and holiday houses and apartments, a list of which can be obtained from the Greek National Tourist Organisation. In country areas accommodation in private houses, simple but clean, is available everywhere.

The hotels are officially classified into six categories – L (luxury), A, B, C, D and E – and most visitors will look for accommodation in one of the first four categories. A new hotel in a lower category may well be more pleasant than an old one in a higher category.

The tariffs shown in the table below are inclusive of service and taxes. Given the present trend of inflation, however, increases are to be expected.

Youth Hostels

There are youth hostels providing accommodation at reasonable prices, particularly designed for young people, both on the mainland of Greece and on the islands of Crete and Corfu. Most of them are open throughout the year. In hostels in the mountains and on the coast advance booking is advisable. The stay at any one hostel is limited to not more than 5 nights. Youth hostellers must produce a membership card issued by their national youth hostels association.

Information from the *Organosis Xenonon Neotitos Ellados* (Greek Youth Hostels Association), Dragatsaniou 4, Platia Klafthmonos, Athens, Tel: (1) 3 23 41 07/3 23 75 90.

Camping and Caravanning

Facilities for camping and caravanning are still in course of development in Greece. Sites are run by the Greek National Tourist Organisation, the Greek Touring Club and private individuals, some of them with bungalows (chalets) available for renting. Most of the sites are in areas of scenic beauty and on the coast. Camping outside authorised sites is not officially permitted.

Information from information bureaux of the Greek National Tourist Organisation and the local Tourist Police.

Hotel Price Range

	Price for 1 night in drachmas	
Type of hotel	Single room	Double room
L (luxury)	6000–9000	9000–30000
A	4500–6000	6000– 9000
B	3500–4000	4000– 6000
C	1800–2500	2500– 4000
D	1000–1500	1500– 2000
E	800–1000	1000– 1500

These prices are intended to act as a rough guide only.

Introduction to Rail Information

Greece has a small rail network which goes by the name of *Organismós Sidir-* *odromón Elládos (OSE)*. Most of the population tends to use coaches and buses for their long distance journeys. The size of the system and its relative unimportance in the overall national transport network means that the stan-

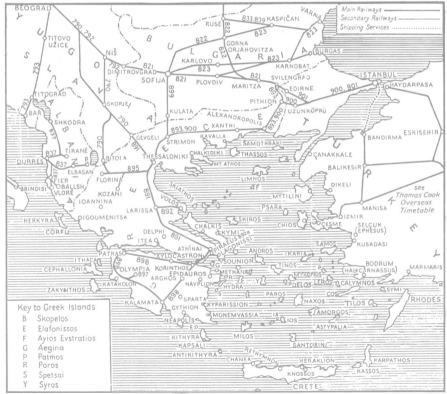

Map supplied by kind permission of Thomas Cook Ltd. The numbers along the lines refer to tables in the *Thomas Cook Continental Timetable*.

dard of service is lower than in other European countries. The government has, however, embarked on a 10 year modernisation programme which aims to improve the service.

Major International Services

Connection	Duration	Frequency
Athens–Belgrade	22–24hrs	3 times daily
Athens–Venice	38–40hrs	once daily

Major Internal Services

Connection	Duration	Frequency
Athens–Llianokladi	2–2½hrs	8 times daily
Athens–Corinth	1½hrs	11 times daily
Corinth–Diakofto	1–1½hrs	6 times daily
Corinth–Kalamata	4½–5½hrs	6 times daily
Athens–Chalkis	1½hrs	19 times daily
Larissa–Volos	1hr	6 times daily
Platy–Thessalonica	30mins	8 times daily

Scenic Routes

The Diakoptò to Kalavrita railway line runs through impressive mountainous scenery. The line rises 700m in 22km and passes along precarious edges and through tunnels hewn in the rock.

Internal Fare Structure

Standard Rate Fares

A return ticket is about 20% cheaper than buying 2 singles and it is valid for 1 month. Some examples of 2nd class single fares are given below.

Athens–Alexandroupolis 1961dr
Athens–Corinthos 276dr
Athens–Megalopolis 724dr
Athens–Olympia 931dr

The Olympieion

Child Reductions

Children under 4 travel free; between 4 and 12 they travel at half fare.

Student Reductions

Students travelling in Greece are advised to consult the International Section for information on the reductions best fitted to their requirements. There are internal student reduction schemes but they are for the benefit of students at Greek universities only.

Senior Citizen Reductions

Senior Citizens travelling by rail in Greece are advised to purchase the Rail Europ Senior Card (see International Section).

Party/Group Savers

A 30% fare rebate is allowed on all single or return fare railway tickets when passengers travel in groups of 10 or more. In addition one free ticket is granted to groups of 16 to 52 (the number of free tickets increases in proportion to the size of the group).

Railrover Passes

The Greek Tourist Card is available for individual passengers or for groups and entitles the holders to unlimited 2nd class travel over the whole network as well as on bus services operated by Greek Railways. The price of the card is dependent upon the number of people it covers and the number of days for which it is valid. In 1990, a 10-day rover for one person costs £19; for five people the cost is only £53.

Basilica B, Philippi

Where to Buy Tickets

In Greece

Tickets may be bought at the major rail stations.

In Great Britain

European Rail Travel Centre
PO Box 303
Victoria Station
London SW1V 1JY
Tel: (071) 834 2345

Beach at Párga

In USA

From *OSE* representatives (see International Section).

Facilities on Trains

Facilities on Greek trains are minimal. Travellers are advised to take food and drink with them, and should be prepared for crowded and 'seatless' rides, particularly in mid summer.

Sleepers and Couchettes

Sleeping carriages are available on some routes. Any ticket holder, on payment of a supplement, may occupy a berth (they are divided into 1st and 2nd class). The supplement can be paid to the sleeping carriage guard but it is preferable to make an advance reservation at the booking office.

Luggage

Every passenger is entitled to free carriage of average-size bags as long as they do not inconvenience other passengers. Responsibility for the safety of personal belongings rests with the individual passenger. Large items may be registered on production of a valid ticket. Registered luggage travels on the same train as the passenger.

Bicycle Carriage

Bikes can be carried on Greek trains. They should be registered about an hour before departure and normally there is no charge.

Animals

Small animals are allowed on trains as long as they are confined in baskets or other suitable containers. Small dogs may be held in the lap as long as they do not annoy other passengers.

Facilities at Stations

Food

Restaurants are open at both the Athens stations between 5am and midnight.

Reservations

It is not possible to reserve seats on internal services. However, it is possible to do so on international services and this should be organised well in advance.

Left Luggage

Passengers may deposit luggage with left luggage offices at major stations upon payment of 28dr per piece per day.

Cape Sounion, the southernmost tip of Attica

Italy

Castel Sant' Angelo, Rome

Introduction

Italy offers a dramatic diversity of scenery with the famous beaches of the Adriatic and the Riviera, the rugged Apennine mountains, the volcanic ranges in the south, and the snow covered Alps rising from the fertile Po plain in the north. This scenery alone attracts thousands of visitors, but when it is added to the wealth of historic remains from the Roman Empire, the magnificent art treasures of the High Renaissance, and the thriving towns and cities of Italy, it makes the country a very appealing prospect to visitors, whatever their particular interest.

Italy has a total area of 324,000sq km including the large islands of Sicily and Sardinia. There are three distinct regions in Italy. Northern Italy consists of the undramatic Po plain, bounded by the Apennines on one side and the Alps on the other. It is the most fertile part of Italy and supports considerably more than half the population. Central Italy possesses a more Mediterranean climate than the north. The majority of its population is centred in the basins of Tuscany and Umbria. Southern Italy where the Apennines form a backbone to the peninsula is an area with characteristic Mediterranean crops, and in the far south an area of intensive volcanic activity, the fault line extends east to west along the north side of the Bay of Naples.

Italy is a country with great climactic as well as scenic diversity. In the north, with the Apennines cutting the Po plain off from the Mediterranean, and with the Alps in the far North, there is a continental climate of warm summers and cold winters. South of the Apennines the summers are hot and dry and the winters moderate. The Riviera, protected by mountains from the cold north winds, enjoys a particularly good climate.

The population of Italy is nearly 57 million, and the main religion is Roman Catholicism. The family is particularly sacred and the family bond is stronger than in most other European countries. It is noticeable that the underdeveloped south is socially separate from the north. The standard of education in the south is significantly lower and much of the population live outside towns and follow a rural existence.

The most notable difference between north and south is in the economy. Northern Italy, enjoying excellent communications has a thriving industrial economy, based on the motor vehicle, engineering, textile and chemical industries. It is also the most productive agricultural region. The south, on the other hand, is almost exclusively agricultural, with only a few developing industries around Rome and Bari. In addition, its agriculture is inefficient and small in scale and yields per acre are low. Sardinia is one of the poorest regions in Europe and epitomises the plight of the south's economy. Tourists play an important role in the country's economy, but again tend to come to northern rather than southern Italy.

A Democratic Republic since 1946, Italy is governed by a Parliament made up of two Chambers. The first chamber has 630 members elected in a general election every five years. The second chamber called the Senate has 320 members elected on a regional basis also for five years. The practical governing of the country is carried out by the Prime Minister and other ministers who form the Cabinet. The Head of State is the President, elected by both chambers of Parliament for a seven year term; his functions are predominantly of a representative nature.

Italian art and architecture enjoyed two particularly prolific periods. The Roman Empire, vividly portrayed in Pompeii and Herculaneum was one of the great cultural achievements. Byzantine influences were uppermost and equestrian statues, mosaics and Roman remains are evidence of a glorious cultural past, underlined by the classical literary works of Livy, Virgil and Ovid.

The second great era was the High Renaissance, a period when Italian art and architecture influenced the whole of Europe. Brunelleschi (1377–1446) was the pioneer of Early Renaissance architecture, Donatello (1368–1466) in sculpture, and Botticelli (1444–1510) in painting. But the two great universal geniuses of the Renaissance, the rebirth of antiquity, were Michelangelo

Leonardo da Vinci's 'Last Supper', Milan

(1475–1564) and Leonardo da Vinci (1452–1519). They spanned painting, sculpture and architecture. The late Renaissance produced perhaps the greatest Italian painter, Titian (1477–1576), while Palladio's (1508–80) architecture served to directly influence European work for many years.

Music flourished in the 17th and 18th centuries and its most successful form in Italy was the opera. Monteverdi (1567–1643) brought opera to all classes, Scarlatti (1660–1725) and Vivaldi (c 1678–1741) championed chamber music and concertos, and the greatest Italian operatic composer was, perhaps, Verdi (1813–1901).

History

753 BC	Legendary foundation of Rome by Romulus, a descendant of the Trojan Aeneas
AD 14–395	The Roman Empire reaches its greatest extent
79	Pompeii and Herculaneum are destroyed by eruption of Vesuvius
800	Charlemagne is crowned Emperor in Rome
951–1268	Italy ruled by German Emperors
1222	Foundation of Padua university
from 1250	Rise of independent city states in Italy
1494–1556	French attempt, without success, to establish their supremacy in Italy
1527	Rome sacked by troops of Charles V
1623	Galileo is compelled by the Roman Inquisition to recant his acceptance of the Copernican picture of the universe
1719	Herculaneum is rediscovered
1796	Napoleon's Italian campaign
1805	Napoleon becomes King of Italy
1848–9	Revolution in Italy and Sicily
1861	Victor Emmanuel II becomes King. First capital is Florence
1915	Italy enters First World War declaring war on Austria-Hungary and Germany
1922	Mussolini granted dictatorial powers by Parliament

1934	First meeting of Mussolini and Hitler in Venice
1936	'Rome-Berlin axis' is established in a treaty with Germany
1940	Italy declares war on France and Britain
1945	Mussolini shot by partisans
1948	New democratic constitution comes into force
from 1957	Rapid movement of people from south to industrial north
1978	Aldo Moro, Chairman of the Christian Democrat party, is kidnapped and murdered by members of the Red Brigade
1981	Pope John Paul II is shot in front of St Peters but survives
1982	Amintore Fanfani the new Prime Minister, presents 42nd post-war Italian government composed of representatives of four different parties
1983	Fanfani resigns; Bettino Craxi forms a government
1985	Italian Defence Minister and two other members of Craxi's coalition cabinet resign over the aftermath of the hijacking of the Italian cruise liner 'Achille Lauro' by Palestinian terrorists
1986	Emergency laws introduced following the poisoned wine scandal which had claimed a number of lives

Major Centres

Rome

EPT di Roma
Via Parigi 11
Tel: (6) 46 18 51

ACI: Head Office
Via Marsala 8
Tel: (6) 49 98

Rome Office
Via Christoforo Colombo 261
Tel: (6) 51 06

Vatican Information Bureau
on south side of St Peter's Square

Embassies:
UK: Via XX Settembre 80 A
Tel: 4 75 54 41, 4 75 55 51

USA: Via Veneto 119/A
Tel: 46 742

Rome is the capital of the Republic of Italy and the country's largest city. Within its precincts is the Vatican city, the residence of the Pope. A major financial and commercial centre, Rome is also a leading light in the world of fashion. Surrounded by the famous Seven Hills of Rome, and situated on the River Tiber, it contains a wealth of cultural institutions, historic

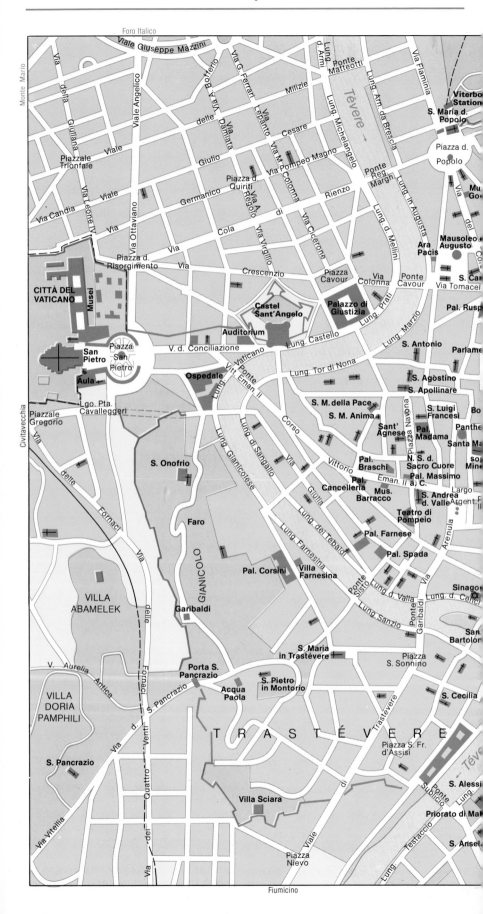

Foro Italico

Monte Mario

Viale Giuseppe Mazzini

Viale Angelico

Via della Giuliana

Piazzale Trionfale

Viale

Via Leone IV

Via Candia

Via Ottaviano

Via A. Bottero

Via G. Ferrari

Via Lepanto

Via M. Colonna

delle

Via Damiata

Giulio

Milizie

Cesare

Germanico

Via A. Regolo

Piazza d. Quiriti

Via Pompeo Magno

Cola

Via

Rienzo

Via Virgilio

Via Cicerone

di

Piazza d. Risorgimento

Via

Crescenzio

Lung. d'Armi

Lung. Matteotti

Ponte Matteotti

Lung. Michelangelo

Tévere

Lung. Arm. da Brescia

Ponte Reg. Margh.

Lung. in Augusta

Via

Via

Viterbo Station

S. Maria d. Popolo

Piazza d. Popolo

Mu. Go.

Via del

Mausoleo Augusto

Ara Pacis

Ponte Cavour

Via Tomacel

S. Ca.

Pal. Rusp.

CITTÀ DEL VATICANO

Musei

San Pietro

Aula

Piazza San Pietro

Piazza Cavour

Via Colonna

Lung. Prati

Lung. Marzio

Lung. d. Mellini

Ponte Cavour

S. Antonio

Parlame.

S. Agostino

S. Apollinare

Palazzo di Giustizia

Castel Sant'Angelo

Auditorium

V. d. Conciliazione

Lung. Castello

Lung. Tor di Nona

Ospedale

Lung. Vaticano

Ponte Vitt. Eman. II

Via d. Conciliazione

Civitavecchia

Piazzale Gregorio

Lgo. Pta. Cavalleggeri

delle Fornaci

S. Onofrio

Faro

Corso

S. M. della Pace

S. M. Anima

Sant' Agnese

Pal. Madama

Piazza Navona

S. Luigi Francesi

Bo.

Panthe.

Santa Ma.

Via

Vittorio

Pal. Braschi

N. S. d. Sacro Cuore

Eman. II a. C.

Pal. Massimo

S. Andrea d. Valle

Largo

son.

Min.

Lung. di Sangallo

Lung. Gianicolense

Via Giulia

Pal. Cancelleria

Mus. Barracco

Teatro di Pompeio

Largo Argent. F.

VILLA ABAMELEK

GIANICOLO

Pal. Corsini

Villa Farnesina

Lung. dei Tebaldi

Lung. Farnesina

Pal. Farnese

Pal. Spada

Arenula

Via

Ponte Sisto

Lung. d. Valla

Lung. Sanzio

Ponte Garibaldi

Lung. d. Cenci

Sinago.

San Bartolor.

Garibaldi

Via delle Fornaci

VILLA DORIA PAMPHILI

V. Aurelia Antica

Via d. Venti

Quattro

Via dei

Fornaci

S. Pancrazio

Porta S. Pancrazio

Acqua Paola

S. Pietro in Montorio

S. Maria in Trastévere

Piazza S. Sonnino

T R A S T É V E R E

Via Trastévere

S. Cecilia

S. Pancrazio

Villa Sciara

Piazza S. Fr. d'Assisi

di

Viale

Piazza Nievo

Tévere

Ponte Sublicio

S. Alessi.

Priorato di Mal.

S. Ansel.

Lung.

Testaccio

Fiumicino

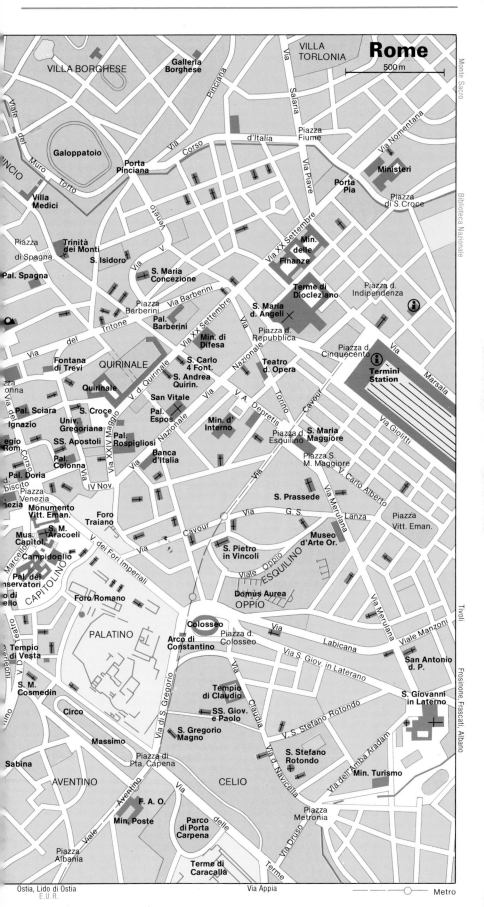

Rome

500 m

buildings and museums and galleries exhibiting art treasures from past ages.

Colosseum, Rome

Sightseeing

Arch of Constantine – a triumphal arch of white marble with a triple opening, erected to celebrate a victory over Maxentius in AD 312

Basilica of Maxentius – enlarged by his conqueror Constantine; noted for its massive barrel vaulting

Rome's Baroque fountains, built on designs by Bernini (1735–62)

Foro Italico – a sports centre built for the Olympic Games of 1960

Forum Romanum – the remains of the old town containing shrines, temples and arches, now fully cleared

Galleria Nazionale d'Arte Antica – sited in the Palazzo Barberini, containing works by Italian and foreign artists of the 13–16th centuries

Galleria Nazionale d'Arte Moderna – contains the largest collection of modern art in Italy from the beginning of the 19th century to the present day

Gesù Church – the principal church of the Jesuit order and one of the richest and most sumptuous

National Monument to Victor Emmanuel II – the largest and most magnificent monument in Italy, built in white Brescia marble in 1885

Museo Nazionale Romano delle Terme – the Roman National Museum, founded 1886

Palazzo Farnese – begun 1514 and continued from 1546 by Michelangelo; now occupied by the French Embassy

Palazzo Venezia – on the west side of the Piazza Venezia, this fortress-like building was built around 1455 and was from 1926–1945 Mussolini's official residence

Palatine Hill – the site of the earliest settlement in Rome, the city was said to have been founded here

The Pantheon after dark

Baths of Caracalla – a gigantic bathing establishment with an area of 109,000sq m, built in AD 216

Capitoline Museum – contains the municipal collection of ancient sculptures

Church of San Giovanni in Laterano – built by Constantine the Great and much altered between the 10th and 16th centuries

Church of Santa Maria del Popolo – built 1472–77 and containing numerous works of art

Church of Santa Maria Maggiore – one of Rome's five patriarchal churches and the largest dedicated to the Virgin

Church of Santa Maria in Trastavere – one of the oldest churches in Rome, founded in the 3rd century and rebuilt in the 12th century

Church of San Pietro in Vincoli – an aisled basilica with 20 ancient columns, originally built 442 to house the chains of St Peter and completely rebuilt in the 15th century

Colosseum – one of the world's most celebrated buildings and the symbol of Rome's greatness

Column of Marcus Aurelius – Stands 29.5m high in the centre of the busy Piazza Colonna

Fontana de Trevi – the most monumental of

Pantheon – built 27 BC by Marcus Agrippa and several times restored, notably by Hadrian 120–26; the only ancient building in Rome which still preserves its walls and vaulting

Ponte Milvio – originally constructed 220 BC, rebuilt in stone 109 BC and restored and improved in the 15th and 19th centuries

St Peters Square and Church – a magnificent collonaded square, 340m long and up to 250m wide, leading up to the most imposing church in Christendom

Spanish Steps – a magnificent Baroque staircase of 137 steps designed by Francesco de Sanctis (1723–26)

Statues of Horse Tamers – two marble statues built in the classical style on Greek models of the 5th century BC

Vatican Palace – originally begun in the 6th century and the Pope's permanent residence from the 14th century

Villa Borghese, Casina Borghese and Galleria Borghese – a beautiful park laid out in the 17th century and containing one of Rome's finest picture galleries

Florence

AACST,
Via Tornabuoni 15;

EPT,
Via A. Manzoni 16;
Tel: (55) 67 88 41

ACI,
Viale Amendola 36;
Tel: (55) 2 78 41

CIT,
Via Cerretani 57–59;
Tel: (55) 29 43 06

Piazza Stazione 51
Tel: (55) 28 41 45

Situated on the River Arno and with the Apennines forming a rugged backdrop, Florence is a delightful city. The cultural centre of Italy since the Middle Ages, it was in Florence that Leonardo

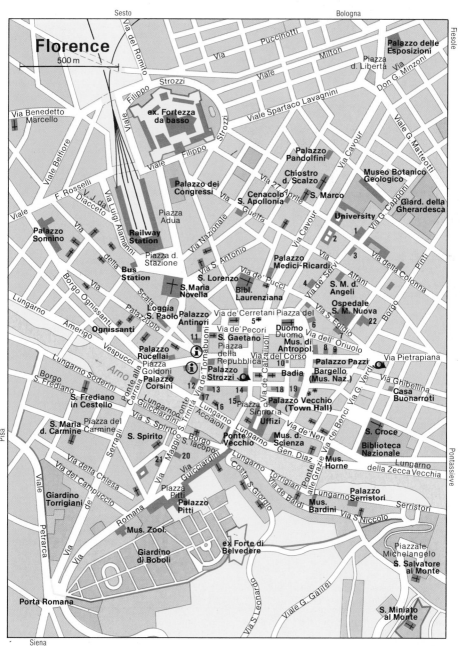

1 Santissima Annunziata	12 Santa Trinità
2 Accademia di Belle Arti	13 Palazzo Bartolini
3 Spedale degli Innocenti	14 Loggia di Mercato Nuovo
(Galleria)	15 Palazzo di Parte Guelfa
4 Palazzo Niccolini	16 Santissimi Apostoli
5 Battistero	17 Palazzo Ferroni
6 Museo dell'Opera del Duomo	18 Palazzo Uguccioni
7 Museo Firenze com'era	19 Palazzo Gordi
8 Palazzo Altoviti	20 Palazzo Rosselli
9 Palazzo Albizi	del Turco
10 Case Alighieri	21 Casa di Bianca Capello
11 Palazzo Larderel	22 Teatro della Pergola

da Vinci and Michelangelo received their training. Literally overflowing with the treasures of Italian art, it is one of the great tourist centres of the world.

Palazzo Vecchio, Florence

Sightseeing

Accademia di Belle Arti – contains the famous statue of David, carved from a single block of stone by Michelangelo

Archaeological Collection – houses a fine collection of Etruscan material and an Egyptian collection

Bapistery – rebuilt in 11th–13th centuries and famous for the three gilded bronze doors by Pisano and the principal door by Ghiberti

Brancacci Chapel – contains famous frescoes on the lives of the Apostles (1424–27)

Cathedral – a mighty Gothic building with an octagonal dome by Brunelleschi (1420–34). The Gothic campanile (14th century), faced with coloured marble, is one of the finest in Europe

Church of San Michele – built 1284–91 as a corn exchange and rebuilt 1337–1404

Church of Santa Croce – a Franciscan church begun 1295, now containing the tombs of many famous Italians including Michelangelo, Rossini and Galileo

Church of Santa Maria Novella – a Dominican church built 1278–1350, containing frescoes by Ghirlandaio

Church of the Santissima Annunziata – built 1250, remodelled 1444–60; forecourt contains frescoes by Andrea del Sarto (1505–14), which are one of the finest achievements of the Florentine High Renaissance

Galleria degli Uffizi – one of the world's great art collections with some 4500 pictures (of which 700 are on display)

Loggia dei Lanzi – an open hall designed for addressing the people (built 1376–82); contains a number of sculptures including Giovanni Bologna's 'Rape of the Sabine Women' (1583)

National Museum (Bargello) – devoted to the history of Italian culture and art in medieval and modern times

New Sacristy – built by Michelangelo (1520–4) as the mausoleum of the Medici family

Palazzo Pitti and Pitti Gallery – a 15th-century palace, now housing over 600 pictures including masterpieces by Raphael, Fra Bartolomeo, Andrea del Sarto and Titian

Piazza della Signoria – the old centre of Florentine life; on the east side of the square stands the Palazzo Vecchio (Town Hall) built 1298–1314

Ponte Vecchio – Florence's oldest bridge (rebuilt 1345) which is lined with jewellers' shops

Florence

Naples – view over bay to Vesuvius

Naples

EPT,
Via Partenope 10/A;
Tel: (81) 40 62 89

AACST,
Palazzo Reale;
Tel: (81) 41 87 44

ACI,
Piazzale Tecchio 49D
Tel: (81) 61 11 04

CIT,
Piazza Municipio 70:
Tel: (81) 32 54 26

Naples, an attractive port with the mighty Vesuvius across the bay, is Ita-

Panoramic view of Naples

ly's third largest city after Rome and Milan. Much of the city has been rebuilt after the destruction of the Second World War, but there are still many historical monuments to be seen in Naples. Of particular interest is the National Museum where many of the treasures recovered from cities engulfed by Vesuvius are exhibited.

Sightseeing

Cappella Sansevero – originally a burial chapel (1590), now a museum with some striking sculptures
Capodimonte Museum – 19th-century militaria, paintings and artefacts
Capodimonte Park – magnificent, extensive park with splendid views
Castel Nuovo – five-towered royal residence, built 1279–83
Cathedral – French Gothic (built 1294–1323), much restored in the 15th century
Church of San Francesco di Paola – an imitation of the Pantheon in Rome; on the main square by the palazzo
Church of San Giovanni a Carbonara – contains tomb of 15th-century King Ladislaus
Church of San Lorenzo Maggiore – recently restored 13th-century Gothic church
Church of Santa Donnaregina – 17th-century Baroque; not open to the public
Monastery of San Martino – 17th-century restoration of 14th-century Carthusian church
National Gallery – a fine collection of paintings, especially works by Titian and Neopolitan artists
National Museum – art treasures and relics of Pompeii; a magnificent collection
Porta Capuana – a beautiful Renaissance gateway dating from 1485
Villa Nazionale – the city's most popular promenade, this park was laid out in 1780

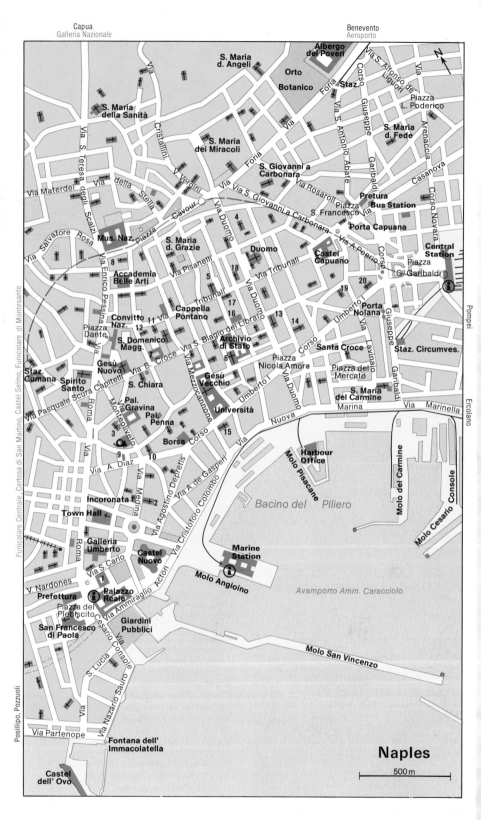

Naples

500 m

1 Teatro San Carlo
2 La Pietà dei Turchini
3 Sant'Anna dei Lombardi
4 Donnaregina
5 San Paolo Maggiore

6 Santissimi Severino e Sossio
7 Palazzo Filomirino
8 Galleria Principe di Napoli
9 Palazzo della Provincia
10 Santa Maria la Nova

11 Conservatoire
12 San Pietro a Maiella
13 San Giorgio Maggiore
14 Sant'Agostino della Zecca
15 San Pietro Martire

16 Palazzo Marigliano
17 San Lorenzo Maggiore
18 Gerolomini
19 SS. Annunziata
20 San Pietro ad Aram

Sicily

EPT Palermo,
Piazza Castelnuovo 34,
I-90100 Palermo
Tel: (091) 58 38 47

EPT, Agrigento,
Viale della Vittoria 255,
I-92100 Agrigento
Tel: (0922) 2 69 26

EPT Caltanissetta,
Corso Vittorio Emanuele 109,
I-93100 Caltanisetta
Tel: (0934) 2 17 31

EPT Catania,
Largo Paisiello 5,
I-95100 Catania
Tel: (095) 31 77 20

EPT Enna,
Piazza Garibaldi,
I-94100 Enna
Tel: (0935) 2 11 84

EPT Messina,
Via Calabria
I-98100 Messina
Tel: (090) 77 53 56

EPT Ragusa,
Via Natalleli
I-97100 Ragusa
Tel: (0932) 2 14 21

EPT Siracusa
Via S. Sebastiano 45
I-96100 Siracusa
Tel: (0931) 6 77 10

EPT Trapani,
Piazetta Saturno
I-91100 Trapani
Tel: (0923) 2 43 85

Greek Theatre, Syracuse

Sicily is the largest (25,708sq km) and most populous (5 million) island in the Mediterranean. With its beautiful beaches and Europe's largest active volcano (the snow covered Etna (3326m)) as its major scenic features, Sicily is a very popular holiday centre.

It also possesses remains from many periods of history including some of the best preserved Greek temples to be found anywhere. It is virtually autonomous, and its healthy agricultural economy gives it a leading place among the farming regions of Italy. The capital is Palermo.

Sightseeing

Agrigento – famed for its magnificent ruined temples, particularly the temple of Zeus, the largest of Greek antiquity at 113m in length

Catania – Sicily's second largest town, almost completely rebuilt after an earthquake in 1693; it is now one of the most important ports in Italy

Cefalù – the cathedral is one of the finest buildings of the Norman period, begun by King Roger in 1131–2

Messina – 91% of Messina's houses were destroyed in the earthquake of 1908; it now has the aspect of an entirely modern city

Palermo – the capital of Sicily and its principal port Palermo boasts many historical and artistic attractions including the Romanesque Cathedral, Archbishops Palace, Norman Palace, National Gallery of Sicily and the Archaeological Museum

Segesta – one of the oldest towns in Sicily, founded by the Elymians in pre-Greek times; the temple, begun 430 BC, is one of the best preserved temples on the island with 36 Doric columns still supporting the entablature and gable

Temple E, Selinunte

Selinunte – the ruins are among the most interesting sites on the island with the Acropolis (450m long and up to 350m across), the Temple of Demeter and the excavated remains of the Greek defensive walls (restored 407 BC)

Syracuse – separated by a narrow channel from the Sicilian mainland, the town has a wealth of ancient monuments and relics of the past including a Roman Amphitheatre, Greek Theatre and some extensive catacombs

Taormina – described by some as the most beautiful place in Sicily, Taormina enjoys a magnificent situation high above the Ionian Sea with the majestic sight of Mount Etna in the background

Trapani – contains a castle built in the time of Frederick II in which Garibaldi proclaimed his dictatorship of Sicily in 1860

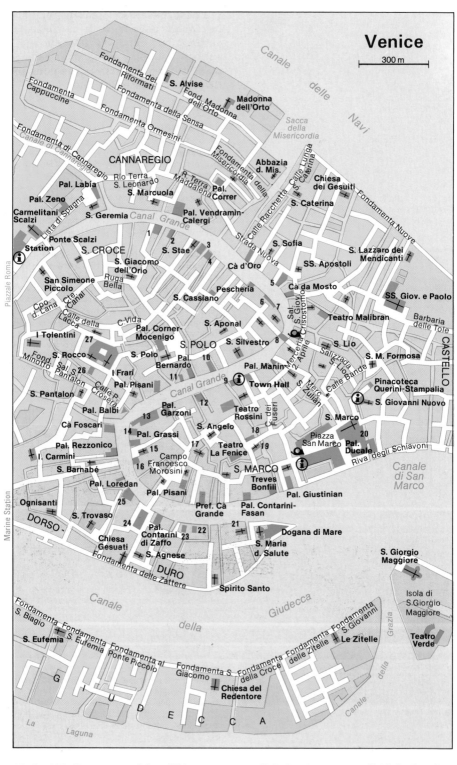

Venice

300 m

1 Fondaco dei Turchi
2 Palazzo Battagià
3 Palazzo Pésaro
4 Palazzo Corner-Regina
5 Palazzo Valmarana
6 Fabbriche Nuove
7 Fabbriche Vecchie
8 Ponte di Rialto
9 Palazzo Grimani
10 Palazzo Papadopoli
11 Palazzo Cappello
12 Palazzo Corner-Spinelli
13 Palazzi Mocenigo
14 Palazzo Moro Lin
15 San Samuele
16 Palazzo Malipiero
17 Santo Stefano
18 Ateneo Veneto
19 San Fantin
20 Ponte dei Sospiri
21 San Gregorio
22 Collezione Guggenheim
23 Palazzo Mula
24 Accademia di Belle Arti
25 Palazzo Contarini
   degli Scrigni
26 Scuola di San Rocco
27 Archivio Centrale

Venice – the Campanile and Doge's Palace

Venice

EPT,
San Marco Ascensione 71C;
Tel: (41) 2 63 56

Information offices
Piazzale Roma
Tel: (41) 2 74 02
Station
Tel: (41) 71 50 16

AACST,
Palazzo Martinengo
Rialto 4089
Tel: (41) 2 61 10

ACI,
Fondamenta Santa Chiora 518A
Tel: (41) 70 03 00

CIT,
Piazza San Marco 48-50
Tel: (41) 8 54 80

Venice, with its unique network of canals and the famous gondolas that frequent them, is a city of breathtaking beauty. Once the centre of a great maritime people, separated from the Adriatic by a series of narrow strips of land, it now has a considerable amount of large scale industry as well as being one of Italy's largest ports. But above all, Venice is a city of fine old palaces and churches, canals and bridges.

Sightseeing

Accademia di Belle Arti – contains more than 800 pictures, mainly by Venetian artists
Bridge of Sighs – built c 1595 to link the Doge's Palace with the Prigioni, the torture chamber and place of execution; the name recalls the sighs of the criminals as they were led to their death
Ca' d'Oro (Golden House) – the most elegant Gothic palace in Venice, built in the 15th century and containing pictures by Titian, Tintoretto, Mantegna and van Dyck among others
Campanile of St Mark – a 99m-high bell tower on the south-east corner of St Mark's Square
Church of San Giorgio Maggiore – a domed struc-
ture begun by Palladio (1565) and completed 1610, set on an island of the same name
Church of Santi Giovanni e Paolo – a Gothic brick-built church (1333–90) and the burial place of many Doges
Church of I Frari – the largest and most beautiful church in Venice after St Mark's; on the altar is Titian's 'Assumption' (1516–18) and in the sacristy Bellini's 'Madonna Enthroned' (1488), two Renaissance masterpieces
Church of Santa Maria della Salute – a magnificent domed church built to commemorate the plague of 1630; contains fine pictures by Titian
Church of San Salvatore – the finest High Renaissance church in Venice, built 1506–34 with a Baroque façade added 1663
Doge's Palace – the official residence of the Doges since c 814; the oldest part of the present building dates from the beginning of the 14th century
Fondaco dei Tedeschi – a hostel and warehouse for German merchants from the 12th to 14th centuries
Grand Canal – 3.8km long and Venice's principal traffic artery
Merceria – the city's main shopping street
Palazzo Grimani – a masterpiece of Renaissance architecture by Sanmicheli
Palazzo Pesaro – the finest Baroque palace in Venice, built by Longhena (1710)
Palazzo Vendramin-Calergi – the finest Early Renaissance palace in Venice, completed c 1509; Wagner died here in 1883
Piazzetta/Old Library – a square containing the Old Library by Sansovino (1536) and the Mint, which houses the celebrated Library of St Mark (founded 1468) with over 500,000 volumes
Ponte di Rialto – a marble bridge built 1588–92, 48m long, lined with shops on both sides
St Mark's Church – begun 830, rebuilt after a fire 976 and remodelled in the 11th century in Byzantine style; until 1981, there stood above the main doorway four bronze horses from Constantinople – they have now been replaced by copies, the originals being in the Museo Marciano of St Mark's Church
St Mark's Square – the hub of the city's life and one of the world's finest squares, giving striking evidence of Venice's past greatness
Statue of Bartolomeo Colloni – the finest statue of the Italian Renaissance, modelled by the Florentine sculptor Andrea Verrocchio (1481–88)

On the Piazzetta di San Marco

Milan

EPT (Tourist Office)
Via Marconi 1
1-20100 Milano
Tel: (2) 80 96 62

Milan, capital of Lombardy and Italy's second largest city, lies in the fertile Lombard plain near the southern end of important passes through the Alps. It is Italy's principal industrial centre, its most important railway junction and its leading banking and commercial city. Milan is a university town with both a state and a Catholic university. It has one of the largest silk markets in Europe and is the see of an archbishop. It is a city of predominantly modern aspect yet full of art treasures and fine old buildings.

Sightseeing

Piazza del Duomo – the life of Milan centres round this square. Flanked by palatial buildings designed by Mengoni and erected from 1876 onwards

Duomo (Cathedral) – dating from 1386 a cruciform basilica in Gothic style faced with white marble, it is one of the world's largest and most magnificent churches. The roof is adorned with 135 pinnacles, the exterior with some 2300 marble statues, and inside the 52 gigantic pillars make a powerful impression. The stained-glass windows (mostly 15th–16th century) are the largest in the world

Palazzo Reale – former Royal Palace, built in 1788 on the site of an earlier palace which had belonged to the Visconti and Sforza families. The **Cathedral Museum** occupies 12 rooms on the ground floor

Galleria Vittorio Emanuele – designed by Giuseppe Mengoni and built 1865–67, it was then the largest shopping arcade in Europe (195m long, dome 48m high)

Teatro alla Scala (1776–78) – one of the largest and most important opera houses in the world. The **Museo Teatrale** traces the history of the theatre and incorporates a Verdi Museum with numerous mementoes of the composer

Museo Poldi Pezzoli – an elegant old patrician house containing pictures of the Lombard, Venetian and Florentine schools, Flemish and Persian carpets, tapestries, jewellery, silver, bronzes and weapons

Museum of Natural History – notable in particular for its large collection of birds (25,000 specimens)

Galleria d'Arte Moderna – housed in the neo-classical **Villa Reale** (1952). 19th and 20th-century paintings and sculpture

Palazzo di Brera (1651–86) – originally a Jesuit college which has been occupied since 1776 by the **Accademia di Belle Arti**. The palace contains a library, an observatory and on the first floor is the **Pinacoteca di Brera**, one of Italy's finest picture galleries (including work by Mantegna, Bellini, Crivelli, Paolo Veronese, Titian, Tintoretto, Correggio, Gentile da Fabriano, Piero della Francesca, Bramante, Raphael, Rembrandt, van Dyck, Rubens and El Greco)

Palazzo dell'Ambrosiana (1603–09) – famous for its library, and an important Picture Gallery founded in 1618 by Cardinal-Archbishop Federico Borromeo; works by Leonardo da Vinci, Botticelli, Ambrogio de Predis, Raphael and Titian

Castello Sforzesco – built in 1368, demolished by the people of Milan in 1447 and rebuilt from 1450 onwards. Houses the **Museo d'Arte Antica** – mainly medieval and modern sculpture, its greatest treasure being Michelangelo's Pietà Rondanini

Former Dominican Monastery – in the refectory is Leonardo da Vinci's 'Last Supper', one of his most famous works, painted on the wall in tempera between 1495–1497

Leonardo da Vinci National Museum of Science and Technology – illustrates the history of science and technology down to modern times

Church of San Satiro – by Bramante (1479–1514) with a campanile dating from 876 and a modern facade. The interior has what appears to be a choir but is in fact an ingenious piece of *trompe l'oeil* painting

Milan – panorama at sunset

Accommodation

Hotels and Pensions

The hotels in the higher categories in large towns and holiday centres offer the usual international standards of comfort and amenity, but in the more remote areas the accommodation available will often be of a more modest standard. The Italian Automobile Club (ACI) and the AGIP oil company have built numbers of *autostelli*, or motels in the larger towns and in spas and seaside resorts there are numerous pensions (*pensioni*) or guesthouses.

The hotels (*alberghi*, singular *albergo*) are officially classified in five categories. Hotel tariffs vary considerably according to season, and are substantially higher in large towns and popular holiday areas than in the rest of the country.

Accommodation in Historic Buildings

All over Italy many historic buildings (convents, castles, villas, medieval palaces, abbeys, country houses) have been converted into hotels.

Villas, Flats and Chalets

Villas, flats and chalets are available for renting at most Italian resorts. Information can be obtained through the local Tourist Office concerned. These offices are also in a position to advise about boarding with families through daily newspapers or through specialised agencies in Britain.

Tourist Villages

Tourist villages consist of bungalows and apartments usually built in or near popular resorts. The bungalows vary in size but usually accommodate four people. The villages have restaurant facilities.

Mountain Huts *(Rifug Alpini)*

The Club Alpino Italiano (Via Ugo Foscolo, 3 Milano, Tel: (02) 802 554) owns most of the huts in the mountain districts (about 500). Equipment and tariffs vary according to grade. As a general guide, the fees are 2200 to 6600 lire for one night's stay. Check with the individual hut before booking. From 1 December to 30 April there is a 20 per cent increase.

Farmhouses

It is possible to rent a country cottage or farmhouse for a holiday. For further information, contact Agriturist, Corso V Emanuele, 101 Roma. Tel: (6) 651 2342.

Youth Hostels

Youth hostels (*ostelli per la gioventú*) provide accommodation at very reasonable prices, particularly for younger visitors. Priority is given to young people under 30 travelling on foot. If the hostel is full the period of stay is limited to 3 nights. Advance booking is advisable during the main holiday season and for groups of more than 5. Hostellers are not allowed to use their own sleeping bags: the hire charge for a sleeping bag is included in the overnight charge. Foreign visitors

Hotel Price Range

Type of hotel	Price for 1 night in lire Single room	Double room
*****	66,000–170,000	133,000–242,000
****	34,000– 85,000	55,000–121,000
***	27,000– 55,000	45,000– 67,000
**	22,000– 31,000	34,000– 49,000
*	14,000– 24,000	24,000– 43,000

These prices are intended to act as a rough guide only.

must produce a membership card of their national youth hostel association. Hostel prices range from about 5700 to 8500 lire per person per night.

Information:
Associazione Italiana Alberghi per la Gioventú
Via Cavour 44 (3 Stock),
I-00184 Rome
Tel: (06) 46 23 42

Camping and Caravanning

Italy has large numbers of good camping sites, most of them in the Alto Adige and the Aosta valley, on the North Italian lakes and on the coasts of the Adriatic, Tyrrhenian and Ligurian Seas. Lists of camping sites are published by the Italian State Tourist Office and the *Federazione Italiana del Campeggio*.

Information:
Federazione Italiana del Campeggio e del Caravanning
Via Vittorio Emanuele II,
I-50041 Calenzano/Firenze
Tel: (055) 88 23 91

Introduction to Rail Information

The Italian rail system is run by the *Ferrovie Italiane dello Stato (FS)*. The main lines run along the coast where building was easier. The most important route is the Milan to Naples line which has recently been modernised. 5 types of train are used to make up the rail service and they run as follows:

TEE (Trans Europ Express) – these are luxury 1st class only trains which run between the major European cities. A special supplement is charged and seat reservation is usually obligatory.

Rapido trains – these are fast-running trains which ply between the major towns. A special supplement is added to the fare.

Espresso trains – these are long distance trains which carry 1st and 2nd class passengers. They stop at main stations only.

Diretto trains – these carry both classes and stop at most stations.

Locale trains – short distance trains which stop at all stations on the route. Most are 2nd class only and very basic.

Major International Services

Connection	Duration	Frequency
Rome–Paris	17–19hrs	3 times daily
Rome–Brussels	19–20hrs	once daily
Rome–Munich	13–16hrs	4 times daily

Major Internal Services

Connection	Duration	Frequency
Rome–Florence	3–4hrs	20 times daily
Rome–Genoa	5–6hrs	15 times daily
Rome–Naples	2–3hrs	34 times daily
Rome–Venice	6–8hrs	12 times daily
Rome–Trieste	10hrs	10 times daily
Milan–Bologna	2–3hrs	Every 15–30mins

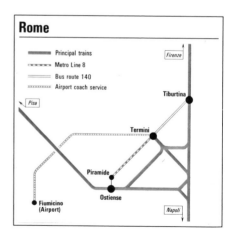

Scenic Routes

Some of the most beautiful and interesting scenery visible from the train can be seen along the coastal routes which run along both sides of the

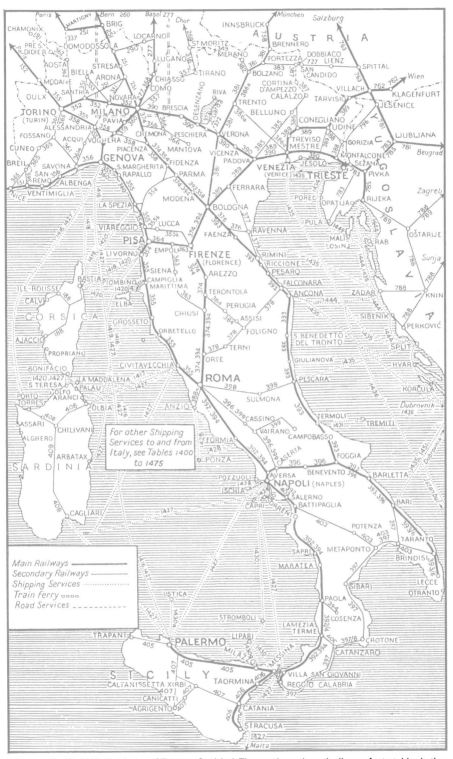

Map supplied by kind permission of Thomas Cook Ltd. The numbers along the lines refer to tables in the *Thomas Cook Continental Timetable*.

peninsula; from San Remo in the north to Taranto at the 'sole' of the 'boot' on the western coast, and from Venice in the north to Lecce at the 'heel' on the eastern coastal route. The Dolomite routes and those through the great tunnels – the Simplon on the Swiss/Italian border and the Mont Cenis (the Rome

Co-Cathedral, Táranto

Express Line between Lyon and Turin) – offer spectacular mountain and Alpine scenery. Finally, the Orient Express, that extravagant recreation of 20s travel, overwhelms the traveller with period decor inside and wonderful views outside – for a price.

The following lines are among those recommended as scenic routes:
Brennero–Bolzano
Domodossola–Locarno
Florence–Bologna
Génova–Pisa
Naples–Sorrento (private railway line)
Rome–Pescara
Udine–Villach

Internal Fare Structure

Standard Rate Fares

Fares are based on kilometric distance travelled, with the actual percentage increase in price becoming lower the greater the distance travelled. For example, the Rome–Florence run costs 15,600L 2nd class and the Naples–Palermo run costs 35,700L 2nd class. A 15% discount is allowed on day return tickets which cover the maximum distance of 50km. A 15% discount is allowed on 3-day return tickets covering a maximum of 250km.

Child Reductions

Children under the age of 4, not occupying a seat, travel free. Between the ages of 4 and 12 they travel for a reduction of 50%.

Student Reductions

There are no special reductions for students travelling in Italy. The International Section gives detailed information on general reductions available to students travelling in Europe.

Family Reduction Cards

These cards are issued to families of at least 3 people travelling together. They are valid for 3 years and give a reduction of 30% for adults and 65% for children on Italian Rail Tickets. They cost 5000L. Applicants must be able to prove their familial relationship.

Senior Citizen Reductions

Senior Citizens travelling by rail in Italy are advised to consult the International Section for information on the reductions available.

Party/Group Savers

Groups of 10–24 people receive a 20% reduction of fares and groups of 25 and over receive a 30% reduction. This is not applicable during the Easter holidays, the peak summer (25 June–31 August), or the Christmas period.

Railrover Passes

Kilometre Tickets

These are valid for 2 months and allow up to 20 trips with a top limit of 3000km. The tickets can be shared by up to 5 people but note that in the case of a shared ticket, the 3000km are divided by the number of passengers so each passenger is entitled to his or her share of kilometres only.

Circular Tickets

These are issued for an itinerary of not less than 1000km and are valid for 2 months. They can commence from any frontier (land, sea or air) and finish at the same or at an alternative frontier. Breaks are allowed *en route*, but since

A scenic view in Northern Italy

tickets must be endorsed at every stop made and since one may not pass through any place more than twice, they are of limited appeal to tourists particularly since they are only slightly cheaper than equivalent sectional tickets unless the journey is very extensive.

Tourist Reductions

Travel at Will Tickets

These allow travel on the entire network of the *FS* including *Rapido* and TEE trains without payment of extra charge. Validity can begin any time within 2 months from the issue of the tickets, but they must be stamped at the station of commencement or by the ticket inspector on the train when crossing the frontier, to establish the validity period from that date. Validity can be extended at any station in Italy only up to double the original validity. They should be bought outside Italy, but are also obtainable on production of proof of foreign residence at International Transit points such as frontiers or international airports and at some railway stations. To give an example, a 2nd class 'Travel at Will Ticket' valid for 15 days costs £60.

Where to Buy Tickets

In Italy

Tickets are on sale at all rail stations throughout Italy. They are also available from *CIT (Compagnia Italiana Tourismo)* offices in the main cities of Italy.

In Great Britain

Tickets and reservations for Italian Railways are issued by:

The Gardesana Occidentale road, Lake Garda

Italian State Railways (CIT)
50/51 Conduit Street
London W1
Tel: (071) 434 3844

Wasteels Travel
22 Gillingham Street
London SW1

L R Stanton Ltd
23a Princess Street
Albert Square
Manchester

Stanton Travel Agency
117 Arndale Centre
Chester Road
Stretford
Lancs

Branches of Thomas Cook and Sons
and
European Rail Travel Centre
PO Box 303
Victoria Station
London SW1V 1JY
Tel: (071) 834 2345

A lane in Spoleto

Tickets from London and from British
ports to many Italian towns are printed
by British Rail and their agents with a
validity of 2 months.

In USA

From CIT representatives in major
cities (see International Section).

Facilities on Trains

Sleepers and Couchettes

Sleepers and couchettes are available
on most services. Sleeper fares vary
according to the size of the compartment and the length of the journey.
Couchettes are also available on long
haul services; a couchette from Paris
to Rome, for example, costs about
16,000L.

Food

Restaurant cars are attached to most
international and long-distance trains.
A luncheon-tray is available on internal
long-distance trains. Snacks, soft
drinks and coffee can be purchased on
many trains. On some specially
selected lines self-service restaurant
cars have been introduced.

Bicycle Carriage

Bikes can be carried as accompanied
luggage on Italian trains (except on the
Rapido). They should be taken to the
Bagagli Partenze office at least 30 minutes before departure. Station staff
will load and unload the bike. Charges
are sometimes disproportionately
high.

Motorail

Applications for motorail reservations
can only be accepted if presented at
least one month prior to departure, as
requests have to be made in writing.
The Central Reservation Office in Milan
does not accept telephone or telex
booking. Name, number of passengers, name of car, length and registration number must be indicated. A
deposit of £20 should be forwarded
with application. The internal motorail
service runs the following routes:
Milan to Rome, Bari, Brindisi and Villa
San Giovanni; Turin to Rome, Bari and
Villa San Giovanni; Genoa to Rome;
Bolzano to Rome; Bologna to Bari;
Rome to Bari and Villa San Giovanni.
Some of these services run only in
summer.

Northern lake scene

Communication Services

Internal telegrams can be sent from
some trains. Those who wish to make
use of this service must ask the guard
for a special form. The telegram cannot
exceed 10 words and costs 1250L.

Facilities at Stations

Food

Station restaurants at the main stations in Italy serve excellent meals.

Reservations

Advance reservation is recommended
for long-distance trains. It is compulsory for the *Colosseum* and certain
other express trains, and for sleeper or

couchette travel. Reservations are
handled by rail and travel agencies.

Luggage

Suitcases and bicycles can be deposited at left luggage offices in all
main Italian railway stations at a small

Naples

charge per item. Some minor stations close during the night, so check beforehand. Porters charge about 400L per case.

Bureau de Change

At most stations there is an exchange office where one can sell foreign currencies. It is sometimes possible to exchange money on the train.

Car Hire

Travellers who wish to hire a car at the end of their train journey can arrange it beforehand by getting in touch with one of the 4 car hire firms offering this service. These are *Autoservizi Maggiore*, *Avis*, *Eurotrans* and *Hertz*, all of whom have branches in the main Italian cities and resorts. If required, the station will send on a telegram to the nearest branch at a fixed rate.

Luxembourg

Lipperscheid in the Luxembourg Ardennes

Introduction

Luxembourg, a small landlocked country of only 2586sq km bordered by Belgium, France and Germany, has always been a natural and historic crossroads for its neighbours. In the past it has come under the control of Spain, France, Austria and Germany. The towns and cities of Luxembourg bear witness to these periods of occupation, yet in spite of their turbulent history, Luxembourgers are proudly patriotic, and since its independence in 1867, Luxembourg has developed into a successful industrial nation.

Geographically, Luxembourg can be divided into two characteristic regions. First, the Ardennes region. This is a relatively infertile area in the form of a rugged plateau. However, the mountain soil has been improved since the beginning of the 20th century and the region now boasts a high level of agricultural productivity. The river valleys of the Moselle are particularly fertile, and provide the grapes for the famous wines. As Luxembourg is far from the sea, its climate, unlike the other Benelux countries is prone to continental influences. Consequently, winters are slightly colder and summers slightly warmer than Belgium and the Netherlands.

The population of the Grand Duchy is 365,000. Of this figure 90,000 are foreigners, and they make up a high proportion (30%) of the working population. The majority of them live and work in the capital city and in the industrial districts of the south. The native Luxembourgers are of German stock and speak Letzburgish, recognised as the official language since 1984. Everybody speaks French and German as well and all three are designated as official national languages. The Roman Catholic faith is practised by over 94% of the population. There are still a small number of Lutheran Protestants practising their faith in the Grand Duchy, a remnant of a religion that was once of great importance in central Europe.

Ever since 1867, Luxembourg has been a hereditary constitutional monarchy, the head of state being the Grand Duke. He appoints a Cabinet of at least three members, one of whom is made the Minister of State and Head of Government. The Grand Duke also appoints the State Council, who are appointed for life to perform a consultative role; the council functions primarily as a second legislative assembly. The parliament of the country has only one chamber, made up of 64 members elected for five years. Ever since 1919 universal suffrage has been enforced and voting is statutory.

The European Parliament Building in Luxembourg

Luxembourg possesses a strong industrial economy, based on the metallurgical industry, which was developed on a large scale at the end of the 19th century. Now the country is a significant world producer of iron and steel; its per capita production of steel is by far the highest in the world. Recently there has been a trend towards the production of finished goods as well. This impressive industrial record is reflected in the high proportion of people employed in mining and industry.

Agriculture employs only 10% of the working population, and a high 85% of farmland is devoted to animal husbandry. Only the grape-growing regions in the Moselle and Lower Sûre valleys are an economic factor of any importance. The annual average production of wine is about 2.2 million gallons.

Tourism plays an important role within the economy. The capital city is the most frequently visited place, although visitors to the Ardennes provide local inhabitants with a significant source of income. Another popular destination is the ancient abbey town of Echternach on the Sûre, where a traditional dance procession of particular interest takes place to commemorate St Willibrord every year on Whit Tuesday.

In Luxembourg, culture has always been something that has been provided by its neighbours. So although there are museums and buildings of interest in Luxembourg, they mostly contain the work of foreigners. These cultural links with foreign countries are still maintained today, and cultural events are frequent and of excellent quality. Nonetheless, Luxembourg boasts its own orchestra, the Orchestra of Radio Luxembourg which is considered outstanding and maintains the traditional strength among the Benelux countries in producing interpreters of music rather than composers.

1914–18 and 1939–45	Luxembourg occupied by German army in both World Wars
1958	Formation of Benelux Customs' Union
1964	Grand Duchess Josephine-Charlotte abdicates in favour of her son, Jean
1976	Prime Minister, Gaston Thorn becomes President of EEC Council of Ministers
1982	General Strike
1984	Centre-left coalition government formed under premiership of Jacques Santer
1986	The Unique European Act was signed at the Conference for the representative of the Governments of the European member states

History

10th–13th centuries	The country of Luxembourg created and linked with Namur, Limburg and Brabant
1354–1477	Luxembourg becomes a Duchy
1555–1814	Luxembourg belongs successively to Spain, France, Austria and France again
1815	Congress of Vienna makes Luxembourg a Grand Duchy and part of *German Bund*
1867	After disintegration of *German Bund*, Luxembourg's independence and neutrality guaranteed

Major Centres

Luxembourg

Office National du Tourisme
Place de la Gare
Tel: 48 11 99

Syndicat d'Initiative et de Tourisme de la Ville de Luxembourg
Cercle
Place d'Armes
Tel: 2 28 09

Embassies:
UK: 28 Boulevard Royal
USA: 22 Blvd. Emmanuel-Servais
Tel: 40123 (4, 5, 6, 7)

Müllerthal (The Valley of the Black Ernz)

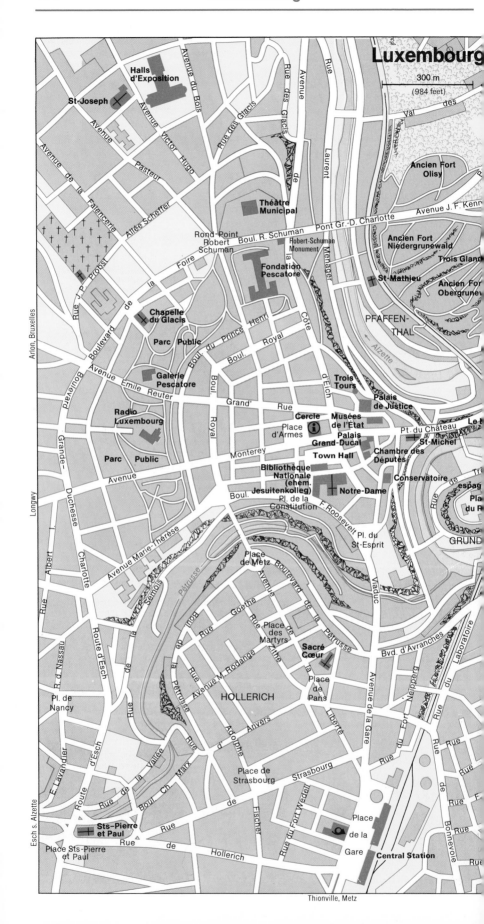

Luxembourg

300 m
(984 feet)

Halls
d'Exposition

St-Joseph

Avenue du Bois

Avenue Victor Hugo

Pasteur

Avenue

Avenue de la Faïencerie

Rue des Glacis

Avenue

Rue des Glacis

Val des

Ancien Fort
Olisy

Avenue J. F. Kenn

Théâtre
Municipal

Rond-Point
Robert
Schuman

Boul. R. Schuman
Pont Gr.-D. Charlotte

Robert-Schuman
Monument

Ancien Fort
Niedergrunewald

Trois Gland

de Foire

Fondation
Pescatore

St-Mathieu

Ancien For
Obergrunev

Chapelle
du Glacis

Rue J.-P. probst

Parc Public

Boul. du Prince Henri

Royal

Boul.

Côte d'Eich

PFAFFEN-
THAL

Alzette

Arlon, Bruxelles

Boulevard

Avenue Emile Reuter

Galerie
Pescatore

Boul. Royal

Grand'

Rue

Trois
Tours

Palais
de Justice

Radio
Luxembourg

Cercle

Place
d'Armes

Musées
de l'État

Pt. du Château

Le

Longwy

Grande- Duchesse

Parc Public

Avenue

Monterey

Palais
Grand-Ducal

Town Hall

St-Michel

Chambre des
Députés

Conservatoire

Tr

espag

Pla
du R

Charlotte

Albert

Rue

Avenue Marie-Thérèse

Bibliothèque
Nationale
(ehem.
Jesuitenkolleg)

Boul.

Pl. de la
Constitution

F. Roosevelt

Notre-Dame

Pl. du
St-Esprit

GRUND

Esch s. Alzette

Semois

Pétrusse

Place
de Metz

Boulevard

Avenue

Boulevard de la

Viaduc

Pétrusse

Bvd. d'Avranches

Laboratoire

Pl. de
Nancy

Route d'Esch

de la

Pétrusse

Goethe

Rue

Place
des
Martyrs

Avenue M. Rodange

Zithe

Sacré
Cœur

Place
de
Paris

Avenue de la Gare

Neipperg

du Fort

Rue

Rue

de

E. Lavandier

Rue d'Esch

Vallée

Boul. Ch. Marx

HOLLERICH

Anvers

d'

Adolphe

Iberté

Sts-Pierre
et Paul

Place Sts-Pierre
et Paul

Rue

Rue

de

Place de
Strasbourg

Fischer

Rue du Fort Wedell

Strasbourg

de

Place
de la
Gare

Central Station

Bonnevoie

Rue

Rue

de

E.

Hollerich

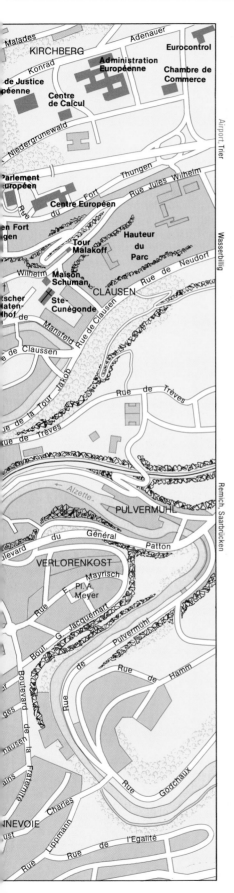

Luxembourg is the capital of the Grand Duchy, seat of the Grand Duke and of the government. Founded in 963, it lies in the southern part of the country and is built on a protruding rock which is surrounded on three sides by rivers and steep cliffs. This natural fortress has been extended over the years and is now one of the strongest fortresses in the world. The city has a particularly beautiful panorama with its hills, valleys, garden terraces and huge viaducts.

The capital city of Luxembourg

Sightseeing

Bock – a steep rocky spur on which the excavated remains of the old castle and gate tower stand
Cathedral of Notre-Dame – formerly a Jesuit church built in the 17th century and enlarged 1935–8
Grand Ducal Palace – a Renaissance building dating from 1572 and enlarged in 1891
Plateau of Kirchberg – site of the headquarters of several international organisations including the European Parliament, the European Court of Justice and the European Administrative Building
State Museum – houses Roman and Frankish antiquities, among them the stone relief of Echternach, the oldest existing altar crown ever found (8th century)

Echternach in the Sûre Valley

Accommodation

Hotels and Inns

Hotels in the larger towns and resorts in Luxembourg provide the usual standard of comfort. Advance booking is recommended, especially in the high season. The inns (in French *auberges*) provide pleasant accommodation in the medium-sized and small towns.

Country-House Hotels

There are a number of country-house hotels in Luxembourg well-known for their high standards and for their attractive locations. Frequently, they provide opportunities for fishing, hunting or riding. Generally, they have only a limited number of rooms and advance booking is therefore recommended.

Clervaux in the Valley of the Clerf

Youth Hostels

The following places have youth hostels:

Beaufort	Ettelbruck	Lultzhausen
Bourglinster	Grevenmacher	Luxembourg
Echternach	Hollenfels	Vianden

Luxembourg Youth Hostels (AJL) are open to all young men and women who have a valid membership card. On the other hand, groups of young people (under 18 years) may use the youth hostels without a membership card, if they are accompanied by one or more adult leaders who are in possession of a Youth Hostels Association Leader's Card. The group leader must lodge with his party at the youth hostel.

The minimum age limit is 8 years and the maximum is 35 years. Hostellers who are over 35 years of age and who hold a valid Youth Hostels card bearing the annual national stamp of their country of residence, are admitted if there are available places, after priority has been given to the younger people.

The price of lodging per night in Luxembourg Youth Hostels is 140LF for everyone under 26 years of age and 180LF for all others (in the new YH in Luxembourg City the prices are 160 and 200LF). Meal prices are as follows: breakfast 70LF; dinner 160LF; packed meal 80LF. Hire charge of a sleeping-bag is 60LF. (The prices for the meals are liable to alterations. No reductions can be granted.)

The Youth Hostels Guide with the detailed list, the interior rules, practical advice and a map showing the paths for walking tours may be obtained free of charge from the Luxembourg Youth Hostels Association, 18 Place d'Armes, Luxembourg-Ville, Tel: (2) 55 88. The catalogue and the pricelist of the

Hotel Price Range

Type of hotel	Price for 1 night in Luxembourg Francs	
	Single	Double
Hotel	700–1540	800–1950
Inn	550–1000	650–1200
Boarding House	550– 750	600– 950

These prices are intended to act as a rough guide only.

'La Corniche', Luxembourg City

ordnance survey maps of the Grand Duchy are all on sale there. The travel department of the LYHA offers package-programs in youth hostels as well as railway tickets at reduced fares for young people under 26 years, such as Inter-Rail Junior and BIGE tickets. It is recommended that an international reply coupon be attached to all requests.

Gîtes d'Etape

The Gîtes d'Etape Luxembourgeois maintain a series of rest houses and vacation homes throughout the country. Each installation includes a well-appointed kitchen and the necessary dishes for proper service. Married people are not admitted except as group leaders.

For all information apply to Gîtes d'Etape Luxembourgeois, 23 Boulevard Prince Henri, 1724 Luxembourg. Tel: (2) 36 98. Open on weekdays from 8 to 12am and from 2 to 6pm.

Holiday Flats and Villas
(Vacation Rentals)

Numerous vacation apartments and villas are available in the popular holiday areas. Here also, advance booking is recommended in high season.

Farm Vacations

Opportunities for farm vacations (*Agrivacances*) are possible in Luxembourg. Camping at farms is also a possibility.

Camping and Caravanning

Luxembourg, like the other Benelux countries, is particularly suited to camping and caravanning. There are well-appointed camp sites in most tourist resorts as well as off the beaten track in quiet river valleys. Holders of an international camping card qualify for a range of price reductions. In high season many sites are filled to capacity. Camping in the open is limited to a few areas because of the population density. It always requires permission from the owner of the land.

Introduction to Rail Information

There are some 870 miles of track within the small Grand Duchy of Luxembourg. All of the lines pass through the capital, Luxembourg City, on their way north/south or east/west through the country. The distances are short, in fact, the entire country can be crossed in an hour. Most of the system is electrified, although the line from Luxembourg City to Troisvierges at the top of the country is diesel powered. All the trains are comfortable and reach reasonable speeds.

Map supplied by kind permission of Thomas Cook Ltd. The numbers along the lines refer to tables in the *Thomas Cook Continental Timetable*.

Major International Services

Connection	Duration	Frequency
Luxembourg–Paris	4–5hrs	9 times daily
Luxembourg–Brussels	2–3hrs	17 times daily
Luxembourg–Cologne	3–4hrs	6 times daily

Major Internal Services

Connection	Duration	Frequency
Luxembourg–Troisvierges	1½hrs	5 times daily
Luxembourg–Wasserbillig	½hr	19 times daily

Veteran Railways

1. **Rodange Train 1900**
   Route: Bois de Rodange–Dhoil–Fond-de-Gras –Pardsstall–Fullssbësch
   Length: 5km
   The line was built between 1873 and 1879 by the Luxembourg Railways and the Prince Henri Mines, in order to use the mining concessions given for the construction of other railways in the country. After closing to traffic in 1964 it re-opened in 1973 with steam engines. There

are three steam locomotives in action. The principal locomotive in use is the No 8, which is a two-axle type built in 1900 in Hanover by Georg Egestorff. The other two locomotives date from the same period and were also built in the ARBED steelworks. The railcar Z 151 and the trailer RZ 1061 operate on the secondary lines and a fuel-driven track motorcar completes the engine collection. The trailer stock comprises a series of three wooden cars with lateral doors (ex-SNCB), some ex-CFL cars and some wagons for service purposes. Operates May to September.
Operated by: AMTF, 10 rue de Noerdange, L-8562 Schweich. Tel: (6) 34 60

Internal Fare Structure

Standard Rate Fares

After a standard charge of 15.2LF for 1st class travel and 10.1LF for 2nd class travel the following rates are applied: 3.93LF per/km for 1st class and 2.62LF per/km for 2nd class.

Child Reductions

Children aged between 4 and 12 pay half the price of the standard one-way fare. Children under 4 travel free if accompanied by a fare-paying passenger over 12.

Student Reductions

There are no special reductions. Students travelling in Luxembourg are advised to consult the International Section for information on general student reductions.

Senior Citizen Reductions

People over 65 years benefit from a reduction of 50% on the normal price of tickets, as long as the journey does not run to or from a point on the frontier or beyond. This reduction is obtained on production of an identity card or a passport.

Party/Group Savers

Groups benefit from a reduction of 70% on the price of a standard fare one-way ticket if a minimum of 5 adults and 1 child are travelling. Each member of the group must be travelling to the same destination and the tickets are valid for 2nd class travel only. Applications should be made 10 days before commencement of the trip.

Mini-groups

Groups of 3–5 adults (or people paying as 3–5 adults) are regarded as a mini-group and enjoy a reduction of 60% on the price of an ordinary ticket. Two children aged between 4 and 12 count as 1 adult. This only applies to 2nd class travel.

Special Excursion/Holiday Rates

These tickets represent a 50% reduction on the standard fare and are valid on weekends and public holidays. They can cover travel throughout the system except to or from frontier points.

Railrover Passes

1-Day Network Tickets

Network tickets, issued for a single day, are valid for an unlimited number of journeys on any of the lines of the Luxembourg railways and buses. They are valid for 2nd class travel only and do not permit journeys which cross the frontier. The price of a 1-day Network Ticket is 217LF.

5-Day Network Tickets

These cover unlimited travel on 1st or 2nd class transport without distinction on all lines of the Luxembourg railway and bus system. They are valid for any 5 days within a period of 15 days. The price of one 5-day Network Ticket is 658LF.

Month Network Tickets

These are valid for 2nd class travel from the first to the last day of one month on the Luxembourg railway and bus system. The price of a month Network Ticket is 1748LF.

Tourist Reductions

Especially attractive for tourists is the Benelux Tourrail card which is available between 1 April and 31 October. It entitles the holder to unlimited travel on any self-selected 5 days out of a specified validity of 17 days over all Netherlands Railways (NS), Belgian Railways (SNCB), Luxembourg Railways (CFL) and by CFL country buses in Luxembourg. It cannot be used in the Netherlands in conjunction with the Public Transport Link Rover. It can be used for travel by D and IC trains without supplement. Holders of this card are required to carry a valid passport for identification purposes. The price of the card for 2nd class travel is £43.50 (adults) and £31 (4–25 years); for 1st class £65 (adults) and £46 (4–25 years). Tickets are available from railway stations in the countries concerned and from Netherlands Railways offices in Great Britain and the United States (see International Section). In Great Britain, the card may also be bought at Youth Hostels Association Travel, 14 Southampton Street, London WC2.

Where to Buy Tickets

In Luxembourg

Tickets are available for international and domestic journeys from the ticket office of Luxembourg Station. Tickets for domestic journeys only are available at each of the 60 passenger stations throughout the country.

In Great Britain

Information on Luxembourg Railways is available through:

Luxembourg National Trade and Tourist Office
36/37 Piccadilly,
London W1V 9PA
Tel: (071) 434 2800

Tickets are available through appointed British Rail agents and European Rail Travel Centre
PO Box 303
Victoria Station
London SW1V 1JY
Tel: (071) 834 2345

In the USA

Tickets for travel on Luxembourg Railways are available from rail representatives in the major cities (see International Section).

Facilities on Trains

Food

Food is not available on the internal routes of the Luxembourg Railway. International trains usually have restaurant cars.

Bicycle Carriage

Bicycles may be carried on the train for a charge of 18LF provided that space is available. The rider must purchase a 'bicycle card' from the ticket office and load and unload the bike without assistance. For a higher charge you can have the bike sent as unaccompanied luggage, handled throughout by CFL staff.

Facilities at Stations

Food

Bar and buffet facilities at Luxembourg City Station are open 5am–11pm.

Reservations

Reservations can be made at Luxembourg City station from 7am–8pm on the day prior to departure.

Tourist Information

The tourist information office at Luxembourg City station is based in the Luxair building right next to the station and opens 9am–6.30pm, Monday to Friday.

Luggage

There is no access to the left luggage lockers at Luxembourg City station between 1.30am and 4am. The fixed tariff for porters is 25LF per case.

Bicycle Hire

Bicycles may be rented from many of the large stations in Luxembourg. A reduced price will be charged for holders of valid tickets.

The Netherlands

Dutch windmills near Kinderdijk

Introduction

The Netherlands, once the strongest naval and commercial power in Europe, is a country that has always thrived on its sea ports and its extensive inland waterways. Like Belgium, it is a very flat country and much of its coastal area is under the threat of flooding, both from the sea and from the innumerable branches of the Rhine and the Maas. This low-lying coastal region is made up of sand dunes, dikes, and sea and river marshes. 20th century technology has enabled much of this land to be reclaimed from the sea. The 'Geest', which lies further inland, consists of sandy plains and heathland while in the south, the scenic foothills of the central European mountain ranges are prominent. The Dutch climate owing to its long North Sea coastline, is subject to oceanic influences, which bring mild winters, cold summers and rainfall in every season.

The population of the Netherlands is 14.4 million and it is spread over an area of 34,800sq km. This makes the Netherlands the second most densely populated country in Europe after Monaco. This fact is also borne out in the population distribution figures as only 20% of the population live in the rural areas, while 40% of the population live in the relatively small 'Randstad Holland' area in the west. The population includes several immigrant communities, the largest groups coming from their former overseas territories of Indonesia, the Moluccas and Surinam. These immigrants practise a number of different religions, while of the indigenous population, 40% are Catholics and 38% are Prostestants.

A characteristic landmark of the Dutch countryside is the windmill. Few are still in use today, but during the 17th and 18th centuries they played a major part in the process of land reclamation and the draining of low-lying areas. With the introduction of steam power the windmill became obsolete. The bulb fields provide another famous scenic feature of the Netherlands. Many tourists travel to the Netherlands solely to see the tulips, which are probably seen at their best at the Keukenhof near Haarlem. The fields here have been described as perhaps the largest 'open-air flower show' in the world.

Windmills in the Netherlands

Windmills are perhaps the best known symbol of the Netherlands. There were at one time about 10,000 windmills in the country, used primarily for draining the polders lying below sea level, and for grinding grain, pressing oil and cutting timber. When the polders were enclosed by dikes after the 11th century it became necessary to reduce the underground water level to make the land habitable and suitable for cultivation. Man or horse-powered bucket elevators were used at first to convey the water into the draining dikes. In the 17th century there were already a great number of wind-pumps north of Amsterdam.

The several types of windmill are distinguishable by their construction. The oldest among them is the support mill ('standermolen'), built on a square plan. In front of the sails and in the back is the *Staart*, a weathervane by which the entire millhouse can be rotated around a vertical axis in order to find the wind direction. These mills were used predominantly for grinding grain and can still be found in the Central Netherlands. The mills in the south of Holland were built on the same technical principles, but on an octagonal plan.

Later the support mills were replaced by another type, where the mill-house was fixed and only the upper shaft rotated with the wind. Inland they were often built on higher terrain or on the town ramparts to make better use of the wind. When these mills were out of action they could be used to communicate news by the positioning of their sails. This system is said to have been used by the Dutch as late as the Second World War to contact pilots of allied aircraft.

Today there remain about 1,000 windmills in the Netherlands, with approximately 300 still in occasional use. Almost all date from the 18th–19th centuries and have been carefully restored and preserved. Every year on the second Saturday in May, National Windmill Day is celebrated and the mills are set in motion.

The best known windmill group is near Kinderdijk, north of Alblasserdam. There nineteen windmills operate every Saturday in summer. Some mills of varying construction can be seen in the outdoor museum in Arnhem, and also near Zaandam. Rampart mills are to be found in Schiedam.

The Netherlands has been a constitutional monarchy since 1815 and, as in the case of its neighbour Belgium, the role of the monarch is a limited one. The practical governing of the country is administered by Parliament, which consists of two chambers. The First Chamber has 50 members who are elected for six years by the 12 provincial parliaments. The Second Chamber has 100 members who are all directly elected by popular vote. There is also a

State Council, headed by the monarch, which serves a purely consultative function.

The Zaanse Schans near Amsterdam

The Dutch economy is a modern industrial one, with a high proportion of the population being employed in the service sector, a sign that the economy has reached a high degree of development. The most important industries are the metallurgical industry, the food and tobacco industries, the traditional textile industry, and the relatively new chemical industry. These provide 45% of the net national product. Despite the fact that farmland covers 60% of total land surface, agriculture provides only 7% of net national product. It is however a very intensive and highly mechanised industry employing only 7% of the total working population. The Dutch economy as a whole depends to a great extent on its excellent inland waterways and the low-cost bulk cargoes that these facilities provide. Tourism since the Second World War has been a growth industry, with the North Sea coastal resorts, the old cities and the famous bulb fields being the main attractions.

Dutch painters have made important contributions to European culture. Dutch theatre and literature have been severely handicapped by the fact that a very small proportion of the human race actually speak their native language. With the political and religious separation of the late 16th century came a cultural separation of north and south. The first great period of Dutch painting was instigated by Jan van Eyck (c. 1390–1441) who, with his brother Hubert, painted the famous Altarpiece of Ghent. His understanding of perspective and fresh sense of realism influenced other Dutch artists like Rogier van der Weyden (c. 1400–64) and Hugo van der Goes (c. 1440–82) and helped to contribute to a Northern Renaissance in Flanders which matched the artistic developments in Italy.

The 16th century produced an outstanding native artist in Pieter Breughel the Elder (c 1525–69) whose peasant scenes illustrating the comedy and tragedy of human life owed much to an earlier Dutch master Hieronymous Bosch (1453–1516). The appearance of Peter Paul Rubens (1577–1640) marked the beginning of the Baroque age in Flanders which reached its peak in the towering personality of Rembrandt (1606–69). He was the undisputed leader of his time both as a painter and as a draughtsman. Together with the master of the portrait Frans Hals (1580–1666) and Jan Vermeer (1632–75) who specialised in interior scenes, he helped to make Dutch painting a leading influence in European art during the 17th century.

Thereafter a decline set in which coincided with the general decline in Dutch supremacy. It only really came to the fore again in the work of Vincent van Gogh (1853–90) who became one of the earliest representatives of Expressionism. Van Gogh's brash use of colour also influenced the Fauvists in France. During the 20th century, the sheer number of modern trends and their

The Westerkerk in Amsterdam

Typical Dutch architecture

internationalism worked against any specific national goals. However, the abstract paintings of Piet Mondrian (1872–1944) who emigrated to New York in 1940, did have great influence on North American art after the Second World War and this overlapped into the fields of sculpture, architecture and design.

Dutch architects occupy a prominent position in the history of 20th century

A stained glass window in the Grote Kerk in Gouda

architecture. Hendrik Petrus Berlage founded the 'Amsterdam School' which turned its back on the eclecticism of the 19th century. An excellent example of his style can be seen in the unfinished Amsterdam Stock Exchange (1893–1903). Breaking away from this school were a group of architects influenced by Cubism: Jacobus Johannes Oud, Robert van 't Hoff, Jan Wils and Gerrit Thomas Rietveld. They founded an organisation called CIAM (Congrès Internationaux d'Architecture Moderne) and developed a new form of West-European Functionalism. The reconstructed city of Rotterdam was one example of a new solution to urban building.

History

8 BC–AD 500	Roman occupation
c 481–843	Low Countries incorporated into Frankish Empire
10th–14th centuries	Emergence of counties, duchies and towns as centres of power
1384–1473	Low Countries united under Dukes of Burgundy
after 1550	Calvinism becomes the dominant creed in the north
1568–84	Northern Netherlands begin fight for freedom from Spanish rule, led by William I the Silent, Prince of Orange
1648	Independence of Netherlands recognised at Treaty of Westphalia
1648–1700	Peak of Dutch supremacy as a naval power and trading nation

Amsterdam – bird's eye view of the Royal Palace

1689	William II of Orange also King of England (with Mary)
1792–4	Netherlands conquered by French Revolutionary Army
1815	Kingdom of United Netherlands created at Congress of Vienna
1830	Rebellion and secession of Belgium
1914–18	Netherlands remain strictly neutral during First World War
1939–45	Netherlands suffer heavily under German occupation during Second World War
1949	Former colonial territories of Dutch East Indies form independent Republic of Indonesia
1958	Customs and Economic Union of Benelux countries
1976	Prince Bernard resigns over 'Lockheed Affair'

1980	Queen Juliana abdicates because of age; Beatrix becomes Queen
1983	Crippling strikes by workers in the public sector in the face of the government's new austerity programme
1986	Lower House of Parliament votes in favour of approving a treaty with the USA to allow 48 cruise nuclear missiles to be deployed on Dutch soil

Major Centres

Amsterdam

VVV Amsterdam e.o.
Rokin 5
NL-1012 KK Amsterdam
Tel: 26 64 44

VVV Amsterdam
Stationsplein (by the railway station)
NL-1012 AB Amsterdam
Tel: 22 10 16

Embassies
UK: British Consort General
Koningslaan 44
1075AE Amsterdam
Tel: 764343
USA: Museumplein 19
Tel: 790321

Known as the 'City of Diamonds', for its leading involvement in the diamond trade, Amsterdam is the focal point and cornerstone of the Dutch economy. However, it holds neither

Dam in Amsterdam

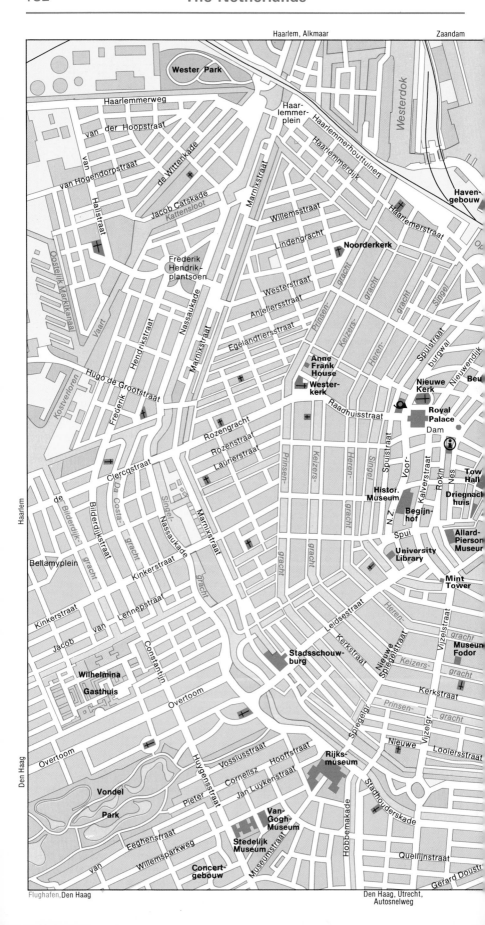

Haarlem, Alkmaar   Zaandam

Wester Park

Haarlemmerweg

van der Hoopstraat

van Hogendorpstraat

Haarlemmerplein

Haarlemmerhouttuinen

Haarlemmerdijk

de Wittenkade

Jacob Catskade

Kattensloot

Marnixstraat

Willemsstraat

Lindengracht

Noorderkerk

Havengebouw

Haarlemerstraat

Westerdok

Frederik Hendrikplantsoen

Westerstraat

Anjeliersstraat

Egelandtiersstraat

Prinsengracht

Keizersgracht

Herengracht

Singel

Spuistraat

Nieuwendijk

Hallstraat

Oostelijk Marktkanaal

Vaart

Hendrikstraat

Nassaukade

Marnixstraat

Anne Frank House

Westerkerk

Raadhuisstraat

Nieuwe Kerk

Royal Palace

Dam

Beu

burgwal

Kostverloren

Hugo de Grootstraat

Frederik

Rozengracht

Rozenstraat

Laurierstraat

Clercqstraat

Singel-Nassaukade

Marnixstraat

Prinsengracht

Keizersgracht

Herengracht

Singel

Spuistraat

Voor-

Kalverstraat

Rokin

Nes

Histor. Museum

Begijnhof

Tow Hall

Driegnach huis

Allard-Pierson Museum

N. Z.

Spui

University Library

de Bilderdijk

Bilderdijkstraat

Kinkerstraat

Lennepstraat

gracht

Bellamyplein

Kinkerstraat

Jacob

van

Constantin

Wilhelmina Gasthuis

Overtoom

Stadsschouwburg

Leidsestraat

Kerkstraat

Nieuwe Spiegelstraat

Keizers-

Herengracht

Vizelstraat

gracht

Museum Fodor

gracht

Kerkstraat

Prinsengracht

Vizelgr.

gracht

Nieuwe

Looiersstraat

Spiegel

Overtoom

Huygensstraat

Vossiusstraat

Cornelisz Hooftstraat

Jan Luykenstraat

Rijksmuseum

Pieter

Vondel

Park

Eeghenstraat

Willemsparkweg

van

Stadhouderskade

Hobbemakade

Van-Gogh-Museum

Stedelijk Museum

Museumstraat

Concertgebouw

Quellijnstraat

Gerard Doustr.

Haarlem

Den Haag

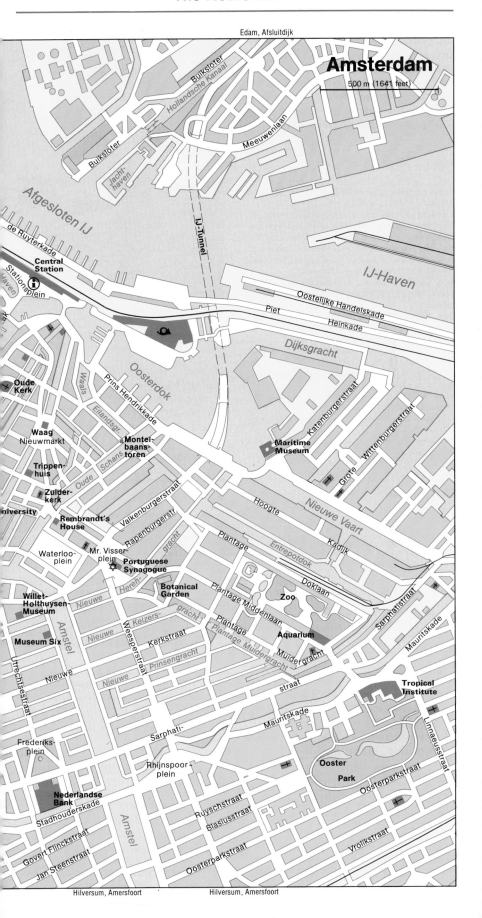

Edam, Afsluitdijk

Amsterdam

500 m (1641 feet)

Bulksloter Kanaal

Hollandsche Kanaal

Meeuwenlaan

Bulksloter

Jacht-
haven

IJ-Tunnel

Afgesloten IJ

de Ruyterkade

IJ-Haven

Central
Station

Stationsplein

Oostelijke Handelskade

Piet

Heinkade

Dijksgracht

Oosterdok

Prins Hendrikkade

Oude
Kerk

Waals

Eilandsgr.

Katenburgerstraat

Wittenburgerstraat

Waag
Nieuwmarkt

Montel-
baans-
toren

Maritime
Museum

Oude Schans

Grote

Trippen-
huis

Zuider-
kerk

Hoogte

Nieuwe Vaart

University

Rembrandt's
House

Valkenburgerstraat

Kadijk

Waterloo-
plein

Rapenburgerstr.

gracht

Plantage

Entrepotdok

Mr. Visser-
plein

Portuguese
Synagogue

Heren-

Doklaan

Sarphatistraat

Willet-
Holthuysen-
Museum

Botanical
Garden

Plantage Middenlaan

Zoo

Mauritskade

Nieuwe

Keizers-

Plantage

Museum Six

Nieuwe

Weesperstraat

Kerkstraat

Plantage Muidergracht

Aquarium

Muidergracht

Amstel

Utrechtsestraat

Nieuwe

Prinsengracht

straat

Tropical
Institute

Nieuwe

Mauritskade

Linnaeusstraat

Frederiks-
plein

Sarphati-

Ooster

Rhijnspoor-
plein

Park

Oosterparkstraat

Nederlandse
Bank

Stadhouderskade

Amstel

Ruyschstraat

Blasiusstraat

Govert Flinckstraat

Jan Steenstraat

Oosterparkstraat

Vrolikstraat

the permanent royal residence nor the seat of government, both of which are in The Hague. Set at the opening of the North Sea Canal into the North Sea, it is a picturesque city of canals and bridges. The older city contains some 6500 architectural monuments.

Sightseeing

Canal Cruise – runs continually in the summer, particularly impressive at night
Kalverstraat – the main shopping street of the city
Municipal Museum – fine collection of Dutch and French paintings from 19th and 20th centuries
National Museum (*Rijksmuseum*) – offers a unique collection of masterpieces and an extensive survey of Dutch cultural development
New Church – built in 15th century and rebuilt several times; inside are tombstones of famous naval heroes
Old Church – built in the 13th century; a 15th century steeple offers a fine view of the city
Rembrandt House – the great painter lived here from 1639–1658; it has been a museum since 1911
Royal Palace – built by Jacob Van Campen in the 17th century; fine Royal Apartments decorated with royal statues
Six's Picture Gallery – one of the most important private collections in the country
Tropical Museum – a world famous museum, well worth a visit
Van Gogh Museum – contains 200 paintings, 500 drawings and 700 letters by the artist

Rotterdam

VVV Rotterdam
Stadhuisplein 19
NL-3012 AR Rotterdam
Tel: (10) 4 14 14 00

Further information:
Centraal Station
Station Hall
Tel: (10) 13 60 06

Rotterdam is the second largest city in the country as well as being the world's largest port in terms of goods handled. The Inner City of Rotterdam was almost completely destroyed by German air raids in 1940. The city as it was reconstructed is one of the most modern cities in Europe.

Sightseeing

Euromast – 185m-high construction built in 1960 on the occasion of the International Gardening Exhibition
Maas Tunnel – a vehicle underpass 1.5km long, connecting the city to its southern suburbs
Museum Boymans-Van Beuningen – world famous museum with many fine exhibits, particularly of Dutch 14th–16th century paintings

Prins Hendrik Maritime Museum – a collection depicting the history of navigation since the 17th century
Zoo Blijdorp – one of the most progressive zoos in Europe, beautifully laid out, with animals in open enclosures

The port of Rotterdam

The Harbour Route of Rotterdam (Rotterdamse Havenroute)

Marked by the sign reproduced here, this is a recommended drive of 90–150km (56–93 miles) through the extensive harbour area of Rotterdam.

● A **Departure point** (from Spaanse Polder)
● 1 **Europoint** (office block)
● 2 **Oud Delfshaven** (originally the port for the town of Delft, incorporated into Rotterdam in 1886)
● 3 **Coolhaven** (an inland port constructed between the two world wars)
   Maas Tunnel (built 1937–42)
● 4 **Sluisjesdikj** (on a peninsula between Nieuwe Maas and Waalhaven; 1888 the first oil tanks)
● 5 **Waalhaven** – *East Side* (originally constructed in 1907–30 for bulk cargo: timber, heavy cargo, container)
● 6 **Waalhaven** – *South Side* (Harbour and transport school, container terminal)
● 7 **Prins Johan Frisohaven** (vehicles, including Japanese cars)
● 8 **Heijplaat** (garden city for shipyard employees)
● 9 **Prinses Beatrixhaven** (opened in 1965 as general cargo port; roll-on, roll-off, large banana unloaders)
● 10 **Prinses Margriethaven** (container terminal; large quay cranes)
● 11 **Pernis** (a fishing village on land reclaimed in the 14th century)
● 12 **1008 km mark on the Rhine** (1008 river kilometres (625 miles) from the first Rhine bridge at Konstanz on Lake Constance; harbour radar station)

- ● 13 **Benelux Tunnel** (opened 1967)
- ● 14 **2nd Petroleumhaven** (Petro-chemical works of Shell and Chevron)
- ● 15 **Rotterdamse Star** ('The Star of Rotterdam', access to highway ring road)
- ● 16 **Petrochemiekomplex** (Shell, Chevron; start of an oil pipeline to Germany; environmental control complex)

- ● 17 **Botlekbrug** (bascule bridge with 45m (148 feet) clearance)
- ● 18 **Gaulhaven** (tug and harbour service boats)
- ● 19 **3rd Petroleumhaven** (Esso Refinery)
- ● 20 **Chemiehaven** (chemical plants; dischargers for copra and tapioca)
- ● 21 **Botiek-Haven** (grain and ore loading; shipyards)

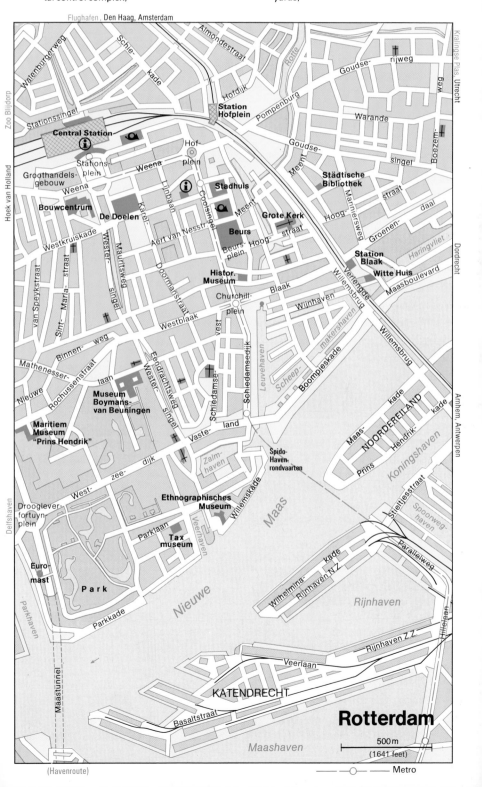

Rotterdam

● 22 **Grain Warehouses** (on the Enclosing Dike of the former Brielse Maas now Brielse Meer, built in 1950; elevators, conveyor belts)

● 23 **St Laurenshaven** (mineral raw materials)

● 24 **Petrochemiekomplex** (storage tanks, chemical plants)

● 25 **Shipyards** (Prins Willem Alexander Dry Dock; waste disposal area)

● 26 **Rozenburg** (village called 'The Green Heart of Europoort', surrounded by reclaimed industrial areas and dikes)

● 27 **Ferry Rozenburg–Maassluis**

● 28 **Calandkanaal** (canal for seagoing vessels between the Europoort docks and the North Sea)

● 29 **Separation Dam** (between Calandkanaal and Nieuwe Waterweg; mooring places for Europoort docks in Scheurhaven)

● 30 **Calandbrug** (bascule bridge with 50m (164 feet) clearance)

● 31 **Calandbrug** (vehicle terminal under construction)

● 32 **Europoort Oost** – *Merseyweg* (plastics factory)

● 33 **Europoort Oost** – *Theemsweg* (chemical plants and cement factory)

● 34 **Rozenburgsesluis** (Rozenburg lock between Hartelkanaal and Calandkanaal; lock size 299m × 233m–981 feet × 764 feet)

● 35 **7th Petroleumhaven** (crude oil transit)

● 36 **'De Beer'** (International Seamen's Institute)

● 37 **4th Petroleumhaven** (Shell, Esso, Chevron, Gulf; mooring station)
5th Petroleumhaven (Gulf Refinery)

● 38 **Beneluxhaven** (ferry services to Britain)

● 39 **Beneluxhaven** (discharge towers, conveyors and silos for grain shipments)

● 40 **Hartelkanaal** (Rhine waterway between the harbour industries of the Maasvlakte and Europoort, and the hinterland)

● 41 **6th Petroleumhaven** (BP Refinery)

● 42 **Europoort** (ore shipment; large discharge towers on the Calandkanaal)

● 43 **Beerkanaal** (pilot station)

● 44 **Oostvoornse Meer** (lake created in the first stage of the Delta plan)

● 45 **Mississippihaven** (natural gas tanks; ore shipments; coal terminal under construction)

● 46 **Maasviakte Power Station**

● 47 **Beach** (along the west coast of the Maasvlakte)
Stone dam (a stone block jetty 4.5km (3 miles) long)

● 48 **Port and industrial area** (a new lighthouse is planned)

● 49 **Manmade dunes** (imitation oil tank; view of the estuary of the Rhone known as 'Maasmond')

● 50 **8th Petroleumhaven** (Maasvlakte oil terminal for giant tankers)

● E **Terminal point** between Brielsebrug and Harmsenbrug

Ceremonial display in The Hague

The Hague

National Bureau voor Tourism
Bezuidenhoutseweg 2
NL-2594 AV Den Haag
Tel: (70) 81 41 91

VVV Den Haag/Scheveningen
Groot Hertoginnelaan 41
NL-2585 EC Den Haag
Tel: (70) 54 62 00

Information
Kon. Julianaplein 8
(at the Central Station)
NL-2595 AA Den Haag

Embassies:
UK: Lange Voorhout 10
USA: Lange Voorhout 102
Tel: (70) 62 49 11

The Hague is the third largest city in the Netherlands and it is the seat of the Dutch government. In the coastal part of the city lies the largest sea resort in the country, Scheveningen. The city is much favoured by retired people, who are attracted to the area by its situation and well cared for appearance.

Sightseeing

Binnenhof – houses Dutch Parliament, once the residence of the Stadholders

The Ridderzaal in The Hague

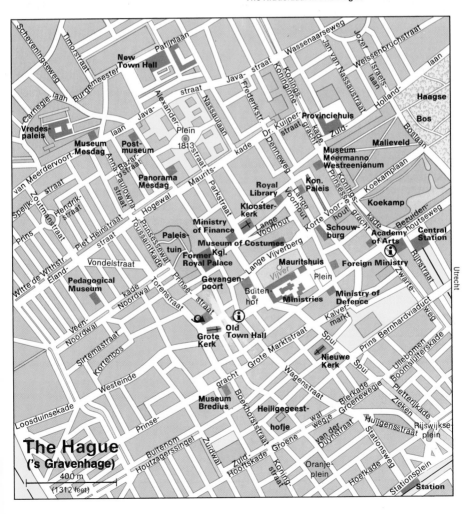

Grote Kerk – 15th–16th-century church with fine vaulted interior
Haagse Bos – wooded park 2km with beautiful tree-lined avenues, leading to
Huis ten Bos – built 1644–6, formerly a royal country retreat and now the residence of Queen Beatrix
Museum Bredius – houses large collection of paintings, furniture and china
Picture Gallery – formed from the collections of the Princes of Orange-Nassau and containing a high standard of exhibits
The Ridderzaal – a 13th-century hall used for the opening of parliament by the Queen in September
Royal Palace – built by Pieter Post in 1640, now the residence of the International Institute of Social Studies
Vijver – picturesque old ornamental lake

Miniature town of Madurodam in The Hague

Accommodation

Hotels and Inns

Hotels in the larger towns and resorts in the Netherlands provide the usual international comfort. Advance booking is recommended, especially in high season. The inns (in French *auberges*) in medium-sized and small towns also provide pleasant accommodation. The traditional Dutch inns, especially in areas off the beaten track, are recommended. They may be quaint and old-fashioned but they are cosy, clean and good value.

The Benelux Hotel Classification system was introduced in 1978. It is com-pulsory for all establishments offering accommodation to carry a sign bearing their classification. There are five categories, 5 being the highest and 1 being the lowest.

Other types of hotel-style accommodation available to visitors are listed below:

Hotel-café-restaurant

An establishment built and fitted out to provide accommodation and in which a café and a restaurant, or a café-restaurant are also operated. The menu and wine list must be available.

Motel

A hotel-café-restaurant integrated with a motorway or trunk road and adapted to the special needs of road users. Menu and wine list must be available.

Hotel-restaurant

An establishment built and fitted out to provide accommodation and in which a restaurant is also operated. Menu and wine list must be available.

Hotel-garni

An establishment built and fitted out to provide accommodation and in which only bed and breakfast are provided.

Apartment-hotel

An establishment built and fitted out to provide accommodation and in which flats or other special accommodation

Hotel Price Range		
	Price for 1 night in guilders	
Type of hotel	Single	Double
*****	220–410	270–500
****	160–350	210–380
***	70–210	100–260
**	50–170	90–240
*	40– 90	65–140

These prices are intended to act as a rough guide only.

units (studio-flats and the like) are let out per day.

Country-House Hotels

In the Netherlands there are a number of country-house hotels well known for their high standards and for their attractive locations. Frequently they provide opportunities for fishing, hunting or riding. Generally they only have a limited number of rooms, and advance booking is therefore recommended.

The Netherlands Reservation Centre is an organisation set up by the Dutch hotel trade. The centre offers you rooms all over Holland in virtually every price category. You may make your reservation by letter, telephone or telex. Within 24 hours the written confirmation will be sent. There is no charge.
NRC
PO Box 3387
NL-1001
AD Amsterdam
Holland
Tel: 020/21 12 11

Youth Hostels

Youth Hostels in the Netherlands provide low-priced accommodation for young people. In the Netherlands there is no age limit and the stay is not restricted to 3 days.
Information:
Vlaamse Jeugdherbergcentrale
Van Stralenstraat 40
B-2000 Antwerpen
Tel: (0 31) 32 72 18

Holiday Flats and Villas
(Vacation Rentals)

Numerous vacation apartments and villas are available on the coast as well as inland. Here also, advance booking is recommended in high season.

Camping and Caravanning

The Netherlands has approximately 2000 camping sites. These are generally well-appointed and can be found in quiet rural areas as well as in the main tourist resorts. Holders of an international camping card qualify for a range of price reductions. In high season many sites are filled to capacity. Camping in the open is limited to a few areas because of the population density. It always requires permission from the owner of the land.

Introduction to Rail Information

The *Nederlandse Spoorwegen (NS)* is the railway system which operates in the Netherlands. It is generally regarded as one of the most modern and efficient in the world. The characteristics of the Dutch landscape are such that travel by train is really one of the best means of seeing the country in comfort. The frequency of passenger services means that a traveller can depart from any one station to any other in the Netherlands (not necessarily by direct train) at least once every hour from early morning until evening. The system makes use of 4 types of train:

InterCity (IC) – international express trains

Intercity – local express trains

D—trains – international express trains

Stoptrains – local slow trains

When travelling on the IC and D trains passengers should expect to pay a small supplement on the fare.

Major International Services

Connection	Duration	Frequency
Amsterdam–London	9–12hrs	7 times daily
Amsterdam–Paris	5–6hrs	9 times daily
Amsterdam–Brussels	2–3hrs	20 times daily
Amsterdam–Cologne	3–4hrs	15 times daily
Amsterdam–Luxembourg	6hrs	hourly

The railway network in the Netherlands is dense

Train Connections from Schiphol Airport

Now Schiphol Airport has a brand new direct and rapid link to Amsterdam Central Station and to all cities in the Netherlands by direct through trains or with one transfer. Trains run every 15 minutes to Amsterdam and the journey lasts 20 minutes. During the night, trains run hourly between Schiphol and Amsterdam Central Station, Utrecht, The Hague and Rotterdam. The Netherlands Railways ticket office at Schiphol gives round-the-clock service.

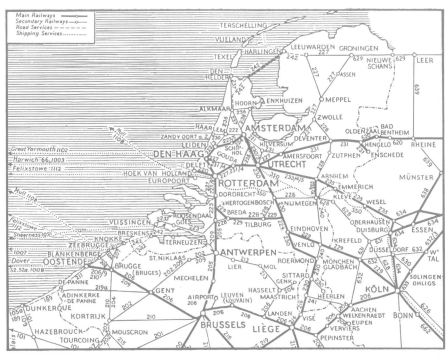

Map supplied by kind permission of Thomas Cook Ltd. The numbers along the lines refer to tables in the *Thomas Cook Continental Timetable*.

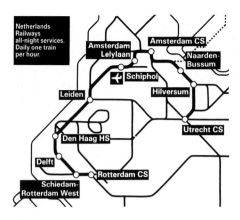

Netherlands Railways all-night services. Daily one train per hour.

Major Internal Services

The journey times of most internal routes are relatively short, in fact only a few rail journeys in the country require more than 3 hours to complete, and many take 1 hour or considerably less. The frequency of the service combined with the short distances involved means that timetables are virtually dispensable. Most Dutch people just go to the station, look at the platform indicator for the next departure in the required direction, and are soon moving towards their destination. Here are some of the principal internal connections:

Amsterdam–Schiphol–Leiden–The Hague
Rotterdam–Dordrecht–Roosendaal–Vlissingen

Amsterdam–Alkmaar–Den Helder

Amsterdam–Alkmaar–Hoorn

Zandvoort–Haarlem–Amsterdam–Utrecht–s'-Hertogenbosch–Eindhoven–Roermond–Maastricht

Amsterdam–Utrecht–Arnhem–Nijmegen

Zwolle–Deventer–Arnhem–Nijmegen–s'-Hertogenbosch–Tilburg–Breda–Roosendaal–Vlissingen

Amsterdam–Amersfoort–Apeldoorn–Deventer–Hengelo–Enschede

Scenic Routes

Some of the best scenic routes in the Netherlands have the added attraction of conveying the passengers in steam trains, for example, the line from Apeldoorn–Dieren travels through the picturesque area of Veluwe. Another attractive line which passes through

the border area of Twente sets out from Haaksbergen and reaches its destination at Boekelo. The Hoorn–Medemblik route is a 'museum line' and maintains the traditions of the old Dutch steam lines. In the south of the country, in the province of Limburg is the popular Miljoenenlijn. Finally, the Heerlen–Valkenborg line operates in the summer only and special tickets are required for this journey.

The train service is highly efficient

Veteran Railways

1. **Apeldoorn–Dieren**
   Route: Apeldoorn VSM–Beekbergen–Loenen–Eerbeek–Dieren USM
   Length: 22km
   Gauge: 1435mm
   This is the only preserved line with two NS-railheads. It runs a service between Apeldoorn and Dieren in the Veluwe area with its attractive sand-dunes and woodlands.
   Open on selected days during summer months
   Operating society: *Veluwsche Stoomtrein, Maatschappij VSM, Dorpsstraat 140, 7361 AZ Beekbergen*. Tel: 05766 2476

2. **Haaksbergen–Boekelo**
   Route: Haaksbergen–Bad Boekelo–Boekelo Dorp
   Length: 7km
   Gauge: 1435mm
   This is an attractive preserved railway which grows in quality (rather than length) every year. Opens on selected days during summer months.
   Operating society: *Stichting Museum Buurtspoorweg (MBS)*, Postbus 1182, 7500 BD Enschede. Tel: 05427 11516

3. **Hoorn–Medemblik**
   Route: Hoorn–Medemblik
   Length: 20km
   Gauge: 1435mm
   This railway project has a wonderful collection of rolling stock. In Hoorn you can visit a museum workshop where maintenance and renovation work is carried out. Regular time-

The Dutch countryside is famous for its tulip fields

table runs during high season (July to September).
Operating society: *Museum Stoomtrain,* Hoorn-Medemblik SHM, Postbus 137, 1620 AC Hoorn. Tel: 02290 14862

4. Hellevoetsluis–Vlotbrug
Route: Hellevoetsluis–Vlotbrug
Length: 2km
Gauge: 1067mm
Europe's only Cape Gauge steam train, in Hellevoetsluis, southwest of Rotterdam. Locomotives and steam-tram coaches date back to the very beginning of this century. You can also see a fine collection of goods vans representing the various types the RTM used in the past.
There is a daily timetable
Operating society: *Stichting Rijdend,* Trammuseum RTM, Postbus 5, 3220 AA Hellevoetsluis. Tel: 01883 15919

5. Rotterdam
Route: mainly static
Gauge: 1435mm
The SSN-depot holds the largest preserved locos in the country. They make occasional journeys on the lines of the Netherlands Railways. If they are not in action, visitors are shown around the shed where the heavy ex-Bundesbahn locos are restored.
Throughout the year, Saturdays 10am–5pm
Operating society: *Stoom Stichting Nederland SSN,* Postbus 541, 2600 AM Delft. Tel: 010 622337

Other Railway Centres

Kaatsheuvel (Noord Brabant)
Narrow gauge steam trains in amusement park De Efteling. Park open April 4 to October 20, daily 10am–6pm. Tel: 04167 80505

Weert (Limburg)
An attractive collection of tramway rolling stock in the Dutch Tram Museum, 6 Kruisstraat. Photoexhibition. Open 2–6pm, closed on Mondays except in July and August. Parties may call for a guided tour from 11am. Tel: 04950 20393

Rotterdam
From April 1 till October 1 daily trip by historic tram (1931) from the Central Station (leaving 1.15pm) with connecting boat trip through the docks. Tel: 010 136000 (Tourist Information).

Erica (near Emmen, Drenthe)
The North Netherlands Museum Railway from May 25 till the end of August. Diesel loco and open coaches on short peat-colonial section. Tel: 05160 13000 Tourist Information or 15160 3520.

Netherlands Railway Museum
Maliebaan Station, Johan van Oldenbarneveltlaan 6, 3581 XZ Utrecht. Tel: 030 318514.
Opening times: Tuesday–Saturday 10am–5pm
Sundays/holidays 1pm–5pm
Closed: Mondays, January, Easter Sunday, Whit Sunday and Christmas Day
Utrecht has been the centre of the Dutch railway scene for as long as people can remember. The Netherlands Railway Museum houses a fine collection of engine models. In addition, there are a number of steam locos and a Mallett loco built for Indonesian Railways by the Dutch Company Werkspoor.

In the Railway Museum of Utrecht

Internal Fare Structure

Standard Rate Fares

Single tickets cover travel between 2 stations on the same day. An ordinary return consists of two separate single tickets (which can be purchased to allow for travel on two different days). Day returns may be used for travel between 2 stations if the return journey is completed on the same day as the outward journey. Day returns work out cheaper than buying 2 single fares and become increasingly better value the longer the distance involved. For example a 2nd class single ticket from Amsterdam to Delft costs f14.90; a day return for the same journey would cost f26.10. Weekend returns may be used for trips which involve an outward journey on the Saturday and a return journey on the Sunday of the same weekend. They are charged at the day return fare plus f2.50.

Child Reductions

Children under 4 are carried free. Children aged 5–11 accompanied by an adult pay f1 only (maximum 3 children per adult). This ticket is only available once in the Netherlands. Unaccompanied children (aged 5–11) pay 55% of the adult single fare or 60% of the adult day-return fare. The best pass for children aged between 10 and 19 is the teenager rover. It is available in June, July and August and entitles the holder to unlimited 2nd class travel over the entire NS network (excluding those trains which require payment of a supplement) on any 4 days within a specified period of 10 consecutive days.

Student Reductions

There are no special student reductions although some students will obviously qualify for the teenager rover pass (see Child Reductions). In addition, students are advised to consult the International Section for information on general student reductions.

Family Rover

This is available in June, July and August and costs £50 2nd class or £62 1st class. It entitles the whole family to unlimited travel throughout the NS network on 4 specified days within a period of 10 consecutive days. Netherlands Railways describe a family as: a man, a woman, a married couple, or 2 persons who have lived at the same address for at least one year and their unmarried children under the age of 19 (including step, foster and adopted children).

Senior Citizen Reductions

Holders of the Rail Europ Senior (RES) card are eligible for a 50% reduction on ordinary single and 40% reduction on day-return fares for journeys over the NS network (not on special return fares, not on rovers and not on supplements). Full information about the RES card may be found in the International Section. In addition, senior citizens may purchase a Senior Citizen railcard which is available for a year. This pass entitles the holder to 7 days free travel in the period and costs f70.

Special Excursion Rates

The NS operate a number of day-excursions (NS-Dagtochen) throughout the year but mainly in late spring, summer and early autumn. They provide one of the best means of visiting the cities, towns, resorts, beaches, places of historical or cultural interest, national parks and recreation centres etc all over the Netherlands. Combined tickets which cover all transport and entrance fees can be easily obtained from most NS stations. A few day-excursions, mainly those which venture into Belgium or Germany, follow a fixed itinerary and should be booked a few days in advance. The vast majority leave the passengers free, within the possibilities of scheduled services and relevant opening hours, to plan the day as they like. There are over 90 excursions on offer, some of these are:

De Efteling (world-famous Recreation Park) April–October

Flevohof (the National Agricultural Centre on a polder) May–October

The Hague-Royal Tour (the Parliamentary centre of the Netherlands and residence of the Queen) April–end September

Volendam and Marken (the picture of Old Holland – dikes, fishing boats and costumes) April–mid October

Giethoorn (the Venice of Holland, Canal-and-punt village) May–end September

Utrecht (city of museums) all year

Railrover Passes

Rover tickets entitle the holder to unlimited travel on all *NS* lines open to passenger traffic. A one-day ticket costs £15.50 for 2nd class travel and £23 for 1st class travel. The 3-day rover costs £24 for 2nd class travel and £30 for 1st class travel. The 7-day rover costs £33.50 for 2nd class travel and £49.50 for 1st class travel. Netherlands Railways 3- and 7-Day Rover tickets are obtainable from the London office of Netherlands Railways (see section 'Where to Buy Tickets').

Passengers intending to use one of these rover tickets must hold the standard *NS* identity card. These can be obtained from any *NS* rail station in the Netherlands for no charge, or at the London office.

Public Transport Link Rover

The Public Transport Link Rover can only be issued in conjunction with a rail rover for the same period and entitles the holder to unlimited travel for that period by the Amsterdam and Rotterdam metro systems, by public transport town and country buses and public transport trams in the whole of the Netherlands.

Multi-Rover

The Multi-Rover entitles from 2–6 passengers (2 children aged 4 or over but not yet 12 are counted as one passenger) to one day's unlimited travel over all *NS* lines open to passenger traffic (D or IC supplements payable if applicable) all day on Saturdays, Sundays and public holidays and after 9am on weekdays.

Tourist Reductions

The Benelux Tourrail Card is available between 1 April and 31 October. It entitles the holder to unlimited travel on any self-selected 5 days out of a specified validity of 17 days over all Netherlands Railways (*NS*), Belgian Railways (*SNCB*), Luxembourg Railways (*CFL*) and by *CFL* country buses in Luxembourg. It cannot be used in the Netherlands in conjunction with the Public Transport Link Rover. It can be used for travel by D and IC trains without supplement. Holders of this card are required to carry a valid passport for identification purposes. The price of the card for 2nd class travel is £43.50 (adult) and £31 (4–25 years); for 1st class £65 (adult) and £46 (4–25 years). Tickets are available from railway stations in the countries concerned and from Netherlands Railways offices in Great Britain and the United States (see International Section). In Great Britain, the card may also be bought at Youth Hostels Association Travel, 14 Southampton Street, London WC2.

Newly opened Schiphol Railway Station

Where to Buy Tickets

In the Netherlands

Tickets for travel within the Netherlands and for international journeys are available at all major Netherlands Railway stations.

In Great Britain

Information for travel within the Netherlands is available from selected travel agents throughout Britain and from:
Netherlands Railways
25/28 Buckingham Gate,
London SW1E 6LD
Tel: (071) 630 1735

Tickets for international journeys which begin in or pass through the Netherlands are not available from this office, but they can be purchased from:
European Rail Travel Centre,
PO Box 303,
Victoria Station,
London SW1V 1JY
Tel: (071) 834 2345
and British Rail appointed agents.

In USA

From NS representatives (see International Section).

Facilities on Trains

Sleepers and Couchettes

There are no sleepers or couchettes on the NS internal services because the journeys are invariably too short. However, there are couchettes and sleepers on some of the international services which set out from stations within the Netherlands.

Food

There are no restaurant cars or hot meals available on trains which travel the domestic routes. Buffet cars are present on most of the longer routes.

These serve hot and cold drinks, sandwiches and cold snacks. Most other trains offer mini-bar service on portable aisle trolleys. These serve cold drinks and snacks.

A two storey NS train

Bicycles

It is possible to take your bike with you on the train between a total of 135 stations in the Netherlands. This facility is restricted during peak travel periods. Loading and unloading is the responsibility of the cyclist. Travel on a particular service cannot be guaranteed and is always subject to the availability of space in the baggage van. A small charge will be added to your fare for this privilege.

All stations use the International Rail Symbols

Facilities at Stations

Food

Most larger stations in the Netherlands have restaurants which are usually self-service. They offer hot and cold meals at varying prices.

Reservations

For travel within the *NS* internal system it is possible to make reservations for large groups of passengers only. For passengers travelling on the international express trains, seat, couchette and sleeper reservations can be made at the major rail stations.

Tourist Information Offices

These may be found at all the major Netherlands railway stations and are fully equipped to answer enquiries and render assistance. English speaking personnel are always on hand.

Disabled Passengers

Assistance for the disabled can be provided by Netherlands Railway staff at departure, changing and arrival stations. This assistance can be requested by telephone (preferably 48 hours in advance) when in the Netherlands through the central telephone number 030 331253.

Wheelchairs and ramps are available at most stations and adapted lifts are built in to some stations.

If a disabled passenger finds it difficult to buy a ticket at the station booking office, he may purchase it on the train at no extra charge after notifying the guard.

Bicycle Hire

A larger number of stations have bicycle depots from which bicycles may be hired per day or per week. A bicycle ticket must be bought from the ticket window of the station on production of the valid rail ticket used for the journey to the station. The cost stands at about f4.25 per bicycle per day. Some identification is required (passport) and a refundable deposit is usually demanded of between f50 and f200 depending on the station.

Railway lines link picturesque parts of the countryside

Norway

Kaupanger Ferry Station on the Sognefjord

Introduction

Norway stretches down the western edge of the Scandinavian coastline and is the fifth largest country in Europe. The west coast is a popular holiday destination. The fjords which are deep valleys cut by glaciers in the Ice Age and filled by the rising sea are a particular attraction for tourists. A large part of Norway lies within the Arctic Circle and is barren and isolated but the hilly countryside around the capital, Oslo, offers some breathtaking scenery.

About three quarters of Norway is unproductive bog and mountain while the rest is mainly forest. The mountains rise sharply in the west and slope gently down towards Oslo in the east. The Norwegian climate varies according to latitude, topography and proximity to the coast. Bergen, on the west coast, is much wetter than Oslo and more subject to severe storms in winter. Winter temperatures average from 1°C at Bergen to −14°C at Hammerfest in the north and summer temperatures from 15°C to 9°C in the same places.

The Norwegian economy has prospered since the discovery of large oil and natural gas fields in the North Sea in 1968. Associated new industries constructing giant tankers and drilling rigs have been developed and unemployment is relatively low. Over 350,000 people are employed in Norwegian industry.

Norway also has numerous small deposits of minerals which it exports. Agriculture is hampered by unfavourable geography and climate but fishing is of central importance to the economy. Herring and cod are attracted to the waters warmed by the Gulf Stream and Norway catches more fish a year than any other European country except the USSR. Norway is a member of the European Free Trade Association (EFTA) and as such has a customs agreement with the EEC.

Norway has a population of some 4 million – mainly Lutheran – making it the least populated country in Europe, after Iceland. The country has produced major composers and writers as well as Arctic explorers such as Nansen and Amundsen. Culturally, perhaps the most famous Norwegian artist is the painter Edvard Munch (1863–1944). Widely regarded as the founder of Expressionism, in his later work he turned away from the gloomy themes of illness, death and destruction to more positive subjects.

Strynsvatn

The wooden 'stave' churches of Norway are the most characteristic achievements of medieval Norwegian architecture. Thirty-one of them survive in Norway and they are distinctive by their construction – vertical planks of 'staves' in contrast to the usual horizontal 'log-cabin' technique. Norway is also famous for its folk art – especially rustic 'rose painting' – which indeed flourished throughout Scandinavia in the 18th and 19th centuries. An example of the remnants of the Viking Age is the 24m-long Gokstad Ship in the Norwegian Folk Museum, Oslo.

Sunset over Alesund

History

9th–11th centuries	While the Vikings raided the coastal regions of Europe, Norway remained a loose association of petty kingdoms
955	Olav Tryggvason returns from England and is accepted as the first King of Norway. At the same time he brings Christianity to the country
11th & 12th centuries	Frequent conflicts with Denmark in a struggle to establish a royal authority
1387–1814	Norway in personal union with Denmark. Norway becomes a Danish province ruled by a governor and Danish becomes the national language
1814	After Napoleon's defeat and the break-up of the Franco-Danish alliance, Denmark is forced to cede Norway to Sweden
1905	A national referendum decides in favour of dissolving the union with Sweden and this is confirmed at the Treaty of Karlstad
1905–57	Prince Karl of Denmark is elected King of Norway and takes the name of Håkon VII

Akershus Castle in the snow, Oslo

1920	Norway joins the League of Nations
1939–45	Norway is occupied during the Second World War and the King and government go into exile in Britain
1949	Treaty with the Soviet Union
1974	Drilling for oil and natural gas begins in the North Sea
1979	A huge field of natural gas is discovered off Bergen
1983	New coalition government formed by Kaare Willoch

1984	Deterioration in relations with the USSR
1986	Conservative coalition government collapses following a decline in oil prices, and a Labour minority government comes into power

Major Centres

Oslo

Landslaget for Reiselivet i Norge
Norwegian Tourist Board
Harnelageret
Langkaia 1
0105 OSLO 1
Tel: (2) 42 70 44

Reisetrafikkforeningen for Oslo og Omegn
Oslo Tourist Board
Rådmannsgården
Rådhusgate 19
N-Oslo 1
Tel: (2) 42 71 70

Tourist Information
Town Hall
Tel: (2) 42 71 70/41 48 63

Embassies:
UK: Thomas Heftyesgate 8,
Tel: (2) 56 38 90/97

USA: Drammensveien 18,
Tel: (2) 44 85 50

Oslo lies in a magnificent setting at the head of the Oslofjord. As well as being the seat of government, it is the busiest port in Norway and therefore of considerable economic importance. The area around Oslo offers excellent wintersports facilities and Lake Mjosa, Norway's largest lake is nearby. The city's principal industries are metal-working, foodstuffs, clothing manu-facture and ship building.

Sightseeing

Akershus Castle – was begun by Håkon V in the late 13th century. Inside the castle are various casemates (chambers built in the walls) and the tomb of King Håkon VII (1872–1957)
Historical Museum – houses a rich collection of materials from the Viking Age (9th–11th centuries)
Munch Museum – a unique collection of some 23,000 items of this famous Norwegian painter's work
National Gallery – offers an excellent survey of Norwegian painting from the 19th century to the present day
Norwegian Folk Museum – lies on the Bygdøy peninsula 6km to the west of Oslo and contains interesting collections of everyday objects. There

is also an extensive open air section and a hall housing three Viking ships

Storting (Parliament Building) – lies in the heart of Oslo, near the main shopping and business street, Karl Johansgate

Bergen

Bergen Reiselivslag (Bergen Tourist Board)
Slottsgt. 1,
5000 Bergen
Tel: (5) 31 38 60

Norway's second largest city and principal port on the west coast, Bergen is the gateway to world-famous fjord Norway. It is the administrative capital of the district of Bergen and the county of Hordaland, the seat of the Lutheran bishop of Bjorgvin, and has a university and a commercial college.

The city has a beautiful situation by the fjord and between seven mountains which are largely forest, although houses climb up the lower slopes. Bergen is one of the most attractive towns in Norway, with a fascinating mixture of old and new.

'Trollhaugen', Grieg's home in Bergen

Sightseeing

Bryggen (The Wharf) – runs along the NE side of the harbour. Here once stood the houses of the German merchants, later replaced by stone-built warehouses in a style characteristic of the Hanseatic period. The **Bryggen Archaeological Museum** and the **Centre for Arts and Crafts** are found here

Hanseatic Museum – ironically housed since 1872 in one of the only buildings in Bryggen preserved in its original condition. The Museum gives a good impression of the Hanseatic warehouses, and display weapons, domestic furnishings and equipment

Bergenhus – fortress which formerly commanded the entrance to the harbour. At the south end is the entrance to the Rosenkrantz Tower, built by Erik Rosenkrantz (1562–7). Beyond this is Hakonshallen (the hall of Hakon) begun in English Gothic style and later restored

Cathedral – originally built as a monastic church in 1248, rebuilt 1537, restored 1870. Fine doorway in tower, beautiful Gothic windows

Rasmus Meyer Collection – bequeathed to the city in 1923 by Rasmus Meyer. Includes paintings by Norwegian artists from 1814–1914 (J C Dahl, H Gude, Edvard Munch, G Munche)

Vestlandske Kunstindustri Museum (West Norway Museum of Applied Art) – applied and decorative art, furniture, carpets, porcelain etc

Municipal Art Museum – collection of work by Norwegian painters of the 19th and 20th century

University Collections – natural history, cultural history and a **Shipping Museum**. Adjoining the **Botanic Garden**

Fløien – restaurant with magnificent views over the city

Accommodation

Hotels

The hotels in Norway, noted for their cleanliness are right up to international standards of comfort and service for the different price categories. The large towns have luxury establishments (advance reservation advisable) but many smaller places have excellent hotels combining international standards of comfort with distinctive national features. Even in the far north, there are good hotels and well-equipped inns (*Gjestgiven*) which provide a very adequate standard of comfort. Many establishments have 'family rooms' with 3–5 beds which provide reasonably priced accommodation for a family group. Some mountain hotels in Norway are open for only part of the year, during the summer and winter seasons. There are also special summer hotels.

Apart from the luxury hotels in Oslo and other large towns, there are a number of alternative types of hotel accommodation. In rural districts there are *turisthotels* and *hoyfjellshotels* which provide a very reasonable standard of comfort. Then there are *turiststasjoner* and *Fjellstuer* (mountain lodges) for the hardy. The *turisthytter* are mountain huts many of which are only accessible on foot. They provide simple accommodation, usually in rooms for 4–6 persons.

For a stay of some length, it is more economic to take a room in a pension (guest-house). There are also a large number of motels in Norway. These usually provide rooms with limited self-catering or cabins with sitting room, kitchen and bedroom. In this category there are also the more simple types of accommodation, eg rooms without private bath/shower/toilet.

Self-catering cabins and apartments are generally of a high standard. They feature a fully equipped kitchen with refrigerator, a shower/toilet, electric heating (some even have a fireplace) and parking space. They all have down quilts and pillows, and linen is usually provided.

Youth Hostels

Norway boasts a large selection of youth hostels of all varieties. NUH (Organisation of Norwegian Youth Hostels) is affiliated with the International Youth Hostel Federation and the same rules apply. For instance, linen bags are mandatory. Most youth hostels have a guest kitchen and at the larger ones it is possible to buy meals. Many have a good standard of catering with many special offers. It is always necessary for groups to make reservations. Everybody is welcome, but members of the NUH in Norway or similar organisations in other countries have a preferential position. If you are not a member of your national organisation, international membership cards are available at most youth hostels. There is no upper or lower age limit. At many youth hostels it is possible for families to have a private room.

Camping and Caravanning

Norway is ideal camping country and there are numerous camp sites. It is advisable (but not essential at the moment) to carry an international camping carnet or the membership card of a

Hotel Price Range		
	Price for 1 night in kroner	
Type of hotel	Single	Double
Luxury	450–950	500–1200
Middle-grade	300–600	380– 800
Modest	120–300	250– 450

These prices are intended to act as a rough guide only. Many hotels offer cheaper weekend rates.

national camping organisation. Lists of camp sites are issued annually by the national tourist organisations, motoring organisation and camping clubs, giving the locations, size, facilities and category (1–3 stars) of the sites. In addition to the usual sanitary and cooking facilities, the larger sites normally have showers and shops selling provisions. On many sites there are also camping huts or chalets (simple wooden huts with sleeping accommodation). In areas of particular natural beauty, there are vacation villages with chalets and log cabins.

Campers who want to camp on their own (wild camping is prohibited in nature reserves and military areas) should always ask the owner's permission before camping on or near private property. In the sparsely populated northern areas, care should be taken to maintain an adequate supply of water.

Introduction to Rail Information

The Norges Statsbaner – NSB (Norwegian State Railways) runs an efficient railway system which is 4000km in length and passes through some of the most scenic areas of Scandinavia. *NSB* carries about 30,000,000 passengers yearly through 775 tunnels and 3000 bridges. The famous Nordland line which was completed in 1962 took 100 years to complete and now constitutes one of the country's most valuable communication services. There are three types of passenger train:

Ekspresstog – these fast trains run between the main cities

Hurtigtog – these are fast, long-distance trains which make intermediate stops

Persontog – these are slow, local trains

Major International Services

Connection	Duration	Frequency
Oslo–Copenhagen	9–10hrs	3 times daily
Oslo–Stockholm	6–8hrs	3 times daily

Map supplied by kind permission of Thomas Cook Ltd. The numbers along the lines refer to tables in the *Thomas Cook Continental Timetable*.

Major Internal Services

Connection	Duration	Frequency
Oslo–Stavanger	8–10hrs	3 times daily
Oslo–Larvik	2–3hrs	9 times daily
Oslo–Roros–Trondheim	8–9hrs	twice daily
Oslo–Dombas–Trondheim	6½–8hrs	3 times daily
Trondheim–Bodø	11–11½hrs	twice daily

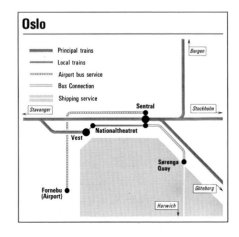

Scenic Routes

Most of the *NSB* lines are tourist attractions as well as being efficient transport and communication services. The Norwegian terrain with its mountains, lakes and barren, windswept plateaux provides a dramatic backdrop for large sections of the rail network. There are, in addition, a number of specific scenic routes:

Nordlandsbanen

The Nordland line between Trondheim and Bodø is one of the few railway tracks in the world to pass across the Arctic Circle. The route travels through rich agricultural districts, neat villages and deep forests.

Bergensbanen

The Bergen railway is described as the line which travels 'across the roof of Norway'. The journey runs from Oslo to Bergen through narrow valleys and across bare windswept heaths complete with glaciers and perpetual snow. From Ustaoset station for over 60 miles westward the line runs above the tree line.

Flåmsbana

The Flåm line passes through a steep, narrow and beautiful mountain valley and it is a masterpiece of engineering. The line is only about 20km long but the journey from Myrdal station down to Flåm station on the Aurland fjord takes about 45 minutes, such is the extremity of the descent.

Veteran Railways

1. **A/L Urskog–Hølandsbanen**
   PO Box 711 Sentrum, Oslo 1
   Tel: (2) 418359.
   Open mid-June to end of August.

2. **Krøderbanen**
   Norsk Jernbaneklubb, PO Box 1492 Vika, Oslo 1
   Open end of June to mid-September.

3. **Setesdalsbanen**
   Grovane, 4700 Vennesla
   Tel: (042) 56482.
   Open mid-June to end of August.

Internal Fare Structure

In Norway, you must purchase a ticket before entering a train unless the station is unmanned (if this is the case tickets will then be issued on the train). Tickets are valid for two months from the date of issue and up until midnight on the date of expiry; they can be used on any train travelling the relevant route unless otherwise stated. On some journeys it is obligatory to purchase seat reservations at a charge of 12Kr per seat (this is reduced to 5Kr for group travel).

Standard Rate Fares

Fares start at 8Kr for a distance up to 3km. For 4–6km the charge is 9Kr and thereafter an increase of 2–3Kr is made for every further 3km up to a distance of 300km. Between 300km and 600km distances the rate stands at 7–8Kr every additional 12km. And between 600km and 2000km distances the rate is 10–20Kr for every further 36km. As an example, a standard single ticket from Oslo–Stavanger costs 429Kr.

Child Reductions

Children under 4 travel free when accompanied by a ticket holder. Children between 4 and 16 travel at half the adult fare.

Student Reductions

Norwegian students are entitled to a 50% reduction on all tickets. Visiting students are advised to consult the International Section for information on the general reductions available.

Senior Citizen Reductions

Passengers aged 67 and over from all countries are entitled to a 50% reduction on all tickets.

Party/Group Savers

For distances of 100km or more, a group of 2–9 people travelling together are entitled to a 25% reduction. This applies on every day of the year and the group can be larger. For groups of 10 or more a 40% reduction is available subject to certain restrictions.

Tourist Reductions

Nordic Tourist Ticket

The Nordic Tourist Ticket is valid for 21 days and entitles the holder to unlimited rail travel throughout Denmark, Finland, Norway and Sweden. It also permits unlimited travel on certain ferry services including Helsingor–Helsingborg; Rodby Faerge–Puttgarden Mitte See; Goteborg–Frederikshavn; Stockholm–Turku; Kristiansand–Hirtshals; Gedser–Warnemunde; and the *NSB* bus section Trondheim–Storlein. Prices are: 2nd class £135 (adult), £101 (12–25) and £67 (4–11); 1st class £181 (adult), £136 (12–25) and £90.50 (4–11). Normal prices apply for seat, sleeper and couchette reservation.

Where to Buy Tickets

In Norway

Tickets are on sale in the major train stations and at the Norwegian State Railway Travel Bureaux.

In Great Britain

European Rail Travel Centre
PO Box 303
Victoria Station
London SW1V 1JY
Tel: (071) 834 2345

In USA

Tickets are available from *NS* railway representatives in the major cities (see International Section).

Facilities on Trains

Sleepers and Couchettes

Sleeping compartments can only be used by those with valid tickets for the journey and a special ticket for sleeping accommodation. Bookings can be made at any Norwegian State Railway Travel Bureau, but when available, bunks can be obtained at the station or on the train.

Luggage

Hand luggage should weigh no more than 25 kilos for adults and 12 kilos for children; it must be stored under or above the passenger's seat.

Bicycle Carriage

Bicycles can be taken on some trains (not express trains) for a charge of 25Kr. Bikes should be registered 20 minutes before departure (30 minutes at Oslo) and you load and unload the bicycle yourself.

Facilities at Stations

Food

Bar and restaurant facilities are open during normal working hours at all the major stations.

Luggage

The left luggage lockers are open during normal working hours.

Tourist Information

Travellers will find that the train information bureaux in major cities have a good supply of maps. Information about accommodation can be found at Oslo Central station from Monday to Saturday 8.30am–11am and 6pm–11pm.

Portugal

The old bridge over the River Lima at Ponte de Barca

Introduction

Portugal is one of the oldest countries in Europe with frontiers that were established in 1297. It is also one of the few countries in Western Europe that has avoided the advent of mass tourism, and many of its interesting historical sites, and its scenic attractions are relatively undiscovered. The only area in which large numbers of tourists gather is in the Algarve, but even there careful planning has ensured that the over-development that characterises the Mediterranean resorts of Spain has not occurred.

The Portuguese mainland occupies one sixth of the Iberian Peninsula and is on the outermost edge of the European continent. The country can roughly be divided into two halves. The northern half, beginning with the Serra da Estrêla which is the highest range of mountains in Portugal (1991m), tends to be more mountainous. The south is characterised by gently undulating lowlands and broad river basins, and has only one mountain range of over 1000m. The country's two most attractive regions are the border region with Spain in the extreme north which houses the ruggedly beautiful Peneda-Gerês National Park, and the Algarve in the extreme south with its spectacular cliffs and sandy beaches. The two Atlantic archipelagos of Madeira and the Azores are also noted for their fine beaches and scenic beauty.

Portugal's long coastline provides the country with a maritime climate resulting in mild winters and quite hot summers. The temperatures in the Atlantic coastal regions are moderated by the prevailing north-westerly winds. The southern Mediterranean coastline enjoys slightly higher temperatures in both summer and winter; further inland, continental influences produce a greater range of variation between summer and winter temperatures.

One notable feature of Portugal's 9.8 million population is its uneven distribution. 35% is concentrated in the urban areas around Lisbon and Oporto, while in some southern border regions there are as few as 19 people per sq km. This uneven distribution has recently been fuelled by the steady drift from rural to industrial areas.

In Portugal, emigration is more prevalent than immigration, although in the 1970s a considerable influx from the newly independent colonies occurred. The Portuguese are a quiet, warmhearted and home-loving people, living in a country that is still not attuned to the hectic pace of modern life.

Since the bloodless revolution of 1974, and the new constitution that resulted in 1976, Portugal has been aiming towards socialism and a classless society in stark contrast to the authoritarian dictatorship of previous years. Although still a long way from achieving these ambitious goals, the revision of the constitution in 1982, which abolished the Military Council of Revolution and joined a Constitutional Tribunal of civilian judges, was a positive move and served to strengthen civilian parliamentary rule. The President is the Portuguese Head of State, and the governing of the country is carried out by the 254-member Assembly of the Republic and the leader of the majority party, who is appointed by the President as the Head of Government.

Cabo Espichel

The Portuguese economy is still predominantly agricultural, despite the emergence of a number of rapidly developing industries around Oporto, Lisbon, Sines and in the Minho region. Farming is largely carried out in small holdings, and there is insufficient mechanisation. The principal crop is wheat, but the most lucrative are wine and cork. From its large areas of forest, Portugal satisfies half the world demand for cork. Its wines, particularly its famous port, are produced in the fertile lower Douro valley and are being exported in increasing quantities. The traditional industries in Portugal concentrate on processing the country's agricultural yield, the largest being cork production, food and fish canning, and the textile industry. More recently, the manufacturing of chemicals and electrical machinery has begun to contribute towards the economy.

Folk-dancers, Ribatejo

The offshore island of Madeira has been an established tourist centre since the 19th century, and it is still one of the most popular destinations for Portugal's foreign visitors. Expansion of the tourist trade has been cautious, but, ever since the set-backs caused by the political troubles of the 1970's, tourism has played an increasingly important part in the country's economy.

It is not until the 13th century that we can see Portuguese cultural development as separate from the rest of the Iberian peninsula. In the late 13th century King Kiniz founded a university at Coimbra. It is the third oldest university in Europe. Although the Portuguese looked to central Europe, particularly France and Italy, for inspiration, (and this can be seen in the magnificent cathedrals), they also developed a unique national style as witnessed by the religious architecture of the late Gothic and Renaissance periods. The Hieronymite Convent at Belém is a fine example of this style. Portuguese art and literature enjoyed productive eras, but few painters or writers of international standing ever emerged. The country's contribution to classical music centres on the operas written in the 18th century. The folk dancing and songs of

Portugal are particularly fine and are still frequently played. A song unique to Portugal is the 'fado', a melancholy song usually in a minor key, sung by a solo male or female voice and accompanied by two guitars. The most celebrated *fadistas* of the 19th century were José Dias (1824–96) and the legendary Maria Severa (around 1840).

History

1197–179 BC	Incorporated into the Roman province of Hispania Ulterior
61–45 BC	Caesar finally subdues Hispania Ulterior after series of revolts
from AD 200	Christianisation
711	Occupation of the Moors, and resulting Reconquista
1095	Alfonso VI of León and Castile establishes the county of 'Portucalia'
1179	Pope Alexander III recognises Portugal as a kingdom
1256	Lisbon becomes capital, displacing Suimarães
1297	Frontier between Portugal and Castile is definitively established
from 1385	Beginnings of voyages of discovery and colonial expansion
1488	Bartolomeu Dias rounds the southern tip of Africa, the Cape of Good Hope
1498	Vasco da Gama discovers sea route to India
1580	Portugal occupied by Spain and ruled by Viceroys
1640	Independence of Portugal restored by revolt led by Duke of Bragança
1755	Lisbon earthquake in which more than 30,000 people were killed
1807	Portugal invaded by Napoleon
1808–10	War of National Liberation against the French. Napoleon beaten with British aid
1910	Revolution after 100 years of civil unrest. Republic established
1916	Portugal enters the First World War on the side of the Allies
1928	Military dictatorship established under General Carmona
1933	New constitution
1939–45	Portugal remains neutral during Second World War
1961	Annexation by India of the Portuguese colony of Goa
1974	Dictatorship overthrown in 'Carnation Revolution' by the Armed Forces
1976	New socialist constitution establishes a democratic Parliamentary Republic
1982	Revision of the constitution
1983	Coalition government formed by Dr Mário Soares
1984	Increased urban terrorism
1986	Portugal joins EEC. Presidential election results in victory for Dr Mario Soares, the Socialist leader

Rulers of Portugal

House of Burgundy

Henrique (Henry of Burgundy) Count of Portucalia	1093–1112
After Henry's death his widow Teresa acts as Regent during the minority of her son Afonso	
Afonso Henriques, the Conqueror King of Portugal	1139–85
Sancho I, the Populator	1185–1211
Afonso II, the Fat	1211–23
Sancho II (deposed 1245, d. 1248)	1223–45
Afonso III, the Restorer (brother of Sancho II)	1245–79
Dinis I, the Farmer	1279–1325
Afonso IV, the Brave	1325–57
Pedro I, the Just, or the Cruel	1357–67
Fernando	1367–83

House of Avis

João I, Defender of the Kingdom (illegitimate son of Pedro I; Grand Master of the Order of Avis) Regent	1383–85
King of Portugal	1385–1433
Duarte His brothers are Pedro (Duke of Coimbra), Henrique (Henry the Navigator), Fernão (d. in Moorish captivity) and João (Grand Master of the Order of Santiago)	1433–38
Afonso V, the African	1438–81
João II, the Perfect Prince	1481–95
Manuel I, the Fortunate	1495–1521
João III, the Pious	1521–57
Sebastião (grandson of João III)	1557–78
Henrique (brother of João III; Cardinal Archbishop of Lisbon)	1578–80

Spanish Kings of the House of Habsburg

Filipe I (Philip II of Spain) King of Portugal	1580–98
Filipe II (Philip III of Spain)	1598–1621
Filipe III (Philip IV of Spain)	1621–40

House of Bragança

João IV (Duke of Bragança) King of Portugal	1640–56
Afonso VI	1656–67
Pedro II (brother of Afonso VI)	Regent 1667–83 King 1683–1706
João V, the Magnanimous	1706–50
José	1750–77
Maria I (wife of Pedro III, who d. 1786)	1777–92
João VI	Prince Regent 1792–1816 King 1816–26
Pedro IV (Emperor Pedro I of Brazil)	1826–28
Miguel (brother of Pedro IV)	1828–34
Maria II (daughter of Pedro IV; m. Duke Ferdinand of Saxe-Coburg-Koháry 1836)	1834–53
Duke Ferdinand rules as Regent during the minority of his son Pedro	1853–55
Pedro V	1855–61
Luis	1861–89
Carlos (assassinated in Lisbon in 1908 together with his heir Luis Filipe)	1889–1908
Manuel II (second son of Carlos I; leaves Portugal 1910, d. in exile 1932)	1908–10

Oporto

Major Centres

Lisbon

Direccão-Geral do Turismo
(Information Bureau)
Palácio Foz
Praça dos Restauradores
Tel: (1) 36 36 53

Comissão Municipal de Turismo
(Municipal Tourist Board)
Rua das Portas de Santo Antão 141
Tel: (1) 36 66 24/36 96 43

Embassies:
UK: Rua São Domingos à Lapa 35-37
Tel: 166 11 91
USA: Avenida das Forcas Armadas
Tel: (1) 726 6600/726 6659

Situated on the north bank of the Tagus, Lisbon ranks among the most beautiful cities in the world. It is the country's principal port and also a city graced by many magnificent buildings and fascinating museums. The city comprises an Old Town, the Lower Town, built after the 1755 earthquake, and the impressively laid out New Town. The aspect of the city has been marred to a certain extent by the influx of large numbers of often destitute refugees from Portugal's former colonies, whose makeshift housing is sadly out of keeping with the rest of the town.

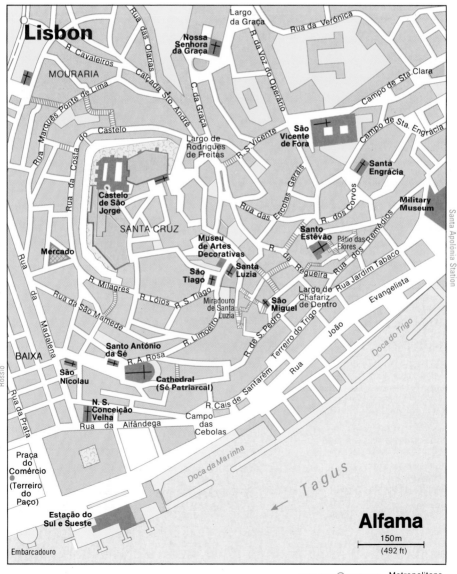

Lisbon

Alfama

150m
(492 ft)

Metropolitana

Lisbon: view from the Castle over the Old Town

Sightseeing

Alfama – the picturesque old town.
Avenida da Liberade – Lisbon's principal traffic artery
Castelo de São Jorge – medieval castle converted from an earlier Moorish fortress
Cathedral – the oldest church in Lisbon dating from 1344
Convento de los Jerónimos de Belém – the world-famous Hieronymite convent, symbol of the power and wealth of Portugal's great colonial age
Monument of the Discoveries – erected in Belém to celebrate the 500th anniversary of the death of Henry the Navigator
Praça do Comércio – a square surrounded by arcades and various public buildings
Rua de São Pedro de Alcântara contains a terrace with superb views of the city and the Tagus
Teatro de São Carlos – Lisbon's famous opera house built in 1792
Tower of Belém – built 1512–21 to protect the harbour of Restelo at the entrance to the Tagus

Museums and galleries

American Library
(Biblioteca Americana),
Avenida do Duque de Loulé 39.

Aquarium
(Aquário de Vasco da Gama),
Dafundo.

Archaeological Museum of the Carmo
(Museu Arqueológico do Carmo),
Largo do Carmo.

A collection of pottery and coins of the prehistoric and historical period, housed in the Gothic church of a Carmelite convent.

Army Library
(Biblioteca da Armada),
Calçade do Combro.
In the headquarters of the Guarda Nacional Republicana.

Azulejo Museum
(Museu do Azulejo),
Rua da Madre de Deus 4B
(church of Madre de Deus).
A valuable collection of azulejos of the 16th–18th centuries.

Biblioteca da Ajuda
Palácio da Ajuda,
Calçada da Ajuda.

Biblioteca Popular de Lisboa
Rua da Academia das Ciências 19.

Botanical Museum
(Museu Botânico),
Rua da Escola Politécnica.

Bullfighting Museum
(Museu Tauromáquico),
Praça de Touros do Campo Pequeno, Gate 20.

Carmo Museum
See Archaeological Museum of the Carmo.

Cathedral Treasury Museum
(Museu do Tesouro da Sé Patriarcal),
Praça de Sé.
Vestments, gold and silver.

Coach Museum
(Museu Nacional dos Coches),
Praça de Afonso de Albuquerque, Belém.

One of the world's largest collections of state coaches and carriages.

Customs Museum
(Museu da Direcção-Geral das Alfândegas),
Ministry of Finance,
Rua da Alfândega.

Fire Brigade Museum
(Museu do Bombeiro),
Avenida de Dom Carlos I.

Folk Art Museum
(Museu de Arte Popular),
Avenida de Brasilia, Belém.
Portuguese arts and crafts, porcelain, silver, pottery, blankets, etc.

Gulbenkian Museum
(Museu da Fundação Calouste Gulbenkian),
Avenida de Berna 45.
Pictures, porcelain, sculpture.

Gulbenkian Planetarium
(Planetarium Calouste Gulbenkian),
Praça do Império, Belém.

Historical Archives of the Ministry of Public Works
(Arquivos Históricos do Ministério das Obras Públicas),
Praça do Comércio.

Library of the Academy of Sciences
(Biblioteca da Academia das Cliências de Lisboa),
Rua da Academia das Ciências 19.

Library of the Government Printing Office
(Biblioteca da Imprensa Nacional),
Rua da Escola Politécnica.

Library of the Gulbenkian Foundation
(Biblioteca da Fundação Calouste Gulbenkian),
Avenida de Berna 56.

Military Archives
(Arquivos Históricos Militares),
Rua do Paraiso 8.

Military Museum
(Museu Militar),
Largo dos Caminhos de Ferro, Santa Apolónia.
Arms and armour from the 9th to the 20th century.

Mineralogical Museum
(Museu de Mineralogia),
Rua da Escola' Politéchnica.

Municipal Archives
(Arquivos Históricos de Cidade),
Praça do Municipio.

Municipal Library
(Biblioteca Municipal Central),
Palácio Galveias,
Largo do Dr Alonso Pena.

Municipal Museum
(Museu da Cidade),
Palácio da Mitra,
Rua do Açúcar 64.
Material illustrating the history of Lisbon.

Museu Antoniano
Praça de Santo António da Sé.
A museum devoted to St Antony of Padua (a native of Lisbon).

Museum of Decorative Art
(Museu de Artes Decorativas),
Largo das Portas do Sol, Alfama.
Portuguese art of the 17th and 18th century, furniture, porcelain, silver, tapestries.

Museum of the School of Decorative Art
(Museu-Escola de Arte Decorativa da Fundação Ricardo Espirito˙Santo),
Rua de São Tormé 90.

Museum of Religious Art
(Museu de Arte Sacra de São Roque),
Praça de Trindade Coelho.

National Archives
(Arquivos Nacionais da Torre do Tombo),
Palácio da Assembleia Nacional,
Largo de São Bento.

National Library
(Biblioteca Nacional),
Campo Grande 83.

National Museum of Archaeology and Ethnology
(Museu Nacional de Arqueolõgia e Etnologia),
Praça do Império, Belém.

National Museum of Art
(Museu Nacional de Arte Antiga),
Rua das Janelas Verdes 9.
Painting, sculpture, ceramics, goldsmith's work, furniture, etc.

National Museum of Contemporary Art
(Museu Nacional de Arte Contedmporânea),
Rua Serpa Pinto 6.

Naval Museum
(Museu da Marinha),
Praça do Império, Belém.
Ship models, uniforms.

Numismatic Museum
(Museu Numismático Português),
Avenida do Dr António José de Almeida.

Overseas Agriculture, Museum of
(Museu e Jardim Agricola do Antigo Ultramar Português),
Calçada do Galvão 1, Belém.
Agriculture, forestry and fishing in the former overseas territories.

Overseas Archives
(Arquivos Históricos do Antigo Ultramar Português),
Calçada da Boa Hora 30.

Overseas Ethnography, Museum of
(Museu Etnográfico do Antigo Ultramar Português),
Rua das Portas de Santo Antão 100.
History and art of the peoples of the former overseas territories.

Pinheiro Museum
(Museu Rafael Bordalo Pinheiro),
Campo Grande 382.
Ceramics; drawings and caricatures.

Postal Museum
(Museu dos CTT),
Rua de Dona Estefânia 173-175.
History and development of the postal and telegraph systems.

São Roque Museum
See Museum of Religious Art.

Teatro Nacional de São Carlos,
Largo de Sáo Carlos 21.
Archives, library and museum.
Seen by appointment.

Zoo
(Jardim Zoológico),
Parque das Laranjeiras,
Estrada de Benfica.

South front of Convento de los Jerónimos, Lisbon

The Algarve

Comissão Regional de Turismo do Algarve
Rua Ataide de Oliveira 100
P-8000 Faro
Tel: 2 40 67

Separated from the rest of Portugal by a range of hills in the north, the Algarve is one of the few provinces in Portugal to show marked evidence of Moorish influence. Thanks to its equable climate, distinctive scenery and fine sandy beaches, the Algarve has become the most popular destination for visitors to Portugal.

Tower of Belém

Albufeira: general view

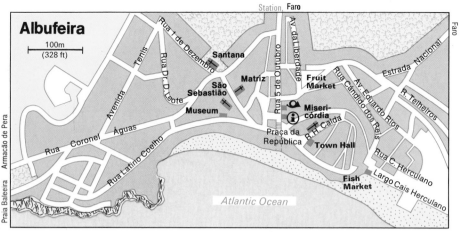

Albufeira

Turismo
Avenida do 5 de Outuburo
Tel: 5 54 28

A beautifully located fishing village that still retains some of its Moorish character. Albufeira has a fine sheltered beach and is now one of the busiest resorts on the Algarve.

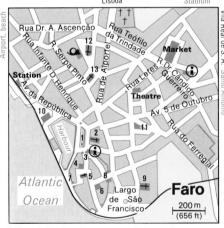

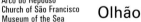

1 Praça de Dom Francisco
   Gomes
2 Church of Miseriocórdia
3 Arco da Vila
4 Town Hall
5 Cathedral
6 Archaeological Museum
7 Arco da Porta Nova

8 Arco do Repouso
9 Church of São Francisco
10 Museum of the Sea
11 Museum of Ethnography
12 Church of Carmo
13 Church of São Pedro

Faro

Turismo
Rua do General Humberto Delgado 20
Tel: (89) 2 40 67

Rua da Misericórdia 8-12
Tel: (89) 2 54 04

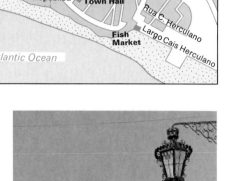

Faro Cathedral

A busy industrial town and port, Faro is the chief town of its district. It contains a Gothic cathedral and several interesting museums. It also has an airport which makes it the focal point of the Algarve's tourist trade. There are good bathing facilities on the offshore island of Praia da Faro.

Olhão

Turismo Faro
Rua da Misericórdia 8-9
P-8000 Faro
Tel: 2 54 04

A picturesque little fishing town with a distinctively Moorish air. The inhabitants are proverbially known in Portugal for their cunning. There is a good bathing beach on the offshore island of Armona.

Rooftop view of the white houses of Olhão

Praia da Rocha

Turismo
Edificio da Santa Catarina
Avenida Marginal
Tel: 2 22 90

One of the foremost resorts in the Algarve with beautiful sandy beaches and all the most modern facilities. It has a particularly mild climate.

Hotel Dom Pedro, Vilamoura

Sagres

Turismo
Municipio
Tel: 6 41 25

Situated on a windswept rocky plateau on the extreme south-west corner of Portugal, Sagres is ideal for those who prefer a harsher climate

and is popular with scuba divers and fishermen. On the Ponta de Sagres are the ruins of the School of Seamanship founded by Henry the Navigator in 1421.

Silves

Turismo Portimão
Largo do 1 de Dezembro
P-8500 Portimão
Tel: (82) 2 36 95

A little country town surrounded by forests of cork-oak, Silves boasts a mighty Moorish castle and a 13th century cathedral. In its day Silves rivalled Granada in splendour and influence.

Tavira

Turismo
in Town Hall
Tel: (81) 2 25 11

Tavira is a small seaside town that was once flatteringly known as the 'Venice of the Algarve' because of its canals. It dates from the latter part of the 18th century when it was almost completely rebuilt following the 1755 earthquake. In the upper part of the town, there are the ruins of an old Moorish castle. There are 37 churches in Tavira.

Tavira – a view from the Ribeira da Asseca

Accommodation

Hotels

In the large towns and resorts the hotels in the higher categories are fully up to international standards of comfort. Off the main tourist routes, however, the standard is often lower than in some other European countries.

There are numerous guest-houses (*pensões*, singular *pensão*), which replace hotels in smaller areas; they are often very similar to hotels.

Albergarias and hotels described as *residencias* have no restaurants. The simplest form of accommodation is provided by *casas de hospedes*.

The *pousadas* are state-owned hotels, mostly in the country, which are excellently equipped and managed; their

Palace Hotel, Bucaco Forest

prices compare favourably with those charged in privately run hotels of similar category. Similar to *pousadas* are the numerous privately run *estalagens* (singular *estalagem*), which are also found in towns.

Hotel Price Range	
Type of hotel	Price for 1 night in escudos Double room
*****	12,500–21,500
****	8,000–15,500
***	5,500–11,500
**	4,000– 8,500
*	2,500– 4,500

These prices are intended to act as a rough guide only. In winter (Nov–Feb) prices are normally reduced by 60%. Prices for a single room are approximately 30% less.

Hotels and pensions are classified in categories designated by stars (from 1 to 5). *Pousadas* are indicated by a special symbol and are not classified in the normal categories.

Tariffs vary within each category according to the area and the situation of the hotel.

It is usual to take meals in your hotel. Hotels are required to keep a complaints book. Prices include breakfast and the rooms generally have a private bathroom.

Youth Hostels

Youth hostels (*pousadas de juventude*) offer accommodation at reasonable prices, suitable particularly for young people (though there is no upper age limit for youth hostellers in Portugal). They are relatively few in number, and advance booking is therefore advisable, particularly in July and August. Parties of more than 5 must book through the head office.

Information:
Associação Portuguesa de Pousadas de Juventude
Rua Andrade Corvo 46,
P-1000 Lisboa 1
Tel: (1) 57 10 54.

Camping and Caravanning

There are at present some 70 camp sites (*parques de campismo*) in Portugal, mostly on the coast. Many sites require the production of a camping carnet.

Information:
Federação Portuguesa de Campismo e Caravanismo
Rua da Voz do Operario 1,
P-1000 Lisboa 2
Tel: (1) 85 23 50.

Introduction to Rail Information

Some railway express services, especially between Lisbon and Oporto, are of a high standard but, for the most

Map supplied by kind permission of Thomas Cook Ltd. The numbers along the lines refer to tables in the *Thomas Cook Continental Timetable*.

part, the service is fairly basic. As in Spain, the main lines are broad-gauge (1674mm compared with the normal European gauge of 1435mm). The trains of the *Companhia dos Caminhos de Ferro Portugueses (CP)* are divided into several classes:

Super-Express and *Express* trains – these run between Lisbon and Oporto.

Rápido trains – these ply between Lisbon and Algarve stations.

Directo and *Semi-directo* – these trains run between Lisbon and other large towns in Portugal.

Major International Services

Connection	Duration	Frequency
Lisbon–Madrid	11–12hrs	twice daily
Lisbon–Paris	28hrs	twice daily

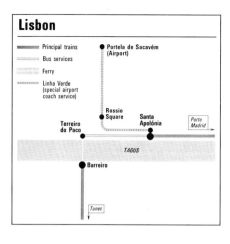

Lisbon

- ▬▬▬ Principal trains
- ═══ Bus services
- ░░░ Ferry
- ════ Linha Verde (special airport coach service)

● Portela de Sacavém (Airport)

● Rossio Square

● Santa Apolónia

Terreiro do Paço

● Porto Madrid →

TAGUS

● Barreiro

Tunes

Major Internal Services

Connection	Duration	Frequency
Lisbon–Oporto	3–4hrs	5 times daily
Lisbon, Terreiro de Paço, Algarve	5–7hrs	once daily
Lisbon–Aveiro	6–7hrs	4/5 times daily
Lisbon–Coimbra	2–3hrs	9 times daily

Scenic Routes

There are two routes of particular value scenically. The first runs from Erme-zinde to Barca d'Alva and the second runs from Vila Nova de Gaia to Porto.

Steam enthusiasts find Portugal of great interest, particularly in the north, where there is a system of narrow-gauge feeder lines and branches ex-tending northward from the Oporto to Barca d'Alva broad gauge line. These metre-gauge trains are worked by immaculately maintained steam locomotives.

Veteran Railways

Portuguese Railways run old-time steam trains on three sections of line.

1. **Historic Railway** (with a German steam locomotive of 1905. German and Belgian sa-loon cars, Portuguese passenger coaches and a French luggage van) runs on the **Tàmega line** between Livração and Arco de Baúlhe.

2. **19th Century Train** (with a British steam locomotive of 1875, Portuguese and French saloon cars, French and Swiss passenger coaches and a French luggage van) runs on the **Minho line** between Valença do Minho and Oporto.

3. Third steam train line still in use runs from Braga to Valença.

Railway Museums

There are 10 museums belonging to Portuguese Railways (*CP*) and these are located in the follow-ing places: Valença, Braga, Santarem, Estremoz, Arco de Baúlhe, Lousada, Chaves, Macinhata do Vouga, Braganca and Faro. Arrangements for visiting these museums must be made one month in advance through *CP*.

Internal Fare Structure

Standard Rate Fares

The fares are calculated on a kilometric basis. At the top end of the scale, the fare from Lisbon to Braganca costs 2080esc (1st class single) and 1395esc (2nd class single). At the bottom end of the scale, the short run from Lisbon to Santarem costs 415esc (1st class sing-le) and 280esc (2nd class single). As a rule fares are inexpensive.

Child Reductions

Children under 4 free; 4 to 12 half fare.

Senior Citizen Reductions

Senior Citizens, on production of their passports, can obtain a *cartão dourado* (gold ticket) which entitles them to a reduction of 50% of the fare for journeys over 100km.

Railrover Passes

Kilometric tickets allow travel for a tot-al distance of 3000km and they are valid for 3 months. Railrover tickets cost the equivalent of £30 per week (supplement payable for rápidos).

Where to buy tickets

In Portugal

The main stations in Lisbon (Rossio, Santa Apolonia, Terreiro do Paco, and Cais do Sodre) and in Oporto (São Bento, Campantia) are open during the day for the sale of tickets. Otherwise ticket offices at the railway stations throughout the country open one hour before the time scheduled for the departure of a train and close five minutes before the train leaves.

In Great Britain

Portuguese Railways do not have an office in Britain. However, information and tickets may be obtained from leading travel agents and:

European Rail Travel Centre
PO Box 303
Victoria
London SW1V 1JY
Tel: (071) 834 2345

Tickets and reservations for the Sud-Express from Paris to Lisbon may be made through:
French Railways Ltd
179 Piccadilly
London W1V 0BA
Tel: (071) 409 1224

In USA

Tickets may be obtained from *CP* representatives in the major cities (see International Section).

Facilities on Trains

The express trains are well equipped with couchettes, restaurant/bar facilities and other modern comforts. The regional trains are generally crowded, uncomfortable and unlikely to have even mini-bar facilities.

Bicycle Carriage

Bikes can be taken as accompanied luggage on trains. The bike should be taken to the luggage office for registration and payment of a moderate flat rate.

Food

The major stations have bar and buffet facilities which are open from early morning until late at night.

Reservations

Reservations are optional on inland trains but reasonably priced. For international and express trains, reservations are free of charge providing they are made the day before departure. In general, trains are crowded so it is best to reserve seats in advance.

Tourist Information

Tourist information is provided by the government-run *Postos do Turismo*. They have stalls at the major stations.

Facilities at Stations

The major Portuguese stations are equipped with reservation facilities, luggage stores, restaurants and bureaux de change.

Fishing off the Portuguese coast

Spain

Casa de las Veletas, Cáceres

Introduction

Spain, with its fabulous beaches on the Mediterranean coast, is a mecca for tourists. But the country has much more to offer the foreign visitor than golden sands and warm seas. Inland, with the rugged mountainous countryside offering a spectacular back-drop, there are many splendid churches and castles. These include Spain's most famous buildings like the Alhambra in Granada, and the mosque of Cordoba.

The Spanish mainland has an area of 492,500sq km, and makes up four-fifths of the Iberian peninsula. The Balearic Islands off the east coast and the Canary Islands 100km south-west of Cadiz, are also Spanish. The peninsula as a whole is mountainous and arid in character, the most important topographical feature being the Meseta, a vast central plateau of between 600 and 1000m. Surrounding the Meseta are a series of mountains, all considerably higher than the plateau itself; this central area is barren, and apart from the capital Madrid, sparsely populated. The most concentrated areas of population are in Catalonia, and in the Erbro basin which lies between the Pyrénées in the north and the Meseta in the south west. The total population of Spain is 38.2 million.

As the Meseta is enclosed by mountains, the central uplands have a continental climate with hot summers and cold winters. The temperature variations in this area are considerable. The Mediterranean coastline enjoys the best climate with hot summers and very mild winters. At Malaga on the Costa del Sol, approximately 195 days of every year are cloudless.

A country famed for its festivals, Spaniards will be celebrating something whenever and wherever you visit Spain. Most often celebrated with colourful processions and bullfights, one of the most famous is the St Fermin Festival which takes place in July in Pamplona. Here the *encierros* (running of the bulls) takes place, enticing the young men of the town to perform death-defying feats as they evade the anger of the bulls. These festivals are also an excellent opportunity to see flamenco dancing and to sample the delicious food and wine that is a central part of Spanish life.

On 22nd November 1975, General Franco was succeeded as Head of State by King Juan Carlos I, and Spain once again became a kingdom. In June 1977 free elections were held for the first time in 41 years. And in July 1978 a new constitution was approved and then endorsed by a national referendum. It provided for a parliamentary monarchy, with a two-chamber parliament consisting of a Congress and a Senate. The 50 provinces are governed by a provincial assembly and a civil governor appointed by the Minister of the Interior.

After suffering considerably during the Spanish Civil War, the Spanish economy has enjoyed a significant upturn in the last 20 years, even if the methods of Franco's right wing government were socially unpopular. Its main exports are machinery and vehicles, chemical and petrochemical products and agricultural products such as oranges, lemons, olives, olive oil and wine. Tourism makes a major contribution to the economy and the foreign currency helps to alleviate Spain's large balance of payments deficit.

Court of Myrtles, Alhambra, Granada

Spanish architecture has always been subject to influences from abroad, the most important being Moorish. Two magnificent buildings that bear witness to this influence are the Mezquita Mosque (785–999), the principal mosque of the western Muslim world, and the Alhambra, built in the 14th century and towering over Granada on a rocky crag. The characteristics of Moorish secular architecture are their unimpressive exteriors and contrasting interiors of magical beauty. With the steady advance of the Reconquista, Moorish styles were gradually replaced by the styles being practised in central Europe. French influences, particularly in Gothic cathedrals, are prominent in the 13th, 14th and 15th centuries, and can be seen at Burgos (1221), Toledo (1227), León (1250) and particularly at Seville (begun 1402).

The mixture of Moorish and Gothic architectures developed into the Plateresque style, which is characterised by intricate detail on the façades of buildings. The cathedrals of Salamanca (1513) and Segovia (1525) are fine examples. The Renaissance affected architecture in Spain, but never to the extent it did in other parts of Europe, and much of the work in this period still betrays a hybrid of different styles. Perhaps the best example is the cloister at Santiago de Compostella (1521–86), the largest of its kind in Spain. The summer palace built for Charles V at Alhambra is one of the few buildings in Spain that can be said to be of purely Renaissance inspiration.

Coinciding with the decline of the Spanish empire by the beginning of the 17th century, architectural achievements in Spain notably decreased. However, fine examples of neoclassical buildings are in evidence. The Royal Palace in Madrid, designed by the Italian, Francisco Sabatini, and the Prado (1785–1819) (also in Madrid) built by Juan de Villaneuva are two examples. Contemporary architecture has been in great demand with the building of resorts at the onset of mass tourism in Spain, but for the most part, the constructions have been of poor quality and often represent an assault on the natural beauty of the landscape.

Spanish painting, particularly of the Baroque period, rates as one of the supreme achievements of European art. El Greco (1548–1614) painted intense religious pictures, while Diego Velázquez (1599–1660) depicted, in a very unflattering style, the life of the Spanish court. Francisco Goya (1746–1828) broke with the stagnation of the 18th century and produced a series of works of great emotional effect, particularly his series of etchings on the disasters of war. Modern art in Spain, and indeed in Europe as a whole, has been dominated by the work of Pablo Picasso (1881–1973). He is one of the most important artists of the 20th century and was instrumental with the Frenchman Georges Braque in creating Cubism. His most important picture, and one which shows his profound concern for human values, is 'Guernica' which shows the destruction of a little town during the Spanish Civil War. Other Spanish 20th-century artists of note are Juan Gris, another exponent of Cubism, and Joan Miró and Salvador Dali, both Surrealist painters of contrasting styles.

From the works of Seneca the Elder (54 BC–AD 39) which were written on Spanish soil through to the epic poems of the 12th century, early Spanish literature has been of lasting importance. However, the golden age really began with Cervantes (1547–1616), who wrote *Don Quixote* and de Vega (1562–1635) who founded the Spanish national theatre and was one of the world's most prolific playwrights. There was a sharp decline in literary achievement in the 17th century, but the 19th century saw the figures of Unamuno (1864–1936) and later Lorca (1898–1936) whose poems, novels and plays are of the greatest importance to European literary development.

Roman Theatre, Mérida

History

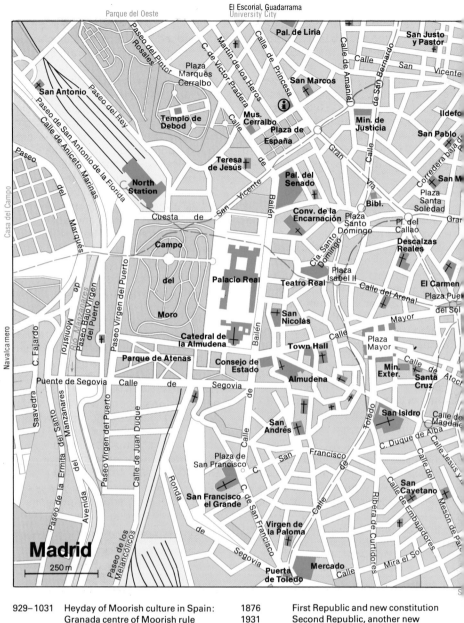

Madrid

250 m

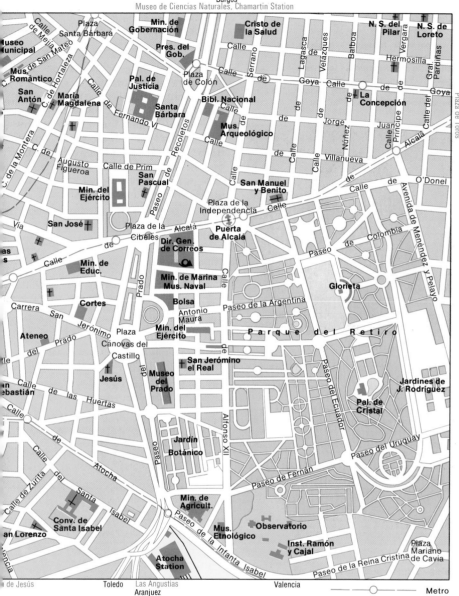

Burgos
Museo de Ciencias Naturales, Chamartin Station

1981	An attempted military coup is foiled after Deputies of the Lower House and the cabinet were held hostage for 18 hours
1983	General election produces a socialist majority
1986	Spain joins EEC. In a referundum, Spain votes to stay in NATO

Embassies:
UK: Calle de Fernando el Santo 16
Tel: (1) 4 19 02 00
USA: Serrano 75
Tel: (1) 276 34 00

Set in the heart of the Iberian peninsula, the Spanish capital covers an area of 531sq km and has a population of over 3½ million. It became the capital as a result of royal patronage, rather than because of the advantages of its position, and is now Spain's second largest industrial centre after Barcelona. When Philip II's court moved there from Toledo in 1861, Madrid became the scene of the flowering of Spanish literature and art, and the many museums and famous buildings bear witness to this development.

Major Centres

Madrid

Oficina de Información de Turismo
Estación de Charmatin (in station concourse)
Tel: (1) 33 10 20

Oficina Municipal de Información
Plaza Mayor 3
Tel: (1) 66 48 74/(1) 66 54 77

Sightseeing

Archaeological Museum – contains prehistoric material and works of art

Ermita de San Antonio de la Florida – a chapel built in 1792 with ceiling paintings by Goya

National Library – founded by Philip V in 1711 and one of the great libraries of Europe

View of the Plaza de Cibeles, Madrid

Plaza de la Cibeles – contains an 18th-century marble fountain

Plaza Mayor – contains equestrian statue of Philip III, cast 1613

Prado Museum – built between 1785 and 1819 and housing one of the most comprehensive art collections in the world

Puerta de Alcalá – a massive triumphal arch erected 1778

Royal Palace and Armeria – built for Philip V between 1738 and 1764 and includes a world famous collection of weapons

Barcelona

Oficina de Información de Turismo
Gran Via
Tel: (3) 01 74 43

Barcelona Cathedral

Oficina Municipal de Turismo
Avenida Puerta de Angel 8
Tel: (3) 18 19 90

One of the largest ports on the Mediterranean, Barcelona is Spain's second city and its largest commercial and industrial centre. Situated in the fertile area round the mouth of the River Llobregat which flows down from the Pyrénées, it has a population of 2 million. Just to the north is the very popular Costa Brava, one of the great centres of mass tourism.

Sightseeing

Barrio Gótico (Gothic Quarter) – the most important surviving part of the medieval town

Casa de la Diputación – formerly the seat of the parliament of Catalonia, now the headquarters of the provincial administration

Cathedral – begun 1298 and completed 1448. The famous front and dome tower were added in 1898 and 1913 respectively

Montjuich – a hill above the city, overlooking the sea, on top of which stands a castle and the Military Museum

Museum of Catalan Art – contains an outstanding collection of Spanish art from the 11th to the 18th centuries

Palacio de la Virreina – the former palace of the Vicereine of Peru, now housing the Museum of Decorative Arts

Picasso Museum – opened 1963, containing probably the best collection of his paintings anywhere in the world

Pueblo Español – the Spanish village, built for the 1929 International Exhibition

Templo de la Sagrada Familia – a monumental Neo-Catalan church built by Gaudi (begun 1882)

The Ramblas Columbus Movement – a succession of tree-lined avenues leading to the 60m-high statue of Christopher Columbus

Andalusia

Andalusia offers a panorama of all the different scenery of the Iberian peninsula, with snow-covered mountains, sun-baked rugged uplands, lush green huertas and the famous beaches of the Costa del Sol. It was also once the centre of the Moorish occupation and the people have preserved something of their Moorish past in race, language and culture.

Córdoba

Oficina de Información de Turismo
Avenida del Gran Capitán 13
Tel: (57) 22 12 05

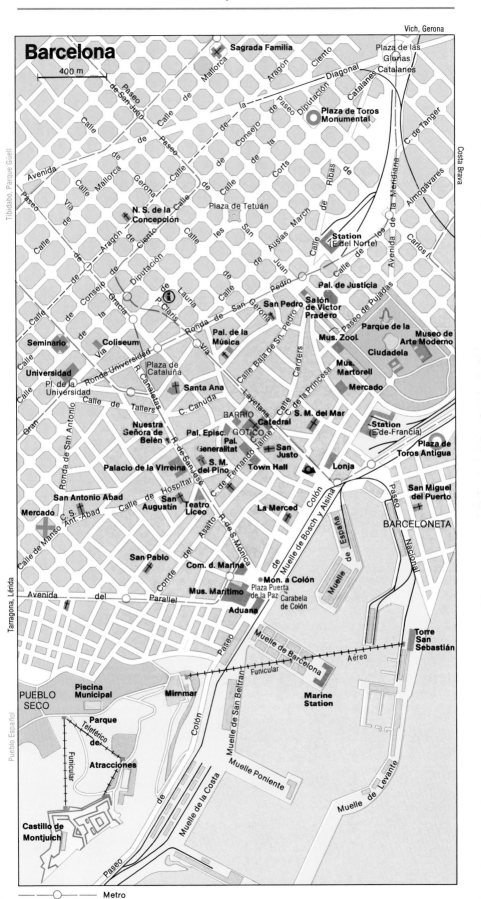

Barcelona

400 m

Vich, Gerona

Costa Brava

Tibidabo, Parque Güell

Tarragona, Lérida

Pueblo Español

Sagrada Familia

Plaza de las Glorias Catalanes

Diagonal

Catalanes

C. de Tanger

Mallorca

Aragón

Ciento

Diputación

Plaza de Toros Monumental

Paseo de San Juan

Calle

Calle

de

Paseo

de

la

Paseo

de

Consejo

de

Corts

Ribas

March

Carlos I

Avenida

Mallorca

Gerona

Calle

Calle

les

san

Ausias

Juan

Almogávares

Avenida de los

Avenida de la Meridiana

Paseo

de

Vía

Calle

de

Calle

de

Aragón

de

Ciento

N. S. de la Concepción

Plaza de Tetuán

Pedro

Station (E. del Norte)

Calle

de

Calle

Calle

Diputación

Calle

de

San Gerona

Pal. de Justicia

Consejo

de

Lauria

Calle

de

San Pedro

Salón de Victor Pradero

Paseo de Pujadas

Seminario

Coliseum

P. Claris

Ronda

Pal. de la Música

Pal. Episc.

Mus. Zool

Parque de la Ciudadela

Museo de Arte Moderno

Vía

R. Canaletas

Vía

Calle Bala de Sn. Pedro

Carders

Mus. Martorell

Universidad

Pl. de la Universidad

Plaza de Cataluña

Calle de la Princesa

Mercado

Gran

Ronda-Universidad

Tallers

Santa Ana

BARRIO

Catedral

S. M. del Mar

Station (E. de Francia)

Calle de

C. Canuda

Layetana

Plaza de Toros Antigua

Ronda de San Antonio

Nuestra Señora de Belén

GOTICO

Pal. Generalitat

San Justo

R. de San José

Pal.

S. M. del Pino

Town Hall

Lonja

San Miguel del Puerto

Palacio de la Virreina

C. de Fernando

R. de S. Mónica

Paseo de España

BARCELONETA

San Antonio Abad

Calle de Hospital

La Merced

Muelle de Bosch y Alsina

Nacional

Mercado

C. S.

Ant.-Abad

San Augustín

Teatro Liceo

Colón

San Pablo

Conde

del

Asalto

Com. d. Marina

Mon. á Colón

Muelle

de

España

Avenida

del

Parallel

Mus. Marítimo

Plaza Puerta de la Paz

Aduana

Carabela de Colón

Torre San Sebastián

PUEBLO SECO

Piscina Municipal

Miramar

Muelle de Barcelona

Aéreo

Marine Station

Parque

Teleférico

Funicular

de

Atracciones

Funicular

Colón

Muelle de San Beltran

Muelle de la Costa

Muelle Poniente

Muelle de Levante

Castillo de Montjuich

Paseo

Metro

Oficina Municipal de Turismo
Plaza de Judá Levi
Tel: (57) 29 07 40

Delegación Provincial de Información
Hermanos González Murga 17
Tel: (57) 22 10 54/22 26 84

The provincial capital Córdoba lies at the foot of the Sierra de Córdoba on a plain which slopes down to the river Guadalquivir.

Sightseeing

Cathedral – begun 875, formerly the principal mosque of the Western Islamic world and still known as the Mezquita. The finest achievement of Moorish religious art in Spain

Puente Romano – originally built after Caesar's triumph over Pompeii. At the southern end of the bridge is the massive Arab Torre de la Calahorra, a defensive tower which also houses the Municipal Museum. It boasts a magnificent view upstream

Granada

Oficina de Información de Turismo
Casa de los Tiros,
Pavaneras 19
Tel: (58) 22 59 90

Delegación Provincial de Información
Plaza Isabel la Católica 1
Tel: (58) 22 62 89

Panoramic view of Granada

Seville: Plaza de España and Palacio Central

Beautifully situated at the foot of the Sierra Nevada is Granada, an old Moorish capital full of history.

Sightseeing

Alhambra Palace – one of the great achievements of Moorish Art, begun in 1333 and largely completed by 1391 by successive Moorish rulers of Granada

Cathedral – begun in 1523, a memorial to the victory of Christian Spain and the country's finest Renaissance-style church

Palacio de Carlos V – begun in 1526 by Pedro Machuca, the finest example of High Renaissance architecture in Spain

Seville

Oficina de Información de Turismo
Avenida de la Constitución 21
Tel: (54) 22 14 04

Oficina Municipal de Turismo
Paseo de las Delicias s/n
Tel: (54) 23 44 65

Delegación Provincial de Información
Avenida de la Constitución 21
Tel: (54) 22 89 90

Seville is capital of Andalusia and Spain's fourth largest city after Madrid, Barcelona and Valencia.

Sightseeing

Alcazar – a medieval fortress built for Pedro the Cruel in the second half of the 14th century by Moorish architects

Cathedral – one of the largest and richest Gothic cathedrals in Christendom, built between 1402 and 1506

Museo de Bellas Artes – exhibits a magnificent collection of Spanish painting, particularly of the 17th century

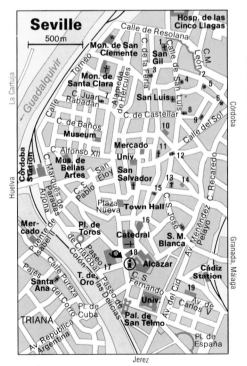

1 Puerta Macarena	11 San Pedro
2 Puerta de Córdoba	12 Santa Catalina
3 Omnium Sanctorum	13 San Ildefonso
4 Santa Marina	14 Casa de Pilatos
5 San Julián	15 San Isidoro
6 Santa Lucia	16 Palacio Arzobispal
7 San Lorenzo	17 Hospital
8 San Marcos	de la Caridad
9 Convento de Santa Paula	18 Casa Lonja
10 Palacio de las Dueñas	19 Bus station

The Costas

In all there are 88 beach resorts with bathing facilities along the Spanish Mediterranean coast. Some are quiet, picturesque fishing villages with few facilities for tourists, others have a great number of hotels, bars and restaurants designed solely to cater for the tourist trade.

Costa Blanca

Patronato Provincial de Turismo
Avda. de General Mola 6
Alicante
Tel: (965) 12 35 31

Dirección Regional de Turismo
Isidoro de la Cierva 10
Murcia
Tel: (968) 21 37 10

Includes the following resorts:
Aguilas
Alicante
Benidorm
Torrevieja

Guadelest, near Benidorm

Includes the following resorts:
Blanes
La Escala
Palafrugell
Rosas
San Feliu de Guixols

Costa Brava

Oficina de Información de Turismo
Ciudadanos, 12
Gerona
Tel: (72) 20 16 94

Oficina Municipal de Turismo
Plaza del Vi 1
Gerona
Tel: 20 16 94

Carnival, Valencia

Costa de la Luz

Oficina de Turismo
Calderón de la Barca 1
Cádiz
Tel: (56) 21 13 13

Includes the following resorts:
Cádiz
Chapiona
Conil de la Frontera
Punta Umbria

Costa del Azahar

Servicio Territorial de Turismo
Plaza María Agustina 5, Castellón de la Plana
Tel: (964) 22 74 04

Asociación Provincial de Promoción del Turismo
Gregorio Mayans 3, Valencia;
Tel: (96) 3 34 16 02

Includes the following resorts:
Benicarlo
Oliva
Oroesa
Valencia

The Balcón de Europa, on the Costa del Sol

Costa del Sol

Costa del Sol Tourist Promotion Board
Palacio de Congresso
Apartado 298
Torremolinos
Tel: (952) 38 57 31

Delegación Provincial de Turismo
Avenida de la Avrora s/n
Málaga
Tel: (952) 34 73 00

Includes the following resorts:
Estepona
Malaga
Marbella
Mortril
Torremolinos

Costa Dorada

Oficina de Información de Turismo
Gran Via de les Corts Catalanes 658
Barcelona
Tel: 3 01 74 43

Oficina Municipal de Turismo
Tarragona
Calle Mayor 39
Tel: (77) 23 48 12

Includes the following resorts:
Avenys de Mar
Calafell
Miami Playa
Tarragona

Costa Brava, Tossa de Mar

Accommodation

Hotels

Spanish hotels are officially classified in various categories according to their function and standard: *hoteles* (singular *hotel*), providing accommodation with or without meals, usually with their own restaurant; *hoteles-apartamentos*, apartment hotels, with facilities similar to hotels but with accommodation in flats or bungalows (chalets); *hostales* (singular *hostel*), modest hotels or inns providing accommodation with or without meals; and *pensiones* (singular *pension*), pensions or guest-houses with a limited number of rooms, providing full board only. Hotels, apartment hotels and hostales may also be run as *residencias*, providing only accommodation and breakfast.

In major tourist centres there are also *Paradores Nacionales de Turismo* (singular *Parador Nacional*), high-class hotels in old castles, palaces and convents, or sometimes purpose-built, excellently run and offering every comfort and amenity as well as an excellent cuisine. They are rather dearer than ordinary hotels in the same category, but provide a unique touristic experience. Advance booking is advisable.

In addition the government has established *Albergues Nacionales de Carretera* (singular *albergue nacional*) on the main tourist routes in places where adequate accommodation is not otherwise available. These provide excellent accommodation (period of stay restricted) and meals, and have a petrol station and garage (car repairs) associated with them.

Motels, on the main roads, offer accommodation for a restricted period of stay. The simplest form of accommodation is provided by *fondas* or *casas de huespedes*.

Under the official classification system hotels are divided into 5 price categories, apartment hotels into 4, *hostales* and *pensiones* into 3, the categories being indicated by the number of stars. Prices vary not only according to category but also according to situation and the size of the town. The dearest are hotels in large cities, bathing resorts and spas.

Hotels in the top category are normally up to international standards of comfort and amenity. Single rooms are rare, particularly in the more modest establishments. Guests are usually expected to take their meals in the hotel so far as possible. Breakfast may be included in the charge for accommodation (no reduction if the guest does not take it). During the main tourist season advance booking is advisable, particularly in the popular areas on the Mediterranean and Atlantic coasts and in the larger towns.

Youth Hostels

There are youth hostels (*albergues juveniles* or *albergues para la juventud*) in towns all over Spain, providing cheap accommodation for young people. They are listed in the annual International Youth Hostel Handbook (Vol. 1, Europe and the Mediterranean) which can be obtained through national youth hostel associations. The hostels are open (usually July–September) to members of national associations. Hostellers are not allowed to spend more than three nights at a time in any particular hostel.

Hotel Price Range	
Type of hotel	Prices in pesetas for a double room for 1 night
*****	18,000
**	5,000
*	4,000
hostel	900

The prices shown are intended to act as a rough guide only.

Camping and Caravanning

There are more than 700 officially approved camping sites (*campings, campamentos*) in Spain, more than two-thirds of them on the coast. They are noted in the annual *Guia de Campings* published by the Secretaria General de Turismo, Calle de María de Molina 50, Madrid 6, which contains illustrations and sketch maps and has an introduction in English.

Camping is allowed outside official camp sites with the permission of the owner of the land. To camp anywhere in Spain you require your passport or identity card which may be asked for at the Reception Office. Although it is not essential for campers to have camping carnets, it is advantageous for them to do so, particularly for those camping outside sites.

Introduction to Rail Information

The Spanish rail system run by RENFE (Red Nacional de los Ferrocarriles Espanoles) is extensive. Fares are low, although supplements are payable for travel on the faster trains. The broad gauge makes it necessary to change at the frontier when arriving from France, unless travelling in through trains with interchangeable bogies.

There are many types of service:

Talgo – these trains are unique to Spain, although services do run between Madrid and Paris and from Barcelona to Geneva and Paris. Luxurious and air-conditioned, these trains give an extremely smooth ride

Electrotren (ELT) and Inter-City – air-conditioned electric multiple units

Rapido (Rap) – locomotive-hauled train with air-conditioned coaches

Estrella (Estr) – long-distance, locomotive-hauled express trains conveying air-conditioned sleeping cars, couchettes and seating accommodation

TER – air-conditioned diesel units

Express (Exp) – long-distance overnight express train

New, fast electric and diesel multiple-units, the latter air-conditioned, have been introduced on many of the commuter services

Map supplied by kind permission of Thomas Cook Ltd. The numbers along the lines refer to tables in the *Thomas Cook Continental Timetable*.

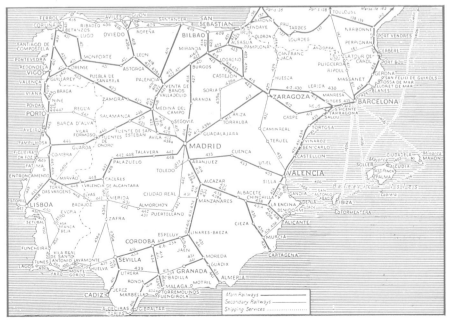

Major International Services

Connection	Duration	Frequency
Madrid–Lisbon	8–11hrs	twice daily
Madrid–Paris	15–19hrs	9 times daily

Major Internal Services

Connection	Duration	Frequency
Madrid–Algeciras	10–12hrs	twice daily
Madrid–Barcelona	8–10hrs	6 times daily
Madrid–Burgos	4–6hrs	4 times daily
Madrid–Santander	6–8hrs	twice daily

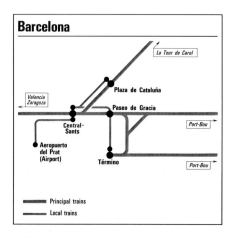

Scenic Routes

The most scenic route into Spain from France is from Toulouse over the Pyrénées and arriving at Barcelona. For picturesque mountain scenery the Léon –Tuy, Córdoba–Málaga and Granada –Almeria lines are particularly renowned.

Veteran Railways

Transcantabrico

The Transcantabrico is the first of Spain's veteran narrow-gauge trains to return to the rails. It covers a longer distance than any other narrow-gauge train in Europe – 625 miles. One of the great advantages of these trains lies in their capacity for taking tight corners and climbing steep gradients. This, of course, makes them ideal for reaching areas of outstanding natural beauty.

The Transcantabrico travels through Northern Spain from Leon to Ferrol or vice versa. The journey lasts a week and all events and entertainments are included in the fare. With daily guided excursions to places of cultural interest, the Transcantabrico provides an unusual and nostalgic means of exploring this beautiful part of Spain.

Al Andalus Express

The Al Andalus Express is made up of 4 vintage coaches – each beautifully crafted – and 4 modern sleeping cars. The train travels through Andalusia visiting Seville, Cordoba, Granada, Malaga, and Jerez de la Frontera. Daily excursions are accompanied by expert guides. Back on board, entertainments include a games room, piano bar, discotheque, videos and Andalucian cuisine.

The tours vary in length from 4 to 6 days and you make a circular trip, returning to the station from which you set off.

Further details of tours on the Transcantabrico and the Al Andalus are available from:
Marsans Travel
7a Henrietta Place
London W1M 9AG
Tel: (01) 493 4934

Internal Fare Structure

Standard Rate Fares

Fares are calculated on a kilometric basis and compared to fares in Britain and other countries on the continent they are relatively inexpensive. On

The Alcázar, Segovia

some types of train a supplement must be paid. There is a small discount for passengers who buy a return ticket rather than two singles. As an example of fare prices, a 2nd class single on an express train between Madrid and Barcelona (683km) varies between 3000ptas and 5120ptas. On *Dias Azules* (blue days) *RENFE* allows tickets to be issued with a 25% reduction. This is applicable to all journeys over 100km in each direction. The blue days fall in the first half of the year and number about 40.

Student Reductions

Students travelling in Spain are advised to consult the International Section for information on the general reductions available.

Senior Citizen Reductions

Senior Citizens travelling in Spain are advised to consult the International Section for information on the general reductions available.

Party/Group Savers

There are reductions of up to 30% for parties of 10 or more travelling in Spain.

Tourist Reductions

The *RENFE* Tourist Card, valid for 8, 15, or 22 days permits unlimited travel on all scheduled domestic trains throughout the *RENFE* network. The pass can be used at any time of the year without date restrictions. The price of a 2nd class *RENFE* Tourist Card is £50 (5 days), £80 (15 days), and £105 (22 days); for 1st class travel, the price is £70 (5 days), £115 (15 days) and £130 (22 days).

Where to buy tickets

In Spain

Tickets may be purchased from major rail stations and from *RENFE* offices and their agents.

In Great Britain

Tickets may be purchased from:
European Rail Travel Centre
PO Box 303
Victoria Station
London SW1V 1JY
Tel: (071) 834 2345

and from
French Railways Ltd
179 Piccadilly
London W1V 0BA
Tel: (071) 409 1224

In USA

Tickets may be purchased from *RENFE* representatives in the major cities (see International Section).

Palencia, on the Rio Carrión

Facilities on Trains

Sleepers and Couchettes

These are available on many of the internal services. As an example of prices, a 4 berth sleeper costs 1340ptas per berth; a couchette stands at about 1000ptas per person.

Bicycle Carriage

Bikes can be taken free, as accompanied luggage on the *Correos*. These trains may be slow but they have the advantage that the bike travels with the rider. For transport on the faster trains, the bike must be registered at the baggage office.

Animals

Domestic pets require special tickets and in general must travel in the luggage compartment chained and muzzled. They should be presented 15 minutes before the departure of the train with the appropriate ticket. Where there is no such compartment, they are allowed to travel with the passenger, provided that they are properly caged.

Facilities at Stations

Rail stations in the large towns are well equipped with food facilities, left luggage lockers, bureaux de change and information.

Reservations

Reservations are not compulsory in internal services, but it is advisable to make them because Spanish trains get very crowded. Seats on express trains must always be reserved. The booking charge is in the region of 200ptas.

Sweden

Typical Swedish lake scenery on the Lake Vänern

Introduction

Sweden occupies the eastern side of the Scandinavian peninsula and stretches for almost 1600km. The most populated and hospitable part of Sweden is the central region with stunning scenery including Sweden's largest lake, Lake Vänern, which has an area of 5546sq km. In all, Sweden has 96,000 lakes covering 9% of the country, many of which are in the cold northern region, called Norrland. Sweden has benefited from a long period of peace to become one of the most socially progressive nations in the world and it has much to offer the visitor.

Sweden's climate is mild for its latitude because of the Gulf Stream of the North Atlantic. The mountains which rise in Norway slope down more gently across Sweden to the Gulf of Bothnia and protect the east coast of Sweden from some of the heaviest rainfall. Average temperatures range from around 15°–17°C in July to well below freezing in winter while in northern Sweden temperatures may remain below freezing for up to 7 months of the year.

Sweden's abundant mineral resources and water power have significantly helped to strengthen the economy. Sweden also has an extensive communications network and relatively low unemployment. The main industries in Sweden include metal-processing, the manufacture of machinery and cars and shipbuilding. Unlike Norway, however, Sweden is obliged to import large amounts of oil and coal for power. Agriculture forms only a small sector of the economy, because of the unsuitability of the land for cultivation, particularly in the north. Sweden is a member of the European Free Trade Association (EFTA) and has a customs agreement with the EEC.

Some of the most notable examples of Swedish art and architecture can be found in and around Stockholm. The Renaissance-style Royal Palace, the Old Opera House and the Exchange are all fine monuments to the cultural advances of the Swedish kingdom.

Modern Scandinavian architecture owes much to the Functionalism of Gunnar Asplund (1885–1940) who designed the halls for the Stockholm Exhibition of 1930. The ideas of the Swedish Arts and Crafts Association on modern design were the starting point for a distinctive Scandinavian school of interior decoration and the design of everyday utensils.

Opera House, Stockholm

History

8th–11th centuries	Swedish Vikings raid the Baltic coastline and establish states in Eastern Europe
12th–13th centuries	Christianity comes to Sweden
1250–1363	The Folkung dynasty consolidates the power of Sweden and completes the conquest of Finland
1319–1523	Sweden is linked with Norway and Denmark
1523	Gustav Vasa defeats the Danes and is elected King of Sweden
1544	Sweden becomes a hereditary monarchy
up to 1718	Sweden enjoys a period of military power gaining territories in the Baltic from all of its neighbours
1814–1905	Union with Norway, during which time a new constitution is established and considerable economic and cultural advances are made
1905	King Oskar gives up the Norwegian crown and the union between the two countries is abolished
20th century	Sweden remains neutral during both world wars. Much improved social conditions and services place an increasing financial burden on the welfare state
1946	Sweden becomes a member of the United Nations
1974	New constitution
1980	Serious labour problems occur due to economic crisis and the effects of a high inflation rate

1981	A Soviet submarine runs aground near a Swedish naval base, leading to diplomatic complications with Russia
1983	Major tax scandal involving Minister of Justice
1986	Mr Olaf Palme, Prime Minister, assassinated in Stockholm

Major Centres

Stockholm

Sveriges Turistråd
Stockholm Tourist Centre
Sverigehuset
Kungsträdgården
Box 7542
S-103 93 Stockholm
Tel: (8) 7 89 2000

Hotellcentralen
Central Station
Vasagatan
S-11120 Stockholm
Tel: (8) 24 08 80

'Miss Tourist' (recorded information service in English)
Tel: (8) 22 18 40

Embassies:
UK: Skarpögatan 6-8
Tel: (8) 67 01 40
USA: Strandvägen 101
Tel: (8) 78 35 300

Stockholm is worth a visit simply for its magnificent setting at the mouth of Lake Mälar where it flows into the Bal- tic. **At this point it forms a deep inlet dotted with skerries and surrounded by woodland. Stockholm is not only Sweden's capital, but also an industrial centre and a university town; it therefore has plenty of attractions for its visitors. The old town of Stockholm is built over three islands but the city now extends onto the mainland. Old and new architectural styles are effectively combined and the new central city is a showpiece of contemporary Swedish architecture. An underground railway system begun in 1930 links the city with its various suburbs.**

Sightseeing

Cathedral – consecrated in 1300, it was not completed until the 16th century and was later remodelled in Baroque style
Djurgården – a park previously a royal hunting preserve
German Church – preserves more than any other church in the city, the character and style of the 17th century
National Museum – houses Sweden's finest art collection as well as major works by other European artists
Royal Palace – a Renaissance-style building in the main part of the old town
Riddarhuset (Knight's House) – Baroque-style hall which used to be the former meeting-place of the Swedish nobility
Riddarholm Church – the burial place of the Swedish monarchs. Its 90m-high steeple is a prominent landmark
Skansen Open-Air Museum – brings together many old Swedish and Lapp buildings and craftsmen's workshops

Riddarholmen – the Old Town of Stockholm

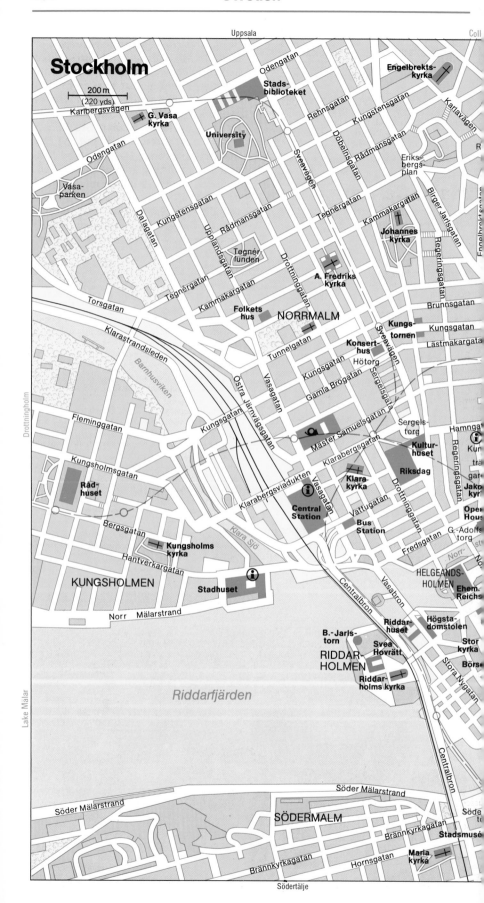

Stockholm

200 m
(220 yds)

Uppsala

Coll

Karlbergsvägen

G. Vasa kyrka

Odengatan

Stadsbiblioteket

Rehnsgatan

Kungstensgatan

Engelbrekts-kyrka

Karlavägen

University

Sveavägen

Döbelnsgatan

Rådmansgatan

Eriks-bergs-plan

R

Vasa-parken

Odengatan

Dalagatan

Kungstensgatan

Upplandsgatan

Rådmansgatan

Tegnérgatan

Kammakargatan

Johannes kyrka

Birger Jarlsgatan

Regeringsgatan

Engelbrektsgatan

Tegnér-lunden

Drottninggatan

A. Fredriks kyrka

Torsgatan

Tegnérgatan

Kammakargatan

Folkets hus

NORRMALM

Brunnsgatan

Klarastrandsleden

Barnhusviken

Tunnelgatan

Kungs-tornen

Kungsgatan

Konsert-hus

Sveavägen

Lästmakargata

Fleminggatan

Östra Järnvägsgatan

Kungsgatan

Vasagatan

Kungsgatan

Hötorg

Gamla Brogatan

Sergelsgata

Sergels-torg

Hamnga

Regeringsgatan

Kungsholmsgatan

Kungsgatan

Klarabergsviadukten

Mäster Samuelsgatan

Klarabergsgatan

Kultur-huset

Kun

trä
gar

Råd-huset

Bergsgatan

Riksdag

Klara kyrka

Drottninggatan

Riksdag

Jako
kyr

Oper
Hous

Klara Sjö

Central Station

Vasagatan

Vattugatan

Bus Station

G.-Adolfs torg

st

Kungsholms kyrka

Hantverkargatan

Fredsgatan

Norr

HELGEANDS-HOLMEN

KUNGSHOLMEN

Stadhuset

Centralbron

Vasabron

Ehem.
Reichs

Norr Mälarstrand

Riddar-huset

Högsta-domstolen

B.-Jarls-torn

RIDDAR-HOLMEN

Svea Hovrätt

Stor kyrka

Börs

Riddar-holms kyrka

Stora Nygatan

Riddarfjärden

Centralbron

Söder Mälarstrand

Söder Mälarstrand

Söde
to

SÖDERMALM

Brännkyrkagatan

Stadsmusé

Brännkyrkagatan

Hornsgatan

Maria kyrka

Drottningholm

Lake Mälar

Södertälje

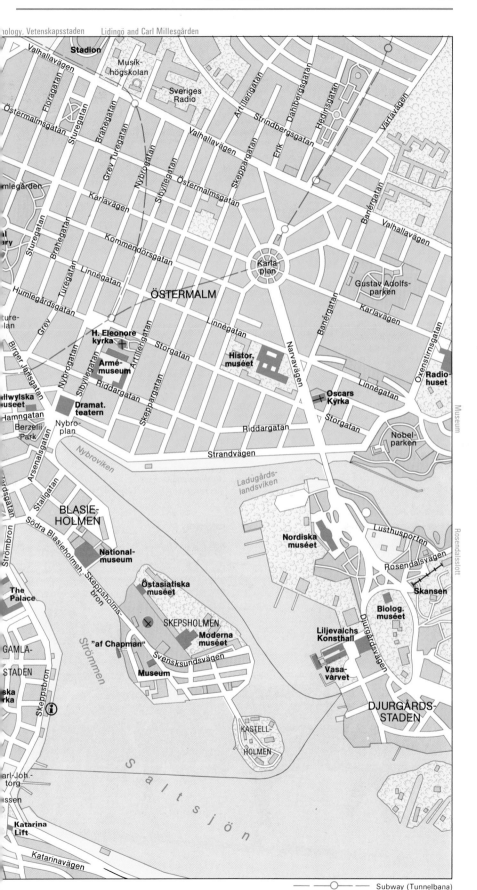

nology, Vetenskapsstaden   Lidingö and Carl Millesgården

Stadion

Musik-
högskolan

Valhallavägen

Floragatan

Östermalmsgatan

Sturegatan

Brahegatan

Grev Turegatan

Nybrogatan

Sibyllegatan

Valhallavägen

Sveriges
Radio

Artillerigatan

Strindbergsgatan

Dahlbergsgatan

Hedinsgatan

Erik

Skeppargatan

Valhallavägen

Bortergatan

Banérgatan

mlegården

Karlavägen

Östermalmsgatan

al
ary

Sturegatan

Brahegatan

Kommendörsgatan

Karla-
plan

Banérgatan

Gustav Adolfs-
parken

Karlavägen

Humlegårdsgatan

Linnégatan

Turegatan

ÖSTERMALM

Linnégatan

Oxenstirnsgatan

ure-
lan

Grev

H. Eleonore
kyrka

Artillerigatan

Storgatan

Narvavägen

Histor.
muséet

Linnégatan

Radio-
huset

Birger Jarlsgatan

Nybrogatan

Sibyllegatan

Armé-
museum

Riddargatan

Skeppargatan

Oscars
Kyrka

Storgatan

llwylska
useet
Hamngatan

Dramat.
teatern

Nybro-
plan

Riddargatan

Strandvägen

Museum

Berzelii
Park

Nobel-
parken

Arsenalsgatan

Stallgatan

ardsgatan

Nybroviken

Ladugårds-
landsviken

Strömbron

Södra Blasieholmsh.

BLASIE-
HOLMEN

National-
museum

Nordiska
muséet

Lusthusporten

Rosendalsvägen

Rosendalsslott

The
Palace

Skeppsholms-
bron

Östasiatiska
muséet

Skansen

GAMLA-

STADEN

Strömmen

"af Chapman"

SKEPSHOLMEN

Svensksundsvägen

Moderna
muséet

Museum

Biolog.
muséet

Liljevalchs
Konsthall

Djurgårdsvägen

Vasa-
varvet

ska
rka

Skeppsbron

DJURGÅRDS-
STADEN

arl-Joh.-
torg

ssen

KASTELL-

HOLMEN

Katarina
Lift

Saltsjön

Katarinavägen

Subway (Tunnelbana)

Stockholm Royal Palace

Opening Times

Most museums, etc., are closed on the following public holidays: 1 and 6 January, Good Friday, Easter (two days), 1 May, Ascension (fortieth day after Easter – Holy Thursday), Whitsun (seventh Sunday and Monday after Easter), Midsummer (the Saturday nearest 21 June), All Saints Day (1 November) and Christmas (two days).

For information about special events and changes in opening times, consult the *Museinyckeln* (key to Museums) column in the Saturday editions of the newspapers, *Dagens Nyheter* and *Svenska Dagbladot*.

Museums and places of interest

Army Museum
(Armémuseum),
Riddargatan 13.

Berzelius Museum
(Berzeliusmuseet),
Roslagsvägen.
Only by appointment.

Biological Museum
(Biologiska Museet),
Djurgården.

Botanic Garden
(Bergianska Trädgården),
Frescati (opposite Natural History Museum).

Gustav III's Pavilion
(Gustav IIIs Paviljong),
Haga.

Hallwyl Museum
(Hallwylska Museet),
Hamngatan 4 (near Norrmalmstorg).

Stockholm Royal Guard

Historical Museum
(Historiska Museet),
Narvavägen.

Kaknäs Tower
(Kaknästornet),
N Djurgården.

Millesgården,
Lidingö.

Modern Museum
(Moderna Museet),
Skeppsholmen.

Municipal Museum
(Stadmuseum),
Slussen, in Old Town Hall.

Museum of Architecture
(Sveriges Arkitekturmuseum),
Skeppsholmen.

Museum of Maritime History
(Sjöhistoriska Museet),
Djurgårdsbrunnsvägen.

Museum of Medical History
(Medicinhistoriska Museet),
Åsögatan 146.

Museum of Photography
(Fotografiska Museet),
Skeppsholmen (W wing of Modern Museum).

National Museum
Södra Blasieholmshamnen.

Natural History Museum
(Naturhistoriska Riksmuseet),
Frescati.

Nordic Museum
(Nordiska Museet),
Djurgården.

Rosendal House
(Rosendalsslott),
Djurgården.

Royal Armoury
(Kungl. Livrustkammaren),
Royal Palace.

Royal Palace
(Stockholms Slott).

Strindberg Museum (Blå Tornet),
Drottninggatan 85.

Thiel Gallery
(Thielska Galleriet),
Djurgården.

Tobacco Museum
(Tobaksmuseet),
Gubbhyllan, Skansen.

Town Hall
(Stadshuset),
Hantverkargatan 1.

Tramway Museum
(Spårvägsmuseet),
Odenplan Underground station.

Waldemarsudde,
Djurgården.

Wasa Museum
Djurgården.

Wine and Spirits Museum
(Vin- och Sprithistoriska Museet),
AB Vin- & Spritcentralen,
St Eriksgatan 121.

Malmö

Turistbyra (Tourist Office)
Hamngaten 1
211 22 Malmö
Tel: (40) 34 12 70

Located on the Öresund in southern Skåne, opposite the Danish capital of Copenhagen, Malmö is the capital town of its province and Sweden's third largest city. It is a major port and an important industrial centre, yet still has the intimate atmosphere of a small country town. Surrounded by canals, the old town in the middle of the city, with many fine old burghers' houses, has preserved much of its original character.

Statue of Charles X, Stortorg, Malmö

Sightseeing

Stortgot – in the 16th century this was one of the largest market squares in any of the Nordic countries. In the middle is an equestrian statue (1896) of Carl X Gustaf who united Skåne with Sweden in 1658

Radhuset (Town Hall) – Dutch Renaissance style, 1546; the cellar (now a restaurant) is in its original state but the exterior was renovated in 1864–9. On the first floor are St Knut's or St Canute's Hall (Knutsalen), in which the influential St Knut's Guild used to meet, and the Council Chamber (Lanstingssalen), with portraits of Danish and Swedish Kings

St Petri Kyrka (St Peters Church) – a handsome 14th-century brick building in Baltic/Gothic style, undoubtedly modelled after St Mary's Church in Lübeck. The steeple is 96 metres high

St Gertrud (1500–1800) – comprising a number of carefully restored buildings and now used as a leisure centre. Awarded the 'Europa Nostra' prize in 1979 for fine restoration work

Malmöhus Castle – a moated fortress built in 1537–42 (restored 1870, after a fire); it now houses the **Municipal Museum** (archaeology, history and art)

Municipal Theatre (1942–4) – the largest theatre in Scandinavia with seating for 1700

Lilla Torg – an attractive small square with 16th–18th century houses. The **Form Design Centre** situated here is well worth a visit

Accommodation

Hotels

The hotels in Sweden, noted for their cleanliness, are right up to international standards of comfort and service for the different price categories. The large towns have luxury establishments (for which advance reservation is recommended) but many smaller places have excellent hotels combining international standards of comfort with distinctive national features. Even in the far north, there are good hotels and well-equipped inns which provide a very adequate standard of comfort. Many establishments have 'family rooms' with 3–5 beds which provide reasonably priced accommodation for a family group. Some mountain hotels in Sweden are open for only part of the year, during the summer and winter seasons. There are also special summer hotels.

There are excellent hotels in smaller towns which are often called *stradshotellet* or *stora Hotellet*. There may be a *Jarnvagshotell* (Railway Hotel) near the station. A *gastgivaregard* is a country inn, in earlier days a post-house. The *turistationer*, run by the Swedish Tourist Board, are usually excellent.

In Sweden there is a system of Hotel Cheques which cover bed, breakfast and reservation of the next night's hotel at a fixed rate. Tourists may buy either 'budget cheques' or 'quality cheques' for use in any one of the 245 hotels which participate in the scheme.

For a stay of some length, it is more economical to take a room in a *pension* (guest-house). There are also a large number of *motels* in Scandinavia. If you are looking for budget priced accommodation, watch out for the *Rum* sign. The word simply means 'room' and that is what you get – a room without breakfast. Local tourist offices have details of *rum* accommodation and prices are inexpensive – about 125Skr per person per night in Stockholm, for example.

Youth Hostels

Sweden has 265 youth hostels which range from mansion houses to renovated sailing ships like the Af Chapman moored in Stockholm harbour. There are no restrictions on motorists using Sweden's hostels.

The hostels are run by the Swedish Touring Club (STF), but if you are a member of the Youth Hostels Association or Scottish Youth Hostels Association you will qualify for a cheaper rate, so don't forget to bring your membership card. Non-members pay an extra 12Skr per night. Normal price for youth hostel accommodation varies between 29 and 39Skr per night. A list of Swedish youth hostels can be ordered direct from: STF, Box 25, S-101 Stockholm (price about 25Skr). The hostels are also listed in the International Youth Hostel Handbook, available through the YHA or SYHA in the UK.

Accommodation for young people visiting Sweden as tourists is provided at the International Youth Centre, Valhallavagen 142, S-115 24 Stockholm. Tel: (08) 63 43 89. Visitors can take a shower free of charge and beds are available for only 40Skr a night.

Camping and Caravanning

Sweden is ideal camping country and there are numerous camp sites (Swedish *campingplats*). Campers should have an international camping carnet

Hotel Price Range		
	Price for 1 night in kronor	
Type of hotel	Single room	Double room
Luxury	800–1100	1050–1350
Middle-grade	450– 800	600–1050
Modest	250– 450	400– 600

These prices are intended to act as a rough guide only.

or the membership card of a national camping organisation. Lists of camp sites are issued annually by the national tourist organisations, motoring organisations and camping clubs, giving the location, size, facilities and category (1–3 stars) of the sites. In addition to the usual sanitary and cooking facilities, the larger sites normally have showers, and shops selling provisions. On many sites there are also camping huts or chalets (simple wooden huts with sleeping accommodation). In areas of particular natural beauty, there are also vacation villages with chalets and log cabins.

Introduction to Rail Information

Statens Järnvågar (SJ) operate a very efficient and modern network of train services most of which are electrified. Trains are comfortable, clean and run frequently, particularly on the main trunk routes linking Stockholm with Gothenburg and Malmö where there is an hourly service.

Major International Services

Connection	Duration	Frequency
Stockholm–Oslo	6–9hrs	3 times daily
Stockholm–Helsinki	14–16hrs	3 times daily
Stockholm–Copenhagen	8–9hrs	7 times daily

Map supplied by kind permission of Thomas Cook Ltd. The numbers along the lines refer to tables in the *Thomas Cook Continental Timetable*.

Stockholm

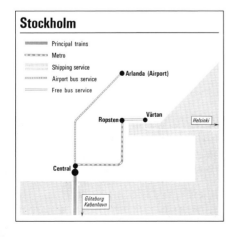

Major Internal Services

Connection	Duration	Frequency
Stockholm–Gothenburg	4–5hrs	18 times daily
Stockholm–Malmö	6–7hrs	16 times daily
Stockholm–Karlstad	3–3½hrs	10 times daily
Stockholm–Kiruna	15hrs	3 times daily

Connection	Duration	Frequency
Gothenburg–Malmö	3–4hrs	10 times daily
Gothenburg–Karlstad	3–4hrs	8 times daily
Malmö–Kalmar	4hrs	7 times daily

Scenic Routes

Any line north of Stockholm is of interest scenically, particularly from Östersund onwards, either to Trondheim in Norway or to Kiruna in the far north. Among the most renowned lines are the following:

Narvik–Kiruna

Östersund–Trondheim

Windmills, Öland

Veteran Railways

1. **Skånska Järnvägar** (South east Skåne)
   Route: Brösarp–St Olof–O Vemmerlöv
   Length: 13km and 9km
   Gauge: 1435mm
   Travel from Brösarp–St Olof by steam train and then in St Olof change to an old railbus bound for O Vemmerlöv. This is Sweden's most southern old time railway.

2. **Ohs Bruks Järnväg** (east of Värnamo)
   Route: Ohs Bruk–Bor
   Length: 15km
   There are three serviceable steam engines and the trip leads up steep inclines with sharp bends through the deep forests of Småland.

3. **Bödabanan** (Böda Crown Forest, Öland Island)
   Route: Fagerrör–Böllingevägen
   Length: 1200m
   Diesel engine 'Simplex' from Britain built 1952. Copy of the King's hunting carriage from 1930 and carriage for forest workers.

4. **Gotlands Hesselby Järnvägar**
   Length: 1km
   Gauge: 891mm
   Veteran railway officially opened 1978. Steam engines and authentic old carriages.

5. **Anten–Gräfsnäs Järnväg**
   Length: 11km
   Gauge: 891mm
   Steam engines, shunting operations, water

filling points, open platforms, cast-iron gates, wooden benches, gas-lit carriages.

6. **Ostra Södermanlands Järnväg**
   Route: Läggesta–Mariefred
   Length: 4km
   Gauge: 600mm
   Steam engine from the turn of the century.

7. **Sollentuna Enskilda Järnväg**
   Length: 1km
   Veteran train drawn by steam engine runs through attractive countryside.

8. **Uppsala–Lenna Järnväg**
   Route: Uppsala–Länna/Fjällnora
   Length: 33km
   Gauge: 891mm
   Railbus and steam train. Nordic countries longest veteran railway.

9. **Jädraås–Tallås Järnväg**
   Length: 5½km
   Gauge: 891mm
   Sweden's most northern veteran railway from the turn of the century. Many steam-operated vehicles including a railbus from 1888, Mallet locomotive, rail trolley.

Internal Fare Structure

Standard Rate Fares

Standard fares in Sweden are based on the number of kilometres travelled. For example, if you travel 2nd class 1–16km costs 12Skr, 50km costs 30Skr and 150km costs 84Skr. Return fares are double the price of the single.

The ordinary fare is either a 'normal fare' or a 'low-price' fare depending on the class and day of travel. The 'normal fare' is charged for 1st class travel every day and for 2nd class travel on Fridays and Sundays. The 'low-price' fare is charged for 2nd class travel between 5pm Monday to 5pm Friday and between 5pm Saturday and 5pm Sunday. The low-price fare reduction is 25%.

Gothenburg

Student Reductions

Students travelling in Sweden are advised to consult the International Section for information about the reductions available.

Group Rates

Groups of 2–5 people travelling together in 2nd class are entitled to a fare reduction. The group may be composed of 2–5 adults or 3–5 children or a combination of adults and children to a maximum of 5. One person (adult or child) pays the adult fare and the others get a reduction of 30%.

Senior Citizen Reductions

A reduction of 30% can be claimed by all Senior Citizens (those over 65) who can produce proof of their age. Senior Citizens are advised to consult the International Section for the alternative reductions available.

Tourist Reductions

Nordic Tourist Ticket

The Nordic Tourist Ticket is valid for 21 days and entitles the holder to unlimited rail travel throughout Denmark, Finland, Norway and Sweden. It also permits unlimited travel on certain ferry services including Helsingor–Helsingborg; Rodby Faerge–Puttgarden Mitte See; Goteborg–Frederikshavn; Stockholm–Turku; Kristiansand–Hirtshals; Gedser–Warnemunde; and the NSB bus section Trondheim–Storlein. Prices are: 2nd class £135 (adult), £101 (12–25) and £67 (4–11); 1st class £181 (adult), £136 (12–25) and £90.50 (4–11). Normal prices apply for seat, sleeper and couchette reservation.

Inlandsbanen go-as-you-please ticket

This ticket gives the visitor unrestricted travel along the Inlandsbanen (inland railway) which runs along the backbone of Sweden from Gällivare in the north to Kristinehamn in the south. The ticket costs 345Skr for a 14-day period

in the summer and this fee provides a discount on overnight accommodation, restaurant meals and sightseeing.'

Where to buy tickets

In Sweden

Tickets are available from major rail stations and travel agents.

In Great Britain

European Rail Travel Centre
PO Box 303
Victoria Station
London SW1V 1JY
Tel: (071) 834 2345

In USA

Tickets are available from SJ rail representatives in the major cities (see International Section).

Facilities on Trains

Couchettes/Sleepers

Couchettes and sleepers are available on some of the longer internal and international routes. Couchettes cost 65Skr each for 2nd class travel and a sleeper costs 90Skr for 2nd class travel.

Food

On virtually all long distance trains there is a restaurant car or buffet for meals, drinks and snacks.

Disabled

Some trains have special seats adapted for the disabled.

Bicycle Carriage

Bikes must be registered for transport at the baggage office. Station staff load and unload the bike, which may take 24 hours to reach its destination (48 hours in summer). A flat rate is payable regardless of distance and if the bike weighs more than 25kg you pay more.

Motorail

SJ have a summer only motorail service on the routes between Malmö and Gothenburg in the south to Luleå and Kiruna in the north. As an example of prices, a car with one adult travelling in a couchette between Malmö and Kiruna costs 1500Skr.

Facilities at Train Stations

Food

Most of the major stations have buffet or restaurant facilities.

Reservations

Passengers are obliged to make reservations on trains which are marked with an R on the timetable. This costs 15Skr and can be effected at the train station up until the moment of departure.

Lake Siljan, near Rättvik

Luggage

Hand luggage which is carried by the passenger is transported free of charge. Heavier items must be registered and for this service there is a small charge.

Switzerland

River Doubs near Les Brenets

Introduction

Switzerland is a country offering a rich variety of landscape to the visitor – from snow-capped peaks and glaciers to green valleys and beautiful lakes. It is divided into three main regions: the Alps in the south-east, which make up 60% of the total area; the Jura mountains in the north-west, which account for 10%; and, in between the two, the low-lying Mittelland occupying the remaining 30%. While the Jura and the Mittelland are well-cultivated and densely populated, the Alps are relatively unproductive and rely heavily on tourism to justify their economic position.

The full Alpine range takes in 24 peaks over 4000m and 70 mountains over 3000m. The highest point in Switzerland is the Dufourspitze at 4634m in the Monte Rosa group. The lowest point is Lake Maggiore (193m) in Ticino. There are over 1500 lakes – both man-made and natural – and 1000 glaciers, as well as five major rivers: the Rhine, the Rhône, the Aare, the Reuss and the Ticino. The less mountainous regions enjoy two different types of climate; to the north of the Alpine chain it is fairly temperate, while in the south, particularly in Ticino and Grisons, Mediterranean influences are already perceptible. In the Alps themselves, weather conditions depend on altitude and the prevailing air currents, both of which produce many local variations.

The population of Switzerland reflects its changing historical development with German, French and Italian influences acting upon an initial Roman base. The country officially recognises four different languages with 75% of Swiss people speaking German, 20% French, 4% Italian and 1% Romansch (a derivative of Latin mainly spoken in remote Alpine villages). Protestants and Catholics are granted equal recognition under the law. During the 16th century, Switzerland became a major centre of the Reformation and came under the reformist sway of Zwingli and Calvin. Their influence is still readily apparent in the form of Protestantism practised in the country today.

The government of Switzerland is carried out through 23 independent cantons, divided into 3000 smaller communes. The cantons make up the Confederation of States which was first established in 1848, and have their own written constitution, governing body and assembly. The key to Swiss democracy lies in the popular devices of the referendum and the initiative. Thus every Swiss citizen who can vote is able to exert influence on national policy.

The high standard of living enjoyed by the Swiss today is as much due to the adoption of national neutrality in 1815 as to the strength of manufacturing industries and legendary Swiss business skills. Switzerland has earned a reputation for exporting high-quality finished products, particularly in the fields of chemicals and pharmaceuticals, instruments and machinery, and man-made fabrics and textiles. At the same time, Switzerland's world-wide trading connections and stable currency have helped to attract a substantial amount of foreign business to its insurance and banking interests.

Bernina Pass

Culturally, Switzerland can offer no one distinctive national style. The neighbouring countries of Germany, France, Austria and Italy have all exerted an effect upon the development of Swiss art and architecture, and many well-known artists from beyond her mountain borders have worked in Switzerland. In fact, most native Swiss artists who have achieved international standing have done so away from Switzerland.

Some key figures:

Konrad Witz (1400–44), founder of Swiss Landscape painting
Ferdinand Hodler (1835–1918), naturalist painter
Paul Klee (1879–1940), the expressionist
Le Corbusier (1887–1965), one of the founders of modern architecture

Centre le Corbusier, Zurich

Alberto Giacometti (1900–66), sculptor in metal
Jean-Jacques Rousseau (1712–78), French educationalist and thinker who made his home in Switzerland
H J Pestalozzi (1746–1827), educational reformer
Carl Gustav Jung (1875–1961), pioneer of analytical psychology
Friedrich Dürrenmatt (b. 1921), novelist and playwright
Arthur Honegger (1892–1955), composer
Henry Nestlé (1814–90), pharmacist and founder of Nestlé

History

Early	The Romans conquer the Helvetii, a Celtic tribe, around 55BC and colonise the area. In turn, they are conquered around AD455 by the Alemanni, a Germanic tribe. Between the 5th & 9th centuries, Switzerland is converted to Christianity. It becomes a part of the Holy Roman Empire under Charlemagne and his descendants
1291	The Forest cantons of Uri, Schwyz and Unterwalden – the 'inner Switzerland' – form the Perpetual Alliance
1367–1471	Common people join the Three Leagues in Rhaetia to defend themselves against oppression by the nobility
1476–77	Burgundian War and the defeat of Charles the Bold by the Confederation and her Austrian allies
1516	Peace with France. The Confederates abandon their role as a belligerent power and declare their complete neutrality
1798	The Helvetian Republic is established by Napoleon
1815	Swiss independence is restored and its perpetual neutrality guaranteed
1848	Adoption by national referendum of a new federal constitution
1864	Signing of the Geneva Convention and formation of the Red Cross
1874	Revision of the federal constitution
1914–18	On the outbreak of the First World War the Swiss army is mobilised, but the country's neutrality is fully preserved
1920	First meeting of the League of Nations in Geneva
1939–45	During Second World War Switzerland again remains neutral
1960	Switzerland joins the European Free Trade Association
1971	Women are granted the right to vote and stand for election in federal elections
1979	Jura becomes a member of the Confederation
1983	Elections confirm stability of four-party coalition government
1985	Vote for a new law giving women equal rights in marriage
1986	In a referendum, Switzerland rejects a government proposal to join the United Nations

Major Centres

Berne

ⓘ

Offizielles Verkehrs- und Kongressbüro
Bahnhof (Station)
POB 2700
CH-3001 Berne
Tel: (31) 22 76 76

Embassies:
UK: Thunstrasse 50
Tel: (31) 44 50 21-26
USA: Jubiläumstrasse 93
Tel: (31) 43 70 11

Berne is the capital of Switzerland and the seat of government. The old part of the town, dominated by the Minister, preserves much of its original layout.

Sightseeing

Bundeshaus (Parliament Building) – Renaissance style building standing on the edge of the high ground above the river

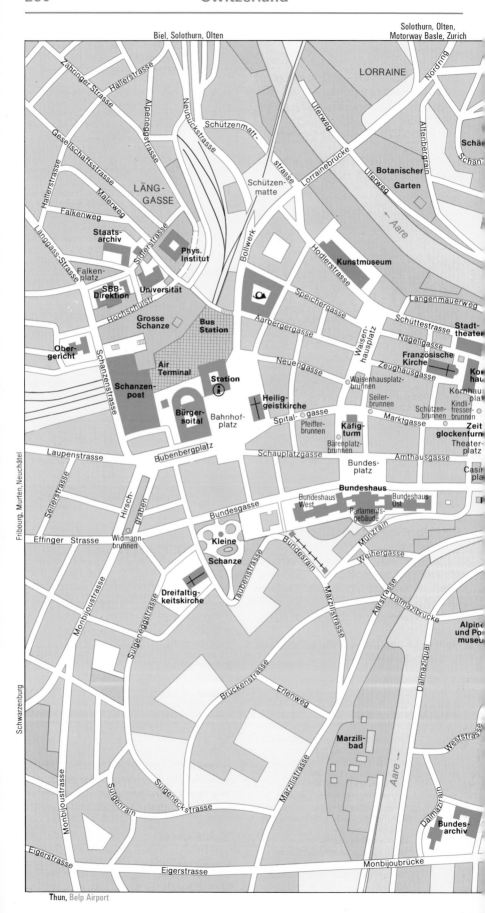

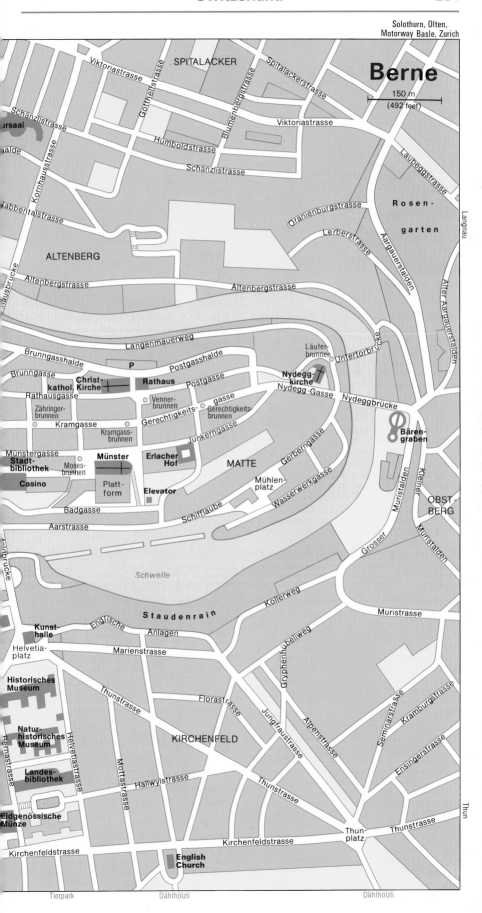

Berne

150 m
(492 feet)

Viktoriastrasse
Gotthelfstrasse
SPITALACKER
Spitalackerstrasse
Schänzlistrasse
Blumenbergstrasse
Viktoriastrasse
Ursaal
Humboldstrasse
Schänzlistrasse
Kornhausstrasse
Oranienburgstrasse
Laubeggstrasse
Langnau
Rosen-
garten
Rabbentalstrasse
Lerberstrasse
Aargauerstalden
ALTENBERG
Altenbergstrasse
Altenbergstrasse
Alter Aargauerstalden
Langenmauerweg
Läufer-
brunnen
Untertorbrücke
Brunngasshalde
P
Postgasshalde
Nydegg-
kirche
Brunngasse
Postgasse
Nydegg-Gasse
Christ-
kathol. Kirche
Rathaus
Nydeggbrücke
Rathausgasse
Venner-
brunnen
gasse
Bären-
graben
Zähringer-
brunnen
Gerechtigkeits-
Gerechtigkeits-
brunnen
Kramgasse
Gerberngasse
Kramgass-
brunnen
Junkerngasse
Münstergasse
Münster
Erlacher
Hof
MATTE
Muristalden
OBST-
BERG
Stadt-
bibliothek
Moses-
brunnen
Mühlen-
platz
Kleiner
Casino
Platt-
form
Elevator
Wasserwerkgasse
Badgasse
Schifflaube
Aarstrasse
Grosser
Muristalden
Schwelle
Kollerweg
Muristrasse
Staudenrain
Englische
Anlagen
Gryphenhübeliweg
Kunst-
halle
Marienstrasse
Helvetia-
platz
Historisches
Museum
Thunstrasse
Florastrasse
Jungfraustrasse
Alpenstrasse
Semrarstrasse
Kramburgstrasse
Natur-
historisches
Museum
KIRCHENFELD
Helvetiastrasse
Ensingerstrasse
Landes-
bibliothek
Mottastrasse
Hallwylstrasse
Thunstrasse
Thun
Eidgenössische
Münze
Thun-
platz
Thunstrasse
Kirchenfeldstrasse
Kirchenfeldstrasse
English
Church

Tierpark
Dählhölzli
Dählhölzli

Berne – panoramic view

Minster – late Gothic (begun 1421). A three-aisled pillared basilica without transept. The **Dance of Death Window** in the Matter Chapel contains 20 scenes from the 'Dance of Death' (1516–19) by Niklaus Manuel-Deutsch

Bärgraben (Bear Pit) – a deep circular den in which bears – the heraldic animal of Berne – have been kept since 1480

Gerechtigkeitsgasse – lined on both sides by arcades and elegant shops. In the middle of the street is the **Justice Fountain**

Rathaus (Townhall) – Burgundian Gothic style, built in 1406–16, much altered in 1866 and restored in the original style in 1939–42

Zeitglockenturm (Clock tower) – a notable Berne landmark, frequently rebuilt – the present stone tower with its pointed spire is 15th century – which was the west gate of the town until about 1250. On the east side of the tower is an **astronomical clock** (1527–30) with mechanical figures which perform four minutes before every hour

Kindlifresserbrunnen (Child-Eater Fountain) – c. 1540. A curious fountain, standing in the Kornhausplatz, with the figure of an ogre devouring a child

Kornhaus (1711–16) – a handsome building with high vaulted wine-cellars (restaurant); on the first floor are the **Industrial Museum** and the **Swiss Gutenberg Museum**

Kunstmuseum (Museum of Art) – built in 1879, with a plain windowless extension of 1935, contains a large collection of Swiss art, pictures by Italian Masters of the 14th–16th century and works by French artists of the 19th and 20th century

Schanzli – once an outer work in the town's defences, now occupied by the **Kursaal** (restaurant, concert hall, casino) from the terrace of which there is a magnificent view of Berne and the Alps

Helvetiaplatz – a large square around the **Telegraph Union Monument** (1922) and surrounded by museums. The **Art Gallery** (Kunsthalle, 1918) has special exhibitions of contemporary art; the **Berner Schulwarte** (1933) with a rich collection of teaching material; the **Swiss Alpine Museum** (1934) presents a fascinating picture of the Swiss Alps; the **Swiss Postal Museum** illustrates the history of the Swiss postal service

Historical Museum of Berne (1892–94) – built in the style of a 16th-century castle, with collections of prehistoric material, folk art and traditions,

ethnography and various types of decorative and applied art

Natural History Museum (1933) – excellently displayed collections of geology, mineralogy, palaeontology, and zoology

Basle

Verkehrsverein
Schifflände 5
CH-4001 Basle
Tel: (61) 25 50 50

Zentrale Unterkunftsvermittlung
(Accommodation Bureau)
Messeplatz 7
CH-4021 Basle
Tel: (61) 691 77 00

Basle is Switzerland's second largest city. It is built on both sides of the Rhine and lies close to the German and French frontiers.

Sightseeing

Minster – standing on the highest point of the hill the Minster dominates the city with its two slender spires, its masonry of red Vosges sandstone and its colourfully patterned roof. Rebuilt in Gothic style after an earthquake in 1356 it was a cathedral until the Reformation

Basle Town Hall

Rathaus (Town Hall) – brightly painted building with arcades in late Burgundian Gothic style (1504–21). The new wing to the left and the tall tower on the right are 19th century additions

Natur-und Völkerkunde Museum (Museum of

Basle – view across the Rhine towards the Minster

National History and Ethnography) – complex also includes the **Swiss Folk Museum** and the **Collection on the History of Paper**

Gemsberg, Basle

Kunstmuseum (Public Art Collection or Museum of Art) – contains the finest collections of pictures in Switzerland, including both old masters and modern art, and also a Print Cabinet

Antikenmuseum (Museum of Antiquities) – Greek works of art from 2500 to 100 BC and Roman and Italian art from 1000 BC to AD 300

Historical Museum – housed in the 14th century church of the Barefoot Friars (Barfüsserkirche). An important collection on the history of culture and art

Zoo – a large and interesting zoo with a vivarium, an excellent monkey house and a children's zoo

Colonia Augusta Raurica – Roman colony founded about 27 BC with a large theatre, an amphitheatre, the remains of several temples, and a reconstruction of a Roman house

Spalentor (1370) – a fortified gate which marks the end of the old town

Spalentor, Basle

Geneva

Office du Tourisme
CH-1211 Geneva
Tel: (22) 28 72 33

The city of Calvin and centre of the Reformation lies in the extreme west-

ern tip of Switzerland at the south-west end of Lake Geneva. It enjoys a magnificent view of the largest of the Alpine lakes and of the majestic peak of Mont Blanc. It has a lively and cosmopolitan atmosphere and attracts the greatest number of foreign visitors of any Swiss centre.

Sightseeing

Cathedral of Saint-Pierre (1150–1232) – situated on the highest point of the Old Town. Romanes-

que church with Gothic elements. The interior is of impressive effect with its harmonious proportions and the austere simplicity characteristic of Calvinist churches

Chapelle des Macchabées, 1406 – with later alterations; restored 1939–1940. A superb example of High Gothic religious architecture, with beautiful window traceries

Reformation Monument (1917) – in the middle are figures of Calvin, Guillaume Farel, Theodore de Bèze and John Knox, and on either side are the statesmen who promoted the cause of the Reformed faith, and bas-reliefs with scenes from the history of the Calvinist Reformation. At the ends are memorials to Luther and Zwingli

University – in buildings which developed out of

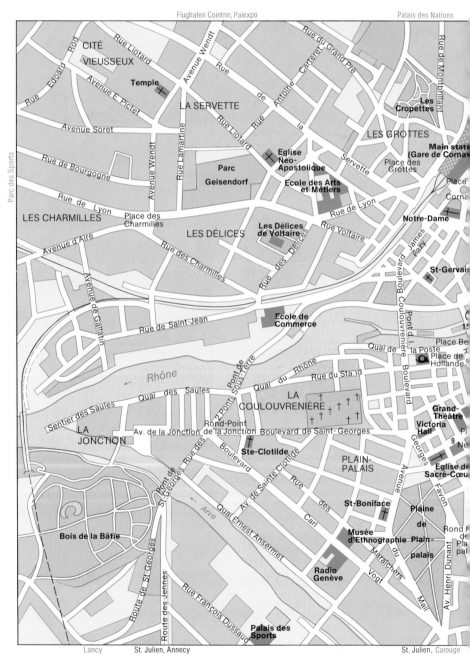

1 Palais de Justice
2 Collège de St-Antoine

3 Musée des Instruments
  Anciens de Musique

4 Musée d'Art et d'Histoire
5 Ecole des Beaux-Arts

6 Athénée
7 Monument de la Réformation

the Academy founded by Calvin in 1559 for the training of Reformed theologians. The **Library** contains some 1,200,000 volumes, a **Rousseau Museum** and a **Reformation Museum**

Musee d'Art et d'Histoire – rich collections of applied art and archaeology, a collection of weapons and a fine picture gallery

Natural History Museum – informatively displayed collections and a specialised library. Of particular interest are the dioramas of regional fauna, the large fossils and palaeontological and mineralogical collections

Institut et Musée Voltaire – housed in a mansion set in a small park. Relics and mementoes of Voltaire

Palais des Nations – a monumental complex of buildings (second largest in Europe after the Palace of Versailles) clad in light-coloured marble. European home of the United Nations. The decorations of the various halls and rooms – usually lavish – were donated by different countries

Ariana – a building in Italian Renaissance style erected in 1877–84 for the Geneva writer and philanthropist P G Revilliod (1817–90). A sumptuously appointed interior now housing the International Academy of Ceramics and a rich collection of ceramics and porcelain

Oecumenical Centre – headquarters of the World Council of Churches, the Lutheran World Federation, the Reformed World Federation and other non-Catholic church associations

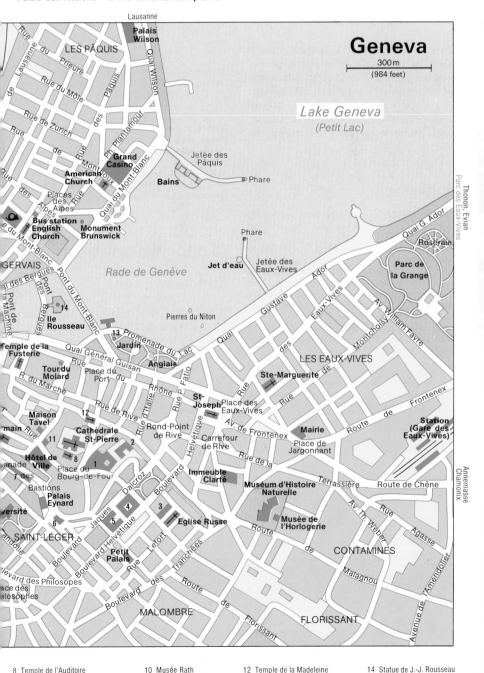

Zurich

Schweizerische Verkehrszentrale
Bellariastrasse 38,
CH-8027 Zurich
Tel: (1) 202 37 37

Offizielles Verkehrsbüro
(Information, accommodation register)
Bahnhofplatz 15, Hauptbahnhof
Tel: (1) 11 40 00

Verkehrsverein Zurich
Direktion, Kongressbüro
Bahnhofbrücke 1,
CH-8001 Zurich
Tel: (1) 11 12 56

Zurich, Switzerland's largest city, is also the country's cultural and economic centre. Despite the fact that a fifth of the country's total national income is earned here, Zurich is still one of Switzerland's most handsome towns, with much to attract and interest the visitor.

Sightseeing

Bahnhofstrasse – the pulsating activity of the city is focussed on this street lined with elegant shops, department stores and banks
Schweizerisches Landesmuseum (Swiss National Museum) – a large castellated building (1893–98) which contains the country's largest collection of material on the history and culture of Switzerland
Kunstgewerbemuseum (Museum of Decorative Arts) – special exhibitions of graphic art, design, architecture and applied art
St Peter's Church – Zurich's oldest parish church with a late Romanesque choir under the tower (13th century) and a Baroque nave of 1705. It has the largest clock-face in Europe
Fraumünster – a three-aisled pillared basilica with a Gothic nave, an Early Gothic transept and a pointed spire. In the imposing Late Romanesque choir are five stained-glass windows by Marc Chagall (1970)
Zunfthaus zur Meisen – a magnificent Late Baroque guild-house (1752–57) in the style of a French hôtel (town mansion). Houses the Swiss National Museum's ceramic collection
Rathaus (Town Hall, 1694–98) – a massive Late Renaissance building overhanging the river, with rich sculptured decoration
Grossmünster – Zurich's principal church which dominates the city with its twin towers. A Romanesque three-aisled galleried basilica (11th–13th century). Notable features are the two modern bronze doors (1935–36), the sculptured Romanesque capitals, remains of Gothic wall-paintings and the Late Romanesque cloister
Kunsthaus (Art Gallery) – important collection of pictures and sculpture from antiquity to the present day. To the right of the entrance is Rodin's 'Gate of Hell' (1880–1917). Swiss painters, French Impressionists, 20th century German painters and the Dadaist's are all well represented
Schauspielhaus (Theatre) – housed in the Haus zum Pfauen (House of the Peacock: built 1888–89,

Zurich

reconstructed 1976–78). One of the most renowned of German-language theatres, completely remodelled in the rebuilding
Kongresshaus (Congress Hall, 1939) – built on the older Concert Hall, it is one of the major focal points of Zurich's social life with its concerts and conferences
Rietberg Museum – housed in a Neo-classical villa modelled on the Villa Albani in Rome. Built in 1857 it became the meeting place of the intellectual élite of Zurich, including Wagner and Meyer. Now contains a fine collection of African and Asian art

Accommodation

Hotels and Inns

The Swiss hotel trade has a long and honourable tradition behind it. Overall, the standard of quality is higher than in other European countries, and even in hotels of the lower categories the accommodation and service are usually among the best of their kind. Outside the larger towns such as Zurich and Geneva, the establishments are mostly of small and medium size.

In many places there are reasonably priced hotels and restaurants which serve no alcohol (*alkoholfrei*). A list of such establishments can be obtained from the Schweizerische Stiftung für Forderung von Gemeindestuben, Brandschenkestrasse 36, CH-8039 Zurich. Tel: (1) 2 01 20 40.

Youth Hostels

Switzerland has some 120 youth hostels (German *Jugendherberge*, French *auberge de jeunesse*, Italian *alloggio*

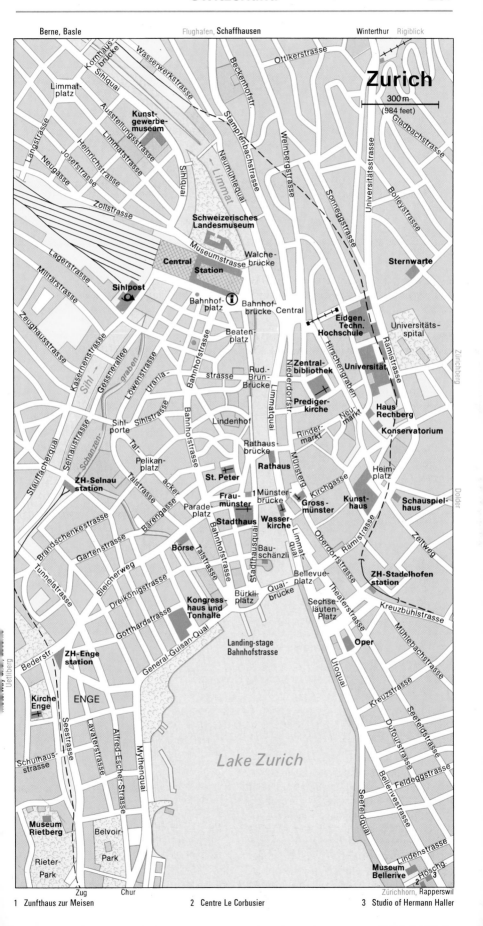

Zurich

300 m
(984 feet)

Ottikerstrasse

Kornhaus-brücke

Wasserwerkstrasse

Sihlquai

Limmat-platz

Langstrasse

Ausstellungsstrasse

Heinrichstrasse

Limmatstrasse

Josefstrasse

Neugasse

Zollstrasse

Lagerstrasse

Militärstrasse

Zeughausstrasse

**Kunst-
gewerbe-
museum**

Beckenhofstr.

Stampfenbachstrasse

Neumühlequai

Limmat

Weinbergstrasse

Sonneggstrasse

Universitätsstrasse

Gladbachstrasse

Bolleystrasse

**Schweizerisches
Landesmuseum**

Museumstrasse

Walche-brücke

Sternwarte

**Central
Station**

Sihlquai

Sihlpost

Bahnhof-platz

Bahnhof-brücke Central

**Eidgen.
Techn.
Hochschule**

Universitäts-
spital

Beaten-platz

Bahnhofstrasse

Rud.-
Brun-
Brücke

strasse

**Zentral-
bibliothek**

Hirschengraben

Universität

Rämistrasse

Zürichberg

Kasernenstrasse

Gessnerallee

graben

Sihl

Löwenstrasse

Urania

Sihlstrasse

Lindenhof

Limmatquai

Niederdorfstr.

**Prediger-
kirche**

Neu-markt

**Haus
Rechberg**

Konservatorium

Dolder

Gartenhofstrasse

Selnaustrasse

Sihl-
porte

Tal-
acker

Pelikan-platz

Rathaus-brücke

Rinder-markt

Kirchgasse

Heim-platz

**ZH-Selnau
station**

Talstrasse

Bärengasse

Parade-platz

St. Peter

**Frau-
münster**

Rathaus

Stadthaus

Münstergasse

**Gross-
münster**

**Kunst-
haus**

**Schauspiel-
haus**

Münster-brücke

**Wasser-
kirche**

Oberdorfstrasse

Rämistrasse

Zeltweg

Stauffacherquai

Brandschenkestrasse

Bleicherweg

Börse

Talstrasse

Bahnhofstrasse

Stadthausquai

Limmat-quai

Bau-
schänzli

**ZH-Stadelhofen
station**

Tunnelstrasse

Gartenstrasse

Dreikönigstrasse

**Kongress-
haus und
Tonhalle**

Bürkli-platz

Quai-brücke

Bellevue-platz

Sechse-
läuten-
Platz

Theaterstrasse

Kreuzbühlstrasse

Mühlebachstrasse

Gotthardstrasse

General-Guisan-Quai

Landing-stage
Bahnhofstrasse

Oper

Utoquai

Bederstr.

**ZH-Enge
station**

Uetliberg

**Kirche
Enge**

ENGE

Seestrasse

Lavaterstrasse

Alfred-Escher-Strasse

Mythenquai

Lake Zurich

Kreuzstrasse

Dufourstrasse

Seefeldstrasse

Feldeggstrasse

Seefeldquai

Bellerivestrasse

Schulhaus-
strasse

**Museum
Rietberg**

Belvoir-
Park

Rieter-
Park

Lindenstrasse

Höschg.

**Museum
Bellerive**

Zürichhorn, Rapperswil

Zug   Chur

1 Zunfthaus zur Meisen   2 Centre Le Corbusier   3 Studio of Hermann Haller

Hotel Price Range

Type of hotel	Price for 1 night in francs	
	Single	Double
*****	110–250	160–380
****	90–200	150–220
***	70–110	120–160
**	50– 95	85–140
*	45– 90	65–130

These are inclusive charges (i.e. including service and taxes). In popular tourist and vacation resorts the rates may be higher, particularly at the height of the season; and it is quite common in such places for hotels to let rooms only with half or full board.

per giovani) providing modestly priced accommodation, particularly for young people (with priority for those under 25). During the main holiday season it is advisable to book places in advance; and the maximum period of stay permitted in any one hostel will vary according to the demand for places. Youth hostellers must produce a membership card issued by their national youth hostel association.

Information:
Schweizerischer Bund für Jugendherbergen
(Swiss Youth Hostel Association),
Postfach 265, Engestrasse 9,
CH-3022 Bern,
Tel: (031) 24 55 03.

Camping and Caravanning

Switzerland now has something like 500 camping sites, some 90 of which remain open in winter. There are special regulations affecting trailer caravans which should be studied before leaving for Switzerland.

Introduction to Rail Information

Since the first Swiss train ran in 1847, the network has expanded rapidly. In 1902, the five major railway companies who operated a total of 2934km of track, were nationalised. However, this still left nearly the same amount of track in private hands. Indeed, these private lines are still of great importance today particularly when it comes to scenic routes. The entire Swiss rail system is electrified as well as being one of the densest systems in Europe. It is second only to Japan in the frequency of its services.

Map supplied by kind permission of Thomas Cook Ltd

Major International Services

Connection	Duration	Frequency
Geneva–Paris	3½–4hrs	5 times daily
Geneva–London	10–17hrs	4 times daily
Zurich–Paris	6–8½hrs	6 times daily
Munich–Geneva	8hrs	4 times daily
Milan–Basle	5½–6hrs	9 times daily
Lausanne–Brig	1½–2hrs	2/3 times per hour
Chur–Basle	2½–3hrs	hourly
Zurich–Berne	1¼–1¾hrs	2/3 times per hour

Major Internal Services

Connection	Duration	Frequency
Geneva–Lausanne	½–¾hr	4 times per hour
Interlaken–Berne	1hr	hourly

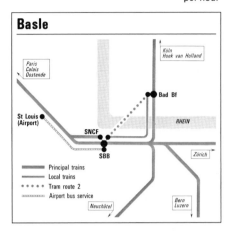

Basle

Koln
Hoek van Holland

Paris
Calais
Oostende

Bad Bf

St Louis
(Airport)

RHEIN

SNCF

SBB

Zürich

Principal trains
Local trains
Tram route 2
Airport bus service

Neuchâtel

Bern
Luzern

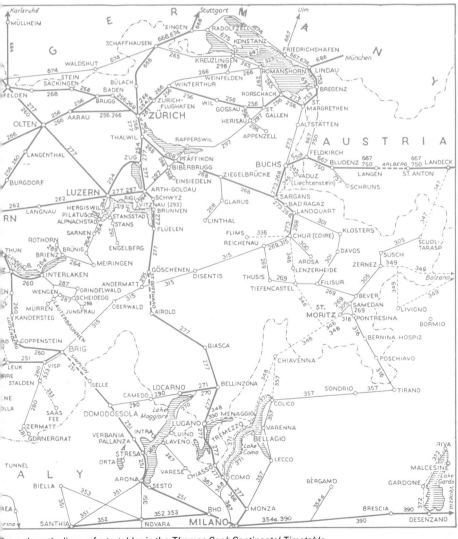

bers along the lines refer to tables in the *Thomas Cook Continental Timetable*.

June 1st 1987 heralded the start of a rail service which runs right up to Geneva Airport. The aim is to provide rail links not only with Geneva and towns in the locality but also to create connections with a large number of the country's major centres.

Scenic Routes

Switzerland has some of the most breathtaking landscape in Europe and this is reflected in the fact that it has the largest number of scenic railways. The various rail companies operating these lines go to great lengths to make sure that the tourist gets the best views possible often extending the window space for this purpose. Contrasting scenes of lush meadows, placid lakes, cypresses, fig and almond trees against a shining backcloth of the snowcapped Alps make for some of the most fascinating rail journeys in the world.

Montreux Oberland Bernois
This magnificent alpine railway passes through 3 countries and many well-known resorts. It provides the only direct access to the Bernese Oberland from Lake Geneva.

Berne–Lotschberg–Simplon Railway

The B-L-S Railway provides an important link between the highly populated areas north of the Alps and Italy. It passes through two popular holiday areas – the Bernese Oberland and the Valais. The line runs through 34 tunnels and over 25 major bridges and viaducts. The countryside provides a fascinating succession of villages, forests, mountains, lakes, rivers and cities. (B-L-S, PO Box 3001, Berne.)

Bernina Express
This train departs from Chur, travels through the Albula Valley, on to St Moritz, over the Bernina Pass to Poschiavo and finally Tirano in Italy. The line includes the impressively long Landwasser Viaduct, the Morteratsch Glacier and majestic ice-capped mountain peaks. The journey lasts 4 hours.

Furka Oberalp Bahn
This panoramic trip over the Oberalp Pass (2033 metres above sea level) takes you through the lovely valleys of Tavetsch (Grisons), Urseren (Uri) and Goms (Valais). Information from: Furka-Oberalp-Railway, CH-3900 Brig.

The Gotthard Line
This famous railway line takes passengers through that remarkable feat of engineering – the Gotthard tunnel. The 9-mile tunnel, which cost 177 men their lives, takes 12 minutes to travel through. Travel from Basle or Zurich through to the plain of Lombardy and the sun-drenched Mediterranean on the Gotthard Line.

Veteran Railways

1. **Appenzeller–Bahn** (Eastern Switzerland)
   Route: Gossau–Herisau–Urnaesch–Appenzell–Wasserauen
   Steam Engine G3/4 No 14 and two passenger carriages, built 1886, renovated and adorned with rustic paintings. Also, one renovated summer passenger carriage runs on special excursions for groups on application during summer months.

2. **Blonay–Chamby** (Lake of Geneva)
   Route: Blonay–Chamby–Blonay
   Chamby–Chaulin (Depot/museum)–Chamby
   Open weekends May to October
   Museum railway line run by enthusiasts

The Blonay-Chamby Railway

3. **Berner–Oberland–Bahnen** (Bernese Oberland)
   Route: Interlaken Ost–Luetschental (near Grindelward) – Interlaker Ost
   Steam Engine BOB/MEFEZ G3/4 No 11 (built in 1902 for Rhaetian Railway). Runs on special excursions for groups on application from April to November.

4. **Brienz–Rothorn–Bahn** (Bernese Oberland)
   Route: Brienz–Rothorn Kulm–Brienz
   Rack-and-pinion mountain railway. Seven steam engines H2/3 (built 1891). Runs daily to set timetable during summer months only. (See official Swiss Railways timetable, table 475.)

5. **Bodensee–Toggenburg–Bahn** (Eastern Switzerland)
   Route: Herisau–Nesslau–Neu St Johann–

Herisau 'Amor Express' including Maffei Steam Engine Eb3/5 and 4 or 5 special carriages. Runs on special excursions for groups on application from April to October.

6. **Brig–Visp–Zermatt–Bahn** (Valais)
   Route: a) St Niklaus–Zermatt
   b) Brig or Visp–Zermatt
   Runs on special excursions for groups on application from May to mid-June and from mid-September until end of October.

7. **Dampfbahn–Verein Zuercher Oberland** (Zurich)
   Route: Bauma–Baeretswil–Hinwil
   'Museum Railway' run by enthusiasts. Selected Sundays during summer months. Seat reservations for groups at Bauma Station SBB. Tel. 052/46 12 41.

8. **Chemin de Fer Fribourgeois** (Fribourg region)
   Route: Paleziux–Chatel-St-Denis–Bulle–Gruyères–Montbovon and Bulle–Broc
   Runs on special excursions for groups on application.

9. **Lausanne–Echallens–Bercher** (Lake of Geneva)
   Route: Lausanne–Chauderon–Cheseaux–Bercher
   Runs on special excursions for groups on application.

10. **Schweizerische Bundesbahnen** (Switzerland)
    Swiss Federal Railways have the following two steam engines in operating condition for historic trains: Eb3/5 No 5819, built 1912 and CZM½ No 31, built 1902 (railcar, formerly Verikon–Bauma–Bahn). They run a number of trips during the summer months. Special excursions for groups are available on application to SBB Zurich.

11. **Schinznacher Baumschulbahn** (Basle/Zurich)
    Route: Railway runs through tree and plant nursery
    Length: 4km
    Gauge: 600mm
    Steam engines
    Weekends April to October. Special excursions for groups on application.

12. **Schynige Platte Bahn** (Bernese Oberland)
    Route: Wilderswil–Schynige Platte–Wilderswil
    Rack-and-pinion steam engine SPBH No 5 (built 1984)
    Special excursions for groups on application June–October.

13. **Sursee–Triengen–Bahn** (Central Switzerland)
    Route: Sursee–Triengen
    Length: 9km
    Two E3/3 steam engines and three passenger carriages
    Runs special excursions for groups on application.

14. **Sensetalbahn** (Bernese Mittelland)
    Route: Flamatt–Guemmenen–Flamatt
    Engine E2/2 'Laufenburgerli'; Engine E3/3 'Lise'; double-headed traction 2 × E3/3.
    Every first Sunday of the month from May until October. Consult Swiss Railways timetable, table 257. Special excursions for groups on application (not November to February).

15. **Region alverkehr Bern–Solothurn** (Bernese Mittelland)
    Route: Worblaufen–Solothurn–Worblaufen
    Length: 36km
    Gauge: narrow
    Selected Sundays during summer months
    Special excursions for groups on application.

16. **Sihltal–Zurich–Uetliberg–Bahn** (Zurich)
    Route: Zurich Selnau–Sihlbrugg–Zurich–Selnau
    Length: 17km
    Gauge: standard
    Historical steam train
    Runs special excursions for groups on application.

17. **Region alverkehr Bern–Solothurn** (Bernese Mittelland)
    Route: Worblaufen–Worb Dorf–Worblaufen
    Length: 12km
    Gauge: narrow
    Daily except Sunday; 4 weeks notice
    Special excursions for groups on application.

18. **Verein 'Mikado 1244'** (Eastern Switzerland)
    The Steam Engine 'Liberation' 141R 1244 (1D1) formerly *SNCF* was renovated by the Society 'Mikado 1244'. It runs special excursions for groups on application (minimum 300 fare-paying passengers required).

19. **Vitznau–Rigi–Bahn** (Central Switzerland)
    Route: Vitznau–Rigi Kaltbad
    Rack-and-pinion mountain railway
    Selected dates during summer months
    Special excursions for groups available on application.

20. **Waldenburgerbahn** (Basle region)
    Route: Liestal–Waldenburg–Liestal
    Length: 13.5km
    Gauge: 750mm
    Steam train WB, Steam Engine Gedeon Thommen' No 5
    Every 3rd Sunday of the month from May to October. Special excursions for groups on application.

Internal Fare Structure

Standard Rate Fares

The standard rate fares are calculated on a kilometric basis. For example, a 2nd class single for 40–42km costs 9.40SF; a 2nd class single for 121–125km costs 28SF and a 2nd class single for 251–260km costs 45SF. It is cheaper to buy a return ticket than it is to buy two singles except for journeys of less than 40km. Many private railways have their own tariffs.

Student Reductions

Students are advised to refer to Half Fare Travel Cards below and to the International Section.

Half-Fare Travel Cards

These may be purchased for 1 year at 100SF or foreign visitors can obtain them for a month (65SF). Foreign visitors may purchase them in their own countries before departure.

Family Card

With the Swiss Family Card children travel free. Those aged between 16 and 25 travel at half rate. The accompanying parents pay full rate or half rate if they hold a Half-Fare Travel Card.

Senior Citizen Reductions

Senior Citizens resident outside Switzerland are advised to consult the International Section for further information on reductions.

The Rhätische Bahn at the Lago Bianco

Party/Group Savers

Parties of adults are entitled to group tickets which offer reductions dependent on the size of the group. For instance, 6–24 adults gain a 20% reduction; 25 or more adults gain a 30% reduction.

Special Excursion/Holiday Rates

Regional Holiday Season Tickets are a competitive alternative to standard rate fares for tourists travelling to certain holiday areas. They are valid for a number of different time spans. As a price example, a Regional Holiday Season Ticket to the Bernese Oberland starts at 102SF. Holders of Half-Fare Travel Cards (or Swiss Holiday Pass) are entitled to a 20% reduction.

Tourist Reductions

The Swiss Holiday pass is available to people who are permanently resident outside Europe. The pass allows unlimited free travel by rail, boat, postal coach and reduced fares on many mountain railways and aerial cablecars. The pass may be purchased at travel agencies outside Europe and from Swiss National Tourist Offices. The prices range as follows: for 2nd class travel, £130 (1 month), £94 (15 days), £78 (8 days), £64 (4 days).

Where to Buy Tickets

In Switzerland

From Swiss rail stations and travel agents.

In Great Britain

From any British Rail station or from:
European Rail Travel Centre
PO Box 303
Victoria Station
London SW1V 1JY
Tel: (071) 834 2345

Swiss National Tourist Office and Swiss Federal Railways,
'Swiss Centre'
1 New Coventry Street
London W1V 8EE
Tel: (071) 734 1921

In USA

From Swiss railway representatives in the major cities (see International Section).

Facilities on Trains

Motorail

There is no motorail service on the Swiss internal services, although there are facilities for transporting cars on some of the international services. Details of these facilities can be obtained from the Swiss National Tourist Office.

Sleepers and Couchettes

Sleeper berths can be reserved against payment of a supplement by the holders of 1st and 2nd class tickets. They may be booked up to 3 months before the date of travel. The supplement payable for the use of a 2nd class couchette is 21SF. There are 4 or 6 couchettes in a 2nd class compartment and 4 in a 1st class one. Reservations can be made through any station or travel agency and couchettes can be allocated up to 2 months in advance.

Food

Most of the inter-city and express trains have dining cars. Reservations are accepted for the restaurant car but not in the self service car. A number of the express trains have a minibar selling refreshments. Swiss stations are well equipped with restaurant and buffet facilities.

Disabled

Tip up seats in the smoking compartments of the new 2nd class coaches provide room for a passenger in a wheelchair to travel in comfort.

Palais des Nations, Geneva

Cog-wheel railway

Facilities at Stations

Food

Swiss stations are well equipped with restaurant and buffet facilities.

Reservations

It is not possible to reserve seats on internal train journeys except for groups of 10 or more. For international trips it is advisable to reserve your seat for a charge of 4SF per seat. Reservations can be made at the ticket retail outlets (see Where to buy tickets).

Disabled

Wheelchairs are available for use within station premises. Inform the station of departure that you will need one and the staff will help.

Bicycle Hire

Bicycles can be hired at most stations in Switzerland although it is advisable to reserve them a day or two in advance. They can be returned to any station.

Car Hire

A joint service is operated between Swiss Federal Railways so that a car can be ordered at any rail station and collected and returned at any other station.

West Germany

Ramsau in the Berchtesgadener Land, Bavarian Alps

Introduction

**From the lowland regions along the
North Sea and Baltic coasts by way of
the rolling forest-clad uplands to the
Bavarian Alps, West Germany provides an endless variety of scenery to
interest the tourist. Despite the destruction caused by the Second World
War, there is still considerable evidence in the north of the wealthy
Hanseatic towns which once ruled the
seas, and in the south, of the old free
imperial cities with their splendid
cathedrals and palaces. Regional
variations are also to be found in the
nature of the German population, in its
cuisine, and in its excellent wines.**

Geographically, West Germany is divided into five zones: the North German
Lowlands, the Central and Southern
German Uplands, the Alpine Foreland,
and the Bavarian Alps. Within these the
attractions of the countryside are
many, ranging from the Rhine Valley to
Lake Constance and the Alps to the
Black Forest. The country's climate is
equally varied as it falls within the un-
predictable, though temperate climatic
zone of Central Europe. The south and
east tend to experience slightly greater
seasonal variations while the north
tends to be wetter.

Nave of St Michael's Church, Hildesheim

The total population of West Germany
amounts to 61.3 million, spread over a
total area of 248,000sq km. There is no
shortage of entertainment to be found
in the country, ranging from the religious, folk and cultural festivals to the
internationally renowned beer festivals. Particularly in Bavaria and the
Black Forest, where traditional folk costumes can still be seen, these festivals
abound.

Religion has always played an important role in German life, as its stormy
past would suggest. Now there are
both Catholics and Protestants in Germany and the continuing importance
of religion can be seen in the fact that
two major political parties are called
the Christian Democratic Union and
the Christian Social Union.

The present system of government
was initiated in 1949, with the formal
assent of the Western occupying
forces. The constitution shows the influence of both the American and British models, and one of its major aims
was to ensure that the Hitler phe-
nomenon would not be repeated. The
formal Chief of State is the President,
who is chosen by a specially covened
assembly and appointed for a term of
five years. He in turn nominates the
Federal Chancellor, who is elected by a
majority in the *Bundestag* (parliament), and also his Cabinet. The *Bundestag* is made up of 496 members
elected by popular vote every four
years. The Chancellor is vested with
considerable independent powers and
initiates all government policy; but at
the same time, these powers are ba-
lanced by those of the President and
Bundestag.

The German economy in terms of its
gross national product is the most successful in the whole of Western
Europe. The economic recovery made
after the devastation of the Second
World War was astounding. Although
Germany possesses a rich variety of
mineral deposits, the backbone of the
economy is the manufacturing industry, which provides 43% of total
domestic production. The auto industry is particularly strong and Volks-
wagen is the fourth largest company in
Europe. Despite the fact that one half of
the country's land is devoted to agri-

culture, Germany still has to import a sizeable amount of its food. The most successful sector is dairy farming, in fact the country is almost totally self-sufficient in all dairy produce.

The artistic and intellectual development of the Federal Republic of Germany is that of the whole of the German language area before the 1949 divisions were created. Sponsored and influenced by the German Imperial Court and the Roman Catholic Church, with the intellectual cross-currents of the Reformation and the Renaissance, Germany fostered many leading cultural and intellectual figures of world renown.

The Romanesque period marks the beginning of an independent German art. The churches and cathedrals built during this time, for example at Mainz and Augsburg, provided opportunities for the religious art forms such as sculpture, carving, and stained glass windows to develop. Gothic styles were slow to assert themselves in Germany, but it is from the Gothic period that the new type of hall-church developed, the two most beautiful being the St Lawrence Church in Nürnberg (1439–72) and the St George in Dinkelsbühl (1448–89).

In Germany the Renaissance was not a period for great works of architecture, and there are few purely Renaissance buildings in Germany. However, it was in this era that Albrecht Dürer (1471–1528), the great master of German painting and Hans Holbein the Younger (1498–1543) were producing the finest works of German portraiture.

The Baroque period saw a great revival in German architecture both secular and religious. The skilled works of the Austrians, J B Fischer von Erlach and Lukas von Hildebrandt, predominently to be seen in south Germany, bear witness to this revival. The Rococo period was one riotous celebration in art, as seen in the palaces at Ansbade and Sanssouci. The neo-classical period on the other hand saw a revolt against the freedom that the French Revolution had inspired and a return to the art of classical antiquity, as seen in the work of Friedrich Schinkel.

The artistic movements of the late 19th century and early 20th century never established themselves in Germany as they did elsewhere in Europe, and it is not until the move towards the new objectivity at the beginning of the 20th century that German art and architecture was once again of great importance. The bastardisation of art for the purposes of propaganda during the reign of the National Socialist Party, put German art into the background again until its recovery after the Second World War with the great opportunities that the reconstruction of Germany afforded its artists and architects.

Perhaps Germany's greatest contribution to the culture of Europe was through music. The revival of the court and town orchestras and choirs after the Thirty Years War encouraged musical life in Germany and three great composers emerged – Georg Philipp Telemann (1681–1767), Johann Sebastian Bach (1685–1750) and Georg Friedrich Händel (1685–1759). Joseph Haydn (1732–1809), Wolfgang Amadeus Mozart (1756–91), and Ludwig van Beethoven (1770–1827) continued the tradition and became masters of the symphony, concerto and piano sonata. The works of Richard Wagner (1813–83) brought German Romantic opera, perhaps, to its highest pitch.

History

919	Henry of Saxony establishes a German Empire and begins medieval struggle with Roman Catholic Church
1184–6	Peak of the Hohenstaufen Empire under Frederick Barbarossa
1517	Beginning of the Reformation with Luther's 95 'theses'
1556	Abdication of Charles V and subsequent division of the Habsburg Empire
1618–48	Thirty Years War
18th century	Age of Enlightenment under Frederick the Great of Prussia
1815	Foundation of the German Confederation of 39 states at the Congress of Vienna
1848	March Revolution in German states
1914–18	First World War
1919–33	Weimar Republic in Germany
1933	Hindenburg appoints Adolf Hitler Chancellor
1939	Blitzkreig against Poland starts Second World War

1945	Germany surrenders (May)
1949	Germany divided into the Federal Republic of Germany and the German Democratic Republic. Berlin divided into East and West
1961	Berlin crisis and the building of the Wall
1973	Treaty with the German Democratic Republic. Both states become members of the United Nations
1974	Helmut Schmidt succeeds Willy Brandt as Chancellor
1978	Controversial law passed on terrorism in an attempt to limit the escalating problem of internal security
1983	Coalition government formed under Chancellorship of Dr Helmut Kohl
1986	East Germany celebrates the 25th anniversary of the Berlin Wall with a martial display, while West Germany deplored partition
1989	Opening of the Berlin Wall with free access from East to West. Followed by the overthrow of the East German leader Erich Honecker.

Major Centres

Berlin (West)

Verkehrsamt
Europa-Center
Berlin 30
Tel: 2 12 34/7 82 30 31

Embassies
UK: British Consulate General
Uhlandstrasse 7/8
Tel: (30) 309 62 92

Schloss Charlottenburg

Gedächtniskirche, Kurfürstendamm, Berlin

USA: 108 Berlin
Neustaedtische Kirchstrasse 4-5
Tel: 22 0 27 41

Berlin is Germany's main industrial city. With a population of nearly two million, two universities, a world famous opera company and Philharmonic Orchestra, West Berlin is also a focal point of political and cultural life.

Sightseeing

Botanic Garden – has fine tropical houses and mountain flora

Brandenburg Gate – built 1788–91 and stands on the boundary between East and West Berlin
Dahlem Museum – its magnificent collection of masterpieces includes 26 Rembrandts
Deutsche Oper Berlin (Berlin Opera House) – opened in 1961
Kaiser-Wilhelm-Gedächtniskirch – built 1891–5, famous for its ruined tower
Kurfürstendamm – runs for 3½km with elegant shops, restaurants and theatres
Olympic Stadium – built in 1936 for the 11th Olympic Games
Schloss Charlottenburg – 17th and 18th century buildings with museums and fine statues in courtyard
Jagdschloss Grunewald – Renaissance-style hunting lodge, originally built in 1542, and altered in the 18th century

Berlin Opera House

Hamburg

Fremdenterkehrszentrale
(Hamburg Tourist Information)
Bieberhaus (at main station)
Tel: (40) 24 87 00

Situated at the mouth of the Elbe, Hamburg is Germany's largest city after Berlin, and is in addition one of the leading centres of international trade. With a reputation as one of the country's foremost industrial cities, it is also the cultural centre of North Germany and offers the tourist a wide range of entertainment.

Sightseeing

Aussenalster – a stretch of water popular for sailing, with beautiful gardens on the west side
Binnenalster – a basin in the centre of the city surrounded by elegant streets and cafés
Hagenbecks Zoo – an excellently laid out modern zoo
Henrich Hertz Telecommunications Tower – finished in 1968; 271.5m high with a revolving restaurant
Port – a tidal harbour with numerous docks; a popular boat trip

Hamburg: the Jungfernstieg on the Binnenalster

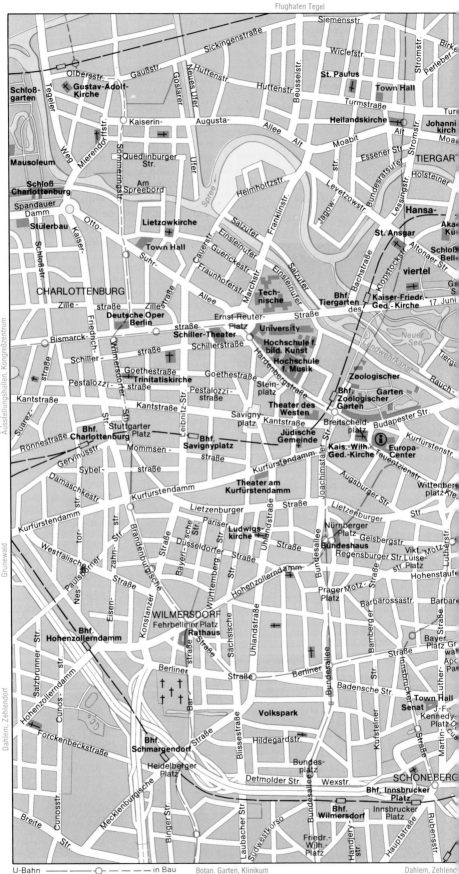

Flughafen Tegel

Siemensstr.

Sickingenstraße

Wiclefstr.

Birke

Olbersstr.

Gaußstr.

Huttenstr.

Beusselstr.

St. Paulus

Town Hall

Perleber

Stromstr.

Schloß
garten

Tegeler

Gustav-Adolf-
Kirche

Goslarer

Neues Ufer

Huttenstr.

Turmstraße

Tur

Kaiserin-

Augusta-

Alt

Moabit

Heilandskirche

Johanni
kirch

Moa

Weg

Mierendorffstr.

Sömmeringstr.

Quedlinburger
Str.

Ufer

Allee

Essener Str.

Alt

Bundesratsufer

TIERGART

Mausoleum

Schloß
Charlottenburg

Am
Spreebord

Spree

Helmholtzstr.

Levetzowstr.

Lessingstr.

Stromstr.

Holsteiner

Hansa-

Spandauer
Damm

Stülerbau

Otto-

Kaiser-

Schloßstr.

Lietzowkirche

Salzufer

Franklinstr.

Jagow-

str.

Bundesratsufer

St. Ansgar

Altonaer Str.

 Klopstockstr.

Aka
Kü

CHARLOTTENBURG

Zille-

straße

Suhr-

Town Hall

Cauerstr.

Einsteinufer

Guerickestr.

Fraunhoferstr.

Marchstr.

Einsteinufer

Salzufer

Technische

Bachstraße

Kaiser-Friedr.
Ged.-Kirche

viertel

Schloß
Bell

17. Juni

Gr
S

straße

Friedrich-

Zille

straße

Wilmersdorfer

Deutsche Oper
Berlin

Allee

Ernst-Reuter-
Platz

Schillerstraße

Straße

Bhf.
Tiergarten

des

Neuer
See

Bismarck-

Schiller-

Pestalozzi-

straße

Goethestraße

Trinitatiskirche

straße

Schiller-Theater

Goethestraße

Pestalozzi-
straße

University

Hardenbergstraße

Hochschule f.
bild. Kunst

Hochschule
f. Musik

Stein-
platz

Landwehrkanal

Rauch-

Tierg

Kantstraße

Kantstraße

Leibnitz-Str.

Savigny-
platz

Kantstraße

Theater des
Westens

Zoologischer

Bhf.
Zoologischer
Garten

Garten
Garten

Breitscheid-
platz

Budapester Str.

Suarez-

Rönnestr.

Bhf.
Charlottenburg

Stuttgarter
Platz

Mommsen-

Bhf.
Savignyplatz

straße

Jüdische
Gemeinde

Kaiser-Wilh-
Ged.-Kirche

Europa-
Center

Tauentzienstr.

Kurfürstenstr.

Gervinusstr.

Sybel-

straße

Kurfürstendamm

Kurfürstendamm

Joachimstaler Str.

Augsburger Str

Wittenber
platz Kle

Damaschkestr.

Kurfürstendamm

tor-

str.

Brandenburgische

Theater am
Kurfürstendamm

Lietzenburger

Pariser

Straße

Lietzenburger

Str.

Westfälischer

Paulsborner

Nestorstr.

zahn-

Str.

Brandenburgische

Württemberg.

Düsseldorfer

Bayer-

Ludwigs-
kirche

Uhlandstraße

Straße

Nürnberger
Platz

Geisbergstr.

Bundeshaus

Regensburger Str.

Vikt.-Motz-

Luise-
Platz

Luther-

str.

Hohenstaufe

Konstanzer

Straße

Straße

Hohenzollerndamm

Bundesallee

Prager
Platz

Motz-
Platz

Barbarossastr.

Barbara

Bhf.
Hohenzollerndamm

Eisen-

WILMERSDORF
Fehrbelliner Platz

Rathaus

Sächsische

Uhlandstraße

Bundesallee

Straße

Bamberger

Innsbrucker

Str.

Straße

Bayer.
Platz

Gr
wa

Apo
Pa

Salzbrunner
str.

Hohenzollerndamm

Cunosstr.

Berliner

Straße

Straße

Berliner

Badensche Str.

Kurfürsten

Straße

Martin-L

Town Hall
Senat

J.-F.
Kennedy-
Platz

Grunewald

Forckenbeckstraße

Bhf.
Schmargendorf

Straße

Heidelberger
Platz

Volkspark

Hildegardstr.

Blissestraße

SCHÖNEBERG

Dahlem, Zehlendorf

Breite

Cunosstr.

Str.

Mecklenburgische

Binger Str.

Laubacher Str.

Südwestkorso

Bundesallee

Bhf.
Wilmersdorf

Friedr.-
Wilh.-
Platz

Bundes-
platz

Detmolder Str.

Wexstr.

Innsbrucker
Platz

Bhf. Innsbrucker
Platz

Handjery-
str.

Hauptstraße

Rubensstr

U-Bahn ――――――○――――― in Bau　　　　Botan. Garten, Klinikum　　　　Dahlem, Zehlend

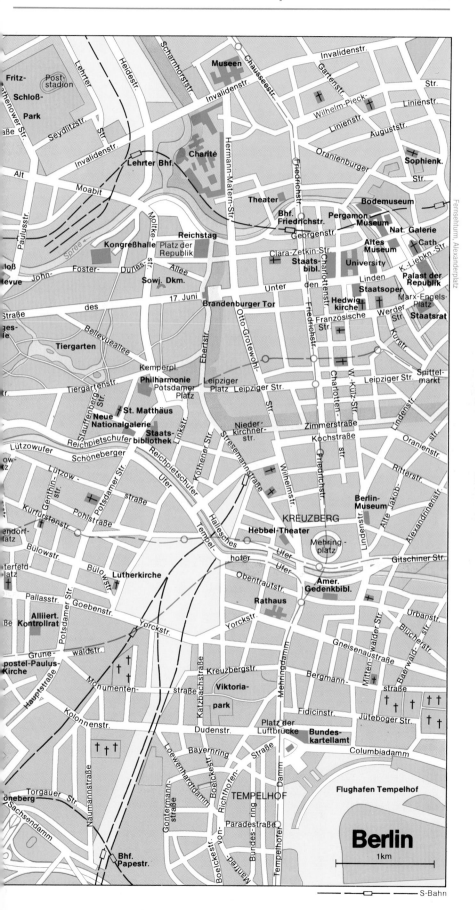

Berlin

1km

S-Bahn

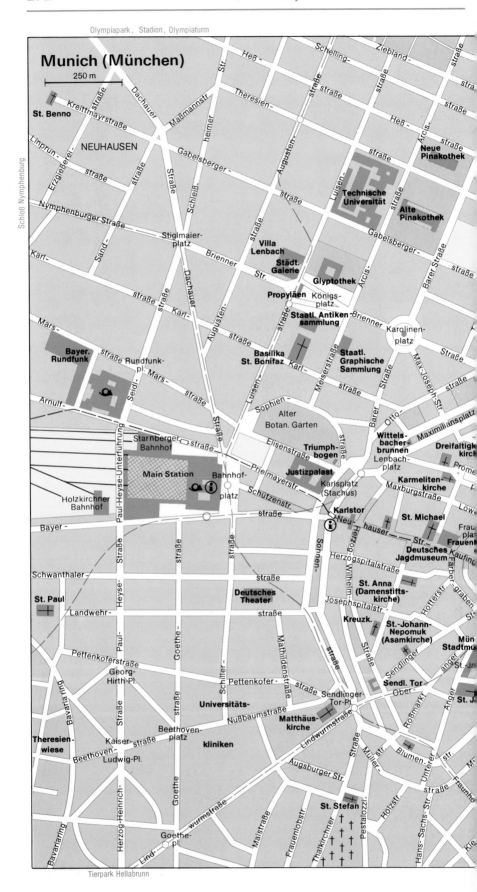

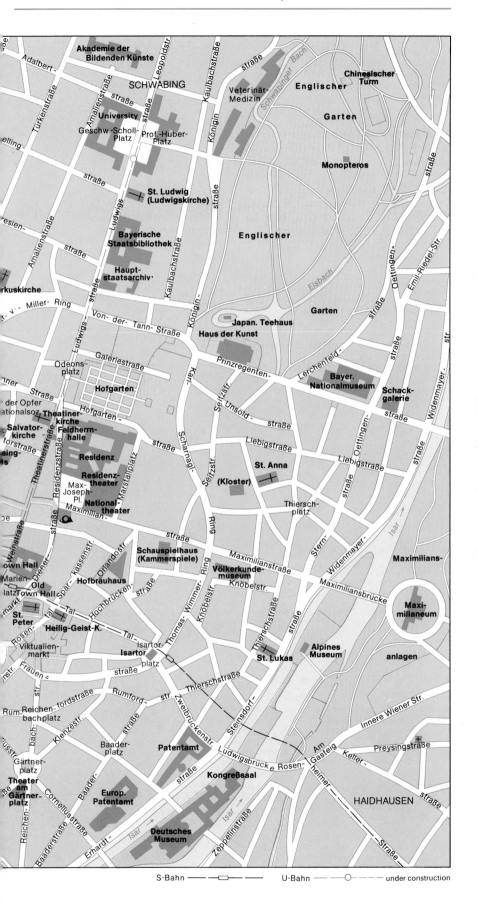

Map of central Munich:

Adalbert-straße · Türkenstraße · Amalienstraße · Leopoldstraße · Kaulbachstraße · straße · Schwabinger Bach · Englischer · Chinesischer Turm

Akademie der Bildenden Künste

SCHWABING

Veterinär-Medizin

Garten

University · Geschw.-Scholl-Platz · Prof.-Huber-Platz · Amalienstraße · straße · Königin-

Monopteros

St. Ludwig (Ludwigskirche)

Bayerische Staatsbibliothek

Haupt-staatsarchiv

Englischer

Ludwigstraße · Kaulbachstraße · Königin-straße

v.-Miller-Ring · Von-der-Tann-Straße

Eisbach

Garten

Oettingen-straße · Emil-Riedel-Str.

kuskirche

Galeriestraße

Japan. Teehaus

Haus der Kunst

Prinzregenten-

Odeons-platz

Hofgarten

Karl-straße · Seitzstr. · Unsöld-straße · Lerchenfeld-

Bayer. Nationalmuseum

Schack-galerie

Widenmayer-straße · str.

Theatiner-kirche

der Opfer nationalsoz

Salvator-kirche · torstraße

Feldherrn-halle

Residenz

Residenz-theater

Max-Joseph-Pl.

National-theater

St. Anna

(Kloster)

Liebigstraße · Oettingen-straße · Liebigstraße

Thiersch-platz

Scharnagl-straße · Scharnagl-straße · Seitzstr. · Ring

Maximilian-straße

Schauspielhaus (Kammerspiele)

Völkerkunde-museum

Maximilianstraße

Stern-straße · Widenmayer- · Isar

Maximilians-

Maxi-milianeum

own Hall · Drener- · kassenstr. · Spar- · Orlandostr.

Hofbräuhaus

Marien- · Old · latzTown Hall

markt · Tal · Hochbrücken- · straße · Thomas- · Wimmer- · Knöbelstr.

Knöbelstr.

Maximiliansbrücke

anlagen

St. Peter

Heilig-Geist-K. · Tal-

Rosen- · Viktualien-markt

Isartor-platz · Isartor · straße

St. Lukas

Thierschstraße

Alpines Museum

Frauen- · Rum · Reichen-bachplatz · Rumford- · str. · Zweibrückenstr. · Steinsdorf- · Thierschstraße

Innere Wiener Str.

Gärtner-platz

Theater am Gärtner-platz

Baader-platz · Klenzestr. · Baader- · Cornelusstraße

Patentamt

Europ. Patentamt

Ludwigsbrücke Rosen-

Kongreßsaal

Am Gasteig · Keller- · heimer- · Preysingstraße

HAIDHAUSEN · straße

Deutsches Museum

Isar · Zeppelinstraße · Straße

Erhardt- · Baaderstraße · Reichen-

S-Bahn ———— ——▭— ———   U-Bahn ———○— — — under construction

Heidelberg

Tourist-Information
at Main Station
Tel: (6221) 2 13 41

Heidelberg, an ancient university town and the old capital of the Palatinate, is picturesquely situated on the River Neckar. Dominated by the famous ruined castle, the old town has a most attractive square surrounded by cafés and there is a rack railway to take tourists up the hill to the castle.

Heidelberg Castle

Sightseeing

Castle – a notable example of German Renaissance architecture. Built in late 16th century and destroyed by the French in 1693, it is now a spectacular ruin
Karl Theodor Bridge – built 1768–88 and affords fine views of the town
Palatinate Museum – contains a fine art and historical collection

Munich

Verkehrsamt
Bahnhofplatz 2
Tel: 23 91 256/259
Information Bureau in Stachus-Passage

Munich is Germany's third largest city and the capital of Bavaria. Despite

Theatinerkirche, Munich

being heavily bombed during the war, Munich is an elegant city with some fine examples of Gothic, Renaissance, Baroque and Neo-classical architecture. It is also a city that offers a wide variety of entertainments, and is especially noted for being a carnival city.

Sightseeing

Alte Pinakothek – one of the oldest and greatest picture galleries in Europe, with large collections of Rubens and Dürer
Bavarian National Museum – contains a fine collection of German art and applied art
English Garden – a park of 350 hectares laid out 1789–1832
Frauenkirch – Munich's imposing late Gothic cathedral, built 1468–88
St Michaels Church – a Renaissance church built 1583–97 with impressive interior
Schack Gallery – contains 19th-century German paintings
Schloss Nymphenburg – built 1664–1728, surrounded by a beautiful park
Theatinerkirch – Roman Baroque style church with a 71m dome

Monopteros, Munich English Garden

Cologne

Tourist Information Office
Verkehrsamt der Stadt Köln
Unter Fettenhennen 19
D-5000 Köln 1
Tel: (2) 21 33 45

This old cathedral city on the Rhine, with its churches and its Roman remains, is one of the focal points of Western culture. Cologne is also one of the most important traffic junctions and commercial centres in Germany, with world-famed trade fairs and busy shipping traffic. It is the see of an archbishop, with a university, a sports college and the headquarters of the WDR (Westdeutscher Rundfunk) radio and television corporation, and is noted also for sport and for the Rhineland Carnival.

Sightseeing

Cathedral – one of Europe's largest cathedrals, it is a masterpiece; the Gothic architecture aspiring to the heavens is second to none. Begun in 1248 it was not completed until 1880. Inside, the Cathedral is breathtaking with its tremendous height, magnificent windows, statues and treasures. Features of this imposing interior are the Reliquary of the Three Kings and the famous Adoration of the Kings
Roman Germanic Museum – the 2000-year-old history of Cologne is presented here in an attractive way: the daily life of the Romans, Roman arts, mosaics, tombs, glassware, jewelery
Wallraf-Richartz Museum – a magnificent gallery of European paintings (works by Rembrandt, Manet, Renoir, Leibl, Liebermann, Slevogt) a rich collection of engravings and large collections of modern art
St Gereon's Church – the city's most unusual Romanesque church, with a long choir (11th century) built onto a decagonal domed structure erected in Roman times and enlarged in 1227
Gürzenich – Cologne's most important old secular building, erected in 1441–44 as a warehouse and banqueting hall
'Ring' streets – a semi-circular circuit of streets laid out in front of the former town walls. Of the old fortified town gates, three remain

Rhine Valley

Fremdrenverkehrsverband Rhinland-Pfalz
Pavilion opposite Main Station
Koblenz
Tel: (0261) 3 13 04

'Father Rhine' is Europe's most important waterway. 1320km in length, the Rhine rises in Switzerland, flows through Lake Constance, Basle, Bonn, and eventually through the Netherlands and into the North Sea. The river offers the prospect of beautiful riverside scenery, and boat trips, especially in the Lower Rhine between Bonn and Düsseldorf.

Sightseeing

Upper Rhine plain – 30–40km wide rift valley, bounded on the east by the Black Forest. Fertile fruit and wine growing region with cathedral cities of Speyer, Mainz and Worms

Lorelei Rock – legendary rock by the Middle Rhine near Koblenz

Burg Stahleck and Bacharach, on the Rhine

Lower Rhine plain – gently undulating region with several major cities: Bonn, Cologne and Düsseldorf

Accommodation

Hotels

The leading hotels in cities and the major resorts are up to normal international standards. Breakfast is usually included in the charge for accommodation. Hotels in West Germany range from fully equipped modern spa-hotels to historic framework houses and romantic castles.

Castle Hotels are ideal for those who wish to stay in picturesque surroundings. Each castle has a unique, unmistakable character with its own particular architecture and history. Most are beautifully situated far off the beaten track.

Useful Addresses

Room Reservation Service

Allgemeine Deutsche Zimmerreservierung (ADZ),

Flower Market

Hotel Price Range	
Type of hotel	Price in marks for a single room
***	50–260
**	40–200
*	30–150

These prices are intended to serve as a rough guide only.

Beethovenstr. 69,
D-6000 Frankfurt am Main 1.
Tel: (69) 74 07 67.

Köningswall 18,
D-4600 Dortmund.
Tel: (231) 14 03 41.

Youth Hostels

Deutsches Jugendherbergswerk,
Hauptverband für Jugenwandern und
Jugendherbergen,
Bulowstr. 26, postfach 220,
D-4930 Detmold.
Tel: (52 31) 74 01 14.

Camping

Deutscher Camping-Club (DCC),
Mandlstr. 28,
D-8000 München 40.
Tel: (89) 33 40 21.

Farmhouse and country holidays

Lists from
Reisendienst der Deutschen Landwirt-
schaftsgesellschaft (DLG),
Agratour,
Rusterstr. 13,
D-6000 Frankfurt am Main.
Tel: (69) 72 28 76/72 08 61.

Landschriften-Verlag,
Kurfurstenstr. 55,
D-5300 Bonn 1.
Tel: (228) 63 12 84.

Riding holidays

Deutsche Reiterliche Vereinigung,
Freiherr-von-Langen-Str. 13,
D-4410 Warendorf 1.
Tel: (25 81) 63 62.

Hobby holidays

Lists of holiday courses published by
Verlag Otto Mayer, Ravensburg
(available through booksellers).

Holidays for the handicapped

Bundesarbeitsgemeinschaft 'Hilfe für
Behinderte',
Kirchfeldstr. 149,
D-4000 Düsseldorf.
Tel: (2 11) 31 00 60.

Introduction to Rail Information

The *Deutsche Bundesbahn (DB)* network offers excellent cross-country
lines which serve all the smaller towns
as well as the principal cities, quickly
and efficiently. There are 5 types of
train:

Trans Europe Express (TEE) – 1st class
only with special luxury features. A
supplementary charge is payable
which incorporates a reservation fee.

Intercity Train (IC) – fast trains which
link the major cities. A supplement is
sometimes payable and this is shown
on the timetable.

Long-distance Express (FD) – a particular kind of express train suitable for
long journeys. A supplement is payable on certain tickets.

Express Train (D) – regular express
train. A supplement is payable on certain tickets.

Semi Fast Train (E).

A special feature of the *DB* network is
the computer reservation procedure.
This not only ensures that passengers
reserve seats in a matter of seconds
but also ensures that should the passenger have to change trains, he or she
needs only to cross the platform to

reach his or her reserved seat in the connecting train.

Major International Services

Connection	Duration	Frequency
Munich–London	20–21hrs	6 times daily
Munich–Paris	8–10hrs	4 times daily
Cologne–Amsterdam	3–4hrs	15 times daily
Cologne–Paris	5–6hrs	8 times daily
Cologne–Brussels	2–3hrs	15 times daily

Major Internal Services

Connection	Duration	Frequency
Aachen–Berlin	8–9hrs	hourly
Frankfurt–Hamburg	5–7hrs	hourly
Berlin–Hanover	4hrs	hourly
Bremen–Munich	7–10hrs	hourly
Düsseldorf–Berlin	6–7hrs	hourly
Hamburg–Munich	8hrs	hourly
Cologne–Frankfurt	2–3hrs	hourly
Nuremberg–Dortmund	6–7hrs	hourly

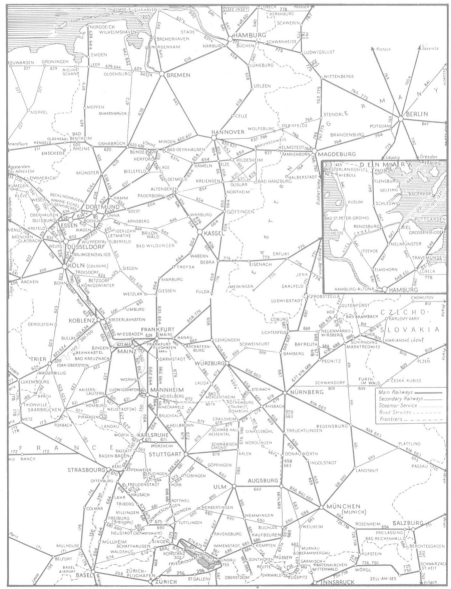

Map supplied by kind permission of Thomas Cook Ltd. The numbers along the lines refer to tables in the *Thomas Cook Continental Timetable*.

Munich

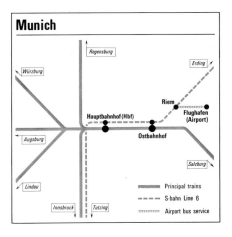

Hamburg

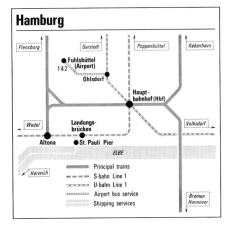

Scenic Routes

Some of the most beautiful, and consequently among the most famous, scenic routes pass through the small villages and towns of the Rhine Valley.

As a special summer excursion (from June to September) a TEE train takes an alternative 'scenic route' between Mannheim and Munich. It travels through some of Germany's most spectacular scenery via Heidelberg, Heilbronn, Stuttgart, Donauwoerth and Augsburg.

Steam train journeys combine stunning scenery with historical interest. The routes available include:

Nürnberg–Amberg

Nürnberg–Bayreuth

Tour of Upper Franconia

Tour of Upper Palatinate

Tour of the Lehen Valley

All routes begin at Nürnberg and operate from mid-May to September. There are reductions for tourists on these routes.

For brochures and for booking purposes apply to:
Bundesbahndirektion Nürnberg
Sandstrasse 38/40
D-8500 Nürnberg 70
Federal Republic of Germany

Other lines renowned for their scenic beauty include:
Berchtesgaden–Salzburg
Freiburg–Donauschingen
Kempten–Garmisch
Koblenz–Giessen
Munich–Lindav
Müngsten Bridge (Solingen–Remscheid)
Niebüll–Westerland
Oberammergau–Murnau
Stuttgart–Singen

Veteran Railways

1. **Schönberger Strand–Schönberg**
   Length: 3.9km
   Gauge: 1435mm
   Steam and diesel traction
   Weekends June–September
   Verein Verkehrsamateure und Museumbahn,
   Dimpelweg 10, D-2000 Hamburg 26.
   Situated 15m from Kiel at the charming Baltic Sea resort Schönberg (Holst), the VVM-Museum has assembled 50 rail veterans constructed between 1869 and 1956. The historic trains run 2.5m from Schönberg Beach to Schönberg on their steam or diesel engines.

2. **Bruchhausen–Vilsen–Heiligenberg–Asendorf**
   Length: 7.8km
   Gauge: 1000mm
   Steam and diesel traction
   Weekends 1 May–end of September
   Deutscher Eisenbahn-Verein e.V. (DEV), D-2814 Bruchhausen-Vilsen. Since 1966 the little trains of the 'First Museum Railway of Germany' have run on the 8km narrow-gauge line between Bruchhausen-Vilsen and Asendorf, County of Hoya, near Bremen.
   Since 1983 there have been four steam engines, two diesels, four railcars and 15 coaches.

3. **Almetalbahn**
   Route: Bodenburg–Almstedt-Segeste–Sibbesse
   Length: 8km
   Gauge: 1435mm
   Steam, diesel and electric traction
   Arbeitsgemeinschaft, Historische Eisenbahn e.V (AHE), Mattiaswiese 6, D-3200 Hildesheim.

4. **Weserberglandbahn**
   Route: Rintein-Nord–Stadthagen-West
   Length: 20km
   Gauge: 1435mm
   Steam traction
   Dampfeisenbahn Weserbergland, Postfach
   1450, D-3260 Rinteln

5. **Minden-Stadt–Hille**
   Length: 13.4km
   Minde-Stadt–Bad Hopfenberg
   Length: 13.3km
   Gauge: 1435mm
   Steam and diesel traction
   Museums-Eisenbahn Minden e.V (MEM),
   Postfach 2751, D-4950 Minden/Westfalen.

6. **Holzhausen-Heddinghausen–Preussisch-Oldendorf–Bad Essen-Bohmte–Schwergermoor**
   Length: 33.8km
   Gauge: 1435mm
   Steam and diesel traction
   Museums-Eisenbahn Minden e.V (MEM),
   Postfach 2751, D-4950 Minden/Westfalen.

7. **Mühlenstroth–Rödelheim**
   Length: 1.8km
   Gauge: 600mm
   Steam and diesel traction
   Dampf-Kleinbah Mülhenstroth (DKBM), Postamm 166, D-4830 Gütersloh 1.

8. **Bochum–Dahlausen Railway Museum–Bochum–Dahlausen DGEG**
   Journey time: 3 minutes
   Gauge: 1435mm
   Steam and diesel traction
   Deutsche Gesellschaft für Eisenbahngeschichte e.V. (DGEG),
   Eisenbahnmuseum Bochum-Dahlause DR-C, Otto-Str., D-4630, Bochlum.

9. **Hespertalbahn**
   Route: Essen-Kupferdreh–Haus Scheppen
   Length: 2.8km
   Gauge: 1435mm
   Steam and diesel traction
   Verein zur Erhaltung der Hespertalbahn e.V.,
   Am Hang 13, D-4300 Essen 17 (Burgaltendorf).

10. **Selfkantbahn**
    Route: Geilenkirchen-Gillrath–Langenbroich-Schierwaldenrath
    Length: 5.2km
    Gauge: 1000mm
    Steam and diesel traction
    Touristenbahnen im Rheinland GmbH, Postfach 1152, D-5133 Gangelt 1

Railway Museums

1. **Aumühle Transport Local Traffic Collection**
   (in locomotive shed)
   D-2055 Aumühle bei Hamburg

2. **Berlin Transport Museum**
   Railway Section, Urania, Kleiststr, 13/14
   D-1000 Berlin (West)

3. **Bochum-Dahlausen Railway Museum**
   Dr-C-Otto-Str. 191, D-4630 Bochum

4. **Darmstrad-Kranichstein Railway Museum**
   Kölner Str. 20b, D-6100 Darmstadt

5. **Rhine-Neckar Railway Museum**
   D-6806 Viernheim, OEG station

6. **Palatinate Transport Collection**
   D-6730 Neustadt an der Weinstrasse (station)

7. **German Steam Locomotive Museum (DDM)**
   D-8651 Neuenmarkt/Oberfranken, Neuenmarkt-Wirsberg station

8. **Transport Museum, Nuremberg**
   Railway Section, Lessingstr 6, D-8500 Nurnberg

9. **German Museum, Munich**
   Railway Section, Museumsinsel, D-8000 München 26

Other railway museums are under construction or planned at Minden and Nordhorn.

Internal Fare Structure

Standard Rate Fares

Rail fares in West Germany are based on the kilometric distance travelled. 1st class travel costs approximately 50% more than 2nd class. For example, a journey of 91–100km costs 19DM 2nd class and 29DM 1st class. Tickets for distances over 50km are valid for 2 months; shorter distances are valid for 4 days. A supplement of 5DM, which includes a seat reservation if required, is payable on IC and 10DM on TEE trains for travel within Germany. Journeys on D trains which are less than 50km are liable for a 2DM supplement. Supplements paid on the train are 1DM extra.

For distances up to 200km return fares are double the single fare but are reduced by approximately 20% for longer distances. This also applies to 'circular journeys' totalling at least 401km. These reduced price returns, when bought in Germany, are called *Vorzugskarte* and are subject to restrictions with regard to time of travel and breaking the journey.

Child Reductions

Children between 4 and 11 travel for half fare and any supplements due are reduced by 50%.

Student Reductions

The DB Junior Rail Pass is available to young people between the ages of 12 and 22 and to students under 27. It is valid for one year and entitles the holder to purchase tickets on all DB trains at a 50% reduction. The pass may be purchased in Britain from the British Rail Travel Centres at Victoria Station and Liverpool Street Station. The *DB* Junior Rail Pass costs 110DM or £36. For alternative reductions students are advised to refer to the International Section.

Tramper Ticket

The Tramper Ticket is available to young people under 23 years and students under 27, for a month. It gives unlimited travel in West Germany and costs 245DM or £87.50 on production of a passport and Student Card.

Family/Party Reductions

Groups of a minimum of 2 children and not more than 5 children travelling together within West Germany can buy a Minigroup Ticket. The first 2 adults pay the normal single fare, further adults pay half fare and children pay quarter fare. These tickets are available in the UK. Refer to the International Section for information on the Rail Europ Family Card.

Senior Citizen Reductions

Senior Citizens visiting West Germany for a one-off short period are probably best served by the Rail Europ Senior Card (refer to International Section). However, Senior Citizens who travel to West Germany on a regular basis may like to purchase the *DB* Senioren Pass. Pass A is for travel between Mondays and Thursdays and costs 65DM for one year. Pass B can be used on any day and costs 110DM for one year. They allow reductions of 50% on journeys over 50km on *DB* lines for 1st class or 2nd class travel. IC and TEE supplements are payable. These passes can work out more expensive than the ordinary return fare unless the holder makes frequent long-distance journeys in West Germany.

Railrover Passes

The *Tourenkarte* (regional railrover) represents excellent value for unlimited 2nd class travel within a chosen area for 10 days within a possible time limit of 21 days. It is available only for journeys over 200km each way and can only be bought in Germany. The *Tourenkarte* can be purchased for any one of 74 areas and costs £20 for a single person, £29 for 2 people travelling together and £35 for a family.

Tourist Reductions

The German Rail Pass allows unlimited travel for 4 days, 9 days or 16 days not necessarily consecutive, within an overall validity period of 21 days, throughout the entire *DB* network. Any train may be used without paying IC or TEE supplements. Seat reservations, couchettes and sleepers are extra, however. The Tourist Card is also valid for the Europa Bus Services, the Rhine Steamers, all *DB* train and coach services, and all services of the Deutsche Touring GMBH within Germany. For 2nd class travel the Rail Pass costs £80 (4 days), £120 (9 days), £170 (16 days); for 1st class travel, £120 (4 days), £180 (9 days), and £250 (16 days).

There is also a German Rail Youth Pass which is available to passengers aged 12–25 inclusive and is valid for 4, 9 or 16 days in 2nd class travel only (12–25 year olds are allowed to purchase the regular Rail Pass, if they prefer). The Youth Pass costs £45 (4 days), £70 (9 days) and £95 (16 days).

Where to buy tickets

In Germany

For IC trains and long-distance connections, tickets must be bought at the station counter; however, for short journeys, tickets may be bought from a machine located at the station.

In Great Britain

Tickets are available at British Rail appointed travel agents, selected railway stations or from the following addresses:

DER Travel Service Ltd
18 Conduit Street
London W1R 9TD
Tel: (071) 408 0111

European Rail Travel Centre
PO Box 303
Victoria Station
London SW1V 1JY
Tel: (071) 834 2345 for enquiries and credit card bookings.

In USA

From *DB* representatives in the major cities (see International Section)

Facilities on Trains

Sleepers and Couchettes

On internal sleeper routes 1st class ticket holders are entitled to a single compartment (175DM or £70.70 per person) or a double compartment (75DM or £30.60 per person). 2nd class ticket holders are entitled to hire a triple compartment at 50DM or £20.60 per person. Couchettes cost 24DM or £8.10 per person and there are normally 6 couchettes to a compartment. For international sleeper journeys the berth supplements may vary according to the distance travelled.

Food

All IC trains and many D trains have a dining car, whilst other D trains have a trolley service offering snacks and drinks. The train restaurants offer varied menus and meals are served all day. A continental breakfast costs around 10DM; a 3-course lunch or dinner, 20DM; and coffee and cake 7DM.

Luggage

Hand luggage should be placed on the rack or beneath the seat in the compartment. Heavy luggage can be registered for a small fee upon presentation of the rail ticket; in this case they will be taken to the luggage van for you. *DB* also offer a service which conveys luggage from the passenger's place of departure to the place of arrival.

Bicycle Carriage

Bikes can be carried on all trains which have a baggage compartment (not Intercity trains) as along as the rider purchases a 7.60DM ticket. This ticket is only valid in West Germany and cannot be used to cross frontiers. You must load and unload the bike yourself whenever you change trains. If there is no room on the train then the bike can be sent as registered luggage. However, this does not guarantee that it gets to the destination at the same time as its rider.

Telephones

All inter-city trains are equipped with coin-operated telephones.

Facilities at Train Stations

Food

The major stations have restaurants and snack bars of varying standards.

Luggage

Almost all stations have a left-luggage office where suitcases, rucksacks, prams and bicycles can be deposited for a small fee. Self service lockers are also available.

Tourist Information

The major stations have efficient tourist information bureaux known as *Verkehrsamt* or *Verkehrsverein*.

Bicycle Hire

Bicycles can be hired from over 200 stations throughout Germany.

Yugoslavia

Brela on the Adriatic Coast

Introduction

Yugoslavia is a country of very diverse scenic beauty, ranging from its karstic limestone mountains to the spectacular Adriatic coast, and in the last two decades it has become one of the great European holiday centres. Positioned at the intersection of the old trading and migration routes into central and south-east Europe, Yugoslavia has been prey to the contrasting influences of many different cultures, and the diversity of its republics and its people reflects this.

The heart of the country is dominated by a rugged series of transverse mountain ridges, running parallel to the Adriatic coast, the most important being the Dinaric Alps which cover roughly half the country's total area of 255,800sq km. The 'strike' of this range runs parallel to the coastline, making access inland very difficult. The mountains support few settlements, and are made even more inhospitable by 'karstic' action that leaves bare limestone lode formations pitted with deep crevices, providing a spectacular but barren landscape. The major settlement areas are in the plains that ring the central mountains, and form nearly a quarter of the country's total area. The final region that completes the picture is the Adriatic coastline, to which hundreds of European tourists have flocked in recent years to enjoy its picturesque beaches and beautiful seascapes.

The transverse mountain ranges have a profound effect on the climate sheltering the narrow coastal strip, which enjoys the mild winters and hot summers of the Mediterranean. The mountainous regions are subject to a moderate continental climate of warm summers and relatively cold winters. The north-east plains are open to the extreme influences sweeping in from central Europe and experience hot summers and cold harsh winters.

The population of Yugoslavia is very diverse. Out of a total of 23 million, 90% is made up of the four major groups, the Serbs, Croats, Slovenes and Macedonians. The other 10% is made up of many different minority groups, the most important among them being the Albanians and Hungarians. 90% of the population speak Slavic languages 75% of whom speak Serbo-Croat. Because of the very different historical patterns of development experienced by each republic, the religious persuasion of its population is also diverse. The majority of the Croats and Slovenes are Roman Catholic, large areas of Bosnia are predominantly Moslem, while the rest of the country belongs to the Eastern Orthodox Church. Inevitably, these religious differences, coupled with varying linguistic and ethnic affiliations, have strongly influenced the country's political and social life and have occasioned fierce conflicts.

Yugoslavia is a federal multi-national state with a socialist social structure. It is a 'non-aligned' state made up of six republics and two autonomous provinces. Marshal Tito, who founded the original Federal People's Republic of Yugoslavia in 1945, was made president for life under the 1974 constitution. Since his death in 1980, the country has been governed by a collective presidency. The legislative body, the SFRY (Socialist Federal Republic of Yugoslavia), consists of a Federal Chamber of 220 members, and a chamber of the Republics and Provinces, which has 88 members. There is only one political party permitted in the country, and that is the Yugoslav League of Communists.

Folk festival in Zagreb (Croatia)

Ever since 1945, under the direction of Marshal Tito, the Yugoslav economy has undergone considerable development. Roughly half the population is employed in agriculture yet they are unable to produce sufficient to meet domestic requirements, and considerable amounts of food, most notably wheat, have to be imported. Yugoslav industry, so backward prior to 1945, is still in the process of developing. One hindrance is the unequal distribution of the country's considerable mineral wealth which favours the north. The lack of resources in the south is a problem that is exacerbated by the predominance of the Islamic religion and family traditions in these areas which makes the successful introduction of industry hard to sustain. The new developing industries, metal-working and electrical and mechanical engineering, are therefore being established in the north-west, although Macedonia in the south houses new metal-working industries. Tourism has, in recent years, been a major foreign currency earner. In the last two decades the growth of this industry has been unprecedented, particularly on the Adriatic coast, and more recently in the Alpine regions where winter sports resorts have been developed. Nearly 7 million tourists now visit Yugoslavia every year.

Djerdap hydroelectric power station

The history of Yugoslav culture is very much a history of foreign cultural figures. During the course of the 17th and 18th centuries, native artists and architects began to grow in stature, but remained merely locally significant. Important figures began to emerge in the 19th century, for example Franc Kavčič (1762–1828) the Slovenian painter, who specialised in heroic and classical themes. After the turn of the 20th century, Iavan Meŝtrović (1883–1962) sculptor, Josip Plečnik (1872–1957) architect, and Anton Ažbe (1862–1905) painter, were the leading figures of their era. Modern art in Yugoslavia has been officially encouraged since 1952. The leading representative is Ivan Generalić (b 1914), who established a school of naive painting at Hlebine.

Of much greater national importance are the country's folk traditions which are perhaps stronger in Yugoslavia than in any other European country. Traditional costumes, which vary from region to region, are still frequently worn, and many secular festivals are openly celebrated. Pagan dances like the Dodok rain dance still survive and folk music is also thriving. The Yugoslav government is attempting to promote and preserve these ancient traditions and customs, which provide colour and enjoyment to enhance any visit to Yugoslavia.

History

7th century BC	Greeks begin to found colonies on the Adriatic coast
229 BC	Roman conquest begins, completed in time of Augustus
AD 9th century	Establishment of a Serbian State and spread of Christianity
11th century	Period of Byzantine overlordship and prosperity despite internal conflicts
1371	Turks conquer south-eastern princedoms
15th–16th century	Most of present day Yugoslavia under Turkish rule
1699	Peace of Karlowitz liberates Slovenia, Hungary and part of Croatia from Turkish rule
1878	Congress of Berlin recognises Serbian independence. Montenegro gains independence
1914	The assassination of the Austrian Archduke Ferdinand in Sarajevo sparks off the First World War
1918	Proclamation of the new kingdom of Serbs, Croats and Slovenes after the end of the war
1929	The state is renamed the kingdom of Yugoslavia
1941	Surrender of Yugoslav army to Germany; large areas of Yugoslavia annexed
1944	Capture of Belgrade by Soviet forces and Yugoslav partisans
1945	Proclamation of Federal People's Republic of Yugoslavia

1948	Tito's 'national communism' leads to Yugoslavia's exclusion from cominform and makes possible a cautious rapprochement with the West
1953	New constitution. Tito elected President of the Republic
1963	New constitution with further decentralisation of government
1974	New constitution. Tito confirmed as President for life
1980	Tito dies
1984	Company launched to quell dissident opinion in the country
1986	Yugoslavia suspends its nuclear power programme until an official commission establishes whether the country can do without atomic energy

Major Centres

Belgrade

Turistički Informativni Centar
Terazije (underpass at Albanija Building)
Tel: (11) 63 56 43

Turistički Informativni Centar
Central Station
Tel: (11) 64 62 40

Belgrade

Embassies:
UK: Generala Ždanova 46
Tel: (11) 64 50 55; (11) 64 50 34 and (11) 64 50 87
USA: Kneza Miloša 50
Tel: (11) 64 56 55

Belgrade, the capital of Yugoslavia, has been destroyed by the country's many conquerors on numerous occasions. It is a modern city and shows the influences of both East and West. Few of the city's historic monuments have survived the attentions of its invaders, but there are still many things of interest to be seen in this fascinating city, which is picturesquely situated on the River Danube.

Sightseeing

Bajrak Mosque – only mosque to survive from Turkish period, built in 1690
Fresco Gallery – contains copies of the finest wall paintings from the medieval period
Kalemegdan – a fortress since Roman times, affords fine views of the Danube
Museum of Contemporary Art – a fine example of modern architecture (built 1960–5); contains 3000 works by 20th century artists
Museum of the Serbian Theatre – illustrates the development of theatre in Serbia
National Museum – one of the finest museums in Yugoslavia, particularly for Serbian culture
Palace of Princess Ljubica – handsome mansion built 1829–31
St Mark's Church – imposing edifice built 1932–41
Skardarlija – the Montmartre of Belgrade; not to be missed
Tomz of Sheikh Mustapha – one of the few relics from the Turkish period built in 1783

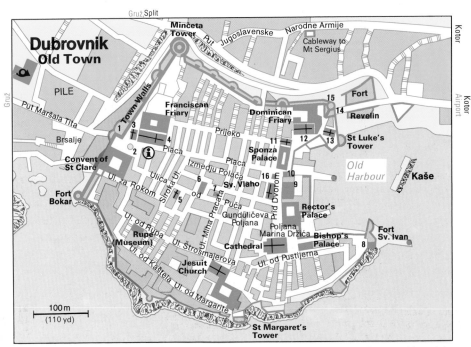

1 Pile Gate	5 All Saints Church	9 Town Hall	13 Church of Annunciation
2 Onofrio Fountain	6 Serbian Orthodox church	10 Clock-Tower	14 Ploče Gate
3 Chapel of St Saviour	7 Icon Museum	11 St Nicholas's Church	15 Asimov Tower
4 Franciscan church	8 Aquarium, Maritime Museum, Museum of Ethnography	12 Dominican church	16 Roland Column

Dubrovnik

Turistički Informativni Centar
Placa
Tel: 2 63 54

Dubrovnik, the Dalmatian capital and showpiece of the Adriatic coast, can guarantee approximately 220 cloudless days in the year, and attracts many visitors in all seasons. Not only does it offer the traditional facilities of a seaside resort, but it also offers its visitors many places of historical interest and has a lively cultural programme.

Dubrovnik

Town walls of Dubrovnik

Sightseeing

Cathedral – rebuilt in Baroque style 1671–1713, contains some fine works of art
Dominican friary – the friary has a magnificently decorated 14th-century cloister
Fort St. John – an imposing and formidable complex of fortifications
Lower Cloister/Pharmacy – founded in 1319 from the Romanesque period
Luža Square – the hub of the town where musicians and singers can always be found
Rector's Palace – finest building in the old town built 1435–51
Town Walls – constructed between 12th and 17th centuries by many different engineers

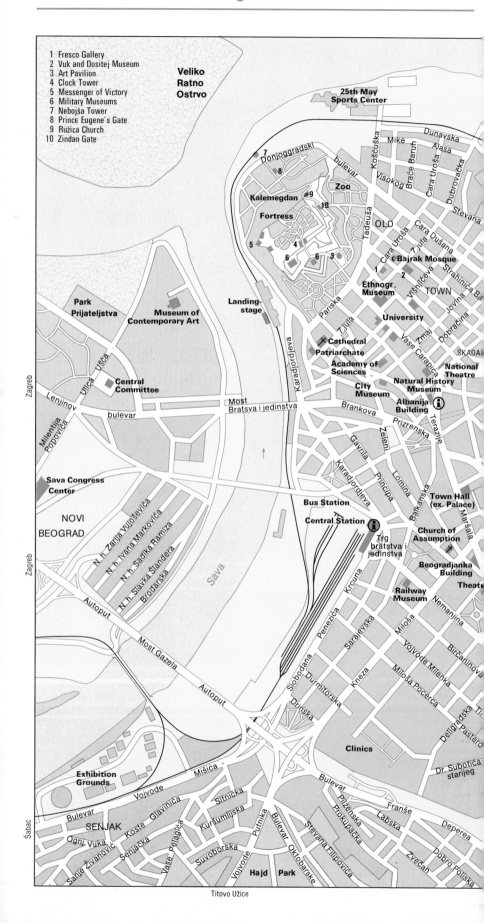

1 Fresco Gallery
2 Vuk and Dositej Museum
3 Art Pavilion
4 Clock Tower
5 Messenger of Victory
6 Military Museums
7 Nebojša Tower
8 Prince Eugene's Gate
9 Ružica Church
10 Zindan Gate

Veliko Ratno Ostrvo

25th May Sports Center

Donjoggradski bulevar

Zoo

Kalemegdan Fortress

OLD

Bajrak Mosque

Ethnogr. Museum

TOWN

University

SKADA

National Theatre

Cathedral
Patriarchate

Academy of Sciences

Natural History Museum

City Museum

Albanija Building

Park Prijateljstva

Museum of Contemporary Art

Landing-stage

Brankova

Prizrenska

Terazije

Central Committee

Most Bratsva i jedinstva

Zagreb

Lenjinov bulevar

Milentija Popoviča

Ulica Tršća

Karadjordjeva

Gavrila Principa

Lomina

Karadjordjeva

Zeleni

Batkanska

Town Hall (ex. Palace)

Marsala

Sava Congress Center

Bus Station

Central Station

Church of Assumption

NOVI BEOGRAD

Zagreb

N.h. Zarija Vujoševiča
N.h. Ivana Markoviča
N.h. Sadika Ramiza
N.h. Slavka Slandera
Brodarska

Sava

Krcuna

Trg bratstva i jedinstva

Beogradjanka Building

Theatr

Peneziča

Railway Museum

Nemanjina

Autoput

Most Gazela

Sarajevska

Miloša

Vojvode Milenka

Birčaninova

Autoput

Kneza

Miloša Pocerča

Slobodana

Durmitorska

Deligradske Ti

Dr. Pastero

Drinska

Clinics

Dr. Subotiča starijeg

Šabac

Exhibition Grounds

Mišiča

Bulevar

Franše

Labska

Deperea

Bulevar

Vojvode

Sitnička

Piženska

Prokupačka

SENJAK

Koste Glavinića

Senjačka

Kuršumlijska

Putnika

Bulevar Oktobarske

Stevana Filippoviča

Dobro Poljska

Ognj. Vuka

Sanje Živanovič

Vaše Petagiča

Suvoborska

Vojvode

Hajd Park

Zvečan

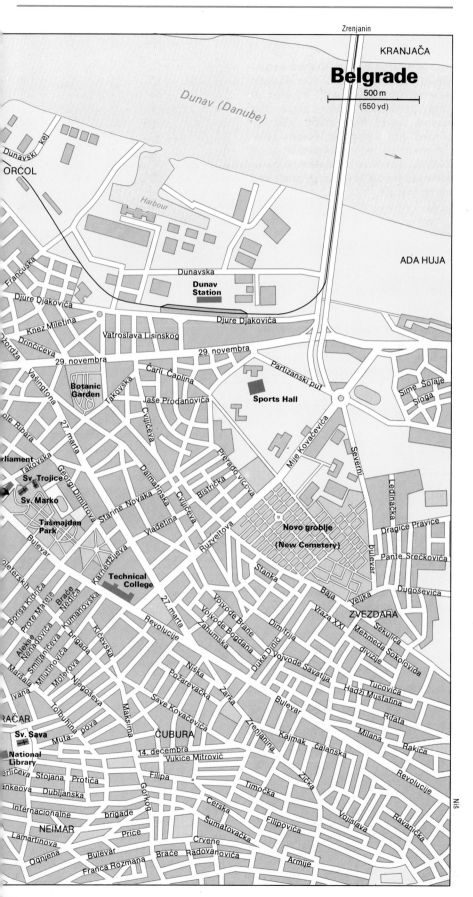

Zrenjanin

KRANJAČA

Belgrade

500 m
(550 yd)

Dunav (Danube)

Dunavski Kej

ORČOL

Harbour

ADA HUJA

Francuska

Dunavska

Djure Djakovića

Dunav
Station

Knez Miletina

Djure Djakovića

Đorđa

Drinčičeva

Vatroslava Lisinskog

29. novembra

29. novembra

Vašingtona

Čarli Čaplina

Partizanski put

Botanic
Garden

Takovska

Jaše Prodanovića

Sports Hall

Sime Šolaje

Sloga

ole Ribara

27. marta

Cvijićeva

Mile Kovačevića

arliament

Takovska

Georgi Dimitrova

Preradovićeva

Severni

Ledinačka

Sv. Trojice

Dalmatinska

Bistrička

Dragice Pravice

Sv. Marko

Starine Novaka

Cvijićeva

Novo groblje

Pante Srećkovića

Tašmajdan
Park

Vladetina

Ruzveltova

(New Cemetery)

Bulevar

pieterskih

Karnadžijeva

Stanka

Baja

veljka

Dugoševića

Borisa Kidriča

Braće
Nedića

Kumanovska

Revolucije

27. marta

Vojvode Brane

Vojvode Bogdana

Dimitrija

Vraža XXI

ZVEZDARA

Technical
College

Prote Mateje

brigada

Kričevska

Zahumska

Duke Dinić

Vojvode Savatija

Mehmeda Sokolovida

Sekulirča

divizije

Aleksa

Nenadovića

Molerova

Niška

Tucovića

Maršala

Smiljaničeva

Milutinovića

Negoševa

Pozarevačka

Žarka

Bulevar

Hadži Mustafina

ivana

Tolbuhina

pova

Maksima

Zrenjanina

Rifata

RAČAR

Save Kovačevića

Kajmak čalanska

Milana

Rakiča

Sv. Sava

Muta-

ĆUBURA

14. decembra

Zicka

Revolucije

National
Library

Vukice Mitrović

erlićeva

Stojana

Protiča

Filipa

Timočka

ankeova

Dubljanska

Gorkog

Cerska

Filipovića

Vojislava

Ravanička

Internacionalne

brigade

Šumatovačka

NEIMAR

Price

Lamartinova

Crvene

Oqnjena

Bulevar

Braće Radovanovića

Armije

Franca Rozmana

Niš

evac

Istria

Istria is a large wedge-shaped peninsula at the north end of the Adriatic coast of Yugoslavia with an area of some 3160sqkm. Ever since the Second World War, Istria has developed into a popular holiday area, with many bathing resorts with good facilities. There is much evidence of Italian influences in its many ports and fishing villages.

Lovran

Turističko Društvo
Šetalište Maršala Tita 68
Tel: 73 10 41

Lovran caters mainly for summer visitors with small beaches overlooked by the beautiful Mt Učka. It contains few buildings of historical or artistic interest.

Opatija

Turističko Savez
Ul. Maršala Tita 10
Tel: 71 17 10

Sheltered from the cold north winds by Mt Učka, Opatija has a luxuriant growth of evergreen sub-tropical vegetation. In the 19th century it used to be a winter health resort, but now it is extremely popular and lively in both winter and summer.

Opatija harbour

Limski Canal, Istria

Poreč

Turistički Biro
Trg Slobode 3
Tel: 3 11 40

An old town with fine palaces and the best preserved example of a 6th-century Byzantine basilica on the Yugoslav coast. A popular place for local holidaymakers, it now attracts over 35,000 visitors per year.

Poreč from the beach

Portorož

Turistično Društvo
Avditorij-Senčna Pot 10
Tel: 7 33 42

The 'Port of Roses' is a select resort with old, established parks and flower gardens. The climate is exceptionally mild all the year round and there is a beautiful beach of fine sand over 1km long.

Roman Amphitheatre, Pula

Pula

Turistički Savez Općine
Trg Republike 1
YU-52000 Pula
Tel: 2 26 62

Arenaturist
Trg Bratstva i Jedinstva 4
YU-52203 Medulin
Tel: 3 43 55

Turističko Društvo Premantura
YU-5200 Premantura
Tel: 7 50 07

Pula has many interesting relics from the Roman period including an amphitheatre still in use today. It is also a commercial harbour which means that bathing is only possible at nearby Medulin and Premantura 10 km away.

Rovinj

Turističko Društvo
Obala Pino 12
Tel: 81 10 77

A picturesque little town with a cathedral and busy harbour. Again there are no bathing facilities and visitors are directed to resorts north and south of the town or to the islands of Katarina and Crveni Otok.

Umag

Istraturist
29 Novembrabbi
Tel: 5 21 11

Istratours Savudrija
Tel: 5 95 41

An ancient little town now flanked by an industrial zone and collection of holiday chalets and apartments. One of the main attractions in the area is scuba diving. Divers flock to explore the ruins of the village of Šipar, originally a Roman settlement, which was destroyed by pirates in the 9th century and as a result of the subsidence of the land is now mostly under sea. The beaches in the area are of shelving rock and the little harbour offers sheltered mooring for boats. Other entertainments in the area include open air plays, dancing and folk singing.

Accommodation

Hotels

In recent years Yugoslav hotels have made great efforts to improve their standards of comfort and amenity and extend their capacity. In the larger towns and resorts most of the hotels are fully up to international standards of quality, and even in smaller places they are entirely adequate. There are, of course differences between various parts of the country: in the north of the country and on the coast, for example, visitors need have no hesitation in putting up at quite modest hotels while in the south and in the interior it is better to choose a hotel in one of the higher categories.

Since a considerable part of Yugoslavia's tourist trade comes to it through the large travel firms which run package tours, it is preferable to book accommodation on an all-included basis through one of these firms if you want to be sure of getting a room in one of the popular resorts. In many places the accommodation available in hotels is supplemented by rooms in private houses, information about which can be obtained from the local Tourist Office.

Accommodation in private houses is available in most tourist resorts. In some households, meals are also provided. To book this kind of accommodation, tourists should apply to tourist offices in smaller resorts or to the town's Tourist Association and, in large resorts, to travel agencies as well. In some places, private accommodation can be booked through hotels. The rooms are graded according to comfort and their prices are very reasonable.

Youth Hostels

The youth hostel (*omladinski turisticki dom*) offers reasonably priced accommodation, particularly for young people. Priority is given to those under 27. There is no restriction on the length of stay. During the main holiday season advance reservation is advisable (accompanied in the case of groups by payment of 50% of the charges). Foreign visitors must have a membership card of their national youth hostels association.

Information from the *Ferijalni Savez Jugoslavije*, Mose Pijade 12/1, YU-11000 Beograd. Tel: (0 11) 33 96 66 and 33 98 02.

Camping and Caravanning

Yugoslavia is a very popular camping country, although at the height of the season the sites are often filled to bursting point. There are large numbers of camp sites in the north of the country and along the coast, but relatively few in the south, and those mostly concentrated in towns near the main trunk roads. Although 'freelance camping' (*camping sauvage*) is not officially permitted, the local authorities and the police (*milicija*) are usually ready to help visitors who want to camp on private or communal land in areas where there are no organised sites.

Hotel Price Range		
	Price for 1 night in US Dollars	
Type of hotel	Single room	Double room
Luxury	50–100	90–130
A	20– 60	30– 60
B	15– 30	10– 50
C	10– 25	15– 40
D	7– 15	10– 30

These rates relate to the main summer season (July and August). In the 'half season' months (June and September) and out of season there are reduced rates. Hotel rates include service charges. Half-board and full-board terms are available for stays of three or more days.

Most of the camp sites are equipped with excellent facilities, supermarkets and self-service restaurants. There may, however, be difficulties in the supply of bottled gas. At the height of the season the sanitary facilities and water supply tend to be inadequate; and at sites on the coast there may not be much room for campers' boats.

A list of camp sites can be obtained from the Yugoslav National Tourist Office.

Package Tours

Most of the hotels on the Adriatic coast and on the islands, as well as large holiday complexes which let chalets and apartments, make sure of being fully booked by entering into contracts with the travel firm which run package tours for the block booking of large numbers of beds. In consequence many establishments are booked up several months before the beginning of the holiday season.

Nevertheless hotels will often accept bookings from individual travellers, on the assumption that the quotas allotted to the travel firms may not be fully taken up. There are, of course, certain risks about this, since visitors making their own arrangements cannot expect to be given priority over the package bookings.

In addition to the usual resorts, many travel firms offer 'special interest' tours, such as motor-yacht trips along the Adriatic cost, study tours and walks in different parts of the country, raft trips on the River Drina, riding holidays at the Lipica stud-farm, shooting holidays, journeys in gypsy caravans 'through the gorges of the Balkans', or seaside vacations with sailing instruction and courses leading to the acquisition of a helmsman's certificate of competence.

Introduction to Rail Information

Jugoslovenske Železnice (JŽ) runs the Yugoslav rail system which consists of 10,000 kilometres of track most of which is electrified. All the major towns in the country are linked by rail but only a few lines go to the coast. Provision for comfort is minimal, particularly on the local services. The service uses the following types of train:

Ekspresni – internal expresses

Poslovni and *Brzi* – fast trains

Putnicki – slow, local trains

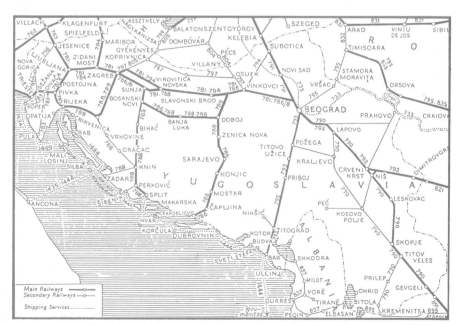

Map supplied by kind permission of Thomas Cook Ltd. The numbers along the lines refer to tables in the *Thomas Cook Continental Timetable*.

Major International Services

Connection	Duration	Frequency
Ljubljana–Paris	19–20hrs	once daily
Zagreb–Salzburg	8–10hrs	7 times daily
London–Split	39–42hrs	once daily

Major Internal Services

Connection	Duration	Frequency
Zagreb–Split	7–10hrs	7 times daily
Belgrade–Bar	7–8hrs	6 times daily
Zagreb–Belgrade	5–6hrs	16 times daily
Ljubljana–Zagreb	2–3hrs	22 times daily
Ljubljana–Rijeka	2–3hrs	11 times daily

Scenic Routes

The most spectacular route in Yugoslavia is the Belgrade–Bar line which runs to the Montenegran coast. Other scenically interesting routes include the Priboj–Bar, Trieste–Zagreb, Vinkovci–Kardeljevo and Zagreb–Rijeka lines.

Veteran Railways

The first Yugoslav Museum Train carries tourists from Jesenice and Bled to the attractive small town of Kanal in the valley of the River Soca.

The engine is almost 70 years old and one of the carriages approaches 103 years old. However, it still functions perfectly and makes good progress along the Karavanke–Bohinj railway.

The journey lasts just under 2 hours and takes its passengers through spectacular, varied scenery and a series of tunnels – one of which is 6km long. At Kanal, the train halts and allows people time to explore the town. At the end of the day the train returns to Bled and Jesenice.

The trips may vary from year to year and information should be obtained from a Tourist Information Centre before booking.

Internal Fare Structure

Standard Rate Fares

Standard rate tickets are valid for 1 day (under 100km), for 2 days (100km–400km) and for 4 days (over 400km). The journey may be broken once within the validity of the ticket but the time limit must still be respected. A return ticket represents a 20% reduction on the price of 2 singles.

Child Reductions

Children aged between 4 and 12 are entitled to a reduction of 50%. Under 4s travel free provided they do not occupy a seat.

Student Reductions

Students travelling in Yugoslavia are advised to refer to the International Section for information about the reductions available.

Senior Citizen Reductions

Men and women aged 60 and over are eligible for a 30% reduction for journeys under 100km. For journeys over 100km, the restrictions for eligibility come into force and Senior Citizens travelling as tourists are advised to consult the International Section for information about alternative reduction schemes.

Boats in Rovinj harbour

Ljubljana

Party/Group Savers

A minimum of 5 people travelling together are entitled to a 20% reduction on internal routes (5 young people gain a 30% reduction). On international routes 10 or more people travelling together can claim a 25% reduction.

Where to buy tickets

In Yugoslavia

At major rail stations and travel agencies.

In Great Britain

European Rail Travel Centre
PO Box 303
Victoria Station
London SW1V 1JY
Tel: (071) 834 2345

In USA

Tickets may be purchased from *JŽ* railway representatives in the major cities (see International Section).

Facilities on Trains

Sleepers and Couchettes

Couchettes are available in a limited number on some of the internal routes. Sleepers are very expensive.

Food

The express trains are fitted with restaurants and dining cars. The other trains generally offer a minibar service.

Luggage

Hand luggage is carried free. Alternatively, heavy luggage may be checked in for a small fee.

Facilities at Stations

Facilities at even the major rail stations in Yugoslavia are limited. Passengers are advised to travel with all bare essentials.

Zagreb